"For over twenty years knowing Scotty as pastor, teacher, counselor, and friend to the Chapman family has been one of God's greatest gifts of grace to us. Being able to 'boldly approach our Father's throne' with this friend every morning through these prayers has been a treasure, and we're so thankful he is sharing them with the world. In these prayers, Scotty invites us into his personal journey with honesty, passion, and profound insight and gives us what we believe will prove to be some of the richest moments of your day. Thank you, friend!" —**Mary Beth and Steven Curtis Chapman**

"All those of us who know Scotty Smith and his ministry know he's a praying man as well as a great preacher, and therefore this book is full of rich resources for our own prayer lives." —**Tim Keller**, pastor of Redeemer Presbyterian Church, New York City

"Scotty's prayers blast my heart every day with the good news and radical implications of Jesus' love for us. Whether Scotty is leading us to pray about the struggles in our hearts, God's work in the world, the beauty of creation, or the taste of good food, Jesus is the focus and hero of all these prayers. I greatly encourage you to get a copy of my friend's new book." —**Michael W. Smith**

"One way to improve the diversity and richness of your praying is to learn how to pray as a function of meditating on Scripture. Scotty Smith here illustrates how. But to get maximum benefit from these pages, you should not only carefully read Scotty's prayerful meditations on Scripture but also imitate him by doing something similar whenever you read the Bible." —**D. A. Carson**, research professor of New Testament, Trinity Evangelical Divinity School

"Each one of these prayers has been a welcome addition to my day. Through the confessional tone and practical human language, Scotty Smith reminds me of the gospel of grace as he further illuminates the great gift it is for us to commune with God." —**Dan Haseltine**, Jars of Clay

"I want to be led in prayer by a man of God whose heart beats with the music of grace. When I read the prayers of Scotty Smith and pray along with him as I do, my heart sings of the glory of God—being soothed, strengthened, and challenged by the greatness of the gospel." —**Bryan Chapell**, president of Covenant Theological Seminary

"Scotty Smith richly, humbly, and honestly engages the crux of what my heart most wants to say and what I most need to hear as I encounter the passage he is reflecting on. I trust him with my heart; his passion is for Jesus and for us knowing him as Lord, Savior, and friend in all his wildness, goodness, and love. I promise this kind of prayer will fill your day with more holy truth, more honest love, and more hope than through any other morning ritual. We need to be led to pray." —**Dan B. Allender**, professor of counseling psychology and founding president of Mars Hill Graduate School

"I so enjoy hearing from Scotty Smith. He is preoccupied with the Good News and is forever seeking out ways to connect us to grace. He is a tremendous communicator in that he seems to feel and think in equal proportions—that is the gift of these written prayers. My heart intersects with these prayers in a new way every time." —**Sara Groves**, singer-songwriter

"It has been a steady and sober joy and a constant encouragement to begin my day with Scotty Smith in recent months. He awakens me to my sin and need of grace and points me to the Savior every morning. Scotty brings a wealth of pastoral experience to his observations, ones that truly prepare us to walk with the Lord each day. Scotty's thoughts are perfect for a daily devotional. With an image, a question, or a well-formed phrase, he engages us, but more than that, he leads us to engage our own souls, and to do so in the presence of the God of the gospel of grace." —**Dan Doriani**, senior pastor of Central Presbyterian Church, St. Louis; professor of New Testament, Covenant Theological Seminary

"In many ways *Everyday Prayers* is a benchmark in the teaching ministry of Scotty Smith. This book finds him talking to God in the public square so that we can find our own prayerful voice in the beauty and craziness of everyday life. Scotty shows us afresh what we instinctually know at our most truthful: the prayers of the people are more messy than they are majestic. Scotty is not afraid to lean into this truth. As a result, the reader finds hope for the day and grace for the journey." —**Charlie Peacock**, co-founder of Art House America; Grammy Award–winning record producer

"*Everyday Prayers* can jump-start your prayer life. Scotty Smith gives our old, dusty hearts a track to run on that opens the door to deeper fellowship with our heavenly Father." —**Paul Miller**, author of *A Praying Life*, www.seeJesus.net

"After many years of straining to hear the voice of God, I now understand that God is equally interested in hearing my voice. God has declared me his friend. He offers me an intimate relationship, one composed of deep conversations, trivial remarks, outbursts of emotion—even jokes. If your relationship with God has become a formal thing, read this book. It will help you deepen your friendship with God." —**Nate Larkin**, founder of the Samson Society; author of *Samson and the Pirate Monks*

"Scotty's prayers breathe the gospel of grace, and as you pray with him you will find your own heart moving away from your fears, selfish desires, and ambitions to rest again in the joy of knowing that God's favor permanently rests upon you." —**Rose Marie Miller**, author of *From Fear to Freedom*

"Scotty Smith's daily prayers have arrived in my inbox between 5:00 and 6:00 a.m. every day for at least two years. I have used them to encourage my counseling clients who are going through particular life struggles. Scotty often challenges and delights with memorable phrases. He is not afraid to share the struggles of his own heart in relation to almost every conceivable area of life with vivid honesty, wit, and humility. These prayers will expand your understanding and experience of prayer, of your own heart, and of the God to whom you pray." —**Richard Winter**, professor of practical theology and director of counseling, Covenant Theological Seminary

"We want to see Jesus *in the midst* of all the heartache and painfulness of this broken world and in all the anxiety, anger, fear, self-pity, and just ordinary discontent that imposes on our days. Are the love and grace of Christ sufficient for these things? Scotty prays to a Lord who answers this question by his own presence. Scotty's prayers lead *us* to pray, which is to speak and listen to the Lord by what Scotty calls 'vital, heart-engaged communion.'" —**Joseph (Skip) Ryan**, chancellor and professor of practical theology, Redeemer Seminary

"Scotty Smith's *Everyday Prayers* is a portal to heaven—not another book on what we ought to do but a delicious reminder of what's been done for us—so that we can enter into the very throne room of heaven knowing that we're welcomed and loved. Buy it! Read it! Pray it! Rejoice!" —**Elyse Fitzpatrick**, speaker and author

Everyday Prayers

365 DAYS
to a Gospel-Centered Faith

SCOTTY SMITH

BakerBooks
a division of Baker Publishing Group
Grand Rapids, Michigan

Published by Baker Books
a division of Baker Publishing Group
P.O. Box 6287, Grand Rapids, MI 49516-6287
www.bakerbooks.com

Printed in the United States of America

Library of Congress Cataloging-in-Publication Data
Smith, Scotty, 1950–
    Everyday prayers : 365 days to a gospel-centered faith / Scotty Smith.
      p. cm.
    ISBN 978-0-8010-1404-8 (pbk.)
    1. Prayers. 2. Devotional calendars. I. Title.
BV245.S615 2011
242′.2—dc22
                                        2011013438

11 12 13 14 15 16 17   7 6 5 4 3 2 1

For

Jack and Rose Marie Miller, my spiritual parents,
who taught me more about prayer than anyone else;

Darlene Smith, my beloved wife,
with whom I'd rather pray more than anyone else;

Finley (Finn) Ward Russell, my awesome grandson,
for whom I pray more than anyone else; and

Jesus Christ, our loving Savior,
whose prayers I count on more than anyone else's

Foreword

Tullian Tchividjian

My friend Scotty Smith gets the gospel—really gets the gospel. He's a grace-soaked, gospel-driven guy. He was, in fact, one of the first to teach me that the gospel is not just for non-Christians. It's bigger than that; it's for Christians too.

You see, like many who grew up in church, I once assumed the gospel was simply what non-Christians must believe in order to be saved, and then afterward we advance to deeper theological waters. But Scotty has helped me to realize that once God rescues sinners, his plan is not to steer them beyond the gospel but to move them more deeply into it—that the gospel doesn't simply ignite the Christian life but is also the fuel that keeps Christians going and growing every day.

In his letter to the Christians of Colossae, the apostle Paul portrays the gospel as the instrument of all continued growth and spiritual progress, even after a believer's conversion. "The gospel is bearing fruit and growing throughout the whole world," he writes, "just as it has been doing among you since the day you heard it and truly understood God's grace" (Col. 1:6 NIV). He means that the gospel is not only growing wider in the world but also growing deeper in Christians.

In other words, the gospel represents both the nature of Christian growth and the basis for it. Whatever progress we make in our Christian lives—whatever going onward, whatever pressing forward—the direction will always be deeper into the gospel, not apart from it or aside from it. Growth in the Christian life is the process of receiving Christ's words

"It is finished" into new and deeper parts of our being. It happens as the Holy Spirit daily carries God's good word of justification to our regions of unbelief.

Through these daily prayers, Scotty teaches frail, fallen, needy people like me how to preach the gospel to ourselves every day. These are prayers filled with heart and hope. They possess a rare combination of gravity and gladness, depth and delight, doctrine and devotion, precept and passion, truth and love. By God's grace you will find yourself (as I did) weeping over your sin, celebrating your forgiveness, and exalting in God's grace. These prayers are intended to make you feel your desperation, cry out for deliverance, and celebrate your pardon.

God used these prayers to sustain me in the most difficult season of my life by reminding me that my relationship to him depends not on my performance for Jesus but on Jesus' performance for me. I learned that because Jesus was strong for me, I'm free to be weak. Because Jesus won for me, I'm free to lose. These prayers served as a daily reminder to me that only the gospel can cause you to rejoice and be glad in your expendability: because Jesus was someone, you're *free* to be no one.

I'm thankful to Scotty for mentoring me; for love and friendship; for seasoned insight; and above all, for reorienting me always to the power of the gospel.

Reader, enjoy!

Tullian Tchividjian, senior pastor of Coral Ridge
Presbyterian Church, Ft. Lauderdale, Florida;
author of *Surprised by Grace: God's Relentless Pursuit of Rebels*

Preface

*E*veryday Prayers is the book I never intended to write. Though I've been published five previous times, I never would have presumed to write a book on prayer. I know some real prayer warriors, and compared to their prayer life, both in time and in depth, I consider myself a novice and neophyte.

In some ways, Everyday Prayers is the book that's been writing me. I never envisioned documenting a whole year's worth of my longings, struggles, and hopes. But that's what I did, along with highlighting a passion to understand and experience more of the gospel of God's grace. The two go hand in hand. The freer we are in acknowledging our messes, the louder our cry will be for God's mercies.

As I began the editing process, I realized it's a good thing I didn't start this project with a book in view. I would have been too self-conscious and audience centered. I would have muted the vulnerability, curbed the spontaneity, and veiled the brokenness reflected in many of these daily entries. I would have been more of a poet and poser and less a thirsty man pouring out his heart to God.

In fact, it's fair to say that spiritual dryness was a main motivation giving birth to these prayers. One of the occupational hazards of vocational ministry is equating doing things *for* Jesus and spending time *with* Jesus. The joy of being used *by* the Lord can mimic the delights of walking closely *with* the Lord, at least for a while. But preaching and applying the gospel to others is not the same thing as preaching and praying it deeper into one's own heart.

The time I invested in Bible study for sermon preparation gradually supplanted time spent marinating in the Scriptures as an act of worship and transformation. But when it comes to growing in grace, double-dipping simply will not do. I needed to get back to my roots—back to the spiritual discipline of a regular "quiet time." However, I needed more than just a new routine for reading through the Bible in a year (which, by the way, is a great thing to do). I wanted a format that would help me accomplish three things.

First, I wanted to be more intentional about looking for Jesus in every part of the Bible, from Genesis through Revelation. I wanted to discover, "beginning with Moses and all the Prophets . . . what was said in all the Scriptures" about Jesus (Luke 24:27 NIV). And since all of God's promises find their "yes" in Christ (2 Cor. 1:20), I wanted to pray those promises with my eyes fixed on the Savior and *his* purposes. God's promises claim us a whole lot more than we claim them.

Second, I wanted a format that would make it easy for me to hear and apply the gospel to my heart on a daily basis. This is a practice I gained from Jack Miller, my seminary professor who became a spiritual father for twenty-one years. Jack taught me that the best way to preach the gospel to others is to first preach it to yourself. He also taught me that there's nothing more *than* the gospel, just more *of* the gospel. We are incessantly to mine the unsearchable riches of Jesus. We do this best, Jack believed, through Bible study and prayer.

Third, I wanted to include an element of journaling in my devotional life—a discipline I've always encouraged others to practice, but one I'd never taken very seriously for myself. I have friends who've kept prayer journals for years, some for decades. I now understand the benefit of chronicling our stories and cries and God's mercies and faithfulness.

So one morning I simply started my day a little earlier than normal, opened the Scriptures, turned on my laptop, and began praying through a few of my favorite verses. Writing my words as I prayed forced me into a slower pace and helped my concentration tremendously, as I am highly distractible. A few weeks into this journey, a new discipline had become an important delight.

I began to share select prayers with friends who were going through some of the same heartaches and difficulties as I. Requests came for permission to pass certain prayers to others. Before long, members of our church family started asking about my prayer devotionals. I started a small email distribution list, which has grown to hundreds of people around the country. Then, at the encouragement of Scott Roley, my best friend and successor as senior pastor, I started posting the prayers as a blog at our church's website, and later on Facebook and on the website of The Gospel Coalition.

The blog became somewhat of a tutorial for gospel praying—an environment for helping members of our church and online community learn how to think the gospel, pray the gospel, and apply the gospel to all sorts of situations. Many members of our church family come from moralistic and legalistic Christian backgrounds. These performance-based spiritualities make it easy to read the Bible as a book of pragmatic rules or formulas for successful living. So discovering Jesus to be the main character in the Bible is new and transforming to a lot of people.

My format remains the same to this day: I begin each day asking Jesus to lead me to a portion of Scripture that speaks to our real and felt needs. When I land on a manageable portion of the Word, I meditate on that Scripture and then pray through it, wearing the "lens of the gospel." I simply write as I pray, trying very hard not to teach under the guise of praying. Some days I feel I do a better job of this than other days.

I try to be sensitive to particular things going on in my heart, in relationships all around me, in the church, in the culture, in our nation, and in our world. I try to strike a balance with all of these, because the gospel speaks to every area of our lives—personal and corporate, local and global, spiritual and cosmic. You will also notice that I interchange personal and plural pronouns. Though the gospel is personal, it is not private. God's grace frees us to be quite specific with things going on in our lives, but it also compels us into deeper community with others. This individual and corporate prayer rhythm is most clearly seen in the book of Psalms.

Praying the gospel involves engaging with all three offices of Christ: Jesus as prophet, priest, and king. Engaging him *as our prophet*, we listen to Jesus and we look for him in every part of the Scriptures (Luke 24:27). Engaging him *as our priest*, we honor Jesus as the perfect sacrifice for our sins, the righteousness we have by faith, and our loving Savior and High Priest who meets and greets us at the throne of his grace. Engaging him *as our king*, we submit to Jesus as the one who is making all things new—including us and the broken world all around us.

Praying the gospel involves "redemptive redundancies." I intentionally always come back to who we are in Christ and who he is in us. Like Luther said, we need the basics of the gospel every day because we forget the gospel every day.

Praying the gospel also involves connecting with the grand metanarrative of the Bible, which runs through and connects all sixty-six books. This redemptive-historical way of praying helps us remember our calling to be characters in and carriers of God's story. God's story unfolds through the fourfold plotline of creation, fall, redemption, and consummation.

Keeping this big story line in mind helps us consistently focus on the person and work of Jesus.

Indeed, the central and operative question in life is not "What would Jesus do if he were here?" Rather, it is "What is Jesus doing?" since he is right here, and everywhere else, right now. The two things that Jesus has "signed on for"—the two things that are central to the history of redemption and echo through every one of these prayers—are his commitment to redeem his bride from every nation and his commitment to restore creation and usher in the new heaven and new earth at his return. These two passions of Jesus are assumed in every one of my prayers.

So *Everyday Prayers* is a whole year's worth of groaning and growing in grace—365 prayers that reflect a lot of gospel lived through a lot of stories and circumstances, joys and sorrows, theological propositions and ongoing questions. I prayed my way through Lent and Advent and in response to other events of pain and joy.

Some of the prayers are poetic, perhaps suffering from preacher-speak and alliteration. Some are raw with confession and longing. Some of the prayers are born of specific crises: the 2010 Nashville flood, the crisis in Haiti, the death of an orca trainer in Orlando—story lines that show believers how to pray the gospel in response to all kinds of hard providences.

Some of the prayers are as broad as heaven, and some are as detailed as gratitude for the smell of baking bread or the taste of chocolate. Some of the prayers are esoteric, demonstrating how to pray the gospel when you bury your ninety-one-year-old, Alzheimer's-stricken father or your beloved sixteen-year-old Yorkie. Some of the prayers are born out of the struggles of specific friends, modeling how we bring our friends to Jesus.

My hope is that *Everyday Prayers* will simply help you, in some small way, to come more fully alive to Jesus on a daily basis and to see how his gospel is "bearing fruit and growing" (Col. 1:6) all over the world and in every sphere of life. "Thanks be to God for his indescribable gift" (2 Cor. 9:15 NIV)!

A Prayer about the New Year and the Gospel

Now therefore fear the LORD and serve him in sincerity and in faithfulness. Put away the gods that your fathers served beyond the River and in Egypt, and serve the LORD. And if it is evil in your eyes to serve the LORD, choose this day whom you will serve, whether the gods your fathers served in the region beyond the River, or the gods of the Amorites in whose land you dwell. But as for me and my house, we will serve the LORD. (Josh. 24:14–15)

Gracious Father, as I sit here sipping fresh coffee and watching flames dance in the fireplace, it's early into the first day of a new year. Tons of confetti cover the streets of Manhattan, and gratitude fills my heart.

I'm thankful I'm beginning this year with a little better understanding of the gospel than I had last year and the previous years. I'm already praying that I'll be able to say the same thing this time next year. For the gospel is not just good news for people getting ready to die—it's good news for people who are now ready to live.

In the gospel you lavish us with your love, liberate us by your grace, and launch us into your transforming story of redemption. What more could we possibly want or hope for, in life or in death?

Because the gospel is true, I don't respond to Joshua's bold charge with a list of New Year's resolutions—promises of what I'm going to do for you. Rather, I begin this year resolving to abandon myself to everything Jesus has done for us. Jesus is the promise keeper, not us. He's the one who has promised to make all things new, including me.

Father, that's why serving you is much more than merely "desirable"; it's the greatest privilege conceivable and the purest delight imaginable. For Jesus is our Joshua—the one who has saved us, is saving us, and one day will completely save us. Without any embarrassment or fear of cliché, I gladly affirm: Jesus saves! What other savior died for us that we might find life in him? What other god sacrificially serves us that we might gratefully serve him?

Because of the gospel, throwing away my idols feels less like a painful sacrifice and more like a liberating dance. For all my "empty nothings" have ever given me is momentary pleasure and lasting regrets. Remind me of this all year long when I'm tempted to think otherwise.

Father, may this be a year of considering our lives worth nothing to us, if only we may finish the race and complete the task the Lord Jesus has given us—the task of testifying (by word and deed) to the gospel of your grace (Acts 20:24). In Jesus' loving name we pray, with great anticipation and much thanksgiving. Amen.

A Prayer about "Blessing" God

To him who is able to keep you from stumbling and to present you before his glorious presence without fault and with great joy—to the only God our Savior be glory, majesty, power and authority, through Jesus Christ our Lord, before all ages, now and forevermore! Amen. (Jude 24–25 NIV)

Heavenly Father, while many clamor about and try to "claim" more blessings from you, may this be a year in which we come alive to the multiplied blessings you've already lavished upon us in the gospel. Already you have rescued us from the dominion of darkness and have placed us in the kingdom of your beloved Son, Jesus (Col. 1:13). Already you have blessed us with every spiritual blessing in Christ (Eph. 1:3). Already we are completely loved by you because of Jesus' completed work on our behalf. As the year progresses, open the eyes of our hearts to see all these glorious riches more clearly and enjoy them more fully (Eph. 1:18–19).

All year long you'll prove your covenant and capacity to keep us from falling. Though we may falter in the journey, the grasp of your grace is steady and secure. When we waver in our adoration of you, you will remain constant in your affection for us. When we are faithless and disobedient, you will remain committed and fully engaged with us. Even when you must discipline us this year, it will be in love, never in disgust or regret that you have adopted us (Heb. 12:7–12). We praise you for being the perfect Father to your daughters and sons.

All year long you'll be at work preparing us for the day when we come into your glorious presence. We're confident and grateful as we face that day, because you have promised to complete the good work of the gospel you've begun in us (Phil. 1:6). Indeed, Father, if this should be the year in which you call me "home," herein lies my humble confidence: I will stand before you without fault because you've placed me in the faultless Righteous One, Jesus.

Our hope is built on nothing less, nothing more, and nothing other than Jesus' blood and his righteousness. Jesus is the only reason we can be sure we'll stand before you with great joy. Your joy is our strength (Neh. 8:10). Because of your great delight in us, we find great delight in you. Because you rejoice over us with singing, we will sing the new song of the gospel forever (Zeph. 3:14–17).

Gracious Father, you are the only God, the only Savior—to you "be glory, majesty, power and authority, through Jesus Christ our Lord, before all ages, now and forevermore!" (Jude 25 NIV). In Jesus' merciful and matchless name we pray. Amen.

A Prayer about Our Called and Shared Life in Christ

To God's elect, exiles scattered throughout the provinces of Pontus, Galatia, Cappadocia, Asia and Bithynia, who have been chosen according to the foreknowledge of God the Father, through the sanctifying work of the Spirit, to be obedient to Jesus Christ and sprinkled with his blood: Grace and peace be yours in abundance. (1 Pet. 1:1–2 NIV)

Gracious Father, we praise you for the gift of community. It's a tremendous joy to begin this New Year together as brothers and sisters in Christ—adopted by your grace, shaped by the gospel, and indwelt by the Spirit. Bring much glory to yourself as you transform us and liberate us for your redeeming purposes.

May this be a year in which we reengage with our corporate calling as your beloved people. We're your *family*, not just your individual sons and daughters. Our selfishness and the busyness and drivenness of our culture conspire to make it easy for us to think only of ourselves. But the gospel contradicts all such isolated and independent living.

You chose *us* by your foreknowledge, redeemed *us* by your Son, and set *us* apart by your Spirit to demonstrate the reconciling and redeeming power of the gospel in cities and among the nations of the world. Indeed, you've called us to live as strangers in this world, not as strange people. If there's to be anything offensive about us, may it only be the gospel of your grace.

Renew our churches and help us plant new churches that make the gospel beautiful and believable. May we live as good citizens of heaven *and* the cities where you've placed us. May our neighbors be glad we are among them. Help us to offer a meaningful glimpse of the future we share because the gospel is true.

Lord Jesus, it's only because you were obedient to death—even death upon the cross—that we can offer back an obedience of grateful faith. Live and love, in us and through us, all year long to your glory. Be magnified in our hearts, revealed in our cities, and revered among the nations of the world. We pray with great anticipation, in your most worthy name. Amen.

A Prayer about Our Wanderings and God's Mercies

Remember my affliction and my wandering,
　　the wormwood and the gall!
My soul continually remembers it
　　and is bowed down within me.
But this I call to mind,
　　and therefore I have hope:
The steadfast love of the LORD never ceases;
　　his mercies never come to an end;
they are new every morning;
　　great is your faithfulness.
"The LORD is my portion," says my soul,
　　"therefore I will hope in him." (Lam. 3:19–24)

*L*oving Father, another day and another fresh batch of your mercies greet us, even before sunrise. We join Jeremiah in calling to mind your great love and your great faithfulness. In fact, we can "call to mind" much more of your love and faithfulness than Jeremiah. Our place in the history of redemption is to be much preferred over his.

Jeremiah lived looking forward to the coming of Jesus and the fulfillment of the promises of the new covenant (Jer. 31:31–34). But we live on *this side* of those blessed events. How much quicker should I be to praise you and how much greater should my hope be!

Lord Jesus, you're the reason I'm not consumed with guilt and paralyzed with fear. Because of you, God has forgiven *all* my wickedness and will *never* remember my sins against me (Jer. 31:34). You became sin for me, and in you I have received the righteousness of God (2 Cor. 5:21). Thus I look at you and loudly proclaim, "The LORD Our Righteous Savior" (Jer. 33:16 NIV)—the Lord, *my* righteousness!

Father, it's because of this gospel, this good news, that I also join Jeremiah in lamenting my wanderings. With humility I still sing, "Prone to wander, Lord, I feel it; prone to leave the God I love." Oh, how I need the gospel every day and every hour.

Don't let me wander far. When I lose sight of Jesus, make the gall *more galling*, make the bitterness *more bitter*, make downcast feel even *more downcast*. I don't want to ever get used to feeling disconnected from the gospel.

In view of your steadfast love and never-failing compassions, I proclaim, "The LORD is *my* portion" (Lam. 3:24). I *will* wait for you, my God. I pray in Jesus' powerful and tender name. Amen.

A Prayer about Flabby Hearts and Love Handles

It is good for the heart to be strengthened by grace. (Heb. 13:9)

While bodily training is of some value, godliness is of value in every way, as it holds promise for the present life and also for the life to come. (1 Tim. 4:8)

Dear Father, the health clubs and fitness centers are packed with postholiday traffic. Yesterday I had to wait twenty minutes before I could even get onto my favorite elliptical machine. Once again, scores of us seem ready to leave the sugar/butter/carbohydrate binge of the past six weeks for the purge of exercise and sweat. This is a good thing, for stewardship of our physical hearts and bodies does have value, and it does bring you glory.

Yet I've never been more aware that spiritual formation based on the "binge and purge" cycle simply doesn't work. Our spiritual hearts need to be strengthened by the grace of the gospel daily, all year long. We cannot afford periods of "cruise control," when we leave the banquet of your love for a buffet of comfort foods, fast foods, and junk foods. Just like the physical hearts you've given us, our spiritual heart muscles will atrophy if we don't take care of them.

So I thank you for the "means of grace"—the good gifts you've freely given us to help us grow in grace and the knowledge of Jesus. Thank you for the Bible, your written Word, through which you reveal yourself and feed us with the riches of the gospel. Thank you for prayer, meditation, and corporate worship, by which you meet and fellowship with us. Thank you for the sacraments of baptism and the Lord's Supper, these tangible expressions of your covenant love and grace.

Father, you won't love us more or less based on our use of these good gifts. But we certainly demonstrate and deepen our love for you as we do so. By the convicting work of your Holy Spirit, let us be far more concerned about flabby, graceless hearts than bigger love handles. Because you love us, don't let us get used to being spiritually lazy. May we come to the point where we'd sooner avoid oxygen and water than the means of grace. Certainly gospel sanity is to be preferred over personal vanity, all the time. We offer our prayer in Jesus' loving and faithful name. Amen.

A Prayer about Resetting My Heart on Jesus

If then you have been raised with Christ, seek the things that are above, where Christ is, seated at the right hand of God. Set your minds on things that are above, not on things that are on earth. For you have died, and your life is hidden with Christ in God. When Christ who is your life appears, then you also will appear with him in glory. (Col. 3:1–4)

Gracious Jesus, I don't think I've ever praised you for a phone with GPS before today. But as someone born with neither an internal compass nor a gyroscope, someone who labors to find his parked car, someone who walks out of a hotel room not remembering if the elevator is to the right or the left . . . I give you praise for the good gifts of modern technology.

Jesus, in a far more profound way, I'm praising you this morning for the Scriptures, for they are constantly redirecting my wandering heart to its true destination. And I'm praising you for the gospel, for the gospel is not only my GPS but the car that gets me home. Indeed, Jesus, I'm resetting my heart on *you* this morning.

You are my destination and my delight. By God's grace, your death is considered to be mine. When you died on the cross, God punished you for all *my* sins. When you were raised from the dead, I was raised with you and was given a whole new life and story.

Right now my life is safely hidden in you, for God has placed me in union with you, Jesus. I'm covered with your righteousness, completely forgiven and acceptable to God, and very much loved by him. I'm destined to become as lovely and as loving as you and to reign with your whole bride in the new heaven and new earth. There's no other story I'd rather be in—and yet, until the day you return, I'll be tempted to think otherwise.

No one and nothing else is worthy of my heart's adoration, affection, and allegiance—only you, though good things and bad things claim otherwise. I set my heart on you today, Jesus, as my ultimate good. Not on my reputation, my children, my marriage, my stuff, my job. Not on my desire to get even, to get out, to be liked, to be happy, to be in control, to be safe.

Jesus, you've done everything *for me*, and now I trust you to do everything *in me* that will bring you glory. In your matchless name I pray. Amen.

A Prayer about Not Being Idle about Idols

Dear children, keep yourselves from idols. (1 John 5:21 NIV)

Dear Father, in Rome I've seen statues of the various gods that filled the temples and lifestyle of that great ancient city. In London I visited the biggest Hindu temple in the city and wandered from station to station as worshipers offered prayers and gifts to deities that looked so strange to me. In Israel I studied decaying remains of various idols that competed for the worship of the people of God. Idolatry is everywhere because there's no such thing as a nonworshiper.

Yet for me to obey John's command to keep myself from idols requires so much more than simply staying away from ancient sites, pagan temples, and man-made idols. Father, I've never been more aware of the invisible pantheon of idols that are constantly angling and clamoring for my heart's worship. How I wish that as soon as you placed me in Christ my struggle with idolatry would have ceased. That's simply not the case, or this Scripture would be entirely irrelevant.

Sometimes the approval or rejection of people has more sway over my heart than what you think about me. Sometimes my need to be right is more compelling to me than being righteous in Christ. Sometimes my desire to be in control of people and circumstances claims much more of my time and energy than seeking your face, savoring your grace, and serving your Son—the true King. These are just a few of the things that bear the marks of idolatry in my heart.

Have mercy on me, Father, and free my foolish heart from giving anything or anyone the attention, allegiance, affection, and adoration you alone deserve. The fact that I'm one of your "dear children"—forgiven, secure, righteous, and beloved in Christ—should be all the motivation I need to keep myself from *any* form of idolatry. May the gospel of your grace relentlessly expose and dethrone all "empty nothings" from my heart. I pray in Jesus' most worthy name. Amen.

A Prayer about God as Abba Father, Not Sugar Daddy

Then Satan answered the LORD and said,
"Does Job fear God for no reason?" (Job 1:9)

There are many who say, "Who will show us some good?
    Lift up the light of your face upon us, O LORD!"
You have put more joy in my heart
    than they have when their grain and wine abound.
In peace I will both lie down and sleep;
    for you alone, O LORD, make me dwell in safety. (Ps. 4:6–8)

Heavenly Father, today we want to affirm that nothing has to change for us to know your joy—neither people nor circumstances. We don't love you simply because you make us happy. We reject Satan's assumption that the only reason we, your children, love you is because you buy our affections with "the good life" (Job 1:9–11).

I never saw a carbohydrate (grain) I didn't like, and I enjoy a glass of good red wine as much as anyone, but my love for you does not depend upon you being a 24/7 convenience store for me. Your name is Abba Father, not Sugar Daddy.

I love you because you bought me back—you redeemed my life from sin and death by the perfect life of Jesus. I love you because you first loved me and gave Jesus as a sacrifice of atonement and propitiation for my sins. I enjoy the many creature comforts you give me, but I love you in response to your great love lavished on me in the gospel.

Though many are asking, "Who can show us any good? Where is your God now? How can you say God is good? Where was your God when . . . ? How could your God possibly . . . ? Why doesn't your God . . . ?" yet, Lord, I will lie down and sleep in peace, for you alone, O Lord, make me dwell in safety.

Father, there's no safer place to be—in life or in death—than in Christ. Because you've hidden our lives in Jesus, not a hair can fall from our heads, not a breath can be taken from our lungs, and not a beat can be missed by our hearts apart from your sovereign purposes and pleasure. And should I die in the next hour, my heart will forever proclaim, "My God has done all things well." I pray with great gratitude, in Jesus' most worthy name. Amen.

A Prayer Warning of Cooling Affections for God

And because lawlessness will be increased, the love of many will grow cold. But the one who endures to the end will be saved. And this gospel of the kingdom will be proclaimed throughout the whole world as a testimony to all nations, and then the end will come. (Matt. 24:12–14)

Jesus, it is pipe-freezing-cold outside this morning, and it's supposed to get even colder. One of my first concerns today is for the poor and elderly in our community—those whose homes are not insulated and heated well enough to withstand this kind of extreme cold. I pray for their safety, but I also realize that loving you involves putting legs on my prayers. To whom would you send me today, in my neighborhood or in my city? Whom should I call and check on?

A concern for the poor is closely connected to your sobering words I just read in Matthew—words warning about the danger of our love growing cold. That's a frightful thought, Jesus. I take it seriously, especially as I take stock of my heart relationship with you. When our affections for you chill, then our concern and compassion for others diminishes as well. What a tragic domino effect. What a disgrace.

May I never stop singing the last line in the hymn "O Sacred Head Now Wounded": "Should I fainting be, Lord, let me never, never outlive my love for thee." That's my earnest, impassioned prayer, Jesus. I don't fear losing my salvation. I will stand firm to the end because of my standing in grace. But what could be worse than for my love for you to cool down, degree by degree, as I get older? Don't let that happen to me, Jesus. Don't let that happen. What could be worse than to finish the race with an ingrown, icy heart?

I do not and will not trust in my love for you, but only in your love for me. I love you, Jesus, because you first loved me and gave yourself as a sacrifice of atonement—as a judgment-exhausting propitiation for my sins. And now it is impossible for you to love me more than you do right now, and you are committed to never loving me less. Hallelujah! Hallelujah! Hallelujah!

Holy Spirit, breathe upon the embers of my heart and rekindle the love I first had for Jesus when the gospel of grace was first applied to my heart, when nothing else mattered. Come, Holy Spirit, come in fire and power. Preach the gospel to my heart today—right now, as though it were the very first time. I pray expectantly, in Jesus' kind and powerful name. Amen.

A Prayer about the Day
Mountains Will Sing

So shall my word be that goes out from my mouth:
    it will not return to me empty,
but it will accomplish that which I purpose,
    and shall succeed in the thing for which I sent it.
For you shall go out in joy
    and be led forth in peace;
the mountains and the hills before you
    shall break forth into singing,
and all the trees of the field
    shall clap their hands. (Isa. 55:11–12)

Gracious Father, you know how much I love mountains of all shapes and sizes. There's just something about mountains that causes my heart to feel the greatness of your glory and grace—the weightiness of your majesty and the endlessness of your mercy. What a Creator! What a creation!

I guess it started with Boy Scout trips to the hills of western North Carolina, then on to exploring the Blue Ridge Mountains around Boone and Banner Elk, North Carolina. And I'll never forget my first sighting of the Rocky Mountains in Estes Park, Colorado—the shimmering aspen leaves against the rich blue of a humidity- and haze-free fall skyline!

But then there was the day I stepped off the train in the village of Interlaken, Switzerland, and got hammered with the holy wonder of three Alps: the Eiger, the Mönch, and the Jungfrau. I can still see, smell, feel, and taste the sensual overload of that day. Indeed, Father, the works of your hands declare your glory, loud and clear. How can I keep from singing your praise?

But, Father, these words of Isaiah envision a day when the mountains themselves will burst into song—the new song of the new creation. Though your glory is clearly revealed in the beauty of your creation, it is revealed *ten thousand times more in the redemption that you freely give us in Jesus.* Jesus is the Alps of your mercy, grace, and love for us!

Because of Jesus, we, your redeemed people, will go out in joy and be led forth into peace, into shalom—the perfect order, society, environment, and world of the new heaven and new earth. You have spoken, you have promised, and *so shall it be!* Your Word will accomplish everything you decree and all your delights. With great hope we pray in Jesus' name. Amen.

A Prayer about Gospel Parenting

Unless the LORD builds the house,
Those who build it labor in vain.
Unless the LORD watches over the city,
the watchman stays awake in vain.
It is in vain that you rise up early
and go late to rest,
eating the bread of anxious toil;
for he gives to his beloved sleep.
Behold, children are a heritage from the LORD,
the fruit of the womb a reward. (Ps. 127:1–3)

Heavenly Father, it's a joy to address you today as the architect and builder of your own house—including the household of faith and my children's place in your family.

As I look back over the years of my pragmatic parenting, I'm saddened, but I am also gladdened, for you've always been faithful to your covenant love, even when I was overbearing and underbelieving. The move from parenting by grit to parenting by grace has been a fitful but fruitful journey. Take me deeper; take me further.

You've rescued me from parental "laboring in vain"—assuming a burden you never intended parents to bear. Father, only you can reveal the glory and grace of Jesus to our children. Only you can give *anyone* a new heart. You've called us to parent as an act of worship—to parent "as unto you," not as a way of saving face, making a name for ourselves, or proving our worthiness of your love.

Oh, the arrogant pride of thinking that by my "good parenting" I can take credit for what you alone have graciously done in the lives of my children. Oh, the arrogant unbelief of assuming that by my "bad parenting" I've forever limited what you will be able to accomplish in the future. Oh, the undue pressure our children must feel when we parent more out of our fear and pride than by your love and grace.

Since our children and grandchildren are *your* inheritance, Father, teach us—teach me—how to care for them as humble stewards, not as anxious owners. More than anything else, show us how to parent and grandparent in a way that best reveals the unsearchable riches of Jesus in the gospel. Give us quick repentances and observable kindnesses. Convict me quickly and surely when I do not relate to your covenant children "in line with the truth of the gospel" (Gal. 2:14 NIV). I pray in Jesus' faithful name. Amen.

A Prayer for Engaging in Gospel Warfare

For I delight in the law of God, in my inner being, but I see in my members another law waging war against the law of my mind and making me captive to the law of sin that dwells in my members. Wretched man that I am! Who will deliver me from this body of death? Thanks be to God through Jesus Christ our Lord! (Rom. 7:22–25)

Jesus, though I'm conflict avoidant by nature and choice, this is one conflict about which I am actually excited. The very fact that there's a war going on inside of me is a *good thing*, especially since the combatants are the gospel and my sinful nature. For this means that the outcome of this war has already been decided. The gospel will prevail! Yet I'm not naïve about the "mop-up" operation. Growing in grace is great, but it sure gets messy and intense.

The only reason I now delight in God's law, in my heart of hearts, is because the demands of the law drove me to you, Jesus. I needed a substitute and a Savior, not a model and a coach. You perfectly met all the requirements of God's law for me, and you've exhausted his judgment against all my law breaking. This is the good news, indeed.

The messy part of knowing you comes from your commitment to make me like yourself. You're more committed to getting "heaven" in me than getting me into heaven. Why couldn't you have just glorified me after justifying me? It would've been so much easier. Why couldn't we have just skipped over the whole sanctification process?

Silly questions, indeed. I'm just very thankful to know that one day I will be as loving and as lovely as you, for the Father will complete his work in each of his children, including me. Until that day, here's my prayer . . .

Jesus, allow me to grieve the sinfulness of sin—the sinfulness of *my* sins. Now that I'm no longer guilty or condemned, let me fearlessly see my sins, ruthlessly hate my sins, and relentlessly repent of my sins. Increase my love for holiness and decrease my self-contempt. Only the gospel can bring me such freedom. Only by seeing more of you, Jesus, will I delight in this journey.

Jesus, *you're* the end of all my wretchedness. *You're* the one who's rescuing me from this "body of death"—all the effects and residue of the fall, all the trappings of my graveclothes, every semblance of every way I'm not like you. Thank you, thank you, thank you. I pray in your most powerful and loving name. Amen.

A Prayer about Not Fretting Evil

Be still before the LORD
  and wait patiently for him;
do not fret when people succeed in their ways,
  when they carry out their wicked schemes.
Refrain from anger and turn from wrath;
  do not fret—it leads only to evil.
For those who are evil will be destroyed,
  but those who hope in the LORD will inherit the land.
    (Ps. 37:7–9 NIV)

Faithful Father, you send your Word with Swiss timing and uncanny precision. Whenever I'm vexed or fretful, you anticipate it. Whenever I'm confused or anxious, you've already spoken wisdom about the matter in multiple places in the Scriptures. Whenever I feel vulnerable or angry, you come to me in the Bible and bring me back to gospel sanity, time and time again. How I praise you for the counsel and consolation of your Word.

Today, Father, I'm a bit worked up over the apparent success of those who bring harm to others and even get rewarded for their madness. Whether it's in the global reach of terrorism, the ongoing shenanigans of Wall Street, the seizing of aid marked for poor countries, or even the self-indulgent world of sports and athletics, violations of beauty and goodness are everywhere. How long, O Lord, before you send Jesus back to put all things right?

Your answer to me today in this Scripture is just what I need. You won't give me a date, but as always, you do give me yourself. I hear you loud and clear, Father. You're speaking stillness and fretless waiting to my heart. No good comes from my obsessing about evil and evil-making. Nothing profitable results from my spending extra time fertilizing my anger and fueling my disgust.

A day is coming when the knowledge of your glory will cover the entire earth as the waters cover the sea. The whole world, not just one small and important bit of real estate in the Middle East, is holy land. The New Jerusalem is coming down from heaven, not a day early and not a day late.

Until that day, I will *seek to seek first* the kingdom of God and the righteousness of King Jesus. How I praise you that the very righteousness with which you have already robed me is the very righteousness with which you are going to fill the earth. You've already made me both your son and an heir of the new heaven and new earth! Hallelujah, what a Savior! Hallelujah, what a salvation! I pray in Jesus' powerful name. Amen.

A Prayer for Preaching the Gospel to Yourself

I am eager to preach the gospel to you also who are in Rome. For I am not ashamed of the gospel, for it is the power of God for salvation to everyone who believes, to the Jew first and also to the Greek. For in it the righteousness of God is revealed from faith for faith, as it is written, "The righteous shall live by faith." (Rom. 1:15–17)

Dear Jesus, even as Paul was eager to preach the gospel to believers in Rome, so I'm eager to preach it to my own heart today. There was a time when I thought the gospel was only for nonbelievers—simply the doorway for beginning a relationship with you. I now realize the gospel is just as much for believers as it is for nonbelievers, because from beginning to end, our salvation is entirely dependent upon the grace, truth, and power of the gospel.

Salvation is not just about going to heaven when we die. It's about becoming like you, Jesus—being transformed into your likeness. Only the resources of the gospel are sufficient for such a task, for we're not just separated from God by a great distance, we are thoroughly broken and corrupted by sin. We need a big gospel for our great need. Indeed, there's nothing more than the gospel, there is just more of the gospel.

So I praise you today, Jesus, that you've already accomplished everything necessary to completely save us. You came into the world as God's promised Messiah. You lived a life of perfect obedience on our behalf—as our substitute, fulfilling all the demands of God's law for us. You died upon the cross for us—taking the judgment we deserve, completely exhausting God's righteous anger against our sin. Hallelujah!

Through faith in you and this good news, all of my sins have been forgiven and I've been given the gift of your perfect righteousness. God has already declared me righteous in his sight. He cannot love me more than he does today, and he'll never love me less. In fact, because of your work for me, Jesus, God now loves me just as much as he loves you, for he's hidden my life in yours. Amazing!

He's adopted me as his child and placed his Spirit in my heart. The Holy Spirit constantly reminds me I'm God's beloved child, because I'm so prone to forget. He's also present in my life to make me like you, Jesus, for I can no more change myself than I could've ever begun a relationship with God on my own. Keep pressing this gospel into my heart, I pray in your priceless and peerless name. Amen.

A Prayer about Jesus'
Shameless Love for Us

Both the one who makes people holy and those who are made holy are of the same family. So Jesus is not ashamed to call them brothers and sisters. He says, "I will declare your name to my brothers and sisters; in the assembly I will sing your praises." And again, "I will put my trust in him." And again he says, "Here am I, and the children God has given me." (Heb. 2:11–13 NIV)

Dear Jesus, I've thought, said, and done a lot of things in my life of which I am truly ashamed. I've been painfully shamed and I've shamed people I dearly love. Shame is a pillaging thief, one that robs us of dignity, freedom, and joy.

So when I hear you tell me that you're *not* ashamed of me—that you're not ashamed to call me your brother—it humbles and gladdens me like nothing else.

You're the only answer for the paralyzing power of shame, Lord Jesus. How I praise you for doing everything necessary to deal with the ways I've been both an agent and a victim of sin—sin that has led to multiple layers of shame. You're the only one who can make me holy, the only one who can "set me apart" for the redeeming and restoring purposes of the one I now know as Abba, Father.

In fact, I only dare cry out "Abba, Father" because you first cried out "My God, my God, why have you forsaken me?" (Ps. 22:1). You took the full guilt and the real shame of my sin on the cross. I really do believe this. I really want to experience it more fully.

And now you sing to me of the Father's love. You declare his praises to my heart every time I hear the gospel, every time I gather with my brothers and sisters to worship the Triune God, every time I take the bread and cup of Holy Communion, every time I read the Scriptures, every time I listen to your voice in creation proclaiming the majesty and mercy of God.

Jesus, you're *not* ashamed of me. This is the theology I defend; make it the doxology in which I delight. I pray in your most compassionate name. Amen.

A Prayer for Seeing with Gospel Eyes

But the LORD said to Samuel, "Do not consider his appearance or his height, for I have rejected him. The LORD does not look at the things people look at. People look at the outward appearance, but the LORD looks at the heart."
(1 Sam. 16:7 NIV)

*L*oving Father, I've worn prescription glasses since high school, moving from regular to progressive focus lenses over the course of years. Recently I've had laser surgery to help me see more precisely than ever. Yet there's an ophthalmological corrective that can *only* take place as the gospel does its work on the eyes of my heart.

Even if I could see with 20/15 or 20/10 vision, if I'm only focusing on the "outward appearance" of people and things, I'm still not seeing as you intend. My plea? Open the eyes of my heart, Lord, so that I may see Jesus—and as I begin seeing Jesus more clearly, help me see everything else from *his* perspective.

Help me to see people with gospel eyes. Father, when I'm only looking at people with the aberrations of a fallen heart, show me what true beauty consists of. When I only see the things in people that irritate or inconvenience me, help me to see their dignity, their brokenness, and *your* image in them. When I only see people in terms of how they might harm or help me, expand my vision beyond my story to your larger story of redemption and restoration. Help me to see what *you* see in my spouse . . . in my children . . . in my friends . . . even in total strangers.

Help me to see creation with gospel eyes. Father, don't let me look at the ocean, mountains, stars, sunrises and sunsets, flora and fauna, or even weather patterns just in terms of me and my plans. As you open and heal the eyes of my heart, enable me to live more as a worshipful steward of your creation and less as a selfish consumer of your creation.

Help me to see pain and suffering with gospel eyes. Father, sometimes looking at all the crucibles, crises, and cruel stories of life makes me want to run, hide, fix, or deny. Help me to see with the eyes of Jesus when overwhelming need is staring me down. I pray in Jesus' healing name. Amen.

A Prayer about Gospel Resolve

But Daniel resolved not to defile himself with the royal food and wine.
(Dan. 1:8 NIV)

Dear Father, the older I get, the more I'm convicted and encouraged by the life of Daniel and his exiled friends. May the gospel bring me greater freedom to live and love as this man did—with passion, conviction, wisdom, and hope.

I used to read the book of Daniel as a survival manual for life in a scary, godless world. But that's not the way *you* wrote the book. I now realize that Daniel is a testimony to your commitment to redeem your people from all the nations, including Babylon. Indeed, you intend to bring the transforming power of the gospel to bear *wherever* you send your people, including Babylon. I wish I'd understood this sooner. But better now than never!

With a better understanding of the gospel, here's my prayer: Father, help me and my friends make the kinds of commitments Daniel made so we can live as instruments of your transforming presence where you've placed *us*.

Keep us wise to the particular "defilements" that wage war against our hearts and your story—not just the things in "Babylon" but the things in the dark continent of our hearts. If only I had to be concerned about just the things outside of me—but the things around me only tend to ignite the lust and greed *within* me.

I'm now convinced that the best way I can "resolve not to defile myself" of the *wrong* kingdom is by feasting regularly upon the royal food and wine King Jesus gives us.

Jesus, I praise you for the bread and the cup of the new covenant. As the Bread of Heaven, feed us till we want no more. As the giver of the water of life, quench our thirst that we might live and love as Daniel did—with passion, conviction, wisdom, and hope. I pray in your loving and holy name. Amen.

A Prayer about Voicing Our Groans and Hope

For we know that the whole creation has been groaning together in the pains of childbirth until now. And not only the creation, but we ourselves, who have the firstfruits of the Spirit, groan inwardly as we wait eagerly for adoption as sons, the redemption of our bodies. For in this hope we were saved. (Rom. 8:22–24)

*L*oving Father, I'm feeling many different things as this day begins. Images of horror and heartache in third and fourth world countries simply will not go away—and they *shouldn't* go away. People being loaded into trucks for mass grave burials . . . infants desperate for formula . . . tens of thousands of newly orphaned children. . . . As much as I would like to tune out, numb out, and check out, the gospel compels me to keep my heart present in the overwhelming distress and dimensions of this crisis.

Paul's words about the intense painful groaning of childbirth seem appropriate to the situation. And there's no epidural, there's no anesthesia, there's nothing to diminish the raw pain of what's going on in many nations of the world's poor, and even in our own nation.

We have only our hope that you, our God, do not lie. In the cries of a whole nation of people, in the moaning of its fragile land, you bid us hear the faint but sure cry of hope. Though to some degree it mocks my sensibilities, I abandon myself to your promise that one day the whole earth will be covered with the knowledge of the glory of God; one day the barren places will have trees again and those trees will clap their hands; one day desolate hills will seem like dancing mountains.

One day you will wipe away every tear from the eyes of your people, and there will be no more death or mourning or crying or pain, for the old order of things will have passed away for your world in waiting (Rev. 21:4). How long, O Lord? How long until that increasingly longed-for day? Oh, that it could be *today* . . .

But because of this hope, we will not tune out, numb out, or check out. We will seek to show up. Lead us, King Jesus. Lead us into your work of redemption and restoration. What will it mean to love mercy, do justice, and walk humbly with you in the broken places of your world?

We praise you that you do not despise our confusion, our despair, or even our railings against heaven and the mysteries of hard providence, but you give us all the gospel sanity we will need to follow you into the heart-wrenching brokenness and chaos. I pray in Jesus' tender and trustworthy name. Amen.

A Prayer about a Benediction and Challenge

Grace to all who love our Lord Jesus Christ with an undying love.
(Eph. 6:24 NIV)

Dear Jesus, I need this benediction like I need oxygen and water, for I *cannot* exist apart from your love. The call to love you with an "undying love" is not a burden or performance. It's simply the privilege we share living in response to the *dying love* and *everlasting love* with which you love us so lavishly. There's no greater demonstration of love in the history of love and affection than your death for us upon the cross. Throughout eternity, we'll feel as though we're just beginning the survey of the wonders of your cross.

You didn't lay down your life for deserving friends but for rebels, fools, and idolaters—like me. You love us, you've freed us from our sins by your blood, and you've made us to be a kingdom and priests to serve our God and Father forever (Rev. 1:5–6). Now, Jesus, please make the familiar sound of these words come alive with holy passion and fresh delight.

Even as we first needed grace to respond to your love (Eph. 2:8–10), so we need grace to stay alive to your love and to love you as you deserve to be loved. Your love for us is the one constant in our lives. Everything else changes. Everything else is subject to whim and fancy. Our brothers and sisters in heaven are more happy than we are, but they are not more loved. But our love for you ebbs and flows.

Jesus, give us grace to love you with an undying love. May the cooling of our affections for you bother us more than the fragile economy, our broken relationships, political upheaval in the world, concerns about our health, getting older, or anything else. Jesus, don't let us get used to status quo, middle-class, business-as-usual love for you.

If by the Holy Spirit we hear you saying to us this morning, "I have this against you, that you have abandoned the love you had at first" (Rev. 2:4), may it seem like a huge kiss from heaven, for it means you are pursuing us, you love us, your desire is for us, your banner over us is love. That you are jealous for *our love* is the greatest compliment you could possibly pay us. Indeed, Jesus, restore to us the joy of being loved by you in the gospel. Restore us to loving you as your much-beloved bride. We pray in your glorious name. Amen.

A Prayer for Days When You Don't Feel Like Praying

In the same way, the Spirit helps us in our weakness. We do not know what we ought to pray for, but the Spirit himself intercedes for us through wordless groans. And he who searches our hearts knows the mind of the Spirit, because the Spirit intercedes for God's people in accordance with the will of God. And we know that in all things God works for the good of those who love him, who have been called according to his purpose.
(Rom. 8:26–28 NIV)

Dear Father, this is one of those days when I could create a long prayer list and methodically go through it, but I'm not sure I would really be praying. I could go through the motions, but to be quite honest, it would be more ritual than reality—more about me than the people and situations I'd bring before you. I'm feeling a bit distracted this morning, scattered and not very focused.

It's one of those days I'm glad the gospel is much more about your grasp of me than my grip on you. I'm grateful your delight in me is not contingent upon my delight in you. I'm very thankful for the prayer ministry of the Holy Spirit.

Gracious Father, I have no problem or reluctance in acknowledging my weakness this morning. In fact, it's freeing to know your Spirit doesn't abandon us when we're weak but helps us in our weakness, faithfully praying in us with "wordless groans" (Rom. 8:26 NIV). Though I don't understand everything that means, I do get that you search our hearts and you know the mind of the Spirit, and that brings me great comfort today.

No one knows our hearts better than you, Father. And you search our hearts to save us, not to shame us; to deliver us, not to demean us; to change us, not to chide us. You know my dignity and my depravity, my fears and my longings, my struggles with sin and my standing in Christ. No one but you knows how little or how much of the gospel I actually get.

And at this very moment your Spirit is praying inside of me, perfectly tuned in to my needs and in total harmony with your will. I cannot measure the peace that brings. I surrender right now, Father. I will gladly groan to your glory. I know you are at work for my good in all things, including this season. You have called me to life in Christ, and you will complete your purpose in me, in each of your children, and in the entire cosmos. I do love you; I would love you more. I pray with thankfulness, in Jesus' merciful and faithful name. Amen.

A Prayer about Nonselective Compassion

You, therefore, have no excuse, you who pass judgment on someone else, for at whatever point you judge another, you are condemning yourself, because you who pass judgment do the same things. Now we know that God's judgment against those who do such things is based on truth. So when you, a mere human being, pass judgment on them and yet do the same things, do you think you will escape God's judgment? Or do you show contempt for the riches of his kindness, forbearance and patience, not realizing that God's kindness is intended to lead you to repentance? (Rom. 2:1–4 NIV)

Heavenly Father, it's a new day, and this is just one more Scripture reminding me of how much I need the gospel. The call to love others as Jesus loves me keeps driving me to you for more grace and for the power of the gospel. I *cannot* change myself.

Meditating on this passage has convicted me about being way too selective in my love for broken people. I'm a selective lover. I'm not an equal opportunity dispenser of your compassion.

Father, it's not difficult for me to shower the riches of your kindness, tolerance, and patience on people whose sins and struggles are *like mine*. But I'm self-righteous and judgmental toward people who deal with brokenness and temptations *different* from mine. Though understandable, it's not excusable. Have mercy on me, for the extending of your mercy *through* me. I'm a mere human. No one has appointed me to be judge and jury.

Here's my prayer today: May your great kindness lead me to repent of my sin more quickly and more deeply. Help me grieve and deal with my heterosexual lust to a greater degree than I am offended by those who struggle with homosexual temptations and entanglements. Help me to be more earnest about repenting of my "Republican" gossip than I am committed to keeping a record of "Democratic" sins. May I be more sad and repentant of my passive-aggressive anger than I am critical of other people's loud-and-large anger. Father, these are just a few things that come to mind. I know there's more . . . much more.

Lord Jesus, you willingly took the judgment I deserve on the cross—the fullness of God's righteous wrath. And now you love me with the fullness of compassion, acceptance, and delight. The greatest non sequitur in life would be for me to show contempt for the riches of God's kindness, tolerance, and patience. Deepen my repentance and deepen my compassion for fellow broken sinners. I pray in your righteous and loving name. Amen.

A Prayer about Rescuing Entangled Friends

Brothers and sisters, if someone is caught in a sin, you who live by the Spirit should restore that person gently. But watch yourselves, or you also may be tempted. Carry each other's burdens, and in this way you will fulfill the law of Christ. (Gal. 6:1–2 NIV)

Heavenly Father, we come to your throne of grace this morning praying for wisdom and gentleness to love our struggling friends well. None of us naturally likes confrontation, and we decry self-righteous busybodies who show up in our lives like self-appointed prosecuting attorneys. But these words of Paul paint a different picture and present a different spirit.

Give us kindness and strength. If a friend loves in all seasons, that certainly must involve the seasons when we get entangled in sin. Sin brings death. We tend to forget this—death. If we saw a friend drinking poison, we wouldn't hesitate to do something. If we saw a friend stepping close to a pit of rattlesnakes, we'd warn them. Help us hate sin enough and love our friends enough to risk getting involved. Better to risk the awkwardness, messiness, and defensiveness than to watch another life or marriage simply go down.

Give us discernment and persistence. It's not about a rush to judgment but about a journey to restoration. Help us to listen before launching. The goal must always be restoration, not just rebuke. Entanglements take a while to get disentangled. We may have to carry some of these burdens longer than we realize. Father, we need the power of the Holy Spirit and the love of Jesus. You promise to give us sufficient grace for all things, and we take you at your Word. We need great grace to do this well.

Give us gentleness and hope. Those who remove specks the best are those who are most aware of the log in their own eye. Keep us humble and keep us aware of our own "temptability." None of us is beyond the need of grace, and none of us is beyond the reach of grace. Keep us gentle and keep us expectant. Our joy is in remembering Jesus is the great Restorer, not us. This is the law of Christ we are fulfilling; his yoke we are bearing; his story that's being written. Fill us with hope. Fill us with the hope of the gospel.

Lastly, Father, we praise you for churches that are stepping up and are seeking to do this hard and heart work of discipline and restoration. Increase their tribe and bless their endeavors. It's never easy. We pray in Jesus' holy and loving name. Amen.

A Prayer for Recovering Legalists

I do it all for the sake of the gospel, that I may share with them in its blessings. Do you not know that in a race all the runners compete, but only one receives the prize? So run that you may obtain it. Every athlete exercises self-control in all things. They do it to receive a perishable wreath, but we an imperishable. So I do not run aimlessly; I do not box as one beating the air. But I discipline my body and keep it under control, lest after preaching to others I myself should be disqualified. (1 Cor. 9:23–27)

Dear Jesus, this is one of those passages I used to avoid as a recovering legalist. Once I came to rest in your righteousness alone for my salvation, it was Scriptures like this one that confused me, at times activating that part of me that still thinks I can make you love me more by my doing. So I praise you for the ongoing teaching ministry of the Holy Spirit. I praise you for showing me more about living in line with the truth of the gospel (Gal. 2:14). I praise you for all the freedoms you have won for us, including the freedom to obey you from our hearts.

The gospel sets us free from working for wages. We now run for a crown. Ultimately, every crown will be laid at your feet, Jesus, for you have earned our salvation for us. Our obedience merits nothing, but it does show that we love you (John 14:15). How can we honestly say we love you if we disregard what you say?

The gospel sets us free from running aimlessly and beating the air. We now live in a story of redemption and restoration. All of history is bound up with your commitment to redeem your people from the nations and to make all things new. We praise you for rescuing us from a little narrative of self-fulfillment for a life of kingdom advancement. There is enough grace for the whole race. We can make no excuses.

The gospel sets us free from beating ourselves up because of shame or pride. We now train ourselves for godliness. We are to bring our appetites and bodies in submission to the gospel (1 Tim. 4:7–8). Forgive us when we are more disciplined out of vanity than out of a commitment to grow as your disciples. Fitting into our pants is not as important as revealing your beauty.

Jesus, you are the one who has "won the prize" for all of us. Only the gospel qualifies us to "share in the inheritance of the saints in light" (Col. 1:12). We do not fear losing our salvation. But do let us fear, and grieve, misrepresenting you and "frittering away" this one short life you've given us. Show us how to do all things for the sake of the gospel and by the grace and truth of the gospel. We gratefully pray, in your most loving name. Amen.

A Prayer for Freedom
from People-Approval

We speak as those approved by God to be entrusted with the gospel. We are not trying to please people but God, who tests our hearts. You know we never used flattery, nor did we put on a mask to cover up greed—God is our witness. We were not looking for praise from people, not from you or anyone else. (1 Thess. 2:4–6 NIV)

*P*atient Father, it's not just apostles who need freedom from living for the approval of people; it's all of us . . . *it's me*. We can't serve people well if our need for affirmation or fear of rejection is greater than our love for you. I need your help in this matter this very week.

As I look at my relational brokenness and sin, I can see how "people pleasing" plays out in two directions. On one hand, there are people to whom I attach my umbilical cord (metaphorically speaking) and expect them to give me life. On the other hand, there are people whose umbilical cords I grab and plug into me, assuming the role of life giver. I grieve both of these patterns, Father.

Because the gospel is true, I can freely confess these things. Because the gospel is powerful, I have hope for change. Because the gospel is entrusted to me, I take this matter very seriously.

Lord Jesus, I don't want to live as an "approval suck." I want to love others as you love me—and as you love them. It's flat-out wrong for me to give anybody the power to control me through their affirmation or their rejection. It's because of your life of perfect obedience that I can be free from living as a poser, pretender, and performer. It's because of your death for me on the cross that I can live with the absolute assurance of God's everlasting approval and his steady kindness.

So, God the Holy Spirit, keep "gossiping this gospel" to my heart. Keep bearing witness with my spirit that I'm a beloved child of Abba, Father. Keep giving me the power to repent of all forms of living for the approval of people, a life-sucking snare indeed. I pray in Jesus' liberating name. Amen.

A Prayer for Bringing
Our Broken Friends to Jesus

Some men came, bringing to him a paralyzed man, carried by four of them. Since they could not get him to Jesus because of the crowd, they made an opening in the roof above Jesus by digging through it and then lowered the mat the man was lying on. When Jesus saw their faith, he said to the paralyzed man, "Son, your sins are forgiven." (Mark 2:3–5 NIV)

Loving Jesus, today I woke up thinking about friends who live with chronic illness—those with mental and emotional illnesses in particular. I come bringing you both the sufferers *and* the caregivers, confident of your great compassion.

Jesus, I cry out to you on behalf of the sufferers—these precious men and women whose capacity to think and feel is painfully distorted. I pray for those who suffer with various degrees of depression. I pray for friends trying to make sense of hard providences and your promises. I pray for those unable to grieve losses and betrayals in a healthy way. I pray for those who live in the angry void of despair and hopelessness. I pray for those whose war with self-contempt makes death look like a good choice. You know the names and the details, and you alone have the grace.

All I know to do is bring these dear ones to you in prayer, much like those who brought their paralyzed friend to you on a pallet. I know you are merciful and I know you are mighty. Only you know what's going on in each of them. I wish a clear and certain diagnosis was easy to secure. It's not always easy to discern what's physiological, psychological, demonic, or just the absence of the gospel. Give us what we need to love and to serve these broken ones well.

When we're fearful and confused, when we are fed up and used up, give us all the wisdom, compassion, and faith to love well. Jesus, it's this kind of suffering that makes me wish for miracles on demand. Help us trust you for supernatural intervention and grace for supernatural long-term caring. Write the stories that will maximize your glory.

How we long for the day when every form of brokenness will give way to the endless joys of spiritual, physical, mental, and emotional health. I pray in your holy and healing name. Amen.

A Prayer in Praise of the Holy Spirit

For those who live according to the flesh set their minds on the things of the flesh, but those who live according to the Spirit set their minds on the things of the Spirit. To set the mind on the flesh is death, but to set the mind on the Spirit is life and peace. For the mind that is set on the flesh is hostile to God, for it does not submit to God's law; indeed, it cannot. Those who are in the flesh cannot please God. You, however, are not in the flesh but in the Spirit, if in fact the Spirit of God dwells in you. Anyone who does not have the Spirit of Christ does not belong to him. (Rom. 8:5–9)

Heavenly Father, I'm particularly grateful today for the person and work of the Holy Spirit. Though I don't understand everything he's up to, these things I gladly affirm today . . .

Just as assuredly as Jesus stood outside of Lazarus's tomb and said, "Come forth," you sent the Holy Spirit to preach the gospel to my heart, and I came out of the tomb of my sin and death. How I praise you for your sovereign goodness and power. Unless you had breathed new life into my spirit, I would have never, could have never believed the gospel.

When you raised me up in Jesus, you baptized me with the Holy Spirit, making me a member of your family and Christ's bride. You sealed me for eternity by the Spirit, marking me as your very own possession. You sent the Spirit to live as a permanent resident in my heart—to constantly preach the gospel to my heart, convict me of sin, make me like Jesus, and tell me that I am your beloved child.

According to the truth of the gospel in your Word, I'm already controlled by the Holy Spirit. I am no longer controlled by my sinful nature. You've given me all the gifts of the Spirit I need to live as a functioning part of the church and a caring servant in your kingdom.

You gave the Spirit to me as the firstfruits and guarantee of the full inheritance of the salvation that Jesus completely earned for me. What a generous and loving God you are!

Therefore, I acknowledge my desire to be more fully and consistently filled with the Holy Spirit, to walk according to the Spirit, to keep in step with the Spirit, to set my mind on what the Spirit desires. All to which I say, "Hallelujah, what a Savior! Hallelujah, what a salvation!" I pray in Jesus' name. Amen.

A Prayer about Burden-Bearing Love

Carry each other's burdens, and in this way you will fulfill the law of Christ.
(Gal. 6:2 NIV)

*C*ompassionate Jesus, the call to shoulder up under the burdens of friends and family drives me to you today. Otherwise I would simply turn and walk away, just like the priest and the Levite in the parable of the Good Samaritan (Luke 10:25–37). Only you know why there's such an avalanche of broken stories converging on my doorstep at this time. Where else can I go but to you?

Jesus, it's only because you bore the burden of the law's demands and judgment for me; only because you say to me, "Cast all your care upon me, for I care for you" (see 1 Pet. 5:7); only because you call to me, "Come to me, all you who are weary and burdened, and I will give you rest" (Matt. 11:28 NIV) that I will risk what's involved in bearing the heavy burdens of others.

Jesus, here's what I ask and need from you today: Help me not to be afraid of the emotional messiness that certain burdens bring. Help me know how to rely on your presence more than I rely on my words. I want to be aware of my limits, for sure, but even *more* aware of your limitless mercy, grace, power, and peace.

For the woman who just got confirmation that the mass in her breast is malignant; for the dad who just lost yet another job in this fragile economy; for the couple whose two-year wait to welcome their adoptive child just ended childlessly; for the parents who've spent all and who are spent from trying to rescue their daughter from the ravages of an eating disorder; for the friend who preaches a powerful gospel that bears fruit in everybody's children but his own; for the friends who are having to pay a great price for a misdiagnosed medical condition; for the couples who are sleeping all alone in the same bed; for those who tell me, "This is too much, I cannot and will not go on."

Jesus, I bring all of these friends to your throne of grace, and I will seek to fulfill "the law of Christ"—the law of love, the way of the gospel—as you give me strength, wisdom, and grace. In your persistent and sufficient name I pray. Amen.

A Prayer about Less Annoyance and More Overlooking

Fools show their annoyance at once,
>   but the prudent overlook an insult. (Prov. 12:16 NIV)

A person's wisdom yields patience;
>   it is to one's glory to overlook an offense. (Prov. 19:11 NIV)

Dear Jesus, I just got "busted" by the gospel while reading these Scriptures this morning. I'm annoyed and have been for several days. I won't try to make excuses; I'll just come to you as the knotted mess that I am.

As I own my bad attitude, I'm thankful that you're the consummate "overlooker." It's not that you don't take my annoying ways seriously, because you do. But you're so forbearing, forgiving, and patient with me.

This side of glorification, I don't really expect to be annoyance free. But certainly the gospel is big enough to help me show my annoyance less quickly, less often, and less harmfully. And certainly the gospel is powerful enough to help me repent quicker when I do act like a fool—taking every insult, offense, cut, quip, and quirk way too seriously.

So, Jesus, give me all the grace and wisdom I need to know what to take seriously and what simply to overlook. Give me gospel bigheartedness and gospel thick-skinnedness.

I don't want to keep a record of annoying things done around me or to me. I don't want to put every intentional or unintentional slight or aggressive or passive-aggressive comment on my iPod and then push the replay button. No good can come from that.

In fact, Jesus, I ask you to help me be far more aware of when *I'm the one* being unnecessarily annoying or irritating to others. Convict me when my sense of humor leads to someone else's harm. Help me to steward my words, body language, and "freedoms." Jesus, help me to give others fewer reasons to need this prayer when they're around *me*. I pray in your loving and kind name. Amen.

A Prayer for Loving Well in Messy Relationships

Some time later Paul said to Barnabas, "Let us go back and visit the believers in all the towns where we preached the word of the Lord and see how they are doing." Barnabas wanted to take John, also called Mark, with them, but Paul did not think it wise to take him, because he had deserted them in Pamphylia and had not continued with them in the work. They had such a sharp disagreement that they parted company. Barnabas took Mark and sailed for Cyprus, but Paul chose Silas and left, commended by the believers to the grace of the Lord. (Acts 15:36–40 NIV)

Gracious Jesus, I start this day so grateful for the stories of brokenness and messiness included in the Scriptures. Thankfully, they weren't edited out, for the stories give me hope. The Bible is so authentic and honest; mere men couldn't possibly have written it without your hand and heart guiding them.

In particular, I'm thankful today for this story of two good friends, Paul and Barnabas, having "such a sharp disagreement that they parted company." Lord, I've been in that situation, and right now I'm watching that story play out between two friends I deeply love and respect. It's sticky and messy, and I hate being caught in the middle.

So I look to you right now for the resources of the gospel. I need wisdom from above; power in my weakness; and grace to love two stubborn, hurting people. My default mode is to not get involved—hoping the whole thing will just blow over or go away. But that's not going to happen.

Jesus, the good news is you've come to destroy hostilities; to tear down walls of division; to make peace and be our peace. You reconcile enemies to God and to one another, so I can trust you to be at work in this tense and complicated situation.

It took time plus grace for Paul and Barnabas to get back together. I don't know what time plus grace will look like for my friends, but show me my role in the story you are writing. Help me listen from the heart and confront in love. Lead my praying and let me feel their hurt. Help me engage with both sides without taking sides. Help me stay present in the chaos without giving in to the pulls. As I serve my friends, show me more of my sin and more of the power of the gospel.

Jesus, no one is better at sticky-situation loving than you, so I abandon myself to you with my fears, my confusion, and my very real hope of your showing up. I pray with confidence, in your powerful and reconciling name. Amen.

A Prayer for Remembering God's Big Story of Redemption

Now the LORD said to Abram, "Go from your country and your kindred and your father's house to the land that I will show you. And I will make of you a great nation, and I will bless you and make your name great, so that you will be a blessing. I will bless those who bless you, and him who dishonors you I will curse, and in you all the families of the earth shall be blessed." (Gen. 12:1–3)

Gracious and sovereign Father, remembering your big story of redemption is not only a great joy but a critical discipline. For so many different narratives compete for our hearts, days, energy, and resources. Remind us today of the main story line that unfolds in the Bible, connects all of history, and reveals your generous heart. And help us once again to find our place in this story.

We praise you for making incredible promises to an unsuspecting pagan, Abram—promises you alone can keep. Indeed, from beginning to end your story is a story of sovereign grace.

Father, thank you for the promise of the land. It began in the Garden of Eden, continued in the land of Israel, and will culminate in the new heaven and new earth. Place and space matter to you. You have promised to redeem and restore your entire fallen world, not just one part of it. We praise you for your inviolate plans and great strength.

Thank you for the promise of the seed. From the one man Abram, you created a great nation as the birthing canal of the Messiah, Jesus. You promised the seed of the woman would crush the head of the serpent (Gen. 3:15), and you did not lie. Jesus came into the world to destroy the work of the devil, and he has succeeded. His cross and resurrection guarantee that just like Abraham, we are counted righteous in your sight by faith (Gen. 15:6; Rom. 4). We praise you for the everlasting gospel of your saving grace.

Thank you for the promise of the blessing. Father, it has always been your plan to redeem a family from all families on the earth. Indeed, you made Abram (Abraham) the father of many nations. All of history is bound up with your commitment to redeem your people "from every nation, from all tribes and peoples and languages" (Rev. 7:9). We praise you for your magnanimous heart and measureless generosity.

Father, thank you for making us characters in and carriers of your great story of redemption. So let us live and so let us love. In Jesus' name we pray, with gratitude and awe. Amen.

A Prayer about Jesus and the Brokenhearted

The LORD is near to the brokenhearted
and saves the crushed in spirit. (Ps. 34:18)

Jesus, I'm increasingly grateful for *all* the reasons the Father sent you into the world. When I look in the mirror of the Word, I'm thankful that you came to set me free from my imprisonment to sin and death and to proclaim the year of the Lord's favor. In the gospel I hear you singing these words over me: "There is therefore now *no* condemnation for those who are in Christ Jesus" (Rom. 8:1). I have *no* righteousness apart from yours, Lord Jesus.

When I look at places like Haiti, Calcutta, and Darfur, I'm so thankful that you came to preach good news to the poor—not just good news concerning spiritual poverty but also the good news of a kingdom that provides food for the hungry, clean water for the thirsty, shelter for the homeless, advocacy for the marginalized, family for the orphan.

When I look at systemic evil in the world—human trafficking, the idolatry of greed, an ideology of terror, the pornography industry, to name a few—I'm so thankful that you've also come to proclaim the day of vengeance of our God. No one is a greater champion of justice than you, Lord Jesus. One day, all the pillaging weeds of unrighteousness will be replaced with mighty oaks of righteousness—"a planting of the LORD for the display of his splendor" (Isa. 61:3 NIV).

Today, Lord Jesus, this very morning, I'm especially thankful that you're close to the brokenhearted and that you save those who are crushed in spirit. To have sat yesterday with a mom and dad as they held their three-week-old son as he drew his last breath . . . *sometimes life feels like too much*, Jesus. Some stories and moments make me wonder, "*Why*, O Lord?" and "*How long*, O Lord?" Thank you for not despising my weakness and weariness.

I'm most thankful, Lord Jesus, that you're very much with our friends, whose wails and wounds you perfectly understand. No one was broken in heart and body like you, no one was crushed in spirit like you, and you did it all for us. In the mystery and in this moment, I praise you that you comfort all who mourn and provide for those who grieve.

O for the day when we will forever be done with a spirit of despair and will only wear the garment of praise. In your kindhearted, ever-present name I pray. Amen.

A Prayer about Ordained Days and Thoughts of God

In your book were written, every one of them,
 the days that were formed for me,
 when as yet there were none of them.
How precious to me are your thoughts, O God!
 How vast is the sum of them!
If I would count them, they are more than the sand.
 I awake, and I am still with you. (Ps. 139:16–18)

Heavenly Father, it's my birthday, and the number just keeps getting bigger. Yet as "vast" and "great" as the sum of my years seems to me today, vaster and greater are my thoughts of you. The number of my years is calculated merely in terms of decades, but if I tried to "do the math" concerning your glory and grace, I'd have to count every grain of sand on every beach that has ever existed. With David I can honestly say, "How precious to me are your thoughts" (Ps. 139:17).

Father, keep on rescuing me from all wrong thinking about you. Keep showing me how little I really see and understand about the greatness of your love for us in Jesus. That won't embarrass me; it will truly thrill me. May the gospel keep on getting bigger and bigger and bigger.

It's a source of incredible peace and freedom to know that you've ordained all of my days for me. That feels not like unfair fatalism but rather Fatherly affection. I'll not live one day more or one day less than you decree, by your sovereign purposes and eternal pleasure.

There's a part of me that would like to turn the clock back for a possible "do-over," especially for certain stretches of my life. But then again, not really. Your name is Redeemer, and you're the God who restores years eaten away by locusts. I choose to rest in your love rather than stew in my regrets. I have great confidence and hope in your commitment to make all things new.

All I ask is that each additional day, week, month, or year you appoint for me in this world will be filled with a greater grasp of the only love that will never let go of us. By your Spirit, Father, continue to reveal to me how wide and long and high and deep is the love of Christ—the only love that surpasses knowledge (Eph. 3:18–19). Everything else will take care of itself. I make my prayer in Jesus' matchless and merciful name. Amen.

A Prayer about the Sufferings of Jesus and the Victory of Justice

Many followed him [Jesus], and he healed them all and ordered them not to make him known. This was to fulfill what was spoken by the prophet Isaiah: "Behold, my servant whom I have chosen, my beloved with whom my soul is well pleased. I will put my Spirit upon him, and he will proclaim justice to the Gentiles. He will not quarrel or cry aloud, nor will anyone hear his voice in the streets; a bruised reed he will not break, and a smoldering wick he will not quench, until he brings justice to victory; And in his name the Gentiles will hope." (Matt. 12:15–21)

Dear Lord Jesus, I'm greatly moved today as I ponder your compassionate heart for the broken and suffering. Surely there's no Savior like you: entering, not running from our chaos; taking, not despising our shame; shouldering, not ignoring our burdens. "Bruised reeds" and "smoldering wicks" love your appearing. Justice will be fully victorious because you have been the willing Sufferer.

For gloriously sure, your sufferings as our sin-bearer are over. As the Lamb of God, you offered yourself once and for all upon the cross. No additional sacrifice for our sin remains to be offered—none. I no longer fear being judged by God for my sin. Your perfect love has driven away all fear of punishment, anxiety about judgment day, and uncertainty about eternity. I boast and rest in your sufferings for me, Lord Jesus, and I also shout a hearty "Hallelujah!"

But I also cry out, "Help me, Lord Jesus . . . help me." Help me go with you into the sufferings of friends and family, further into the groans of my own heart, and into the injustices and brokenness of my community. Like most, I have an aversion to pain and suffering. Like many, I'd love the Christian life to be an antidote for all discomfort and distress. Like some, I get overwhelmed and overtaxed by the sufferings of others.

Here's my peace, my consolation, my ballast, Jesus: you're not calling us to suffer *for you* but to suffer *with you*, and that makes all the difference in the world. We're called into the fellowship of your sufferings, not into the isolation of our sufferings.

You'll never lead us into hard places where you're not present. You'll never ask us to do anything all by ourselves. You'll never leave us or forsake us, Jesus. You will lead justice to victory, and in your name all the nations will put their hope. I pray in your kind and compassionate name. Amen.

A Prayer about Perpetually Coming to Jesus

As you come to him, a living stone rejected by men but in the sight of God chosen and precious, you yourselves like living stones are being built up as a spiritual house, to be a holy priesthood, to offer spiritual sacrifices acceptable to God through Jesus Christ. For it stands in Scripture: "Behold, I am laying in Zion a stone, a cornerstone chosen and precious, and whoever believes in him will not be put to shame." (1 Pet. 2:4–6)

Heavenly Father, I used to think that "coming to Jesus" was a phrase whose meaning is exhausted when we first trust your Son to be our Savior. For sure, that is the most glorious and essential "come to Jesus" meeting we'll ever have. How I praise you for showing me how much I needed your Son and for giving me the faith to trust Jesus plus nothing for my salvation.

It's obvious to me now, however, that the whole Christian life is about coming to Jesus. We need Jesus today as much as the first day he entered our lives. In fact, we'll never exhaust our need for what Jesus alone can give. We'll forever discover more and more reasons to give him the worship, adoration, and praise of which he alone is worthy.

Indeed, Jesus, you are the life-giving living stone for your beloved people; the precious cornerstone of the living temple called the body of Christ; the rock of refuge that's higher than I am (Ps. 61:2–3); the rock from which God gave water in the wilderness in Moses' day (1 Cor. 10:1–4). You are the honey-giving rock of whom Asaph spoke (Ps. 81:16), and you are Daniel's stone, cut from a mountain by the hands of God, which will become an everlasting kingdom of redemption and restoration (Dan. 2:36–45).

Jesus, we exalt you and delight in you. The more precious you become to us, the more we watch our shame melt away. The more we see you for who you really are, the more we see all other precious currencies as fool's gold. The more we come to you, the more we realize that it's you who is always coming to us first.

Jesus, we come to you right now—we come bringing our emptiness to the fountain of your fullness. We bring our brokenness to the storehouse of your kindness. We bring our weakness in the great assurance of your endless mercies. We come to you right now for enough gospel manna to meet the demands of this one day. We pray in your precious and shame-freeing name. Amen.

A Prayer about Our Tireless, Weariless God

The LORD is the everlasting God,
   the Creator of the ends of the earth.
He will not grow tired or weary,
   and his understanding no one can fathom.
He gives strength to the weary
   and increases the power of the weak. .
Even youths grow tired and weary,
   and young men stumble and fall;
but those who hope in the LORD
   will renew their strength.
They will soar on wings like eagles;
   they will run and not grow weary,
   they will walk and not be faint. (Isa. 40:28–31 NIV)

Gracious Father, this was one of the first Scriptures I memorized as a young believer, yet reading it today is like finding a new treasure in an old field. That's one of the things I most love about your Word. It's never antiquated or redundant but always vintage and ever new. You're the God who speaks in specifics and without stuttering. You're the Father who knows what we need even before we ask, and you provide before we ask.

This passage from Isaiah is underlined multiple times in my favorite Bible, and for good reason. It reminds me that you're not like me, in so many ways. You never get tired or weary. I do and I am. Accepting limitations, finiteness, and weakness has never been one of my strengths. But I must. Since youths grow tired and weary and young men stumble and fall, why do I think I'm exempt from "running on empty" and hitting a wall?

Father, I'm not asking to soar like an eagle, as fun as that might be, and I'm not seeking to run like a sprinter or a marathoner. Just walking upright with a renewed heart, a steady gait, and a replenished energy will be enough.

My hope is in you, Father—merciful Abba, who brings refreshment into the wilderness; generous Lord, who promises sufficient grace every day; mighty God, who raises the dead. Right now I look to you for all the spiritual, emotional, mental, and physical strength I'll need to live out the implications of the gospel just today. I'm not depleted, though heading there, but I have no doubts about your great compassion for me in Jesus.

Because Jesus embraced the ultimate weakness and weariness of the cross, I'm confident of your burden-bearing love. I may be weary in my servanthood, but I'm thriving in my sonship. Nothing can separate us from your love. I pray in Jesus' tender and triumphant name. Amen.

A Prayer about Devilish Footholds

"In your anger do not sin": Do not let the sun go down while you are still angry, and do not give the devil a foothold. (Eph. 4:26–27 NIV)

Dear Jesus, I can think of certain door-to-door salespeople I wish I'd never let across the threshold. One toe through my front door, one minute into their pitch, and I'm wishing I could usher them on their way. Oh, that I'd be that wise when the devil approaches my heart and home.

Of course, if he came knocking in a red jumpsuit with a three-pronged pitchfork in hand, sporting sixties-style beatnik facial hair, I'd have no problem turning him away. Unfortunately, he often comes in the back door through my impatience, irritation, aggravation, and anger.

Jesus, help me steward my anger. It's always been a confusing emotion to me. I've been on the destructive end of anger and rage. I remember the fear, the confusion, the shame, the ambivalence. I don't wish such a crushing of the spirit on anyone, but I certainly own the ways my anger has nonetheless brought harm to people I love.

You're not telling me never to be angry but to be careful not to sin in my anger. Jesus, help me be angry at the right time, for the right reasons, in the right way. Only you can melt this icy tension in my heart. Only you can change my rigidity into playfulness. Only you can redirect the wasted energy of my anger into patience and loving-kindness. Only you can replace my idol of control with a greater worship of you and submission to your purposes.

Right now, Lord Jesus, I throw open every door and window of my heart. Come on in and establish multiple footholds of mercy, grace, and compassion. I abandon myself to your beauty and bounty today. I pray in your peerless and priceless name. Amen.

A Prayer about the Comfort
of Jesus' Tears

Jesus wept. (John 11:35)

Lord Jesus, we all know this verse answers the question, "What's the shortest verse in the Bible?" But it's also a candidate for the most profound and comforting verse in the Bible. Your aching and compassionate tears, shed outside of Lazarus's tomb, are one of the greatest showers that has ever fallen upon the face of the earth.

You knew that within a matter of moments, your friend would breathe again. You knew he'd walk again. You knew you'd get to enjoy his company again. And yet you wept convulsively in the presence of his death. It was well said by those honored to see your sacred fury and great sadness, "See how he loved him!" (John 11:36).

Jesus, I'm glad to know you as a tenderhearted Savior . . . especially today. In just a few hours I'll help a couple bury their three-week-old son. Oh, the pain, the loss, the confusion, the second-guessing. Understandably, we cry, "Lord, if only you'd been there . . ."

Jesus, no one hates death more than you. *No one.* No one feels its horrid implications more profoundly. No one grieves its ugly violation more deeply. No one longs for the day of "no more death" (Rev. 21:4 NIV) more earnestly than you.

Perhaps some of your tears outside of Lazarus's tomb were offered knowing he'd have to go through the whole rotten dying process again—such is your hatred of death.

Today I rest my sobered and saddened heart on your shoulder and on the hope of being able to call you "the resurrection and the life" (John 11:25). Jesus, your death on the cross secured the death of death itself—the last enemy (1 Cor. 15:26). And because of your resurrection, we sing in advance of *our* resurrection, "O death, where is your victory? O death, where is your sting?" (1 Cor. 15:55).

How we praise you! How we exalt you! How we rest our heavy hearts in your loving hands! I pray in your grave-robbing name. Amen.

A Prayer about What or Who Brings Us Peace

"Blessed is the king who comes in the name of the Lord!" "Peace in heaven and glory in the highest!" Some of the Pharisees in the crowd said to Jesus, "Teacher, rebuke your disciples!" "I tell you," he replied, "if they keep quiet, the stones will cry out." As he approached Jerusalem and saw the city, he wept over it and said, "If you, even you, had only known on this day what would bring you peace." (Luke 19:38–42 NIV)

Jesus, the ache within our hearts for peace is unrelenting. Let me get specific: the ache within *my* heart is unrelenting. Though I already rest in you plus nothing for my forgiveness and righteousness, I still get sucker punched by the tantalizing illusion that peace can be found in something or someone else.

Some days, Jesus, I'm like Esau. My peace pangs take over, and in the moment, I'll gladly settle for a bowl of hot porridge over the hope of a future banquet. The provision of a snack in hand blinds my eye, deafens my ear, and dulls my taste buds to the sumptuous fare of the wedding feast of the Lamb—the day when my longing and demanding heart will be fully set free to delight in you. "Maranatha!" Even so, Lord Jesus, come . . . hasten that day!

Some days, Jesus, I get lost in the world of "if only." If only there were no tensions in any of my relationships, I'd be a happy man. If only the phone wouldn't ring again, demanding a little more of me than I have to offer, I'd be fine. If only I lived somewhere else, worked with different people, had a different body, had more money, had fewer hassles, had a different spouse, had never been deeply wounded, were twenty years younger . . .

But right now I hear you saying to me, "If you, even you, had only known on this day what would bring you peace" (Luke 19:42 NIV). Indeed, Jesus, you alone, this day and every day, are the Prince of Peace. Only in union with you, only in communion with you do I find the true and sufficient peace for which I long.

I join the chorus of those who cry out, "Blessed is the king who comes in the name of the Lord!" (Luke 19:38 NIV), for you, Jesus, are the king of glory and grace. Until the day of consummate peace, continue to free me from the delusion that peace can be found anywhere else but in you. I pray in your faithful name. Amen.

A Prayer about Formerly "Useless" People

Accordingly, although I am bold enough in Christ to command you to do what is required, yet for love's sake I prefer to appeal to you—I, Paul, an old man and now a prisoner also for Christ Jesus—I appeal to you for my child Onesimus, whose father I became in my imprisonment. (Formerly he was useless to you, but now he is indeed useful to you and to me.) (Philem. 8–11)

Dear Jesus, what a great story these few verses tell—the story of how one man's "useless" slave became another man's beloved son. Stories like this make the gospel so beautiful and believable. I see myself in this story, both as Onesimus and as Philemon.

Jesus, thank you for not giving up on me, for coming after me when I was running away from you as fast as I could, just like Onesimus ran from Philemon. Overtly and covertly, I did everything I could to avoid you and ignore you, but you found me, you bound me to your heart through the cords of the gospel, and slowly but surely, you're changing me. The journey from slavery to sonship hasn't always been easy.

Jesus, I also know what it's like to be Philemon. I've been failed and I've been hurt. I've been betrayed and suffered loss. But forgive me for labeling *anyone* as useless. Paul saw something in Onesimus that Philemon didn't see. Jesus, you saw something in me that no one else saw. Please give me your gospel eyes to see what you see in others: broken people just like me.

Who have I branded "useless," with either my actual words or unspoken words? Who have I written off? Who have I renamed "failure," "worthless," "you'll never amount to anything," "never to be trusted again"?

I know you're calling me to be wise, but I also know you're calling me to love others as you love me. None of us is beyond the *need of your grace* and none of us is beyond the *reach of your grace*. I pray in your chain-breaking name. Amen.

A Prayer about Jesus' Dining Mates

Levi [Matthew] held a great banquet for Jesus at his house, and a large crowd of tax collectors and others were eating with them. But the Pharisees and the teachers of the law who belonged to their sect complained to his disciples, "Why do you eat and drink with tax collectors and sinners?" Jesus answered them, "It is not the healthy who need a doctor, but the sick. I have not come to call the righteous, but sinners to repentance." (Luke 5:29–32 NIV)

Dear Jesus, I can't read this story without fueling my longing for the banquet of all banquets. Who will sit and be served by you at the wedding feast of the Lamb?

Only those who've been saved by grace alone through faith alone; only tax collectors and "sinners" and Pharisees and teachers of the law who've been clothed in the wedding garments of your righteousness.

I praise you for making me a part of your broken-yet-beloved bride; for calling me, healing me, saving me. I have no problem acknowledging my sickness and receiving your remedy. Jesus, there's no greater friend of sinners than you. Thank you for eating and drinking, reclining and dining, fellowshiping and communing with the likes of us.

It would actually be a good thing if our churches were places where Pharisees and "older brothers" (Luke 15) criticized us for all the sick people, broken sinners, and cultural misfits who gathered there. May we grieve when your welcoming heart is not extended as you intend.

Oh, to be more like Levi—to be so impacted by your love, Lord Jesus, that I'm constantly throwing mini-banquets for my friends. Turn every one of my lunch appointments into a threesome, with you and a friend. Turn my family gatherings into occasions where you're always filling the empty seat.

Make this concave heart of mine far more convex, far more friendly to outsiders, far more like yours, Jesus. I pray in your merciful and mighty name. Amen.

A Prayer for a Friend Doubting the Faith

Keep yourselves in the love of God, waiting for the mercy of our Lord
Jesus Christ that leads to eternal life. And have mercy on those who doubt.
(Jude 21–22)

Dear Jesus, the liar and thief is at it again, and a good friend has a
bull's-eye painted on his chest. The one who maliciously asked,
"Did God really say . . . ?" (Gen. 3:1) continues his unrelenting assault,
seeking to twist, undermine, and sabotage the only Word that gives life. I
long for the day when our already-defeated foe becomes our fully eradicated
enemy. Hasten the day, Lord . . . hasten that day.

Jesus, as you know, this is a friend who's helped many people find peace
in you, but right now he's not really sure what he believes. He's beyond
anger. There's a scary void in his eyes. He feels abandoned by you and
cruelly punished. This could be burnout, but it feels like more.

I ache for him, Jesus. I groan for my friend and grapple for his heart. Help
me love him well. Give me patience to stay present in his chaos. Help me
wade through what feels like a smoke screen of theological questions to
get to the real issues of his heart. What's really going on inside of him,
Jesus? Give me discernment. Give me good answers for honest questions,
but give me great mercy for his real needs, whatever they are.

And please keep him from medicating in destructive ways. Pain makes
us vulnerable, and isolation intensifies our demand for relief. He's pulling
away from those of us he's walked with for years. That's what concerns
me the most.

Jesus, I'll keep pursuing and praying, but I put much more stock in your
prayers than mine. You never stop interceding for us (Rom. 8:34); you
ever live to pray for us (Heb. 7:25). I cannot imagine your prayers failing.
Restore the joy of your salvation in my friend. Bring him home to your
heart. As you prayed for the protection of your disciples, I'm confident of
your prayers for my friend (John 17:15). I pray with peace, in your tender
and tireless name. Amen.

A Prayer for Gospel Pharisees and Scribes

And the Pharisees and the scribes asked him, "Why do your disciples not walk according to the tradition of the elders, but eat with defiled hands?" And he said to them, "Well did Isaiah prophesy of you hypocrites, as it is written, 'This people honors me with their lips, but their heart is far from me; in vain do they worship me, teaching as doctrines the commandments of men.' You leave the commandment of God and hold to the tradition of men." (Mark 7:5–8)

Jesus, these are strong words. What could be more tragic than to hear you say, "You talk about me a whole lot, using plenty of spiritual language and Bible quotes. You're very quick to recognize and correct false teaching. You're even zealous to apply what you know to others. But your heart is very far from me"?

It would be one thing if such a rebuke came to us because we were acting like Mosaic Pharisees and scribes—distorting and misapplying Old Testament law; putting people under the yoke of performance-based spirituality; replacing your commandments with our traditions. But it's an altogether different thing to be a gospel Pharisee and scribe.

Forgive us, Jesus, when we love exposing false gospels more than we love spending time with you in prayer and fellowship.

Forgive us when we are quick to tell people what obedience is not but fail to demonstrate what the obedience of faith and love actually is.

Forgive us when we call ourselves "recovering Pharisees" or "recovering legalists" when in actuality, we're not really recovering from anything.

Forgive us when we talk more about "getting the gospel" than how we've been "gotten" by the gospel.

Forgive us for being just as arrogant about grace theology as we were obnoxious about legalistic theology.

Forgive us when we don't use our freedom to serve one another in love, but rather use it to put our consciences to sleep.

Forgive us when our love for the gospel does not translate into a love for holiness, world evangelism, and caring for widows and orphans.

Forgive us for having a PhD in the indicatives of the gospel yet failing so miserably when it comes to the imperatives of the gospel.

Forgive us when we love "the gospel" more than we actually love *you*, Jesus, as impossible as that may seem.

Change us by your grace and for your glory. We pray with convicted and humbled hearts. Amen.

A Prayer about a Fleeing Devil

"God opposes the proud, but gives grace to the humble." Submit yourselves therefore to God. Resist the devil, and he will flee from you. (James 4:6–7)

Gracious Father, at times I make things more complicated than they need to be (an enormous understatement). This is certainly the case when it comes to spiritual warfare. When I look back over the years at all the different teaching I've had about "fighting the devil," much of it promoted more fear than faith, more phobia than freedom, more preoccupation with darkness than fascination with the Light of the World. Somewhere along the line, I missed the image of a fleeing devil. Alas, another arena for gospel sanity.

I know that we can't afford to be naive about the destructive schemes of the enemy. Because of the cross of Jesus, the devil knows his time is short, and he is filled with fury. En route to his sure demise, he ramps up his seducing, tempting, and condemning ways, every opportunity he gets.

I know even more surely that I can no longer afford to be ignorant of how to resist the devil with the gospel. So today, Father, because the gospel is true, I humble myself before you. Only the gospel frees me to see and own my weakness and susceptibility to the devil's schemes.

I'll not be sucker punched by my arrogance and pride. I need the gospel today as much as I did the first day you declared me to be righteous in your sight. I trust you in this moment for all the grace I'll need to live for your glory this very day.

Accordingly, Jesus, right now I submit to you as my Prophet, Priest, and King. You're my wisdom and my righteousness, my holiness and my redemption (1 Cor. 1:30). I boast in you plus nothing, for there's nothing boastworthy in me.

I'll resist the devil's deceitful and damning ways by looking unto you, Jesus, pondering your beauty and bounty. With the eye of faith, I set my gaze on you, the author and perfecter of my faith (Heb. 12:2). I'm not even going to glance at the devil as he flees, and flee he must. I pray in your powerful and triumphant name. Amen.

A Prayer about Early Morning Love

Let me hear in the morning of your steadfast love,
for in you I trust. (Ps. 143:8)

Dear Lord Jesus, I understand that breakfast is the most important meal of the day. What we consume early will greatly determine the rhythms of the rest of the day. I know this to be true, especially on the mornings when meager sleep segues into a way-too-busy day, and I choose to break the evening fast with too much caffeine and sugar. As they say, "Up like a rocket, down like a rocket."

But on a far, far more profound level, what I put into my mind and heart as the day begins affects a whole lot more than my energy level and how soon I'll need a "power nap."

Out of equal measures of delight and desperation, I make the psalmist's cry my own: "Let me hear in the morning of your steadfast love" (Ps. 143:8). That's what I need more than *anything* else.

Only your love is better than life, Jesus. Only your love meets the deepest needs of my whole being and satisfies my most intense longings. Only your love is unwavering, Jesus, for all other loves are filled with conditions and contingencies. Only your love is unfailing, Jesus, for all other loves are fickle and finite.

Only your love can expose and replace my idols. Only your love can break my self-indulgent chains and set me free to love well. Only your love can heal the greatest heart-wounds I carry. Only your love can move me from navel-gazing to kingdom living. And I can think of a lot more "onlys," Jesus.

So this morning and every morning—afternoons and evenings too—Jesus, preach the gospel to our hearts by the Holy Spirit. The gospel is the word of your unfailing love, and only in the gospel do we hear and experience your unfailing love. We pray in your trustworthy name. Amen.

A Prayer about the Ultimate Romance

I am my beloved's,
and his desire is for me. (Song of Sol. 7:10)

Gracious Jesus, it's the day in our culture in which red hearts, over-priced cards, dark chocolates, and cut flowers abound—Valentine's Day is upon us. For some, it's a day of incredible kindness, sweetness, and gratitude. For others, it's a day in which brokenness, loneliness, and emptiness are magnified. For all of us, it should be a day in which our deepest longings for intimacy and connection find their way home to you, Jesus, the consummate lover.

I praise you for your generosity, Jesus. You've given me incredible tastes of sensual wonder and joy in my marriage. There've been times when I've wondered how heaven itself could hold more joy than what I've known with my spouse.

I equally praise you for showing me, time and time again, that no one human being (or any number of them), no human romance story, no torrid love affair can possibly fill the vacuum in my soul that's uniquely Jesus shaped. Even the best marriage is made of two broken people, two redeemed sinners who will ultimately not be enough for the other.

Grant me, no, *grace* me with a deeper and richer experience of belonging to you, Jesus. *You're the ultimate Spouse.* I believe this, but I want to *know* it. One moment I believe you truly desire me, and the next I'm filled with disconcerting unbelief.

It's in those times when I'm not alive to your pursuit of me, love for me, and delight in me that I place unrealistic demands on other relationships. Instead of being a steward, I become a user of others. Instead of being a servant, I take up a scorecard to measure them by my expectations. Forgive me and free me from all such nonsense.

Let me love as you love me, until the day my betrothal becomes the day of great banqueting—the day I long for more than any other—the wedding feast of the Lamb. I pray in your tender and tenacious name. Amen.

A Prayer in Praise of the God Who Knows Our Hearts

Lord, you know everyone's heart. (Acts 1:24 NIV)

Heavenly Father, there are so many things attributed to you in the Scriptures that are clearly not our domain. Heart-knowing is one of them. We often speak of being drawn to someone's heart, or of being offended, confused, or shut out from their heart, but only you really know what's in each of our hearts.

That's why we pray with humility and joy, "Search me, O God, and know my heart" (Ps. 139:23), for we cannot and must not trust our own diagnosis. There is nothing more deceitful on the face of the earth than the heart, including our hearts (Jer. 17:9). Only you understand the ways of the heart, Father. Only you can cure its great sickness.

Sometimes we think of ourselves much more highly than we ought—so wanting to believe we're more like Jesus than reality affirms. Sometimes we fall into shame and contempt and act like strangers to your mercy and grace, like orphans without a Father above or your Spirit within. Sometimes we just think about ourselves too much, period. Way too often we arrogantly assume we know what's in the hearts of others, playing judge and jury. Forgive us and free us from such meanness and madness.

Father, here's our sure and only hope: Through Jesus, you've already sprinkled clean water on us and have declared us to be clean. You've cleansed us from our impurities and are freeing us from our idols. You've already given us a new heart and placed your Spirit within us. You removed our stony hearts and gave us hearts of flesh—hearts that beat for you and your glory (Ezek. 36:24–27). What a generous and powerful God you are!

And you will complete this good work you've begun in each of us and in all of creation (Phil. 1:6). Justified sinners are destined to be your glorified children (Rom. 8:30). Oh, how we praise you for the peace and assurance we enjoy, all because the gospel is true. Help us to walk in greater humility before you and in observable kindness toward one another. We pray in Jesus' loving and heart-transforming name. Amen.

A Prayer in View of the Brevity of Life

Come now, you who say, "Today or tomorrow we will go into such and such a town and spend a year there and trade and make a profit"—yet you do not know what tomorrow will bring. What is your life? For you are a mist that appears for a little while and then vanishes. Instead, you ought to say, "If the Lord wills, we will live and do this or that." (James 4:13–15)

Heavenly Father, you have made us not for "fifteen minutes in the spotlight" but for an eternity of glorifying you and enjoying you forever. As this day begins, I praise you for such a hope and future—a future that's already begun for us in Jesus. Our eternal life began the day you "raised us up with Christ and seated us with him in the heavenly realms" (Eph. 2:6 NIV), to the praise of your glorious grace (Eph. 1:6).

Yet, Father, these verses in James remind me that our life span in this body isn't very long at all. We're more like a brief mist than an aging oak. I feel this more than ever, and I'm both sobered and gladdened by the thought.

Here's my question and prayer: How would you have me live the rest of my "misty moment"? Only you know when I'll "vanish" from this body. Only you know what'll happen tomorrow. I'll keep on planning, but it's you who orders my steps (Prov. 16:9).

In light of the gospel, what should I spend *more* time doing and *less* time doing? What have I been putting off that really matters to you? With whom do I need to spend more face-to-face and heart-to-heart time? Who am I still holding hostage by the chains of my unforgiveness and bitterness? What am I allowing to bug me that isn't all that "bugworthy"? Where should I invest more of your money and less of my worries?

Father, I praise you that I'm not going to merit any more of your affection by doing a better job with *any* of these things. None of these questions has a scorecard attached to it. It's Jesus' performance and record I boast in, but your grace frees me to ask the right questions and live a freer, more intentional life. Make my "gospel bucket list" for me. I pray in Jesus' matchless and magnificent name. Amen.

A Prayer for Being a Little Less Stupid

Whoever loves discipline loves knowledge,
but he who hates reproof is stupid. (Prov. 12:1)

The ear that listens to life-giving reproof
will dwell among the wise. (Prov. 15:31)

Heavenly Father, I'll never tire of thanking you for the joy of calling you Father—Abba, Father. There's no greater privilege, there's no safer refuge, there's no better address than to call your heart my home.

Once I was separate from Christ, excluded from citizenship in the true Israel, a foreigner to your promise-filled covenants, without hope and without you in the world. But through the work of Jesus, you brought me near—you made me one of your beloved children (Eph. 2:12–13). I worship, praise, and adore you for such a rich and firm standing in grace.

It's only because you love us as your children that you discipline us as you do (Heb. 12:4–11). All of your rebukes are "life-giving." None of them are meant to be guilt inducing, shame producing, or contempt fueling. You humble your children, but you don't humiliate us. You're firm but never harsh. You have my eternal glorification in view, but too often I'm only thinking about my instant gratification.

On the cross Jesus exhausted the punishment we deserve. Now you delight in us, even when you confront our immaturity and irresponsibility. That's why I'm a foolish man to play dodge ball with the convicting work of your Holy Spirit. You only purpose our freedom through the gospel. I'm a simpleton and stupid when I get defensive and try to make excuses for myself. What's there to defend?

Indeed, "stupid" has nothing to do with my IQ, my SAT score, or my GPA from various schools. Stupid is what we are when we hate correction, despise your discipline, or run from your admonitions.

I want to be at home among the wise, Father, so whether you speak to me from your Word, by the voice of your Spirit, or even through my spouse, colleagues, children, or friends, I'll trust you for a humble heart and submissive spirit. By the grace, truth, and power of the gospel, make me a little less stupid. I pray in Jesus' life-giving name. Amen.

A Prayer for Times of Troubling News

Do not let your hearts be troubled. You believe in God; believe also in me.
(John 14:1 NIV)

In the world you will have tribulation. But take heart; I have overcome the
world. (John 16:33)

Jesus, yesterday's troubling stories shape today's morning prayer. I went
to bed late last night, wearied with woes of good friends. I arise today
hungry with hope in you, our great and gracious Savior.

Thank you for being so honest with us about life this side of the new
heaven and new earth. You're not an on-demand panacea, promising the
elimination of hardships and heartaches. But you're a very present help,
pledging your presence in every circumstance and trial. Troubling news
doesn't have to cripple our hearts. Indeed, may it carry our hearts to you
today, for you are ever so trustworthy, Jesus.

For our friends stunned with heartbreaking health news, we declare
our trust in you, Jesus. How we long for the day when words like *cancer*,
dementia, and *heart disease* will no longer appear in our vocabulary. Until
that day, we unabashedly and earnestly pray for healing, and we trust you
for all-surpassing peace and more-than-sufficient grace.

For our friends saddened with heart-ripping issues with their children,
we declare our trust in you, Jesus. Few troubling reports carry more power
to dishearten than those related to our children. Whether they've been
vandalized by others' darkness or victimized by their own foolish choices,
it hurts real bad and real deep. We appeal to your covenant faithfulness
and your powerful reach: capture the hearts of our children, Jesus, and
help us love them well in the chaos and the crisis.

For our friends saddled with heart-wrenching financial burdens, we
declare our trust in you, Jesus. There's a growing number among us who
have more month left over at the end of the check. There's a growing
number of us who are facing losing homes and hope. But things that are
impossible with man are possible with you, Jesus. We pray not only for
your provision but for our generosity with one another. May the law of
love be fulfilled as we bear one another's burdens—spiritually, emotionally,
physically, and financially.

Jesus, we can trust in you as we trust in God, for you are God—the Son
of God and God the Son. We can "take heart" because you have already
overcome the world for us. In the world we will have tribulation, but in
you we find all the peace we need. We pray in your kind and overcoming
name. Amen.

A Prayer for Centering and Settling Our Hearts

"Be still, and know that I am God.
  I will be exalted among the nations,
  I will be exalted in the earth."
The LORD Almighty is with us;
  the God of Jacob is our fortress. (Ps. 46:10–11 NIV)

Sovereign Father, whenever I hear the command to "Be still," my default mode takes me back to several elementary school teachers who consistently told me to "Sit still!" They had to, because I was a squirmy, restless little person. I had a hard time staying in my seat. But you're telling me to *be* still, not *sit* still . . . and there's a world and gospel of difference.

You're not impatient or frustrated by me. I'm not disrupting your classroom, but I do have a disrupted heart, and you notice and you care. I'm squirmy and restless on the inside.

I know that you're with me and for me. I know this because of everything you've done for me in Jesus. You're a fortress of comfort for broken people like Jacob and me; you're a haven of rest, a strong tower of grace.

When I'm still I remember that you are God and nothing and no one else is. That's the best news of this or any day. You have no competition—counterfeits, but no competition. There are demigods, semi-gods, wannabe gods, but only you are God.

Kings and nations are not God, for one day you will be exalted among all the nations. The nations are like droplets in your bucket. Storms and environmental disasters are not God, for you will be exalted in the earth. You send the earthquake and harness the hurricane for your purposes.

Neither are my circumstances God, nor the opinions of others; nor is getting older, nor the choices of people I love, the mistakes I make and the sins I commit. In fact, the second most comforting news of the day is that *I'm not God*, though at times my attitude, prayerlessness, and unbelief would indicate a measure of self-worship.

Father, be exalted in the dailiness of my today. Let me see your hand and heart at work in everything. I don't want to be a practical atheist about anything, not any little thing. You are working all things together after the counsel of your will. You are working in all things for the good of those who love you, and that means me, but only because you first loved me in Jesus.

I probably won't sit still, but because the gospel is true, I will *be still*. With palms up in surrender and praise, I enter this day. I pray in Jesus' excellent and exalted name. Amen.

A Prayer for Moving from Cynicism to Servanthood

Submit yourselves for the Lord's sake to every human authority: whether to the emperor, as the supreme authority, or to governors, who are sent by him to punish those who do wrong and to commend those who do right. For it is God's will that by doing good you should silence the ignorant talk of foolish people. Live as free people, but do not use your freedom as a cover-up for evil; live as God's slaves. Show proper respect to everyone, love the family of believers, fear God, honor the emperor. (1 Pet. 2:13–17 NIV)

Heavenly Father, it is Presidents' Day in our nation—a perfect day for praying these words from the apostle Peter. But as this day begins I stand convicted of how little I've prayed for our past presidents and how very little I pray with faith for our sitting president. Forgive me, and by the power of the gospel, please give me a better attitude.

I confess, I've been more of a cynic than your servant with respect to supporting our government. I haven't been living with the confidence that *you* set up and sit down kings, presidents, premiers, and governors at *your* bidding.

In many ways, I'm one of the "foolish people" Peter wrote about in this passage—someone whose "ignorant talk" should be silenced by the gospel. Show me what "doing good" looks like as a dual citizen of the United States and the kingdom of God. Show me how to use my freedom wisely and how I'm to show proper respect to everyone, including our president. You're not calling me to be passive, but neither are you calling me to be a pest.

Father, I'm ashamed and humbled to realize that when Peter wrote this letter, the megalomaniac Nero was the sitting "president" in Rome. It's obvious that Peter lived with more faith in the King of Kings than fear of the madman of madmen. Help me to do the same, Father; help me to do the same.

Lord Jesus, *yours* is the only everlasting kingdom, and *you* are the only King worthy of my unqualified submission and obedience. I honor you as my King. I worship you as my Savior. I love you as my bridegroom. I pray in your name, above all names. Amen.

A Prayer for Gospel-Saturated Local Churches

We always thank God, the Father of our Lord Jesus Christ, when we pray for you, since we heard of your faith in Christ Jesus and of the love that you have for all the saints, because of the hope laid up for you in heaven. Of this you have heard before in the word of the truth, the gospel, which has come to you, as indeed in the whole world it is bearing fruit and growing—as it also does among you, since the day you heard it and understood the grace of God in truth. (Col. 1:3–6)

Gracious Father, we bring our church families before you today, with all their brokenness and beauty. It's not only a privilege but a central calling to pray without ceasing for one another in the body of Christ. For until the day Jesus returns, the church is your chosen means for revealing your glory, lavishing your grace, and advancing your kingdom. No wonder she is constantly being assailed by the world and assaulted by darkness.

In keeping with the way Paul prayed for every church he planted, we ask you to inundate, saturate, and liberate our churches by the gospel of your incomparable grace—new church plants and aging communities alike. There's no other power sufficient for the task. There's no other story, motivation, or resources adequate for the calling you've given your beloved people.

By the glorious gospel, bear great fruit in our midst, Father. Deepen and strengthen our faith in Jesus. It's not the size of our faith but the object of our faith that matters most, so keep revealing more and more of the beauty and bounty of Jesus to us. Let us boast in his work, not ours. May the name of Jesus be the most heard, loved, and trusted name in our churches.

By the powerful gospel, make us great lovers. By your mercy and grace, give us love for all the saints. Help us to love one another as Jesus loves us—the surest and most necessary mark of our discipleship. Tear down our divisions. Rescue us from our prejudices. Eradicate our petulance and pettiness. Demonstrate the difference the gospel makes in our worship, in our conflicts, in seasons of disconnect and delight. Don't let us ever get used to loving poorly.

By the hope-filled gospel, liberate our hands, hearts, and resources for the work of your kingdom in our cities and among the nations. With us or without us, the gospel will continue to bear fruit and grow throughout the world. We want it to do so with us, Father.

By the gospel, revive us, transform us, and free us for your sovereign and saving purposes. We pray with longing hearts, in Jesus' exalted name. Amen.

A Prayer for a Gospel-Saturated Lent

And Jesus said to them, "Can the wedding guests fast while the bridegroom is with them? As long as they have the bridegroom with them, they cannot fast. But days will come when the bridegroom is taken away from them, and then they will fast in that day." (Mark 2:19–20)

Dear Jesus, it's Ash Wednesday, the beginning of the season of Lent. For the next forty days we have the privilege of surveying your cross and preparing for the greatest of all celebrations: Easter Sunday, the foundation of our hope and the fountain of eternal joy.

For your glory and our growth, we ask you to inundate us with fresh grace in the coming weeks. We don't want an ordinary Lenten season, Jesus. Saturate it with the gospel. It's all about you, Jesus. It is all about what you've done for us, not what we promise to do for you.

Sadly, I used to dread Lent like late summer football practice—a lot of striving and sweat mixed in with much uncertainty and fear. "What's the coach thinking about my performance? Am I doomed to sit on the bench? Will I even make the team this year?" What a misuse of the season of Lent. What a complete misrepresentation of the gospel. What a dismal way to live the Christian life. We're your betrothed bride, not a beleaguered people.

Indeed, Jesus, we begin Lent today anticipating our wedding, not our funeral, for you're the loving bridegroom who died to make us your cherished bride. The work's already done; the dowry has been paid in full; the wedding dress of your righteousness is already ours; the invitations have been sent out; the date has been secured; you'll not change your mind! Hallelujah! Hallelujah! Hallelujah!

Over these next forty days intensify our hunger, our assurance, and our longing for the day of your return—the day of consummate joy, the wedding feast of the Lamb. In light of that banquet, we choose to deny ourselves (fast from) certain pleasures for this brief season. But we're not looking to get one thing from you, Jesus—just more of you. Fill our hearts with your beauty and bounty, we pray in your holy and loving name. Amen.

A Prayer about a Very Slow Fast

Jesus answered them, "Truly, truly, I say to you, you are seeking me, not because you saw signs, but because you ate your fill of the loaves. Do not labor for the food that perishes, but for food that endures to eternal life, which the Son of Man will give to you. For on him God the Father has set his seal." (John 6:26–27)

Then Jesus declared, "I am the bread of life. Whoever comes to me will never go hungry, and whoever believes in me will never be thirsty." (John 6:35 NIV)

Dear Jesus, I'm barely twenty-four hours into Lent and already I realize how weak I am, how powerful my appetites are, and how much I take the gospel for granted. This may be the slowest fast I've ever tried. At this rate, this might be the longest forty days of my life.

Who would've thought that one little piece of corn bread staring up at me from a Styrofoam dinner box could present such a challenge to my "no bread during Lent" fast? I choose to deny myself one little thing—with a world of other culinary options open to me—yet my mouth waters, my taste buds engage, and I want to chow down.

Oh, that my hunger for you would be as compelling as my hunger for every other kind of bread. No bread endures to eternal life except the bread that you give. Indeed, all breads except the Bread of Life will ultimately spoil.

During this season of Lent, renew our craving for the manna of the gospel. Intensify our longings for the day when we will feast together at the wedding feast of the Lamb. Ignite our hearts to sing with vigor, "Bread of heaven, feed me till I want no more!" To come to you today is to never hunger for eternity.

Help me and my friends as we seek you in fresh ways over these next six weeks. Jesus, may the gospel come alive in profound and transforming ways. Satisfy our appetites as no other bread can. Because the Father has placed his seal of approval on you, we find our approval in you. We pray with hope, in your satisfying and sufficient name. Amen.

A Prayer about Planting Tears for a Friend

Those who sow in tears
  shall reap with shouts of joy!
He who goes out weeping,
  bearing the seed for sowing,
shall come home with shouts of joy,
  bringing his sheaves with him. (Ps. 126:5–6)

Gracious Jesus, I'm a grieving, weepy man this morning. It's not the first time and it won't be the last time I get word of a hard fall—of a friend being "caught" (Gal. 6:1 NIV) and "entangled" (Heb. 12:1 NIV) in the short-lived pleasures of sin (Heb. 11:25).

As I pray for my friend, may my tears be like seeds of hope. If I only think about him, I get mad. Because of the gospel, I want to trust you for a harvest of a restored life and sheaves of redemption, all to your glory.

What he did is serious, and he knows and owns it with brokenness and pained contrition. But what happens next is equally serious. Jesus, he loves you; no one doubts that. But his affection for you is miniscule compared to your love for him. As some would take up stones to harm him, speak these words to him: "Who is it that condemns you? Go and sin no more" (see John 8:10–11).

Early in this season of Lent, let him survey your wondrous cross, upon which you, the Prince of Glory, died for rebels, fools, and idolaters just like me and just like my friend. As the accuser of the brethren screams condemnation, may the cross drown out those damning indictments with its louder boast, "You are fully and eternally accepted in the Beloved! Jesus became sin for you that in him you might become the righteousness of God!" (see 2 Cor. 5:21).

Surround my friend with those who understand the difference the gospel makes in the face of failure, betrayal, and addiction. Raise up spiritual men and women who understand the ways of gentle restoration (Gal. 6:1) and the journey to gospel sanity. Provide good counseling and the healing community he will need. Show us, his friends, how to love up close and afar.

Jesus, grant my friend deep repentance—a repentance that will result in the fruit grace alone can grow. Keep him humble, teachable, and patient in the coming days. In your tender and tenacious name I pray. Amen.

A Prayer about Our Fears and Treasure

Do not be afraid, little flock, for your Father has been pleased to give you the kingdom. Sell your possessions and give to the poor. Provide purses for yourselves that will not wear out, a treasure in heaven that will not be exhausted, where no thief comes near and no moth destroys. For where your treasure is, there your heart will be also. (Luke 12:32–34 NIV)

Dear Jesus, it's early in the season of Lent, and I'm poised to hear your calming voice and to experience your transforming presence. I gladly own my place among your little flock—one of your beloved lambs who's no stranger to uncertainty and fear. The best news is that this little flock is your little flock. There's no safer place than to be in your hand and heart.

Jesus, I completely understand why you warned us against setting our hearts on the wrong treasure when we feel vulnerable. When threatened, we often look to the wrong things and wrong people for safety, stability, and security. But I've lived long enough to see what happens when we choose anything or anyone besides you as our ultimate treasure.

I have friends who've inherited millions and others who've inherited the wind. I've seen families deeply stressed as they prepare for the reading of a will and then permanently divided over the execution of the same will. I've seen windfall profits turned into landfill waste in a matter of months. I've seen dads and moms drink away enough money in a couple of years to have built two orphanages in Haiti and educated their kids and grandkids for a couple of decades.

There are all kinds of wear and tear and thieves and moths that diminish and destroy the temporal things and temporal places, but nothing, absolutely nothing threatens you and your everlasting kingdom. Right in the middle of our chaos and confusion, we reaffirm that you, Jesus, are our priceless treasure and most to be desired inheritance. Because of you we call God "Abba, Father" and the new heaven and new earth our inheritance. Hallelujah!

Jesus, during the whole season of Lent, melt our fears with your peace; strengthen our hearts with your grace; and send us forth into kingdom service with your irrepressible love. We pray with gratitude, in your sane-making, soul-centering name. Amen.

A Prayer about Plural Pronouns

For those God foreknew he also predestined to be conformed to the image of his Son, that he might be the firstborn among many brothers and sisters. And those he predestined, he also called; those he called, he also justified; those he justified, he also glorified. (Rom. 8:29–30 NIV)

Gracious Father, one of the many things you're convicting me about during Lent is the big family into which you've placed me. In the gospel, none of us is an only child. Though I came from the womb a selfish man, was raised in a culture of individualism, and am an introvert by temperament and often a loner by choice, nevertheless, you've made me for rich relationship and engaged community.

I'm seeing this everywhere in the Scriptures, but especially in the plural pronouns. The "we's" outnumber the "I's," and the "our's" outnumber the "my's" about ten to one.

I praise you that the gospel is powerful enough to make a concave heart convex. I know of no other power that can free me for knowing and being known by others and for actually thinking more of others than I think of myself (Phil. 2:1–11).

Indeed, there are no ordinary people or unnecessary people in the body of Christ. There are no big people or little people in your family. We're all the right size. Not one of us is more justified than the other or more precious in your sight. We'll all be equally glorified when Jesus comes back—each one of us will be just as lovely and loving as our Savior.

Forgive me when my attitude and actions contradict these grand affirmations. Forgive me when I give more credence to my Myers-Briggs profile than my identity in Christ in trying to explain and defend my relational style. Forgive me when I use way too many singular rather than plural pronouns in my prayers.

Father, one day we will gather as your completed family in the New Jerusalem as sons and daughters from every race, tribe, language, and people group, eternally diverse and perfectly united. As we will love then, enable us to love in small yet observable ways now—one family, many children, all to your glory. We pray in Jesus' unifying name. Amen.

A Prayer for More Freedom

If the Son sets you free, you will be free indeed. (John 8:36)

Dear Jesus, I'm still not as free as you intend. Though you've already freed me from trying to earn my salvation by anything I do or based on anything in me; though you've already liberated me from the illusion that I can earn more of God's love by ramping up my obedience and decreasing my foolishness; though the chains of condemnation have already been broken and the fears of death, judgment day, and the future have been sent packing—I'm still not as free as you intend.

I'm still a babe, a neophyte, a raw rookie in so many gospel freedoms. Only the gospel helps me see and acknowledge these things. Only your grace keeps me from going to shame and self-contempt as I offer these prayers.

Jesus, please free me so I can be less irritated, and less often, with fewer people. Please turn my hair-trigger reactions into slower, wiser responses. Please help me to use fewer words and more listening when engaging others. Please unshackle me from the illusion of control and my commitment to a pain-free heart.

Jesus, please liberate me from thinking about the next thing, so I can be present in the current moment. Please help me make better eye contact and heart connection with others. Please help me to be more intrigued with people I don't know and less timid around strangers.

Jesus, please break even more of the chains of my insecurities. Please free me from the graveclothes of feeling incompetent about important things in life. Please unfetter me from thinking too much about what I'm not by showing me more of you and who I am in you.

Jesus, please free me for greater spontaneity, louder laughter, saltier tears, and quicker repentances. I pray in your most compassionate name. Amen.

A Prayer for Loving God
Just Because He's God

"Does Job fear God for nothing?" Satan replied. "Have you not put a hedge around him and his household and everything he has? You have blessed the work of his hands, so that his flocks and herds are spread throughout the land. But now stretch out your hand and strike everything he has, and he will surely curse you to your face." (Job 1:9–11 NIV)

Gracious Father, I sometimes wonder if Satan watches American religious television, because there's a lot there to fuel his accusations. Much of it could substantiate his charge that the only reason we love you is because of the goodies you give us.

It's hard not to be cynical, but I've got to be careful, because as far as creature comforts go, I don't have anything "whineworthy" going on. There's nothing right now presenting a challenge to my faith. I've got good health; there's more check left over at the end of the month; none of my family members are in crisis. Nothing beyond the normal fallenness and brokenness of life is happening around me or within me.

Father, I presume on none of this kind providence. I take none of your good gifts for granted. It's only by your grace that I don't struggle with entitlement as much as I used to. The gospel has convinced me that everything I have comes from you (1 Cor. 4:7).

So as I think today about Job's story, it's not with gritted teeth or clenched fists. But Satan's question always remains current: Why do we love you? What's our motivation for worshiping you? How will I think about you the next time *I* suffer loss, betrayal, and pain? That, no doubt, *will* happen.

I want to be a man who loves and worships you simply because you are God. There's no other god besides you, and there's certainly no other god like you. I'm grateful for your gifts, but I want to love and worship you, the Giver, as the primary treasure of my heart. I pray in Jesus' holy and loving name. Amen.

A Prayer about Jesus' Way with Words

A soft answer turns away wrath,
    but a harsh word stirs up anger.
The tongue of the wise commends knowledge,
    but the mouths of fools pour out folly. (Prov. 15:1–2)

Patient Jesus, as with so many other Scriptures, this passage makes me think of you. There's no one more filled with kindness and gentle answers than you. There's no wiser tongue than yours. Even when I rush into your presence with demands dressed up like questions, arrogance pretending to be confusion, clenched fists rather than raised hands, you remain unnerved, nondefensive, and ever so welcoming.

You're firm with me but never harsh. You don't have to be, because you never get irritated, you don't have any insecurities, and you don't fear losing an argument. Jesus, you're not into "saving face" but *saving me*.

When I ignore your wooings or act immature in response to your warnings, I simply reveal how little of the gospel I really understand. For there's nothing about you that justifies any other response from me but humility, gratitude, and submission.

Jesus, I'm so glad Lent is about repentance and faith in you and not penance and work done by me. As we get closer and closer to Holy Week, let your cross get bigger and bigger in my gaze. For if I had to atone for all the ways I misuse my tongue, if I had to finance redemption to pay for my poor stewardship of words, if I thought I had to gentle my own heart—I would surely despair.

Jesus, you never gush folly, but only the gospel—the very words of life that are changing me. By the Holy Spirit, preach the gospel to my heart all day long. Free my tongue for your praise and the building up of others. I pray in your ever-so-glorious name. Amen.

A Prayer for Friends Struggling in the Ministry

But it displeased Jonah exceedingly, and he was angry. And he prayed to the LORD and said, "O LORD, is not this what I said when I was yet in my country? That is why I made haste to flee to Tarshish; for I knew that you are a gracious God and merciful, slow to anger and abounding in steadfast love, and relenting from disaster. Therefore now, O LORD, please take my life from me, for it is better for me to die than to live." (Jon. 4:1–3)

Dear Jesus, you're stirring my heart today to pray for weary men and women serving in the ministry of the gospel. I wish it weren't so, but sometimes it takes my own challenges and hardships in ministry for me to hit my knees with compassionate intercession for others. Before your throne of grace, I bring you missionaries, pastors, elders, counselors—a wide range of friends you have called and gifted to share and apply the gospel of your grace.

Many of them are living Jonah's story. In their heads they still know you to be a God who is gracious and compassionate, slow to anger and abounding in steadfast love. But in their hearts they are displeased and angry, disconnected and disillusioned, and some, like Jonah, aren't sure they want many more days in this world. Have mercy on them, Lord; have great mercy today.

Jesus, you know all the issues. You know what's under the anger; what's compounding the contempt; and what's fueling the flight. Meet these dear servants of yours right where they are. I pray for their spouses and children as well, for sometimes it's the family members who suffer ministry pangs the most.

Comfort them with your compassion. Grant them a renewed perspective of eternity. Rekindle hope in their hurting hearts. Where needed, may your kindness drive them to appropriate repentance. Refresh them with whatever means of grace you choose.

Until you return, Jesus, Satan will continue to mount an all-out assault against you by attacking your bride, and especially those called to nourish and prepare your church for the great wedding day. Satan knows he's lost us for eternity, so he will do anything and everything within his power to bring havoc, heartache, and hell. Use us, however you choose, to encourage your servants, and all the more as we see that great day approaching. We pray in your holy and loving name. Amen.

A Prayer about Lenten Weeping and Dancing

Now may the God of peace himself sanctify you completely, and may your whole spirit and soul and body be kept blameless at the coming of our Lord Jesus Christ. He who calls you is faithful; he will surely do it.
(1 Thess. 5:23–24)

Holy and loving Father, as I continue to pray and read my way through Lent, it's portions of your Word like this one that make me want to weep and dance at the same time. I feel like weeping over the years I spent in gospel ignorance, a stranger to the ways of grace. I am grateful that you brought me to Jesus but clueless about how you actually change your sons and daughters—I suffered much under the hands of bad theologies, man-centered remedies, and Christless formulas.

This one passage alone tells me that you're the God who called me to life in Jesus; you are thoroughly transforming me to be like Jesus; you are keeping my whole being blameless until the day you send Jesus back to finish making all things new—including me! The God of peace you are indeed! Where else can such peace, joy, and assurance be found?

How did I miss the really good news of the gospel for so long? Why was I such an easy target for performance-based spirituality? Why wasn't I able to recognize corruptions of the gospel sooner?

I lament the years I spent in seeing Jesus more as my perfect model than as my perfect Righteousness, rededicating my life to Jesus, trying to make him Lord of all things, holding out for a second and third and ninth and seventeenth baptism in the Spirit, instead of savoring a life of union and communion with Jesus. How did I miss so much of the gospel for so very long?

Enough of looking back in sadness. I choose to look up in gladness, for you've turned my mourning into dancing, Father. You've removed the sackcloth of my self-righteousness and have clothed me with the wedding garments of the Lamb. With the music of a coming banquet already emanating from heaven, my prayer is simply this: Dear Father, more and more, and through and through, *make me like Jesus*. You are faithful and you will do it. I pray with profound gratitude and assurance, in Jesus' holy name. Amen.

A Prayer for Friends Struggling with Pornography

Although I want to do good, evil is right there with me. For in my inner being I delight in God's law; but I see another law at work in me, waging war against the law of my mind and making me a prisoner of the law of sin at work within me. What a wretched man I am! Who will rescue me from this body that is subject to death? . . . Therefore, there is now no condemnation for those who are in Christ Jesus, because through Christ Jesus the law of the Spirit who gives life has set you free from the law of sin and death.
(Rom. 7:21–24; 8:1–2 NIV)

Jesus, my heart goes out today for friends and their spouses whose lives are being assaulted by the ravaging and enslaving grip of pornography. I know of no other power sufficient for the task but the gospel. This is why I run to you today with grave concern, but also with great hope.

O Lord of resurrection and redemption, bring your mercy and might to bear in stunning fashion. Things impossible for us are more than possible for you. You have come to set captives free and to heal the brokenhearted. Pornography is creating an overabundance of both.

Jesus, for friends somewhere in the pornography continuum of titillation to addiction, we ask you to reveal yourself in the deepest place of their hearts. We ask for the holy gift of godly sorrow, not the short-lived remorse of worldly sorrow. For your noncondemning love has great power to deliver those who cry, "What a wretched man I am! Who will rescue me from this body that is subject to death?" (Rom. 7:24 NIV).

Lead them to that cry, Jesus. They need a lot more than embarrassment and fear; they need contrition and hope. Where pornography has desensitized our friends, resensitize them so they can see and feel the horror of their entrapment and more so—much more so—the wonder of your deliverance.

For our friends who are married to someone in the talons of pornography, dear Jesus, theirs may be the greater pain and struggle. No one but you can help them with the anger, the disgust, the wound, the shame, and the mistrust that goes with this story. Help us walk with our friends who are right in the middle of this dark vortex. Show us how to validate their feelings without confirming hurt-driven conclusions. Bring patience and perspective, forbearance and faith.

Only you can rebuild the trust. Only you, Jesus, can bring a willingness to hope again. Only you can heal the places in our hearts that have suffered the greatest violation and harm. Absolutely no one understands all this like you, Jesus, and absolutely no one redeems these messes but you. We pray with hope, in your great and glorious name. Amen.

A Prayer about All-Weather Friendship

A friend loves at all times,
  and a brother is born for adversity. (Prov. 17:17)

Jesus, there's no question about your commitment to love us well in every season of life. You will never leave us or forsake us, and there's no ebbing or flowing with your compassion. You stick much closer than a brother, because you're so much more than a brother. You humbled yourself to become a spouse to us—the bridegroom who died to make rebels, fools, and idolaters like us your cherished wife. What wondrous love is this, indeed?

Your lavish, constant affection should spell the end of all our poutings and pity parties, all our whinings and worryfests. It should also radically affect how we relate to our friends. I come before you today convinced of your love and therefore convicted about the way I relate to my friends, especially those who are in various stories and stages of adversity. I've been too busy even to pray for them. That's a confession of sin, not an excuse or an alibi.

I repent, and I bring before your throne of grace a friend who is stuck in the throes of a toxic marriage. He simply doesn't know what to do. His heart is treading water in the Bermuda Triangle of hopelessness, rage, and numbness. Show me how to love him well. I need wisdom. I need courage. O God of resurrection, bring the power of the gospel to bear. Give his wife hope that men can change—that her husband can change. Please redeem this marriage for your glory.

I pray for another friend who's suffered sequential betrayals and losses. He's beyond being angry, and he doesn't have many tears left. He loves you as only a broken man filled with the gospel can, but Jesus, he needs relief. His willingness to trust and hope is gone. How much is too much? How much more can this one brother sustain? It is one thing to be brokenhearted, but he is nearly broken down. Please intervene, Jesus.

Gracious Lord, give us fire and faith for loving as all-weather friends. What do we do next? Do we get in our cars, buy an airline ticket, call up, show up? How can we best come alongside of our hurting friends? Show us, Jesus; lead us. We pray in your faithful and compassionate name. Amen.

A Prayer about Contagious Gospel Renewal

This is what the LORD Almighty says: "In those days ten people from all languages and nations will take firm hold of one Jew by the hem of his robe and say, 'Let us go with you, because we have heard that God is with you.'" (Zech. 8:23 NIV)

Gracious Father, every day, without exception, we need to be reminded of where history is heading. For we're forgetful and fearful people, way too easily influenced by the spin of pundits and the banter of newspeak.

But a great promise you made through a minor prophet is the major headline we need to remember today and every day. History is the unfolding story of your commitment to redeem your pan-national family and make all things new through the work of your Son, Jesus. This outcome isn't merely a great possibility or a grand probability but a covenantal certainty. For nothing will keep you from magnifying the excellencies of your glory through the work of Jesus.

Indeed, Lord Jesus, you are fulfilling everything in Zechariah's vision. You are the "one Jew" of the Father's promise. You are the faithful remnant of Israel. You are the second Adam—the only Nazarene in whom there was no guile; the Lord who became the Lamb; our substitute in life and in death. We lay hold of the hem of your robe only because you grasp us in the gospel.

Jesus, in light of who you are and what you've already accomplished on our behalf, how can we not leap for joy? How can we not be moved to pray with great hope for our churches, communities, and cities?

We need renewal and we need revival, Jesus. We need you to send your Spirit to stir us up. We long for a contagious gospel renewal to break out in our local congregations. We long for substantiated rumors of your transforming presence to run through our cities. We long to have the rich and the poor, the educated and the uneducated, the religious and the irreligious, the washed and the unwashed, the found and the lost, the unrighteous and the self-righteous come together to hear, believe, and live the gospel.

Why not us, Jesus, and why not now? We're tired of playing church. We're bored with ourselves. Magnify your name in our midst and in this hour. We pray in your most majestic and merciful name. Amen.

A Prayer about Thirsty Panting for Jesus

As the deer pants for streams of water,
  so my soul pants for you, my God.
My soul thirsts for God, for the living God.
  When can I go and meet with God? (Ps. 42:1–2 NIV)

Loving Jesus, there's no craving more demanding than thirst. It's neither patient nor polite. When we get thirsty, we're usually quick to slake its unrelenting demand, one way or another. Thirst will not be denied. We'll do almost anything to satisfy our thirst.

Because this is true, we join the psalmist in crying out: Jesus, intensify our thirst for you. Keep us panting like the deer that pants after streams of water—the unpolluted, undistilled, never-ending brooks of your bounty.

Quickly drain the broken cisterns of our own making. Don't let us be even momentarily satisfied with any other beverage than the draft you draw, the potion you pour, the life-giving libation you alone can give.

If we take up King David's lament, "When can I go and meet with God?" you answer back without delay, "Right now, my beloved; do not wait. If you're thirsty, come to me and drink." "Whoever believes in me, streams of living water will flow from within them" (John 7:38 NIV).

If we should say, "But Jesus, where can we find you?" you answer back even quicker, "Not in the law; not in your strivings; not in your labors; not in your earnestness; not in your self-loathings; not in your vain promises; but only in the gospel. Come and fall into the rivers of my love. Stand under the cascading waterfalls of my grace. Open your heart wide to my supply, and I will fill you to overflowing with everything you need and more than you want."

Even so and evermore, Jesus, school us well in panting after you. Fill us afresh that we might be a people to the praise of your glory and grace. We pray in your all-glorious and all-generous name. Amen.

A Prayer about "Blessed Are the Refreshers"

One person gives freely, yet gains even more;
    another withholds unduly, but comes to poverty.
A generous person will prosper;
    whoever refreshes others will be refreshed.
      (Prov. 11:24–25 NIV)

Lord Jesus, I cannot read these words without lifting my heart and hands toward heaven. I cannot read the words "whoever refreshes others" without thinking of you, for no one refreshes a dry and weary heart like you. Your mercies are new every morning, and your steadfast love never comes to an end. Great is your faithfulness.

No one gives more freely than you, Jesus. You'll never be charged with withholding any good thing from your people. You'll never come to poverty through hoarding, because you freely chose the poverty of the cross as a means of making us rich (2 Cor. 8:9). This is the gospel, and nothing is more refreshing than the gospel, for it is the power of God for salvation (Rom. 1:16), for this moment, for this weary heart.

Indeed, you're calling to us in a loud voice, "Let anyone who is thirsty come to me and drink" (John 7:37 NIV). Jesus, I join my brothers and sisters in coming to you right now with my heart as wide open as the gospel enables. I humble myself before you. I own the need that you alone can meet. I am not ashamed to let you know just how much I need to be refreshed by you, Jesus. You love to give, and I love to receive from you.

And as grace runs downhill to the needy, so it flows freely to others. To whom would you send us today—to whom would you send me? Freely I receive; freely I will give. I pray in your most generous name. Amen.

A Prayer for Decision-Making Peace

Trust in the LORD with all your heart,
and do not lean on your own understanding.
In all your ways acknowledge him,
and he will make straight your paths. (Prov. 3:5–6)

Dear Jesus, as this day begins, many of us are facing big decisions. We need the wisdom, guidance, and peace you alone can give. It's a joy to come before your throne of grace confident of your audience, grateful for your advocacy, and resting in your authority.

Indeed, Jesus, you're an engaged Shepherd, not an absentee landlord. Even as we make plans in our hearts, you are actively ordering our steps (Prov. 16:9). Oh, the freedom and peace this brings! You are the Lord who "opens doors no one can shut" (Rev. 3:8). And the converse is just as true; you also shut doors no one can open. Our future is tied not to making the right decisions but to trusting the right Lord.

Because of your great love for us in the gospel, we're learning to trust you with all the stuff in our hearts—with our longings, fears, hurts, and dreams. To acknowledge you in all of our ways isn't to *make* you Lord but to recognize and to rest in your lordship. We can no more make you Lord of something than we can make water wet or chocolate good. You *are* who *you are*, Jesus. Hallelujah! So in surrender to the occupied throne of heaven, we anticipate straight paths as we move ahead into these difficult decisions.

For those of us dealing with job changes, financial stresses, and health issues, show yourself to be both merciful and mighty, Jesus. May your mercy keep us gentle and your might trump our impatience. For those of us having to make important decisions for the people we love, be huge and present. Long-term care for aging parents, the "right" education for our kids, the best treatment for family members and friends in the destructive whirlwind of addictions—make the way clear, Lord. As Prince of Peace, give us your peace as we wait upon you.

Jesus, in these coming days write stories of redemption that will reveal your glory, showcase your grace, and leave us reveling in your goodness and timing. We pray in your trustworthy and beautiful name. Amen.

A Prayer for the Restoration of Our Joy

Restore to me the joy of your salvation,
and uphold me with a willing spirit. (Ps. 51:12)

Jesus, knowing you is a personal but not a private affair. I may come before you alone, but I cannot remain alone. As soon as I bring my longings and needs before you, you enlarge my heart and expand my gaze to see the faces and hear the cries of others. Such is the way of the gospel.

Your words to Peter in John 21 echo in the chambers of my meditation. "Do you love me? Then feed and care for my lambs." When you feed me, it's always for the nourishment of others.

Today I'm bringing you a bevy of family members, friends, and colleagues. Everybody is hungry and everybody needs bread. Every one of us is like King David, with stories of failure and fear, brokenness and weakness, heartache and heart need. The details of our stories differ, but each of us needs you just as much as the other.

So I ask with confidence and I appeal with hope, restore to us the joy of your salvation for us, Lord Jesus. It's your salvation, because we could never, ever save ourselves. Like Jonah, we humbly cry from within our own hard places, "Salvation comes from the LORD" (Jon. 2:9 NIV). Bring us back to the joyful, childlike love we had for you at first, Jesus (Rev. 2:4)—a love totally generated in response to the undeserved, unparalleled, unwavering love you have for us (1 John 4:19).

For *your* joy is our strength, Jesus—strength for repenting, strength for obeying, strength for hoping, strength for serving others, and above all, strength for adoring you, for you alone are worthy of our hearts' attention, affection, and allegiance.

The only sacrifice we cling to is yours, Jesus. Only your cross, only the gospel enables us to offer up a contrite heart free of all condemnation, a broken spirit free of all self-contempt. And we cry out together, "Hallelujah, what a salvation! Hallelujah, what a Savior!" I pray in your most holy and loving name. Amen.

A Prayer about a Future
without Chaos and Evil

Then I saw a new heaven and a new earth, for the first heaven and the first earth had passed away, and the sea was no more. (Rev. 21:1)

Loving Father, as fresh coffee helps me transition from a good night's sleep into a new day's mercies, so your Word is quickening all of my senses. As you greet me this morning with your steadfast love (Lam. 3:22–24), I can hear the roar of waves breaking along the Gulf Coast. It's a stormy morning—one that connects me with John's hope-filled vision of our sealess future.

I praise you that this very cosmos, this very earth, this very beach has been bought back by Jesus. I praise you that even as you're presently redeeming your big family from the nations, so you're restoring the world in which you placed us.

As surely as the waters cover the sea, so the knowledge of your glory will cover the earth one day (Hab. 2:14). The "passing away" of the first heaven and the first earth doesn't speak of its replacement but of its restoration, to which I say a very loud "Hallelujah!"

I smile really, really big when I try to imagine the glorified beaches of the new heaven and new earth. I can hardly wait for the day when I get to hear "every creature in heaven and on earth and under the earth and in the sea, and all that is in them, saying: 'To him who sits on the throne and to the Lamb be blessing and honor and glory and might forever and ever!'" (Rev. 5:13).

Indeed, Father, John's vision is not about a "beachless" future but about a "sealess" one—an eternity and a world delivered and devoid of all chaos and evil—no more sea beasts, only beauty; no more angry leviathan, only dancing dolphin; no more tempest, only the triumph of the Lamb!

I can only imagine such a glorious state of affairs, but may John's vision compel and propel me and my friends to engage, not retreat; to show up, not disappear; to be filled with missional hope and gospel servanthood as we seek first your kingdom and the righteousness that is by faith—as we wait expectantly for that day. I pray in the name of our resurrected and reigning King, Jesus. Amen.

A Prayer about Spirit Homicide

The human spirit can endure in sickness,
   but a crushed spirit who can bear? (Prov. 18:14 NIV)

The LORD is near to the brokenhearted
   and saves the crushed in spirit. (Ps. 34:18)

But he was pierced for our transgressions,
   he was crushed for our iniquities;
the punishment that brought us peace was on him,
   and by his wounds we are healed. (Isa. 53:5 NIV)

Jesus, I begin this day filled with both great sadness and profound hope. The sadness is born from witnessing a parent commit "spirit homicide" on a child who couldn't have been older than two or three. Walking through the store parking lot, I watched as an exasperated mom targeted her son's spirit for crushing. I literally saw that little fellow shrivel under the weight of her impatience, harshness, and anger. The image lingers— maybe because I know what a crushed spirit feels like.

In all fairness, I have no clue what was going on in that mom's heart. I have no idea what preceded her cruel eruption, but nothing could justify or excuse her behavior—nothing. And in all honesty, I wanted to treat her just as harshly as she was treating her son. For a moment I was more angry at her than concerned for her son. I need your mercy as much as she does.

That's precisely where you come in, Jesus—where you come real close, for you are near to the brokenhearted and you save those who are crushed in spirit. This is why I also feel profound hope today, for you took the ultimate crushing of the cross that we might know your tear-wiping hand and a peace you alone can bring. Jesus, continue to heal those places, those wounds in my heart where I lost face and heart, where I simply went limp with shame.

Again, Jesus, I don't tower in judgment over this mom, but I stand convicted by her actions. All of us are just as capable and culpable of crushing the spirits of others—children, spouses, friends. Melt the madness of meanness with the grandeur of your grace. I pray in your near and healing name. Amen.

A Prayer about the Freedom of Being Completely Known

Come, see a man who told me everything I ever did. Could this be the Messiah? (John 4:29 NIV)

Jesus, I wish I could have been present to watch this stunned Samaritan woman recount the tale of her collision with the gospel—her story of meeting you and coming alive to the transforming power of grace (John 4:1–42). Water from Jacob's well was superseded by the water you alone can give, the living water that slakes our death-doling thirst.

You exposed to her the sinfulness of her sequential affairs, yet instead of ridiculing her, you redeemed her; instead of condemning her, you cherished her; instead of shaming her, you saved her.

En route to the nations, you brought the gospel of the kingdom to the dark continent of her heart. As she stood so vulnerable in the public square of her community, she'd *never* been so free. No more need to pose or pretend. I wonder if some of the six men with whom she'd been heard her proclaim, "Come, see a man who told me *everything* I ever did. Could this be the Messiah?" (John 4:29 NIV).

Nothing but the gospel can free us for being thoroughly known without fear. Jesus, your love is unlike anything else we can experience in this life. In fact, your love is better than life itself. We adore and praise you this day as the Christ—the Messiah, our Lenten Lord, the heart knower, our holy lover, our righteousness from God, our only hope of glory!

You know every vain, foolish, and evil thought we've ever conceived; every lustful, greedy fantasy in which we've engaged. Only you hear every grace-robbing, grandstanding, gossipy word we speak. Only you know the broken cisterns of our choices—our idols, the many things to which we turn to find life somewhere else than in you. Yet you *pursue* us, *welcome* us, and *love* us, and you are *changing* us.

What a wonderful, merciful Savior you are, Jesus. Life, temporal and eternal, can only be found in you. We joyfully pray in your transcendent and transforming name. Amen.

A Prayer for a Jesus-Centered Prayer Life

The prayer of a righteous person is powerful and effective. (James 5:16 NIV)

Dear Jesus, my prayer life, like many other parts of my discipleship, has suffered the damaging effects of bad teaching through the years. This one verse in James used to intimidate and discourage me from praying. First of all, I used to assume that the only "powerful and effective" prayer was one to which you said yes, and secondly, I thought the health of my prayer life was directly related to my maturity as a Christian.

I thought that the more righteous I was, the more inclined you would be to answer my prayers, and if I wasn't getting my prayers answered, it was probably because of unconfessed sin in my life. What a horrible misunderstanding of prayer and self-centered approach to discipleship. No wonder it was easier for me to talk about you than to talk to you.

Thankfully, the gospel has been deconstructing and rebuilding my prayer life. Jesus, I now understand that you are the "righteous man" whose prayers are powerful and effective. You are our great prayer warrior—ever living to pray for us and ever so graciously purifying our prayers as they rise to heaven. We don't have any righteousness except the righteousness that we have freely received in the gospel.

Because our lives are now hidden in you; because of our unbreakable union with you, Jesus; because our permanent address is "in Christ," we've been set free to pray with palms-up boldness. You are the sovereign King who is reigning over all things, not a computer waiting to be programmed by us. You are our great bridegroom who enjoys communing and fellowshiping with us in prayer, long before we even ask anything of you. Oh, the joy of knowing your good answers to our prayers include "Yes," "No," "Maybe," "Not yet," and "Not telling you"!

Because the gospel is true, we will dance before you when you choose to release Peter from prison in answer to our prayers (Acts 12:5–17), and we will seek no less to delight in you when James is beheaded in prison, even as we plead otherwise (Acts 12:1–2). Throughout eternity our testimony will be, "You have done *all* things well." Why pray? Because you are God and we are not. Why pray? Because you command it, commend it, and commune with us through it. We pray in your high-priestly and most trustworthy name. Amen.

A Prayer for Adorning the Gospel

Teach slaves to be subject to their masters in everything, to try to please
them, not to talk back to them, and not to steal from them, but to show that
they can be fully trusted, so that in every way they will make the teaching
about God our Savior attractive. (Titus 2:9–10 NIV)

Gracious Father, while jogging today I came upon your Son's name
in a recently poured sidewalk. "Jesus loves you" was scribbled in
the cement with either a finger or a stick. The elder brother in me
reared his ugly head, and I wanted to find the culprit and ask, "What were
you thinking? You defaced private property, identified yourself as a Christian, and *this* is supposed to make the gospel attractive to nonbelievers?"

But it didn't take me long to move from being a self-appointed prosecuting attorney to a convicted son. For I realize you have every right to
ask me, "What are *you* thinking when you and your friends carry on a
conversation about me in a restaurant, then undertip your server? And
what are you thinking when you drive like a madman on the interstate
with a fish symbol on the back of your car? And what are you thinking
when you overindulge in food and beverage and call it 'Christian liberty'?
And what are you thinking when you cop an attitude when lines, traffic,
and servicepeople don't move fast enough for you?"

Father, the gospel is attractive all by itself. You're not calling me to
"spice it up," put a bow on it, or add anything to it, for there's no such
need. I simply must be more careful not to hide its beauty by my foolishness and lack of manners. Continue to show me what it means to do
all things in line with the truth of the gospel (Gal. 2:14). I pray in Jesus'
peerless name. Amen.

A Prayer about Reservations
Only by Grace

God has not rejected his people whom he foreknew. Do you not know what the Scripture says of Elijah, how he appeals to God against Israel? "Lord, they have killed your prophets, they have demolished your altars, and I alone am left, and they seek my life." But what is God's reply to him? "I have kept for myself seven thousand men who have not bowed the knee to Baal." So too at the present time there is a remnant, chosen by grace. But if it is by grace, it is no longer on the basis of works; otherwise grace would no longer be grace. (Rom. 11:2–6)

Holy Father, at least seventeen times a day I need to be reminded of how I got into your story of redemption and how I stay there. Occasionally I'm like Elijah, assuming I'm special because I'm one of the few who really "gets" the gospel—no longer bowing the knee to performance-based spirituality, moralism, or legalism. At other times I know myself to be an idolater—not worshiping Baal, but worshiping almost anything or everything else—and wondering how I could possibly be yours.

Then, like a rebuke or a kiss from heaven (depending on my attitude), I hear the Holy Spirit speak these words to my heart: "I have reserved for myself . . ." As in the days before Elijah, of Elijah, and long after Elijah, you've reserved and are preserving a much-loved people for yourself.

Many of them have Israeli passports, but most don't. In fact, no nation or people group will be excluded from your family, so great is your covenant of grace. My only claim to being your son is the reservation you made for me by grace. "But if it is by grace, it is no longer on the basis of works; otherwise grace would no longer be grace" (Rom. 11:6). If I'm not careful, I can even turn "getting the gospel" into a work—as though I were smart enough, hip enough, or spiritual enough to be a member of an elite gospel club.

Father, because of past grace, present grace, and future grace, I want to live with bowed knees and palms up toward you. I seek to worship other things less by loving you more. I pray in Jesus' exalted name. Amen.

A Prayer about Friends Finishing Well

See to it, brothers and sisters, that none of you has a sinful, unbelieving heart that turns away from the living God. But encourage one another daily, as long as it is called "Today," so that none of you may be hardened by sin's deceitfulness. We have come to share in Christ, if indeed we hold our original conviction firmly to the very end. (Heb. 3:12–14 NIV)

Dear Jesus, I'm so grateful for the dear friends you've woven into my life. Since I'm an introvert, the journey of investing my heart in long-term relationships has required, and still requires, a lot of your grace—grace that you've been faithful to supply.

I've already gripped the handle of a couple of friends' caskets, and other friends will do the same for me one day. More than ever, I want us to finish well together in the gospel. What will this look like and what will it take, Jesus?

My temptation is to treat my easiest friendships like a broken-in pair of Birkenstock sandals—I just enjoy them without much thought or effort. It's a great gift to have a few friends who can finish each other's sentences, endure one another's jokes, appreciate each other's quirks, and accept one another's weaknesses. Surely this is a gospel gift.

Yet, Jesus, we're still foolish people, capable of acting out in very destructive ways, prone to wander, easy targets for temptation. With all of my being, I trust in the grip of your grace and the security of your bride. But your Word is so very clear that continuance in gospel faith is a sign of a real faith. That doesn't scare me, but it does sober me.

Help us know how to hold each other accountable for believing the gospel. Help us take each other's heart struggles seriously. Help us never to minimize or marginalize the deceitfulness and hardening power of sin. Help us know how to preach the gospel to our own hearts daily, and to each other, until today gives way to the day of your longed-for return. I pray in your all-glorious name. Amen.

A Prayer of Desire for Fresh Grace

And he began to teach them that the Son of Man must suffer many things and be rejected by the elders and the chief priests and the scribes and be killed, and after three days rise again. And he spoke this plainly. And Peter took him aside and began to rebuke him. But turning and seeing his disciples, he rebuked Peter and said, "Get behind me, Satan! For you are not setting your mind on the things of God, but on the things of man." (Mark 8:31–33)

Jesus, one of the many things I cherish about the Bible is the way it robs me of my penchant for hero worship. Who but God would write a book documenting the foibles and failures of so many of his sons and daughters? Who but God would chronicle the ways his chosen leaders limp along and prove themselves to be in constant need of mercy and grace?

This gives me great encouragement and hope. It also gives me freedom to acknowledge that I need the gospel today just as much as the first day I believed it. This will be just as true tomorrow, and the next day, and the next. Keep me convinced, Jesus, because I'm much like Peter.

It's one thing for me to stress and stew about the ways this generation is distancing itself from your cross. But it's quite another to see the subtle ways I try to *keep you* from the cross. Deal with me as you dealt with Peter.

When I mute my heart to the insult of grace, I deny your cross. When I think, even for one moment, that my obedience merits anything, I deny your cross. When I put others under the microscope and measure of performance-based living, I deny your cross. When I wallow in self-contempt and shame, I deny your cross. When I'd rather do penance than repent, I deny your cross.

By the gospel, help me to mind the things of God more than the things of men. May your cross get bigger, and may my boast in it grow louder. Jesus, you're the only hero in the Bible, and I'm fine with that. I pray in your patient and persistent name. Amen.

A Prayer about Being Claimed
by God's Promises

Since we have these promises, dear friends, let us purify ourselves from everything that contaminates body and spirit, perfecting holiness out of reverence for God. (2 Cor. 7:1 NIV)

Through these he has given us his very great and precious promises, so that through them you may participate in the divine nature, having escaped the corruption in the world caused by evil desires. (2 Pet. 1:4 NIV)

Patient Father, the "farther up and further in" I go into the gospel, the more you challenge and change the way I think about everything. It's another kind example of your commitment to complete the good work you've begun in your children and in the entire creation. At times this process is quite painful, but it's always about more glory for you and more Christlikeness in us. We praise you for the perfection of your plan and the persistence of your heart.

Recently I've been thinking about your promises, so generously and copiously given in your Word. I now see, and grieve, how as a young follower of Jesus, I was pretty much trained to be a computer programmer, and you were the computer. I acted as though you were passively waiting for me to tell you what to do. Your hands were bound by the limitations of my faith. All I had to do was "claim the promises" without negative thoughts or a wavering will, and you would spring to action.

I confess and repent of my cynicism, but you know how long this way sounded really good to me. Thankfully, I now see that your promises are primarily about changing us, not programming you. Through your promises, we increasingly share in your divine nature—that is, you're making us more and more like Jesus. By your promises, we can escape the corruption in the world, not simply accumulate more of its treasures.

Father, every one of your promises directs our gaze away from us to Jesus, who is the ultimate "Yes!" to every promise you've made (2 Cor. 1:20). Oh, the difference the gospel makes in how we view all things. We don't claim your promises—they claim us! If we're going to "name and claim" anything, may it be to have greater passion for your glory. May our "standing on your promises" lead to living under your authority and serving well in your kingdom until Jesus returns. We pray in Jesus' triumphant and transforming name. Amen.

A Prayer about Hearty, Gospel-Saturated Service

Whatever you do, work heartily, as for the Lord and not for men, knowing that from the Lord you will receive the inheritance as your reward. You are serving the Lord Christ. (Col. 3:23–24)

Jesus, I begin this day profoundly grateful for your relentless, never-ceasing work in my heart. You never sleep; you never slumber. You don't just give me sleep but you give to me in my sleep. You're the only reason that one day I will be free from all sin and as loving as you.

Oh, the hope this gives me—the invigorating, liberating, consecrating hope this generates as I begin my day. It's why this admonition from Paul feels more like a kiss than a kick today. I want to work more heartily at all things because of your finished work on the cross, your present work in the world, and your future work in the new heaven and new earth. Even in eternity you will shepherd us and lead us to springs of living water (Rev. 7:17). No one will ever outserve you, Jesus.

Therefore, here's my cry: continue to free me from doing anything for the approval of people, out of the fear of people, or to gain power over people. I work for you, Lord Jesus, not for mere men.

Free me for doing all things as unto you: loving my wife without manipulation, doing my job without self-congratulation, and serving your people without unrealistic expectations, to name a few.

How I praise you, Jesus, that the gospel is the end of any sense of a wage-earning relationship with God. I work for you because you first worked for me. (What a humbling, staggering, and astonishing truth!) I serve you because you ever live to serve me, as my advocate and intercessor. Indeed, I love you because you first loved me and gave yourself as a propitiation for my sins. You are always first and last—the Alpha and the Omega.

I'll receive an inheritance only because of your work, not mine. And should I receive any rewards or crowns, they will be thrown at your feet, giving credit where credit is due. I pray in your quintessentially glorious name. Amen.

A Prayer in Praise of Jesus, the Perfect Savior

Because Jesus lives forever, he has a permanent priesthood. Therefore he is able to save completely those who come to God through him, because he always lives to intercede for them. (Heb. 7:24–25 NIV)

Gracious Jesus, driving into my home state recently, I came upon a billboard that pushed some buttons before it raised my palms. Just through the mountains of North Carolina, there it was, in bold, big, red letters: "Are You Saved?"

I'll be honest. My first response was, "What an uncool, cost-ineffective, out-of-date, impersonal way to do evangelism. People who put up highway signs like that are *clueless* about the gospel. They're usually legalists and moralists and have no idea about a theology of imputed righteousness. They're culturally disengaged and don't realize what a turnoff that kind of signage is."

But then your Spirit gently disrupted my signage tirade with this thought: "You completely avoided the question. *Are you saved?*"

I continued driving, but one palm went up anyway. For, indeed, I am saved, Jesus—unabashedly and unashamedly so. And there's only *one reason* and there's only *one basis*: I have come to God through you. You are the permanent priest who offered the perfect sacrifice for me, once and for all. You completed your work on the cross, and you will complete your work in me.

You live forever, and forever you live to thoroughly save me and your whole pan-national, transgenerational bride. Your life and death were given in substitution for me, and now I wear your righteousness and enjoy your advocacy before the Father. Am I saved? Most definitely and most delightfully!

I don't have to like highway billboards, but may I never ever tire of responding to the question "Are you saved?" for there's no question more humbling to me and honoring to you. I pray, Jesus, in your merciful and mighty-to-save name. Amen.

A Prayer for Parents Learning to Love Their Gay Children

God is our refuge and strength,
    a very present help in trouble.
Therefore we will not fear though the earth gives way,
    though the mountains be moved into the heart of the sea,
though its waters roar and foam,
    though the mountains tremble at its swelling. (Ps. 46:1–3)

Dear Jesus, this Scripture seems appropriate in light of the phone call I just finished: a mom and dad in tears, shame, and great confusion—devastated to discover their son is gay. They feel like the earth has given way and the mountains have jumped into the ocean, for the world as they know it has just been turned upside down.

Jesus, there's no safer or more welcoming refuge than you. You give us strength when hard stories and fresh crises sap our energy and buckle our knees. No one is better suited to provide gracious help for troubled hearts than you.

I bring my friends to your throne of grace. They have no clue what this means or what to do next. Please keep them free from stereotypes, bad information, and uninvited helpers. Make your presence palpable to them.

Unfortunately, like me, they were led to believe that same-sex attraction is the most egregious and twisted form of sin. Because of this, their shock and fear makes them want to assign responsibility and find someone to blame. Don't let them turn on one another, Jesus. More than anything else, they need you and the grace and wisdom you promise.

In the next hours and days, calm their hearts and give them kindness beyond their own—your kindness. I pray for a bridge of compassion and communication. Help them see their son not as a leper but as their son. Help them love him as a sinner-saint like they are, not as someone to fix.

And I pray for their son, Jesus. Help me know how to best serve and care for him. He's confused about you now that he's convinced about his homosexuality. Bring your mercy and grace to bear in powerful ways. Keep him far from those who would try to exploit his vulnerability—especially from those with evil intent.

Though this young man's story, sin, and weakness are different from mine, I don't need you any less than he does, Jesus. Help me make that clear as we lean into this next season together. I pray in your gracious and powerful name. Amen.

A Prayer Calling Us to Goodness

Be subject for the Lord's sake to every human institution, whether it be to the emperor as supreme, or to governors as sent by him to punish those who do evil and to praise those who do good. For this is the will of God, that by doing good you should put to silence the ignorance of foolish people. Live as people who are free, not using your freedom as a cover-up for evil, but living as servants of God. Honor everyone. Love the brotherhood. Fear God. Honor the emperor. (1 Pet. 2:13–17)

King Jesus, what but the gospel can explain the change in Peter's life? The same disciple who nervously tried to protect you from being arrested by the authorities by cutting off the ear of the high priest's servant (John 18:10–11), the same disciple who then fled into the night and denied you three times out of fear—this same disciple calls us to fear only God and to live as model citizens in our broken world filled with broken kings, governors, and authorities. What but the gospel can explain his movement from fear and frenzy to faith and freedom?

And who but you, Jesus, who reattached Malchus's ear to his head (Luke 22:51); who but you, who could've dispatched "more than twelve legions of angels" (Matt. 26:53); who but you can give us the freedom and courage we need to "silence the ignorance of foolish people" (1 Pet. 2:15) as we live to your glory in our cities?

Though your kingdom is "not of this world" (John 18:36 NIV), your kingdom has broken into this world and one day will utterly transform this world. Because this is true, Jesus, I need you to free me from both extremes of naive passivity and fear-mongering aggression. Very practically, show me what "obeying God and not men" looks like when the claims of your kingdom clash with the values of this world. How do I submit to the authorities for your sake while primarily only bowing my knee and heart to you as my King?

Please, Lord Jesus, may I only suffer for doing good—not for being fearful, obnoxious, or paranoid. May I be busy with your kingdom and not simply be a busybody (2 Thess. 3:11). Keep changing me the way you changed Peter. I pray in your most glorious name. Amen.

A Prayer about Being Smitten with Jesus

Do not be led away by diverse and strange teachings, for it is good for the heart to be strengthened by grace, not by foods, which have not benefited those devoted to them. We have an altar from which those who serve the tent have no right to eat. (Heb. 13:9–10)

Jesus, throughout Lent, you've made me glad about several things. I've never been more grateful for the family you've given me. We're a broken but beloved bunch—each of us is on the path of groaning and growing in grace. And I praise you for a handful of very good friends, a "gospel posse" with whom to share longings and laughter and the bleakness and bounty of life. We finally know how to provoke one another to love and good deeds, and not just provoke one another.

In particular, I'm thankful for the ways that you continue to show me more of yourself, for you are the author and perfecter of my faith. I can afford to be flexible about a lot of theological issues, but I can ill afford to be wrong about you.

Over the past four decades, you've been faithful to rescue me from all kinds of "strange teachings," especially from gospels that are no gospel at all (Gal. 1:6–9). You've rescued me from illusions such as graceless legalism and obedienceless grace, from politicized gospels and sentimental gospels, from gospels that privatize knowing you and gospels that compartmentalize serving you, from gospels that despise the poor and gospels that empower the rich.

Lord Jesus, well beyond this current season of Lent, continue to smite my heart with more of your glory and your grace. I want to boast much more in your righteousness than in my being right. Strengthen my heart with your grace. Continue to feed me from the altar in the tabernacle of the gospel. Though I know you only in part, you know me perfectly, and that is enough. I pray in your peerless and powerful name. Amen.

A Prayer for God's Transforming Presence in Our Worship

The secrets of their hearts are laid bare. So they will fall down and worship God, exclaiming, "God is really among you!" (1 Cor. 14:25 NIV)

Gracious Father, I'm not afraid for the secrets in my heart to be laid bare today—to be openly exposed and revealed. For I'm confident that you will deal with me not according to my sin but according to the unsearchable riches of the gospel. Otherwise, I would surely fear and despair of such exposure. For in the gospel I find the generosity and kindness of your heart "laid bare" and poured out—your welcome and provision for rebels, fools, and idolaters just like me.

Indeed, the gospel is the sanctuary where my heart cries the loudest, "God is really among you!" Only the gospel of your grace frees me to fall down and worship you in humility, not humiliation; in gratitude, not groveling; in repentant faith, not uncertain penance; in the assurance of Christ's righteousness, not the condemnation of my unrighteousness.

Father, I pray our whole church family will enjoy this same freedom—especially as we gather each Lord's Day to worship you. In a day when we seem to need more gadgets and gimmicks to create "worship experiences," free us from needing anything more than the gospel to worship you the way you deserve and delight to be worshiped.

Teach us how to be stewards of technology, not slaves to technology. Teach us how to be creative, not cute; faithful, not manipulative; simple, not spectacular. Reel us back in anytime we move away from the "sincere and pure devotion to Christ" (2 Cor. 11:3). And let us never forget that you are not seeking "great worship" but true worshipers—those who worship you "in the Spirit and in truth" (John 4:23 NIV).

May our worship be so saturated with the truth and grace of the gospel that nonbelievers will be overwhelmed with your presence and captured by your love. We pray in Jesus' most wonderful and worthy name. Amen.

A Prayer about God's Delight and My Hope

His delight is not in the strength of the horse,
nor his delight in the legs of a man,
but the LORD takes pleasure in those who fear him,
in those who hope in his steadfast love. (Ps. 147:10–11)

Compassionate Father, once again I come before you as a repeat offender, a man suffering from doxological dementia, one of your sons who gives you so much opportunity to demonstrate the wonder of your "immense patience" (1 Tim. 1:16 NIV). It's like I'm a perpetual candidate for summer school in the gospel.

Why is it that every time I feel a little disconnected from you; every time I get appropriately disappointed with me; every time I experience the accusations of the enemy; every time I see other believers more zealous, missionaries more passionate, and young converts more committed than me—why is it that my default mode is to lace up my running shoes and get busy for you? Instead of running to you for grace, I start running to do something to assuage my guilty conscience and calm my disquieted heart.

But as this Scripture says, you don't find any pleasure or delight in the strength and movement of my "legs"—of what I can do for you. You find great pleasure as I put my hope in what you've done for me in Jesus. Indeed, where can I find your unfailing, unwavering, unending love? Only in the gospel of your grace. This is so counterintuitive, so contrary to the way I'm wired and the way the world literally works.

Holy Father, to fear you is the beginning of wisdom, and we fear you the most when we hope most fully in your unfailing love for us in Jesus. Should I forget where I parked my car, the address of my home, or even my own name, may I never forget this glorious gospel. I pray in Jesus' most grace-full name. Amen.

A Prayer Asking Jesus to Intensify Our Thirst for Him

O God, you are my God; earnestly I seek you;
  my soul thirsts for you;
my flesh faints for you,
  as in a dry and weary land where there is no water.
So I have looked upon you in the sanctuary,
  beholding your power and glory.
Because your steadfast love is better than life,
  my lips will praise you.
So I will bless you as long as I live;
  in your name I will lift up my hands.
My soul will be satisfied as with fat and rich food,
  and my mouth will praise you with joyful lips. (Ps. 63:1–5)

Dear Jesus, we come before you today asking for the gift of thirst. Renew and intensify our thirst for you. Make us so faint that unless you hydrate our hearts with the gospel, we will surely perish.

It's a dangerous thing to no longer deeply crave fellowship with you, Jesus. It's a deceptive thing to enjoy but no longer actually need you. It's a deceitful thing to be satisfied with correct theology about you, without experiencing rich communion with you. It's a demonic thing to find our ultimate satisfaction in anyone or anything else but you.

Only your steadfast love is better than life, Jesus—only your contra-conditional, irrepressible affection for us. Nothing else will do. You have created a gospel-shaped vacuum in our hearts—a screaming empty place that fits only you. Forgive us when we try to cram human love, creature comforts, or anything else into that place. Don't let us be so easily satisfied. Give us redemptive discontent until our hearts rest again in you.

Jesus, we're asking this not just for ourselves as individuals, but for our churches as well. Forgive us when we get so organized, creative, and "right" that we no longer miss your presence. Is it really you we are worshiping, or are we just worshiping worship? Is it really you we are serving, or are we just serving ourselves as religious consumers?

If you actually "left the house," how long would it take before we knew the difference? In all honesty, Jesus, how much of what we do in our churches doesn't require the Holy Spirit at all? Show us, convict us, forgive us, and change us.

Let us see and experience your power and glory in fresh ways, Jesus. We want to lift our hearts, voices, hands, and whole lives to you as a sacrifice of praise. May the truth and grace of the gospel satisfy us as fat and rich food. We pray with longing hearts. Amen.

A Prayer about Longings for Healing

Then the angel showed me the river of the water of life, bright as crystal, flowing from the throne of God and of the Lamb through the middle of the street of the city; also, on either side of the river, the tree of life with its twelve kinds of fruit, yielding its fruit each month. The leaves of the tree were for the healing of the nations. (Rev. 22:1–2)

Merciful Jesus, I begin today with one clear image and many pronounced longings. The image is John's vision of the New Jerusalem, our future home of perfect health. Because of the tree of Calvary, the tree of life will stand tall in the New Jerusalem, bearing the fruit of your great sacrifice, extending its leaves for our complete healing. Oh, to live, play, and praise in the shade of that tree, where every disease, disintegration, and distress will be gone forever!

My longings are connected to people I love—people in need of all kinds of healing. I pray for marriages of friends to be healed; for the minds of those suffering with mental illness to be healed; for the fabric of our racially torn community to be healed; for the emotions of the demonized to be healed; for friends with stories of abuse, cancer, and heart disease to be healed; indeed, for the nations to be healed . . .

Even as I pray for these things, Jesus, I don't understand—and I don't have to understand—the "already and not yet" of your healing ministry. Why, how, and when you choose to bring a foretaste of perfect health in the present state of our brokenness is up to you. You are the King who does all things well. You don't need our permission to do anything.

But help me avoid two extremes: keep me free from faith formulas that treat healing like an on-demand right, and keep me free from a theology that has no expectation of your kingdom breaking in with power and healing.

More so than ever, I intensely and deeply long for the day of perfect health. Until that day, help me and our church family to anticipate and extend various dimensions of your healing ministry to one another, to our community, and to the nations. I pray in your holy and healing name. Amen.

A Prayer about the Names
by Which We Live

He who has an ear, let him hear what the Spirit says to the churches. To
the one who conquers I will give some of the hidden manna, and I will
give him a white stone, with a new name written on the stone that no one
knows except the one who receives it. (Rev. 2:17)

Gracious Jesus, who'd have thought that a quick run to the super-
market would result in a painful study in "naming"? I'm sure that
little boy who was straining for his favorite box of cereal has another
name than "So Much Trouble" and "Such a Bother." I hope the husband
who shared the paper goods aisle with me calls his wife other things than
"Slow," "Indecisive," and "Wasteful." It seems like we live and die by the
names we are given, and we harm or heal by the names we give.

Jesus, you have the name that is above *every* name. It's by your name
and everything your name signifies that I'm forgiven, I'm declared righteous in the sight of God, I'm being healed of every disease, I'm being
set free from every bondage, and I'm being "shalomed" and fitted for life
in the kingdom. And it's at your name, Jesus, that one day I will gladly
bow my knees with everyone in heaven and on earth and under the earth
(Phil. 2:9–11).

It's only because you overcame sin and death for me that I call myself
an "overcomer." It's only because you drank the cup of my judgment that
I will feast on the "hidden manna" of eternity. It's only because you are
renaming me in the gospel that I'm being delivered from every wrong,
cruel, damaging name I've ever received or given myself.

And it's only through the power, grace, and glory of your name that I'm
learning to be so very careful what I call, label, and name others.

Whether or not there's literally a new name you'll give me in heaven, I
don't know. I'll just have to wait and see. That today you call me "beloved"
is enough for now and eternity. I pray in your merciful and matchless
name. Amen.

A Prayer about Weary Friends and a Caring Jesus

Come to me, all who labor and are heavy laden, and I will give you rest. Take my yoke upon you, and learn from me, for I am gentle and lowly in heart, and you will find rest for your souls. For my yoke is easy, and my burden is light. (Matt. 11:28–30)

Merciful Jesus, though I slept well, I begin today restless with concern. I've got a few friends dangerously depleted, spiritually numb, and close to giving up.

One can no longer fight the strong undertow of rage she faces every single day in her home. She'd rather drown than continue to fight the cruel current. Another brother lives in a swirling vortex of shame, either unable or unwilling to believe you won't crush him if he comes to you. Then there's the married couple who've lost sight of the issues and are simply trying to out-mean each other. They seem oblivious to the ways their bitterness and bickering are impacting their children.

Jesus, I am weary and burdened for my friends, and I do bring them to you right now. Out of the strength of your gentleness and the power of your humility, give me what I need to love them well. Show me how to pray and wrestle in the Holy Spirit for them. I take on your yoke because it unites me to you. I simply cannot do this alone.

Free me to be comfortable with not being able to fix anything. None of this is about my competency; it's about their crises and your glory. Indeed, more than anything, I want you to receive much glory in each of these three very broken stories.

Write stories of redemption for your name's sake. Bring your resurrection power to bear in each of these three situations, I pray. The things that are impossible with me, as a mere man, are more than possible with you.

Keep me restless for my friends, Jesus, but keep me fully resting in you. I pray in your gentle, humble-hearted name. Amen.

A Prayer for Discerning the Will of God

In their hearts humans plan their course,
but the LORD establishes their steps. (Prov. 16:9 NIV)

Sovereign Father, this promise brings me immeasurable peace, humility, and joy. You're vitally engaged in determining and directing every one of my steps. You're working all things together after the counsel of your will. You're working in all things for your glory and for our good. You open doors no man can shut and you shut doors no man can open. Indeed, you're no mere life coach; you're the Lord of all things—including me.

Many years I labored under the arrogance and anxiety of assuming that if I prayed hard enough and long enough, that if I was really filled with and "tuned into" the Holy Spirit, I could know the specifics of your will for my life well in advance of any decision that needed to be made. Of course, my assumption was that if I was in your will, life would be enjoyable, pleasant, and hassle-free.

If I bought the right car, it would never break down. If I bought the right house, the roof would never leak. If I married the right person, we would never disagree. If I went to the right college, I'd get the right job and life would be all right. If I sent my kids to the right school, they would never act out and would end up on the mission field. If all of this were true, I wouldn't really need you.

Father, you're certainly honored when we work hard to make good plans in keeping with our understanding of the Scriptures. It's important for us to seek and heed the wise, prayerful counsel of good and godly friends.

But help us to live with more confidence that Jesus is the Good Shepherd, not a consulting partner; a very present Lord, not an absentee landlord; the reigning King, not an impotent bystander.

Because of Jesus, I'm confident your will is being done, on earth as it is in heaven. I pray in his exalted name. Amen.

A Prayer about Palm Sunday Wonder

Rejoice greatly, O daughter of Zion!
   Shout aloud, O daughter of Jerusalem!
Behold, your king is coming to you;
   righteous and having salvation is he,
humble and mounted on a donkey,
   on a colt, the foal of a donkey.
I will cut off the chariot from Ephraim
   and the war horse from Jerusalem;
and the battle bow shall be cut off,
   and he shall speak peace to the nations;
his rule shall be from sea to sea,
   and from the River to the ends of the earth.
As for you also, because of the blood of my covenant with you,
   I will set your prisoners free from the waterless pit.
Return to your stronghold, O prisoners of hope;
   today I declare that I will restore to you double. (Zech. 9:9–12)

Lord Jesus, I'll exhaust the wonder of this passage as soon as I drink Niagara Falls dry, as soon as I memorize the names of every star you've launched into the heavens, as soon as I finish climbing all the Alps in Switzerland, Italy, Germany, and France.

On this Palm Sunday morning, I'm overwhelmed with your humility and your sovereignty. What other king could conquer warhorses and warriors by riding the foal of a donkey? What other king could break the battle bow and the backbone of all warfare by the brokenness of the cross? What other king could ever replace the politics of tyranny with a reign of peace?

What other king would offer his life and death for the redemption and restoration of rebels, fools, and idolaters like us? What other king could possibly make prisoners of sin, death, and "waterless pits" into prisoners of hope?

Jesus, you are that King. There is no other such king. Who is the King of Glory? It is you, Lord Jesus, and only you. Who is the King of Grace? It is you, Lord Jesus, and only you. Who is the King of Kings and the Lord of Lords? It is you, Lord Jesus, and only you.

Our joy is great as this Holy Week begins, for you have come to us righteous and victorious. May your cross and your crown continue to free us from other imprisonments so that we may live as prisoners of hope and agents of redemption. We pray in your peerless and priceless name. Amen.

A Prayer about the Very Reason Jesus Came

"Now is my soul troubled. And what shall I say? 'Father, save me from this hour'? But for this purpose I have come to this hour. Father, glorify your name." Then a voice came from heaven: "I have glorified it, and I will glorify it again." The crowd that stood there and heard it said that it had thundered. Others said, "An angel has spoken to him." Jesus answered, "This voice has come for your sake, not mine. Now is the judgment of this world; now will the ruler of this world be cast out. And I, when I am lifted up from the earth, will draw all people to myself." (John 12:27–32)

Lord Jesus, it's Monday of Holy Week, and I'm deeply moved as I reflect on how profoundly troubled you were as the events of that week began to unfold. There was no doubt in your mind why you came into Jerusalem riding the foal of a donkey. There was great conflict, but no doubt.

There would be no surprises. You knew what was coming. In a matter of days, you would take the holy wrath of judgment day for all who will trust in you. At the end of the week, your "bruised heel" (Gen. 3:15) would secure the ultimate crushing and "casting out" of the "ruler of this world" (John 12:30)—Satan himself. At the end of the week, you would pay the supreme price that alone guarantees the redemption and "drawing" of men and women from every single nation, tribe, people, and language—a number as great as the stars in the sky, the sand of the beaches, and the dust of the earth.

For this very reason you came from eternity into time and space. For this very reason you emptied yourself of your glory by taking the form of a servant-man—the Lord's Servant. For this very reason the Father spoke thunderous words from heaven for our benefit. For this very reason you became obedient—even obedient to death on the cross. Understandably so, your heart was greatly troubled, Lord Jesus.

As the events of our week now unfold, grant us grace to survey the wonders of your cross with greater awe and gratitude than ever. In a time when many in our culture are marginalizing and minimizing, denying or dismissing your cross, may our boasting in your cross grow by all-time exponential proportions. We pray in the beauty and bounty of your most glorious name. Amen.

A Prayer about Jesus' Compassion and My Blindness

As he [Jesus] approached Jerusalem and saw the city, he wept over it and said, "If you, even you, had only known on this day what would bring you peace—but now it is hidden from your eyes." (Luke 19:41–42 NIV)

Dear Jesus, everything about Holy Week reveals the depth of your compassion for sinful, broken people just like me. The tears you wept coming into Jerusalem, even the anger you showed in driving the money changers out of the temple—every encounter, parable, and action gives staggering clarity to Paul's words, "You see, at just the right time, when we were still powerless, Christ died for the ungodly. Very rarely will anyone die for a righteous person, though for a good person someone might possibly dare to die. But God demonstrates his own love for us in this: While we were still sinners, Christ died for us" (Rom. 5:6–8 NIV).

Paul was writing about me. I'm the powerless, ungodly sinner for whom you died, demonstrating God's incomparable and irrepressible love for me. I was God's enemy when you reconciled me to him through your death on the cross (Rom. 5:10). May I never believe otherwise.

I would still be blind to what alone brings me peace if you hadn't opened my eyes to see my need of you and your death for me. The gospel would still remain hidden from my eyes unless you had given me sight to behold you as the Lamb of God who takes away my sin. I can't and I won't sneer at a single Pharisee, Sadducee, priest, teacher of the law, or anyone else who tried to trick or trap you during Holy Week. I am just as worthy of judgment as they.

How I long for the day when I will no longer even be tempted to look for peace, for shalom, anywhere else but in you, Jesus. I yearn for the day when I will see you as you are and I will be made like you (1 John 3:1–3). This is my great hope. Until that day, keep healing the eyes of my heart of all spiritual myopia, astigmatism, or anything else that keeps me from seeing the magnificence of your glory and the full measure of your grace. I pray in your tenacious and tender name. Amen.

A Prayer about the Main Question in Life

While the Pharisees were gathered together, Jesus asked them a question, saying, "What do you think about the Christ?" (Matt. 22:41–42)

Dear Jesus, it's Wednesday of Holy Week. The question you directed to the Pharisees, you still put before us: "What do you think about the Christ?" There's no more important question for us to wrestle with in life. Continue to free us from all wrong notions we have about you—those generated in our fallen hearts; the ones that come to us from the father of lies, Satan; others that simply reveal the wrong and incomplete teaching we have received through the years.

But what do I think about you today, Jesus? What do I believe in my heart? You are everlasting God, and I am a mere man. I would despair if you were anything less, and I am weary of trying to be more. You are the Creator, Sustainer, and Restorer of all things. You don't just care about my soul; you care about everything you have made.

You are the second Adam—our substitute in life and in death. You lived a life of perfect obedience for us, and you exhausted God's judgment that stood against us. By you, we have been completely forgiven, and in you, we have received perfect righteousness. I humbly stake my life and my death upon what you've done for us. Jesus, you are all this and so much more. Eternity will be an endless revelation of your glory and grace.

But this holy week, what stuns me the most is to realize you are always thinking about us. We are in your heart and on your mind all the time. You are always praying for us and advocating for us before the Father. You're the One who knows us the best and loves us the most. With fresh gratitude and awe, we worship you. We make our prayer in your gracious name and for your everlasting glory. Amen.

A Prayer about the Mandate Jesus Gave Us

Now before the Feast of the Passover, when Jesus knew that his hour had come to depart out of this world to the Father, having loved his own who were in the world, he loved them to the end. (John 13:1)

A new command I give you: Love one another. As I have loved you, so you must love one another. By this everyone will know that you are my disciples, if you love one another. (John 13:34–35 NIV)

Lord Jesus, as I meditate and pray my way through these Scriptures, I'm quite literally undone. What but the gift of faith can enable me to grasp the wonder of these words and the magnificence of this moment? What but the power of the gospel can enable me to believe and obey them? Grant me both, I pray; grant me both.

On our calendar we call this day Maundy or Mandate Thursday. It is a day of Holy Week and a day in the history of redemption brimming over with glory and grace. Passover will soon become the Lord's Supper—your supper. The promises of the old covenant will soon be fulfilled by the blood of the new covenant—your blood.

Having shared eternal glory with the Father, you now show stunning grace to your disciples. Having loved this ragtag bunch of broken men—who squabbled with each other hours earlier for positions of honor and who within a few hours would all scatter and deny you—having loved them so well, you now show them even greater manifestations of your love. Your disrobing to wash their feet was with a full view to your being stripped naked to wash their hearts and our hearts. What wondrous love is this indeed! How wide, long, high, and deep!

"Love one another. As I have loved you, so you must love one another" (John 13:34 NIV). This is the new and never-ending mandate we're now under as your disciples. Don't let me ever forget that the measure of your love is not just the basin and towel of the upper room but your cross and your death at Calvary. There simply is no greater love—none.

Jesus, as my heart comes more fully alive to how you loved me by your death and how you love me now in your resurrection glory, I'll seek to make fewer excuses for loving poorly and to offer quicker repentances when I do. As you continue to show me the full extent of your love for me in the gospel, love through me to your glory. I pray in your name. Amen.

A Prayer about the Good of Good Friday

And Jesus said, "Father, forgive them, for they know not what they do."
(Luke 23:34)

Jesus cried out with a loud voice, saying, "Eli, Eli, lema sabachthani?" that
is, "My God, my God, why have you forsaken me?" (Matt. 27:46)

*L*ord Jesus, it's the day in Holy Week we call "Good Friday." I've always felt conflicted about calling the day of your crucifixion "good." It seems quite a bit insensitive and self-serving. That there had to be a day when you, the God who made us for yourself, would be made sin for us is not good at all.

But on the other hand, that you would so freely and fully give yourself for us on the cross is never-to-be-surpassed goodness. There never has been and there never will be anything that is more deserving of the appellation "good" than your death for us.

For out of the same heart and the same mouth came these two cries from the cross: "Father, forgive them" (Luke 23:34) and "My God, my God, why have you forsaken me?" (Matt. 27:46). The first required the second. The second secured the first. Together, both of them buckle my knees, still my heart, and loose my tongue.

Yet how can I begin to express the wonder, love, and praise I feel in response to what you've done for me on the cross? It's like wanting to paint the most magnificent spring landscape I've ever seen, but with a palate of three colors and both of my arms in a cast. It's like having a passion to write a great symphony in honor of you but knowing I'm just a kazoo player who doesn't read music. It's like desiring to cook you a great banquet with my microwave oven, a loaf of white bread, and a can of processed cheese.

There's simply no way I can possibly offer a response congruent to the magnificence of your mercy and the measure of your grace for me at Calvary. So like everything else I have to offer you, Jesus, take my humble praise and purify it, magnify it, and cause it to be a sweet aroma in your heart. No one could ever take your life from you, and I could never find life on my own. Because you were fully forsaken, I am forever forgiven. Because you exhausted God's judgment against my foul sin, I now live by the gift of your perfect righteousness. Hallelujah! Hallelujah! Hallelujah! I pray in your all-glorious, all-gracious name. Amen.

A Prayer about Resurrection Promise

The next day, the one after Preparation Day, the chief priests and the Pharisees went to Pilate. "Sir," they said, "we remember that while he was still alive that deceiver said, 'After three days I will rise again.' So give the order for the tomb to be made secure until the third day. Otherwise, his disciples may come and steal the body and tell the people that he has been raised from the dead. This last deception will be worse than the first." (Matt. 27:62–64 NIV)

Jesus, as Good Friday gave way to silent Saturday, the range of emotions following your crucifixion was as broad as the Grand Canyon. I can only imagine the degree of shock and the depth of sadness that filled the hearts of your disciples, your family, and your friends. And yet there were also those who were filled with glee and relief that you, "the deceiver," could no longer threaten their existence.

As the sun rose on Saturday, no one could have possibly understood that the most undeserved death imaginable would yield the greatest return calculable. As you were nailed to the cross, the written code—God's law, with all its regulations and requirements—was taken away from us, losing all its condemning power over us. As you drew your last breath, you were actually disarming the powers of darkness and triumphing over all authorities marshaled against the reign of God (Col. 2:14–15).

No one yet grasped that your mortal punishment would bring our eternal peace, that your fatal wounding would secure our everlasting healing, and that your being crushed would lead to our being cherished by the thrice holy God (Isa. 53). Though they had the Scriptures, they had no clue.

And yet the chief priests and the Pharisees did remember your promise of resurrection. They weren't sad about your death; they were mad with fear about the possibility of your life. Having already plotted to put to death a resurrected Lazarus, they weren't about to indulge a resurrected rabbi.

Oh foolish, silly, sinful men—they could sooner hold back the rising of the sun than the rising of the Son of Man, the Son of God, God the Son! Resurrection Sunday was coming, and there was absolutely nothing they could do about it. The silence of Saturday would soon be shattered with the shouts of Sunday: "The Lord is risen! He is risen indeed!"

Jesus, continue to astonish and nourish our hearts—my heart—with the whole Easter story and the full glory of who you are and everything you have done. I pray in your peerless name. Amen.

A Prayer about Resurrection Firstfruits

But in fact Christ has been raised from the dead, the firstfruits of those who have fallen asleep. For as by a man came death, by a man has come also the resurrection of the dead. For as in Adam all die, so also in Christ shall all be made alive. But each in his own order: Christ the firstfruits, then at his coming those who belong to Christ. Then comes the end, when he delivers the kingdom to God the Father after destroying every rule and every authority and power. For he must reign until he has put all his enemies under his feet. The last enemy to be destroyed is death. (1 Cor. 15:20–26)

Exalted and resurrected Jesus, I offer a threefold "Indeed!" and a threefold "Hallelujah!" early this morning. You *have* been raised from the dead! Preaching the gospel is not useless; it's essential. Faith in you is not futile but fertile. We're no longer encased in our sins; we're fully wrapped in your righteousness. Those who have "gone to sleep" in you are not slumbering in the void; they are savoring your resurrection glory.

We are *less* to be pitied than anybody and *more* to be grateful than everybody (1 Cor. 15:14–19). Because you have been raised from the dead, everything changes, Jesus. You are the firstfruits and guarantee of a whole new order—the "new creation" dominion of redemption and restoration. The decay in our earthly bodies will give way to the delights of our resurrection bodies.

The kingdom of this world has already become, and will be fully manifest as, the kingdom of our God and of you, his Christ. You are already reigning, and you will reign forever and ever. All evil dominions, wicked authorities, and malevolent powers have already been defeated by you and one day will be completely eradicated by you.

Jesus, your death is the death of death, and your resurrection is the resurrection of all things. Oh, the wonder, the glory, the grace! In light of this great hope, because this gospel is true, free me and my friends from the pettiness and emptiness of living for ourselves. Because of your compelling love, show us how to live for you, for you died for us and have been raised again! Again I shout it, a threefold "Indeed!" and a threefold "Hallelujah!" I pray and shout, in your most glorious name! Amen.

A Prayer about My Foolish, Slow Heart

And he said to them, "O foolish ones, and slow of heart to believe all that the prophets have spoken! Was it not necessary that the Christ should suffer these things and enter into his glory?" And beginning with Moses and all the Prophets, he interpreted to them in all the Scriptures the things concerning himself. (Luke 24:25–27)

Gracious Jesus, of all your postresurrection appearances (1 Cor. 15:3–7), I treasure the visit you paid disheartened friends on the road to Emmaus the most (Luke 24:13–35). That you met with a shattered and shamed Peter was incredibly kind and healing. That you appeared to the apostle Paul, who in his own words was a man unworthy of even being called an apostle, marked him forever. All of us have enjoyed the fruit of that visitation through Paul's life and writings.

But I love how you came alongside of the Emmaus men, for I am so much like them. I am a foolish, slow-of-heart man who constantly needs you to preach the gospel to my heart by the Holy Spirit. How I praise you for your tender forbearance, unlimited patience, and grace-full persistence.

As you dealt with my brothers, so deal with me. Continue to reveal yourself as the main character and hero in all the Scriptures. Don't let me read the writings of Moses without thinking about you, Jesus—especially the law. May Moses's words always drive me to you. For you have fulfilled the demands of the law for me, and you are now fulfilling the beauty of the law in me as the gospel changes me. I don't want to forget that, even for a nanosecond, lest I lapse into graceless guilt or performance-based pride.

And continue to show me how you are fulfilling everything the prophets have spoken—not just the things concerning your sufferings on the cross and your resurrection from the dead but also all the promises of your present work in the world as a redeemer and restorer. May a vision of your present reign and coming kingdom give me "redemptive heartburn" like that which you ignited in the hearts of my Emmaus brothers. Continue to open the Scriptures to me, Jesus, until the day you return to finish making all things new. I pray in your holy and transforming name. Amen.

A Prayer about My Cluttered Spirit and God's Kindness

God raised us up with Christ and seated us with him in the heavenly realms in Christ Jesus, in order that in the coming ages he might show the incomparable riches of his grace, expressed in his kindness to us in Christ Jesus. (Eph. 2:6–7 NIV)

Loving Father, I'd be a crazy man to start this particular day without immersing my heart in the truth and riches of the gospel. I already feel a busy, cluttered spirit rearing its ugly head inside of me. Whether it's poor management or providence, I'm supposed to see more people and get more done than is realistic. The control-meister in me is at work, planning my day as though everything is up to me—as though I'm an orphan without a heavenly Father. In short, I really need the gospel today. It's good to know your mercies are more than a match for my heart today and every day.

So here's what I choose to remember right now: you not only raised Jesus from the dead on Easter Sunday, but you raised up all your children in him, including me. I'm seated with him in the heavenly realms, no longer cemented to the earthly way of seeing people and doing things.

You've called me to live today as a man of resurrection, not resentment. All day long, in the coming ages and throughout eternity, you are committed to showing me the incomparable riches of your grace and kindness toward me in Jesus. I do believe this, but not as much as you intend.

Father, thank you for being so tenaciously compassionate with me. It's the riches of your kindness, tolerance, and patience that lead me to repent in this very moment. Right now, as your Spirit convicts my heart; right now, with palms up, I both worship you and release my tightfisted grip on this day.

You will give me all the grace I need to do anything you ask of me today. You will give me all the kindness I need to be kind to the people you are bringing to me. You will give me all the mercy I need to be present in the moment and not anxious about the next thing on today's schedule.

At the end of today, you will be the God who yet again worked in all things for my good and your glory. I pray with hope, in Jesus' centering and freeing name. Amen.

A Prayer about God's Sovereignty and Our Sanity

At the end of the days I, Nebuchadnezzar, lifted my eyes to heaven, and my reason returned to me, and I blessed the Most High, and praised and honored him who lives forever, for his dominion is an everlasting dominion, and his kingdom endures from generation to generation; all the inhabitants of the earth are accounted as nothing, and he does according to his will among the host of heaven and among the inhabitants of the earth; and none can stay his hand or say to him, "What have you done?" (Dan. 4:34–35)

Almighty Father, I need to bookmark this passage and return to it often, for it doesn't just tell the conversion story of a pagan king; it's the ongoing story of my heart. We're never more sane than when we raise our eyes toward heaven and focus our attention on you. Navel-gazing, circumstance watching, and daily news fixating never serve us well.

Father, help us to understand the glorious implications of your perpetual enthronement. Your dominion is the only eternal dominion. November elections and political insurrections; the world economy and temperature instability; earthquakes and oil leaks; multiplied conspiracies and grass-roots organizing don't affect your reign one microbit for one nanosecond.

For your kingdom endures from generation to generation. There never has been, nor will there ever be, any nervous sweat, furrowed brows, or anxious pacing in heaven. There will be not one moment of consternation or vexation in the corridors of paradise; no need for a plan B to emerge from the big boardroom.

Father, you do as you please with the powers of heaven and the peoples of earth. I praise you for marshalling the powers of heaven for the salvation of ill-deserving rebels like me and the ultimate transformation of the entire cosmos. Though many tried to hold back your hand and many said, "What are you doing?" nevertheless you chose the sacrifice of your Son and the "foolishness" of the cross (1 Cor. 1:18) as the greatest demonstration of your sovereignty and grace.

The only King who could say, "Behold the world I have made," is the only King who would say, "Behold the people for whom I die." Father, the greatest sanity is gospel sanity. Keep us sane, Father; keep us gospel sane.

We choose to lift our eyes to heaven today and fix our gaze on Jesus, the author and perfecter of our faith, and we cry with unfettered, unabated joy, "Hallelujah, what a Savior! Hallelujah, what a salvation!" We pray in the name and for the glory of the true King, Jesus. Amen.

A Prayer about Pain-Generated Compassion

Therefore, as God's chosen people, holy and dearly loved, clothe your-selves with compassion, kindness, humility, gentleness and patience.
(Col. 3:12 NIV)

Jesus, the gospel should be all the motivation I need for living as a compassionate, kind, humble, gentle, and patient man—especially when I consider this is how you relate to me 24/7, in full view of my ill-deserving ways. I'll never experience you as insensitive, unkind, proud, harsh, or impatient. Indeed, through the gospel, I've become a member of God's chosen, holy, dearly loved people.

Yet it does take more: sometimes it takes pain. Today is just such a day. As I pray, I'm hurting big-time. Today it will be easier for me to clothe myself with compassion than with cotton. Yesterday afternoon I forgot that exercising at the gym doesn't qualify me to be a refrigerator mover. But as I hurt, I'm moved to pray today for chronic sufferers—those who cry, "How long, O Lord?" for better reasons and with more tears than I have.

Jesus, I pray for people with unrelenting pain in their bodies—those who no longer get any relief from physical therapy or medication. I pray for people with emotional and mental diseases, who live in the cruel world of delusional thinking and sabotaging emotions. I pray for their families and caregivers.

I pray for the unconscionable number of children in the world who are suffering from hunger and malnutrition and for their parents who feel both shame and helplessness. Lord, these and many more stories of great suffering I bring before you.

I also pray for the worst chronic suffering of all: for those who are "sepa-rate from Christ, excluded from citizenship in Israel and foreigners to the covenants of the promise, without hope and without God in the world" (Eph. 2:12 NIV). Come, Holy Spirit, come, and apply the saving benefits of Jesus to the religious and the nonreligious alike—to those who may be in the church or in the culture but who are not in Christ.

Jesus, I anticipate getting over this back pain pretty soon, but I don't want to get over compassionate praying and compassionate living. I pray in your kind and caring name. Amen.

A Prayer for the Spiritually Distressed

O Lord, you have deceived me, and I was deceived;
  you are stronger than I, and you have prevailed.
I have become a laughingstock all the day;
  everyone mocks me. (Jer. 20:7)

Why did I come out from the womb
  to see toil and sorrow
  and spend my days in shame? (Jer. 20:18)

Gracious Father, this is some pretty raw praying by one of your prophets. Jeremiah's lament makes me thankful today for the freedom you give us to bring our unfiltered and unfettered feelings to you. If we don't bring our painful emotions to you, we will take them *somewhere*. Somebody besides ourselves will feel the brunt of our anguish and anger.

But only you have the big enough heart and broad enough shoulders to walk with us through the chaos and confusion. I praise you for the constancy of your welcome. If you're not put off by Jeremiah's struggle, surely you will take on ours.

And to think, the same prophet who assured others of your gracious promise and good plan—a plan for prosperity, not harm (Jer. 29:11); the same prophet who gave us a vision of the glory and the grace of the new covenant (Jer. 31:31–34); this same prophet, like us, experienced seasons in which he felt deceived, betrayed, and abandoned, even grieving the day he was born. We're all weak and broken. We all need the gospel.

This gives me courage as I seek to steward my own feelings. But today it gives me compassion as I pray for a few friends who are feeling exactly what Jeremiah felt.

For the friend I sat with yesterday who's feeling set up, chewed up, and spit out by you, bring the gospel to bear. She loves you, but she feels abandoned by you. She knows better, but she feels bitter. My instinct is to "fix her," but the way of the gospel is to listen and love before launching. Give me patience and kindness as I trust you to restore her to gospel sanity.

For my friend whose spiritual melancholia is heading to an even darker place, Father, give me wisdom. What's purely physical? What's to some degree demonic? What's just plain ol' pity party? I don't know. I just don't know.

Help me, Lord, and heal my friends. Meet them as you met Jeremiah. I pray in Jesus' strong and loving name. Amen.

A Prayer Celebrating Jesus' Active Advocacy

But he [Stephen], full of the Holy Spirit, gazed into heaven and saw the glory of God, and Jesus standing at the right hand of God. And he said, "Behold, I see the heavens opened, and the Son of Man standing at the right hand of God." (Acts 7:55–56)

Gracious Jesus, this scene from Stephen's costly discipleship shouts your engagement, care, and love for us, your people. With stones bouncing off his brow, Stephen saw you *standing* at the right hand of the Father—rising for the very occasion of Stephen's greatest challenge and forthcoming death. Indeed, you are the Good Shepherd, who cares so faithfully for your lambs even from heaven.

May this story supplant every wrong notion I've ever had about you "sitting at the right hand of the Father." Your "sitting" doesn't speak of passivity or inactivity. On the contrary, you are "sitting" as one in session—as the One already enthroned as the King of Kings and the Lord of Lords.

When you completed your work of redemption for us on the cross, then and only then did you take your seat at the right hand of God the Father, celebrating the victory of your cry, "It is finished" (John 19:30). And since that time all of your enemies are becoming your footstool, as your kingdom advances in time and space (Heb. 10:12–13).

Jesus, forgive me for ever thinking that you've forgotten about me, don't really care about me, or have even abandoned me. I confess that sometimes, especially when life seems the hardest, loneliest, most unfair, and most broken, I entertain these foolish, unfounded, disbelieving notions.

Holy Spirit, do the same for us as you did for Stephen. Open the eyes of our hearts to see more of Jesus. Let us see "heavens opened, and the Son of Man standing at the right hand of God" (Acts 7:56), no matter if the sky is filled with foreboding, dark clouds or if the sky is totally cloudless and Carolina blue. Just let us see Jesus, and it will be enough. I pray in Jesus' exalted name. Amen.

A Prayer about the Ultimate Oxymoron

Peter took him aside and began to rebuke him. "Never, Lord!" he said. "This shall never happen to you!" (Matt. 16:22 NIV)

Patient Jesus, if an oxymoron is the juxtaposition of incongruous terms—like deafening silence, jumbo shrimp, planned spontaneity, or peace offensive—then the ultimate oxymoron is "Never, Lord!" Those two words just don't belong together. Yet, like Peter, I often match them up.

When you tell me that my need of salvation is so great—that I am so broken, so sinful, so diseased, so rebellious that only the gospel of God's grace can save someone like me—and yet I persist in trying to merit the righteousness of God or at least "supplement" what you've done for me on the cross, I pull you aside, rebuke you, and say, "Never, Lord! You haven't done quite enough for me."

When you assure me that your grace will be sufficient for me and that in my weakness your strength will be made perfect, and yet I persist in unbelief and start looking for sufficiency somewhere else, I say to your face, "Never, Lord! Your grace won't be quite enough for me."

When you call me to participate in your big story of redemption—of making all things new and gathering your bride from every nation—and yet I persist in living a little narrative of personal peace and fulfillment instead of finding my place in your story, I am saying to your face, "Never, Lord! Your glory is not as important as my happiness."

Have mercy on me, Jesus. Not on Peter, on me!

Lord Jesus, "Yes!" A thousand times "Yes!" to whatever you have said, have promised, and are up to in my life and in your world. Please take me aside and rebuke me with the gospel on a daily basis. I pray in your most wonderful and awe-worthy name. Amen.

A Prayer about Freedom from My Imprisonments

Bring me out of prison,
that I may give thanks to your name! (Ps. 142:7)

Jesus, great Lord and Liberator, when King David prayed for freedom from his prison, he wasn't behind iron bars; he was hiding in a cave. It's obvious he felt pursued, trapped, and alone. It's also obvious he enjoyed great freedom to own his desperation and abandon himself to you. I begin today doing the same.

You've already set me free from many slavish imprisonments: the fear of dying, for you robbed the grave of its victory through your resurrection; the fear of judgment, for you were condemned in my place upon the cross; the tyranny of false gospels, for it's your obedience and righteousness that make me acceptable to God; the myth of autonomy, for you alone are the sovereign Lord and the King of Kings. When I consider these liberties, why would I doubt your ability or willingness to set me free from other imprisonments?

Jesus, set me free from vain regrets—those haunting memories of what could have been and what should have been. I want to learn from the past, not be enslaved to the past. Your name is Redeemer.

Set me free from the fear of incompetency. I still feel insecure and underequipped in some important areas of life, mostly relational. I yearn for more freedom from the fear of man, truly a snare (Prov. 29:25). Be big in my life, Jesus, that people may assume the right size. I long to be a courageous peacemaker—not looking for fights but working for shalom.

Set me free from the power of old wounds. I'm a victim, but that's not my identity. Some things will be fully healed only by your second coming. Let me be okay with that, even as I trust you to use my pain for the benefit of others.

The more freedom you give me, the more fully I will seek to praise your name. I pray in your merciful and mighty name. Amen.

A Prayer of Big Thanks for Big Grace

> Praise the LORD, my soul;
>> all my inmost being, praise his holy name.
>
> Praise the LORD, my soul,
>> and forget not all his benefits—
>
> who forgives all your sins
>> and heals all your diseases,
>
> who redeems your life from the pit
>> and crowns you with love and compassion,
>
> who satisfies your desires with good things
>> so that your youth is renewed like the eagle's.
>>> (Ps. 103:1–5 NIV)

Dear Jesus, though I'm growing forgetful, I pray I will never forget you or a single benefit you've given me so freely in the gospel. But irrespective of changes in my brain chemistry, you will never, ever forget me. This is my great hope and peace. While my memory is fully functioning, here are a few things for which I am especially grateful as this day begins.

I praise you for forgiving all my sins—past, present, and future—sins of thought, word, and deed. I used to think you forgive only confessed sins, but now I realize I'm probably aware of only 4 percent of my sins. But your blood covers the other 96 percent as well.

I praise you for healing all my diseases—diseases in my body, heart, and mind. Though I wish you would completely heal me before you return, nonetheless, I have this sure hope: one day I will be perfectly whole. Praise the Lord, O my soul, for present, ongoing, and a secured complete healing!

I praise you for redeeming my life from all pits—the pit of eternal separation from God, the pits others throw me into, the pits I naively fall into, and the pits I foolishly dig for myself! Praise the Lord, O my soul, for an all-pit redemption!

I praise you for crowning me with your love and compassion. You have taken away all my guilt and you've borne my shame. I now live under grace, not law. Praise the Lord, O my soul, for a coronation of mercy and grace!

I praise you for satisfying my desires with good things. Lord, I praise you for the kiss of my wife, the taste of dark chocolate, and the rainbow painted on a trout and in the sky, to name a few. Praise the Lord, O my soul, for a God who delights in delighting us!

Jesus, may the unsearchable, innumerable, and inexhaustible riches of the gospel renew me today with youth-like energy, that I may soar like an eagle and live to the praise of your glorious grace! Amen.

A Prayer about a Gospel Garden

Now he who supplies seed to the sower and bread for food will also supply and increase your store of seed and will enlarge the harvest of your righteousness. You will be enriched in every way so that you can be generous on every occasion, and through us your generosity will result in thanksgiving to God. . . . Thanks be to God for his indescribable gift!
(2 Cor. 9:10–11, 15 NIV)

Heavenly Father, once again you've given us a beautiful spring. I absolutely love this time of year. Every day begins and ends with the most refreshing cool. The browns and grays of winter step aside for the kaleidoscopic colors and aromatic wonder of a brand-new season.

As tiny buds segue into full leaf and bloom, I'm reminded of your covenant faithfulness. The cycle of seedtime and harvest will continue until the completed harvest of your pan-national family and the emergence of the ultimate garden city—the New Jerusalem. Oh, hasten that day! Hasten the day of the sneezeless, allergyless new heaven and new earth!

Father, thanks for including us in this whole redeeming and greening process. You've not only promised to turn the barrenness and fallowness of our lives into a "well-watered garden" (Isa. 58:11; Jer. 31:12), you've also promised to use us as a means of making all things new, beautiful, lush, and fruitful.

Gardening is hard, Father, with its weeds, pests, and drought. But the gospel is our surety. You've planted and raised the perfect seed, Jesus, as the firstfruit of the final harvest. There's no possibility of crop failure.

Some of us plant, some of us water, but only you cause things to grow (1 Cor. 3:6). You are causing things to grow, and you will continue to do so. Indeed, "the gospel is bearing fruit and growing throughout the whole world" (Col. 1:6 NIV).

O Father, make us and our church families gardens of grace and righteousness, for your glory and the benefit of our communities. We pray in Jesus' fruitful and faithful name. Amen.

A Prayer in Praise of God's Goodness

May the God of endurance and encouragement grant you to live in such harmony with one another, in accord with Christ Jesus. (Rom. 15:5)

May the God of hope fill you with all joy and peace in believing, so that by the power of the Holy Spirit you may abound in hope. (Rom. 15:13)

May the God of peace be with you all. Amen. (Rom. 15:33)

Gracious Father, your Word never ceases to astonish, nourish, and cause my heart to flourish. Today I'm reveling in the fact that you delight to be known, and I'm rejoicing in who you reveal yourself to be. In this one chapter alone (Rom. 15) out of nearly 1,200 in the Bible, you come to me this very day as . . .

The God of endurance and encouragement. O Father, you know how much I need both of these grace gifts. I'm tired and worn out, and on top of that, I haven't been sleeping well at all lately. Why can't our crises be spread out a little more evenly in life? I may be exaggerating out of exhaustion, but it seems like I've had an inordinate number of broken people asking of me more than I have to give. Please grant me strength, Father, and encourage my fainting heart.

The God of hope. It's an increasingly complex world, Father. It feels more uncertain and fragile than ever. Fill my heart with a vision of your finished story. Quicken my senses with the sounds of the new heaven and new earth, the smells of that garden city, the beauty of what it's going to be like when Jesus finishes making all things new. May this living and sure hope give me courage to serve you sacrificially, with the joy given by the Holy Spirit. Indeed, Father, I want to overflow with hope, not just be a slow drip.

The God of peace. Father, you are the consummate peacemaker— reconciling enemies and restoring broken things. I only have peace with you because you have made your peace with me through the work of Jesus. May this profound assurance free me today to live as a conduit of your shalom-making love and power. To know that you are with me and for me will be enough.

I pray in Jesus' matchless name. Amen.

A Prayer about Relational Messes and God's Mercies

For you were called to freedom, brothers. Only do not use your freedom as an opportunity for the flesh, but through love serve one another. For the whole law is fulfilled in one word: "You shall love your neighbor as yourself." But if you bite and devour one another, watch out that you are not consumed by one another. But I say, walk by the Spirit, and you will not gratify the desires of the flesh. (Gal. 5:13–16)

Forbearing Father, thank you for documenting the relational failures, foibles, and foolishness of your people. It helps me repent of idolizing the perfect community. It also keeps me from giving up and running away from other Christians. The fact that you've chronicled just how poorly we love one another is a witness to the steadfastness of your love and the depth of our brokenness. We need the gospel every day—every hour.

These stories of relational madness also serve as a warning and wooing to much healthier ways of relating. That we indulge our sinful nature and "bite and devour one another" (Gal. 5:15) is a sad fact. But it's not our fate and it's not okay. One day we will be made perfect in love. Sear and seal this hope upon our hearts, and may it be the fuel for earnest reflection and change.

Come, Holy Spirit, come. Grant us godly sorrow and deep repentance for the ways we hide the beauty of Jesus in our churches by our pettiness, immaturity, and selfishness. Let us grieve as those who really "get" the gospel and as those who realize what is at stake. In a day when the culture is looking for reasons not to believe the gospel, forgive us for adding to their ammo and salvo.

Forgive us, Jesus. You've made it clear that the world will know that we are your disciples by the way we love one another. You've also made it clear that the quality of our relationships is one of the ways the world will believe that our Father sent you to be the Savior of the world (John 17:20–23). No wonder they remain unconvinced.

Bring the power of the gospel to bear upon our shared and broken life in the body of Christ. Grace doesn't free us to love poorly but to love generously, extravagantly, in keeping with how Jesus loves us. Grace is not a green card for self-indulgence. It's our only hope for serving one another in love. We pray in your holy and loving name. Amen.

A Prayer about the Beauty
and Brokenness of Sexuality

And God raised the Lord and will also raise us up by his power. Do you not know that your bodies are members of Christ? Shall I then take the members of Christ and make them members of a prostitute? Never! Or do you not know that he who is joined to a prostitute becomes one body with her? For, as it is written, "The two will become one flesh." But he who is joined to the Lord becomes one spirit with him. Flee from sexual immorality.
(1 Cor. 6:14–18)

Holy and loving Jesus, so many thoughts are swirling through my head this morning. I've never been more aware of the pervasiveness of sexual brokenness—everywhere I go, everywhere I look, including in the mirror. It's like we're living in the Corinth of Paul's day. So many of us bear the wounds, feel the shame, know the disconnect of our sexual brokenness and sin. And yet the gospel dares us to hope.

Indeed, hope—that's the greater impulse of my heart this morning. In fact, as I ponder what Paul was saying to the Corinthians, I am left speechless—overwhelmed at the beauty, Jesus, of belonging to you, being desired by you, being "known" by you in the most intimate of all ways.

Dare I say it, Lord Jesus? Whatever the "best sex" is between a husband and wife, it's only a hint and a whisper of the intimacy you intend for yourself and your bride. Jesus, give me a greater capacity to understand, believe, and enjoy the wonders of the relationship you've established with us.

Why should I flee all forms of sexual immorality? Simply because it's what I'm supposed to do as a Christian? Only because it's "the rules"? That would never be enough to keep me from acting out in selfish and destructive ways. I'll flee sexual immorality because you flee to us in the gospel.

You've died for us; you've been raised for us; you've married yourself to us; you've united everything that we are to yourself. We're already one with you "in spirit," and we await your return and our resurrection. Whatever the future and fulfillment of sexuality is, it belongs to you.

Until then, Lord Jesus, help us flee all forms of sexual immorality by fleeing to you, our great and gracious bridegroom. In our marriages, in our singleness, in our brokenness, in our need for repentance and healing, be glorified. I pray in your peerless name. Amen.

A Prayer about a Holy Rage for Justice

Arise, LORD! Lift up your hand, O God.
Do not forget the helpless.
Why does the wicked man revile God?
Why does he say to himself,
"He won't call me to account"?
But you, God, see the trouble of the afflicted;
you consider their grief and take it in hand.
The victims commit themselves to you;
you are the helper of the fatherless. (Ps. 10:12–14 NIV)

Holy Father, there are times when it's good to get fed up and hacked off, to get red in the face and fire in the pants, to get angry with holy rage. Looking into the eyes of helpless victims and hearing the sneer of agents of terror is just such a time. Today we take up the psalmist's impassioned cry, "Arise, LORD! Lift up your hand, O God. Do not forget the helpless" (Ps. 10:12 NIV).

It's inconceivable and unconscionable that there are twenty-seven million human slaves today who live (barely) in bondage to other human beings. I've seen it firsthand. Never let me forget the day I walked the streets of Bangkok looking for an afternoon snack, only to be offered little girls for my pleasure by street vendors, as though these priceless seven-, eight-, and nine-year-olds were nothing more than an ice cream cone—a usable commodity, fodder for evil's fantasies.

Righteous Father, "break the arm of the wicked man; call the evildoer to account for his wickedness that would not otherwise be found out" (Ps. 10:15 NIV). I don't ask this arrogantly but with a longing for justice to flow like a river through the streets of Bangkok and Nashville, and every city and hamlet, and for your righteousness to be the never-failing stream that cuts its life-giving way throughout the earth (Amos 5:24).

Lord Jesus, because the gospel is true, we pray with confidence, "The LORD is King for ever and ever; the nations will perish from his land. You, LORD, hear the desire of the afflicted; you encourage them, and you listen to their cry, defending the fatherless and the oppressed, so that mere earthly mortals will never again strike terror" (Ps. 10:16–18 NIV).

Because of your cross, terror is terrified and one day will be no more; Satan knows his time is short, and demons tremble with fear. Because of your resurrection, your kingdom will come, your will will be done, on earth as it is in heaven. We pray in your name, with holy rage and humble gratitude. Amen.

A Prayer for Wise Choices

O Lord, make me know my end
    and what is the measure of my days;
    let me know how fleeting I am!
Behold, you have made my days a few handbreadths,
    and my lifetime is as nothing before you.
Surely all mankind stands as a mere breath!
    Surely a man goes about as a shadow!
Surely for nothing they are in turmoil;
    man heaps up wealth and does not know who will gather!
And now, O Lord, for what do I wait?
    My hope is in you. (Ps. 39:4–7)

Sovereign Father, though I have no desire to know the exact day or means by which you will take me home, I'm more committed to live with that day in view. Because the gospel is true, I have no fear of dying. I really believe that to be absent from my body will mean that I am immediately present with you. The sting of my death has been removed. The grave has been robbed of its victory over me and my body. I can honestly say with Paul that it is better by far to depart and be with the Lord (Phil. 1:23).

But until that departure, how do you want me to invest the rest of my days? I've spent enough years bustling about in vanity, heaping up stuff that will only end up on the ash heap one day. Should you give me one more, ten more, twenty-five more years, how can the gospel of your kingdom and the riches of your grace claim and fill the span of those very brief years?

What do I need to make a bigger deal about—and a lesser deal of? What things do I simply need to let go of? Who should I be spending more time with or, quite honestly, less time with?

The two things that define the rest of history are your commitment to redeem your people through the gospel and your commitment to make all things new through Jesus. How do you want me to engage with both of those stories with my friends and church?

Indeed, give me greater love for people who don't know Jesus, Father. I spend way too much time just with other Christians. And help me live more intentionally as an agent of redemption and restoration in my community and neighborhood. I pray in Jesus' magnificent name. Amen.

127

A Prayer about Consummate Longings

And the angel said to me, "Write this: Blessed are those who are invited to the marriage supper of the Lamb." And he said to me, "These are the true words of God." Then I fell down at his feet to worship him, but he said to me, "You must not do that! I am a fellow servant with you and your brothers who hold to the testimony of Jesus. Worship God." (Rev. 19:9–10)

Jesus, it's not hard to understand why John fell down to worship the angel who delivered this stunning vision. For our oldest longings, greatest cravings, and deepest yearnings are claimed by what John saw: the wedding supper of the Lamb—the fullest expression of your great love for us.

We only foolishly think there's some set of circumstances, some person, some relationship, some change in our world, some sensual experience that can satisfy the restlessness in our hearts. But we're made for you, Jesus—designed to be fulfilled and completed only by you. You are the most loving and tender bridegroom who cherishes a most unlikely and ill-deserving bride.

Jesus, because we're called and guaranteed a place at this banquet; because you've set your affection upon us and find great delight in us; because we will spend eternity celebrating the only love that was ever enough, the only love that would never let us go—O Lord, for these incomparable gifts, we too fall down and worship you, for you alone are God and you alone are worthy.

Jesus, until that day when you consummate your marriage with us, help those of us who are married to love our spouses as you love us. Free us from unrealistic expectations of one another. Free us from having no expectations of one another. Free us from thinking you cannot renew broken, boring, passionless, purposeless marriages. In these temporary marriages of ours, bring childlike wonder and grace-full kindness to bear once again. We pray in your merciful and mighty name. Amen.

A Prayer about Focused Wanting

I press on to take hold of that for which Christ Jesus took hold of me. Brothers and sisters, I do not consider myself yet to have taken hold of it. But one thing I do: Forgetting what is behind and straining toward what is ahead, I press on toward the goal to win the prize for which God has called me heavenward in Christ Jesus. All of us, then, who are mature should take such a view of things. (Phil. 3:12–15 NIV)

Gracious Jesus, it's good to be free from the "paralysis of analysis"—an unhealthy, navel-gazing preoccupation with me. But it's equally good to be free to examine my life through the lens of the gospel.

I don't know how old Paul was when he wrote these words—maybe in his sixties or seventies—but it's obvious that with an increase in age came an increase in gospel astonishment. He never grew bored exploring the unsearchable riches of Jesus, and he never seemed to tire of wrestling with the kingdom implications of the gospel.

Jesus, make me that kind of man. Give me this kind of maturity in the gospel. I'm thankful that it's your grasp of me and not my grasp of you that defines this way of life. Sometimes I lift my hands in awe and gratitude for the way you love me. Sometimes I shake my fists at heaven like a pouting, demanding child. Sometimes I wring my hands in anxious unbelief, like a hapless orphan. But I live and I will die secure in your palms and written upon your heart.

Jesus, I praise you that as with Paul, you've given me a prize to win, not a wage to earn. I never earned my way into a relationship with you, and I don't maintain a relationship with you by my efforts either.

What do I want for the rest of my days? I cannot say it any better than Paul, Lord: I want to know you, Lord Jesus, more intimately than ever. This is the one thing I want more than anything else. And I want to experience more of the power of your resurrection, for I have no power in myself to love others as you love me.

I want to enter more fully into the fellowship of sharing in your sufferings, living out the birth pangs of new-creation life in this broken world, which groans for its release from the bondage to decay—a release that is sure to come (Rom. 8:18–25). Our labors in you are not in vain, Jesus (Phil. 3:10–11).

This is what I want. Help me to be done with lesser things and be more taken up with the things that matter most to your heart. In your most glorious name I pray. Amen.

A Prayer about Depression
in Its Many Forms

Why, my soul, are you downcast?
Why so disturbed within me?
Put your hope in God,
for I will yet praise him,
my Savior and my God. (Ps. 43:5 NIV)

Kindhearted Father, my heart goes out today and my prayers reach up on behalf of those who struggle with depression. I have friends who live all along the axis from mild melancholy to the relentless pangs of suicidal depression. Father of mercies, teach me how to love in the dark places.

Thank you for rescuing me from simplistic views of depression. It's not as simple a condition as I used to think. I grieve the ways I used to counsel the depressed, and it saddens me to realize how much pressure I put on them to get better and "get over it."

David asked the right question in a season of duress: "Why, my soul, are you downcast?" (Ps. 43:5 NIV). Indeed, Father, what are the various reasons for a downcast, disturbed soul, and what does hoping in you look like for each?

Father, for my friends who are depressed for no other reason than living with a graceless, gospelless heart, keep them miserable until they rest in the finished work of your Son, Jesus. May they despair of their own unrighteousness and their wannabe righteousness until they are driven to the righteousness that comes from faith in Jesus.

Father, for my friends who suffer from depression generated by anatomical anomalies, lead them to the right kind of medical care. Help us in the community of faith to be patient and understanding of the complexities involved in their care. The risk of abusing medications is always there—give us wisdom together.

Father, for my friends who suffer from depression fueled by the demonic, I really need humility and wisdom. A part of me doesn't even want to acknowledge that this is an issue, but how can I read your Word and dismiss the demonic so lightly? His condemning, blaming, and shaming voice is enough to generate the deepest forms of despair. Yet those things don't exhaust his evil arsenal. How are we to care for those under the spell and sway of our defeated, fury-filled foe (Rev. 12:12)?

I do and I will yet praise you, my Savior and my God. My hope is in you, Father—for me and for all of my brokenhearted friends. I pray in Jesus' compassionate and victorious name. Amen.

A Prayer for Staying Teachable

Now a Jew named Apollos, a native of Alexandria, came to Ephesus. He was an eloquent man, competent in the Scriptures. He had been instructed in the way of the Lord. And being fervent in spirit, he spoke and taught accurately the things concerning Jesus, though he knew only the baptism of John. He began to speak boldly in the synagogue, but when Priscilla and Aquila heard him, they took him and explained to him the way of God more accurately. (Acts 18:24–26)

Patient Jesus, there are many things I love in this story. I'm so thankful that as with Apollos, so it is with us: we're useful long before we've got every theological *t* crossed and every *i* dotted just right. Ultimately, it's not how much we know but *who* we know that wins the day. I praise you for revealing yourself to Apollos and to me.

And, Jesus, I treasure the picture of a husband and wife offering hospitality and ministering the gospel together. The little I know of Priscilla and Aquila leads me to pray for marriages in general. Oh, that more of us would live as partners in the gospel, as cosaboteurs of the kingdom of darkness, rather than frittering our years away on less noble pursuits and passions. There are so many different story lines clamoring for our marriages—so many distractions and seductions. A marriage, just like singleness, is too precious a gift to spend on pettiness and nonintentional living. Bring more gospel sanity to our marriages, Jesus. Rescue us, resuscitate us, refresh us.

Lastly, Jesus, I'm convicted and drawn to Apollos's teachability. Make and keep me that kind of man. I don't want to suffer from "hardening of the categories" as I get older. Continue to explain to me "the way of God more accurately" (Acts 18:26) through whomever you choose—children, PhDs, married couples, my wife, saints of old long since in heaven—that's your call, Jesus. Free me from my provincialism, prejudices, and presumption.

I'm hungry for you to expand my understanding and experience of life "in line with the truth of the gospel" (Gal. 2:14 NIV), until the day when knowing in part gives way to worshiping you in full. I pray in your all-sufficient and glorious name. Amen.

A Prayer about Why God Loves Us

The LORD your God has chosen you to be a people for his treasured possession, out of all the peoples who are on the face of the earth. It was not because you were more in number than any other people that the LORD set his love on you and chose you, for you were the fewest of all peoples, but it is because the LORD loves you and is keeping the oath that he swore to your fathers. . . . Know, therefore, that the LORD your God is not giving you this good land to possess because of your righteousness, for you are a stubborn people. (Deut. 7:6–8; 9:6)

Dear Father, I've been thinking about our future life in the new heaven and new earth a lot lately. The more aware I am of my brokenness and the brokenness all around me, the more I long for the amazing inheritance you've promised your children.

The more I ponder images of the New Jerusalem (Rev. 21:1–22:6), the more I experience doxological overload. A life devoid of chaos and evil and a world permeated with goodness and grace has never looked so good.

Forgive us when we're still tempted to believe there's something we can do to make you love us. Forgive us when we think there's something we can do to fuel you to regret and make you renege on your promises. Our arrogance and unbelief have infected every cell of our being.

We're your treasured people because you chose to make us your treasure. We didn't choose you. Apart from the gospel we'd still be hating you, rebelling against you and trying our best to ignore you. But you set your love upon us in eternity and revealed this great affection when you sent Jesus to be our Redeemer. And we wouldn't love Jesus unless you'd given us a new heart by the Spirit and the faith we need to receive eternal life.

The only reason we'll enjoy life in the ultimate land—the new heaven and new earth—is because of the righteousness of Jesus. Apart from Jesus' righteousness, we have none. We're still a stubborn people, in desperate need of more and more grace. Our stubbornness is seen most clearly in our refusal to believe the gospel; in the ways we still give our hearts to other gods and saviors; and in our multiplied failures to love each other as Jesus loves us.

Father, change us. By the same grace you justified us, sanctify us—make us like Jesus. By the same Spirit who brought new life to our hearts, extend new life through us into the world. We pray in Jesus' beautiful name. Amen.

A Prayer about the Gospel and Loving God's Law

The law of the LORD is perfect,
reviving the soul;
the testimony of the LORD is sure,
making wise the simple;
the precepts of the LORD are right,
rejoicing the heart;
the commandment of the LORD is pure,
enlightening the eyes;
the fear of the LORD is clean,
enduring forever;
the rules of the LORD are true,
and righteous altogether.
More to be desired are they than gold,
even much fine gold;
sweeter also than honey
and drippings of the honeycomb. (Ps. 19:7–10)

Holy and gracious Father, apart from the gospel, there's no way I would be able to join King David in singing this robust praise song about your law. For apart from the gospel, the law didn't revive me; it condemned me. Apart from the gospel, it didn't give joy to my heart; it brought terror to my soul. Apart from the gospel, the law wasn't like the sunshine lighting my way; it was like a searchlight exposing my sin.

The law didn't lead me to fear you with an affectionate reverence but to be afraid of you with a guilty conscience. Apart from the gospel, I didn't value the law like precious gold; I avoided it like a deadly plague. It wasn't sweeter than honey from the comb but more bitter than zest from a lemon.

But Father, when the law drove me to Jesus—when you gave me faith to trust Jesus as my forgiveness and my righteousness—everything began to change. I'm now learning to love your law as fatherly instruction to your beloved children, as a revelation of the good, the true, and the beautiful, not as a formula for merit, acceptance, and favor. What a life-giving, liberty-fueling difference!

May the gospel continue to free me from "cheap grace" that ignores your law and from graceless legalism that ignores your Son. I long for the day when Jesus, who has perfectly fulfilled the law for me, perfectly fulfills the law in me. I pray in his holy and loving name. Amen.

A Prayer about the Promise
of Perfect Peace

You keep him in perfect peace
  whose mind is stayed on you,
  because he trusts in you.
Trust in the LORD forever,
  for the LORD GOD is an everlasting rock. (Isa. 26:3–4)

Most kind and trustworthy Father, you haven't promised me a stormless, hassle-free, disappointment-empty life. You offer me no formulas for decreasing the probability of sad things happening around me or disillusioning things happening to me. But you have promised something that transcends the chaos and fear of uncertainty.

You've promised to keep me in perfect peace, in the midst of whatever happens. Given the circumstances of the past week, I treasure the promise of being kept by you. I've been convinced afresh that I cannot keep myself. I'm out of bootstraps to pull up; there's no magic happy pill to take, no fix-it button to push. Thank you for being a Father who will never forget or abandon your children—who will never forget or abandon me.

But you've promised even more: you've promised to keep me in perfect peace. All I have to do is mine the riches of the gospel and keep in mind the wonders of your love. For you are the Lord—the eternal Rock that is higher than me, the Rock of refuge, the Rock of ages.

Because the gospel is true, because Jesus is the precious "living Stone" (1 Pet. 2:4–8), I will not despair when I am weak in concentration and focus. Indeed, Father, you're not calling me to trust in my ability to trust, but to trust in you—in your trustworthiness, not in mine. For you've even promised your children a peace that passes, surpasses, and at times even bypasses all understanding. Hallelujah!

What a God you are! There is none like you, Father; no, not one! How great are your mercies, how profound your kindnesses, how more-than-sufficient your grace! I pray in the name of Jesus, the Prince of Peace, the basis and bounty of all my peace. Amen.

A Prayer about the Fierce Good-bye
of Suicide

And they went to a place called Gethsemane. And he [Jesus] said to his disciples, "Sit here while I pray." And he took with him Peter and James and John, and began to be greatly distressed and troubled. And he said to them, "My soul is very sorrowful, even to death. Remain here and watch." And going a little farther, he fell on the ground and prayed that, if it were possible, the hour might pass from him. And he said, "Abba, Father, all things are possible for you. Remove this cup from me. Yet not what I will, but what you will." And he came and found them sleeping, and he said to Peter, "Simon, are you asleep? Could you not watch for one hour?" (Mark 14:32–37)

Gracious Jesus, twice in a year would be sobering, twice in a month would be shocking, but to have two families in our church lose a loved one to suicide in one week is simply too much. Have mercy on us, Lord; have mercy. How could this happen? What did we miss? What are we to do now?

We're to run to you, Jesus. Where else can we go with our disbelief, numbness, shock, and profound sadness? No one has suffered overwhelming sorrow like you. What you sustained in Gethsemane and endured on the cross makes the path into your presence so very welcoming.

There are so many things we don't understand about suicide. We feel guilt. We feel fear. We feel vulnerable. Please help us in the middle of our shock and confusion.

Oh, the holy and horrible mystery that you were made sin for us, Jesus—the victim and agent of sin. *No one* understands like you how disintegrated and distressed the heart can become, even to the point of losing all desire to live. *No one* understands like you the guilt and shame of sin. *No one* understands like you betrayal, loss, forsakenness, emptiness.

And *no one* knows how to love in the most broken of all stories like you, Jesus. Because you drank the cup of God's judgment, you now give us the cup of your grace. How are we to love and serve these families in the coming hours and days? What will being present and keeping watch look like?

Though you were abandoned by sleeping disciples, you will never abandon us. Jesus, help us know how to love in the darkness. Bring your limitless, tender mercies to bear. No one can offer tears of hope and a tear-wiping hand like you, Jesus. We pray in your solace-laden name. Amen.

A Prayer in Response to Environmental Disasters and Hard Providence

> The voice of the LORD makes the deer give birth
>   and strips the forest bare,
>   and in his temple all cry, "Glory!"
> The LORD sits enthroned over the flood;
>   the LORD sits enthroned as king forever.
> May the LORD give strength to his people!
>   May the LORD bless his people with peace! (Ps. 29:9–11)

Sovereign Father, it's not just media footage from a faraway place. It's my neighborhood, my friends, my family, and it's right now. The floodwaters have already forced evacuations and damaged many homes, and there's much more rain coming.

Before the sun rises, veiled by threatening storm clouds, I lift my gaze and heart to you. I come—I run—to the one who sits enthroned over the flood, the eternal King, who does all things well. I come praying for our situation but also for people and places where similar stories of hard providences are being written today.

Father, I don't ask "Why this crisis? Why us?" for I know the rain falls on the righteous and the unrighteous, even as the sun rises on the evil and the good (Matt. 5:45). And I know the present world will never again be destroyed by floodwaters (Gen. 8:21). But there are two things I do ask for, two things you have promised: strength and peace.

Grant us all the strength we will need today to serve one another in love. As the floodwaters continue to rise, many more people will be despairing, displaced, and disheartened. Strengthen our backs and arms for what lies ahead. This is a time for neighbor love, not just looking out for ourselves and our own stuff. Grant us the power of the Holy Spirit and extra energy for neighbor love.

And grant us all the peace we will need today to act wisely, trust boldly, and love deeply. We will probably need to negotiate and navigate some fear and panic. Help us care for those most vulnerable and anxious. May your peace rule as an umpire in our hearts—centering us, focusing us, and leading us to make good choices for one and all.

In this crisis we praise you for Jesus, the high and safe Rock, the ultimate trustworthy foundation for any and every storm of life (Matt. 7:24–27). Thank you for rescuing us from building our lives on all kinds of shifting sands. I pray in Jesus' strong and peace-giving name. Amen.

A Prayer about the Every Nation Day of Prayer

After this I looked, and behold, a great multitude that no one could number, from every nation, from all tribes and peoples and languages, standing before the throne and before the Lamb, clothed in white robes, with palm branches in their hands, and crying out with a loud voice, "Salvation belongs to our God who sits on the throne, and to the Lamb!" (Rev. 7:9–10)

Loving Father, on this "national day of prayer," it's easy to think of several things to bring before you. First of all, I praise you for heavenly citizenship. Thank you for making me a citizen of the realm from which I eagerly await the return of the true King, our Savior, the Lord Jesus Christ. He's already reigning, and one day he will return to transform all things—including transforming my body to be like his glorious body (Phil. 3:20–21). What comfort and what joy that good news brings!

Secondly, as broken as our country is, I'm very thankful to be an American citizen. I praise you for the many freedoms we still enjoy and the multiplied privileges that go with being a citizen of this great nation. I bring our sitting president before the occupied throne of heaven, and I ask you to be at work in his heart and through his hands.

As with all "kings," you set them up and you sit them down at your discretion, so I trust you for the accomplishment of your sovereign purposes through our president, in keeping with the eternal wisdom of your heart. I don't look for a lasting city in our country but for the City whose builder and maker is God—that would be you!

Lastly, the more I understand the gospel, the more I find it easy to pray in light of the apostle John's vision of the "every nation" day of prayer. Oh, for the day when men and women from every nation, tribe, people, and language will be wearing the white robes of grace-secured salvation while waving palm branches of praise and shouting in perfect harmony, "Salvation belongs to our God who sits on the throne, and to the Lamb!" (Rev. 7:10).

Because that day is coming, free me to be a better citizen of two countries until the kingdom of God arrives in fullness and the King of Glory arrives in splendor. I pray in his sovereign and saving name. Amen.

A Prayer about God Overriding Our Unbelief

He [Peter] went to the house of Mary the mother of John, also called Mark, where many people had gathered and were praying. Peter knocked at the outer entrance, and a servant girl named Rhoda came to answer the door. When she recognized Peter's voice, she was so overjoyed she ran back without opening it and exclaimed, "Peter is at the door!" "You're out of your mind," they told her. When she kept insisting that it was so, they said, "It must be his angel." But Peter kept on knocking, and when they opened the door and saw him, they were astonished. (Acts 12:12–16 NIV)

Heavenly Father, thank you for chronicling this almost comical prayer meeting in your Word. As much as it exposes our unbelief, in a far greater way it highlights your faithful commitment to do exceedingly beyond all we can ask or imagine. This story describes the kind of praying that's going on in my heart way too often. I dutifully pray, but I faithlessly doubt. Forgive my unbelief; override my unbelief.

There are many things I'm praying about right now for which I want to hear "Peter knocking at the door." I have no need to be considered a great prayer warrior. I'm not looking for wonderful stories to tell others as a testimony to my faith. I simply want you to bring a whole lot of glory to Jesus. Astonish us, Father; astonish me.

Father, I pray for those in the persecuted church and for their leaders. Strengthen them, encourage them, and grant miracles of provision and deliverance. Cause the gospel to spread like wildfire. Give them so much joy, peace, and love that their persecutors will be convicted and fall down and worship you.

Father, I pray for the courageous men and women who are laboring in the dark world of human trafficking. Bring justice to bear; deliver women and children from the evil of slavery in every form. Protect the rescuers and provide good aftercare for those rescued.

Father, I pray for an outpouring of your Holy Spirit on our church family. Let us have done with "lesser things" that we might more fully give ourselves to the things that matter the most to you. We're spoiled; we're dull; we're bored and we're boring. The main vision we need is a renewed vision of Jesus gathering his bride from the nations and making all things new. Free us from ourselves for yourself. Astonish us, Father; astonish us as you override our unbelief. I pray in Jesus' exalted name. Amen.

A Prayer Asking God to Do More Than We Can Ask or Imagine

I pray that you, being rooted and established in love, may have power, together with all the Lord's holy people, to grasp how wide and long and high and deep is the love of Christ, and to know this love that surpasses knowledge—that you may be filled to the measure of all the fullness of God. Now to him who is able to do immeasurably more than all we ask or imagine, according to his power that is at work within us, to him be glory in the church and in Christ Jesus throughout all generations, for ever and ever! Amen. (Eph. 3:17–21 NIV)

Heavenly Father, as I read these words addressing the churches in Ephesus, I am more grateful than ever that you have rooted and established us in your love. You have planted our roots deep in the fathomless depths of your agape love. Our eternal health and fruitfulness are not in doubt. We will flourish and thrive forever. The gates of hell will not overcome the growth and forward movement of your beloved people (Matt. 16:18).

However, until that day, so much can happen to us and among us as your people. Satan hates the church, and we are an "in Christ" but still sinful people. It's what makes Paul's prayer so critical for each day. What but a bigger and better grasp of the love of Jesus can keep us focused on the things that really matter and repentant for the ways we fail one another?

Father, it's sobering to realize that Paul's letter to the Ephesians wasn't the only time the churches of Ephesus were addressed about love. Many years later Jesus spoke these words to the same churches, "I hold this against you: You have forsaken the love you had at first. Consider how far you have fallen! Repent and do the things you did at first" (Rev 2:4–5 NIV). Really good churches can fall into really big messes. Only the love of Jesus can win the day.

I'm glad you can do so immeasurably more than we can ask or imagine, but I will settle today for what I can ask and for what I can imagine. I ask you to restore me to my first love relationship with Jesus. And I ask you for power—for an outpouring of your Holy Spirit that will enable me and the brothers and sisters in Jesus to grasp how wide, long, high, and deep is the love of Jesus.

May the love of Jesus humble us. Help us remember the height from which we have fallen, repent, and do the gospel things we did at first. I can imagine this, Father, and I do ask for it, so that your glory will be revealed in the church and throughout all generations. I earnestly and passionately pray in Jesus' beloved name. Amen.

A Prayer about the Sacredness
of Human Life

I heard a loud voice from the throne saying, "Behold, the dwelling place of God is with man. He will dwell with them, and they will be his people, and God himself will be with them as their God. He will wipe away every tear from their eyes, and death shall be no more, neither shall there be mourning, nor crying, nor pain anymore, for the former things have passed away." And he who was seated on the throne said, "Behold, I am making all things new." Also he said, "Write this down, for these words are trustworthy and true." (Rev. 21:3–5)

Most loving Lord Jesus, your loud voice and tear-wiping hand together give us the courage and compassion we need to live as faithful advocates for human life. How we long for the day when "death shall be no more." Today we are especially thinking about the death of unborn children.

Jesus, give us gospel courage to rise and contend against the dark oxymoron called "legal abortion." Because you are making all things new, with undaunted hope we will fight the good fight of faith for children who are still being knit together in their mother's womb.

There is a day coming when abortion will be no more. In light of that day, give us wisdom. Give us strength. Give us fire. Give us perseverance. Give us the sufficient grace we need to advocate for unborn children in this day—in our communities and among the nations of the world.

We also cry out for gospel compassion. Jesus, show us how to love and care for women and men whose stories are marked by abortion—either as victims or agents. Only the gospel is sufficient for the guilt. Only the gospel can bring healing. Only the gospel can transform an agent of darkness into a warrior for justice and mercy.

Jesus, we also long for the day of no more miscarriages and stillbirths. Our hearts break for those families who would love a child to your glory, but must endure the pain of giving up their children before birth. Show us how to love and serve them well. Extend your tear-wiping hand through us.

We also ask for courage and compassion to adopt the millions of orphaned children who have safely made it into this world. May our zeal against abortion be matched by our zeal for adoption. Surely the gospel is big enough for this calling too. We pray in your holy and loving name. Amen.

A Prayer Praising Jesus
for His Persistent Love

Those whom I love, I reprove and discipline, so be zealous and repent. Behold, I stand at the door and knock. If anyone hears my voice and opens the door, I will come in to him and eat with him, and he with me. (Rev. 3:19–20)

Dear Lord Jesus, every day we have the privilege of living the hymn "O Love That Will Not Let Me Go," for you love us tenaciously and you pursue us constantly. As hard as it is to imagine, you desire fellowship with us, and not occasionally but continually. It's even harder to imagine that you actually enjoy being with us. We believe; help our unbelief.

In the gospel we enjoy eternal union with you, but for various reasons, we tend to flow in and out of vital communion with you. The sad thing is, sometimes we don't recognize our heart drift for quite a while—days, even months. It's usually the people around us who first recognize our being out of communion with you, for rich fellowship with you changes the way we relate to everyone.

Jesus, there's no greater rebuke than to hear you knock on the door of our hearts, yet that knock comes like a kiss. Nothing is more convicting than to hear your voice on the other side of that door, yet your voice is that of a bridegroom wooing his beloved bride. It's because you love us that you confront us and discipline us. All of your rebukes are life-giving, and when you discipline us, though it's painful, it's for our good and our freedom. It's your kindness that leads us to repentance.

Jesus, your knock and your voice in the gospel are so powerful, and by faith we rise to greet you. Come in and let us feast together this very day. You are the bread we need the most. You give the water that alone quenches our thirst. Until the day when daily fellowship meals are replaced with a wedding feast, may we have to hear your knock on the outside of the door way less often. We pray with gratefulness, in your loving name. Amen.

A Prayer about Feeling Overwhelmed by the Odds

When the servant of the man of God rose early in the morning and went out, behold, an army with horses and chariots was all around the city. And the servant said, "Alas, my master! What shall we do?" He said, "Do not be afraid, for those who are with us are more than those who are with them." Then Elisha prayed and said, "O LORD, please open his eyes that he may see." So the LORD opened the eyes of the young man, and he saw, and behold, the mountain was full of horses and chariots of fire all around Elisha. (2 Kings 6:15–17)

Gracious Father, there are times when the "odds" feel quite stacked against us, as your people. With the naked eye, the enemies of justice, truth, and the gospel greatly seem to outnumber your "troops." Serving you feels quite overwhelming, at times even futile.

But just when I begin to retreat into a basement of fear or question your concern and faithfulness, once again you open the eyes of my heart and show me the way things *really* are. You're such a patient and merciful God.

Though serving you is not like a childhood game of kickball, when we did our best to choose the best players for our team, nevertheless, it is good—no, *vital* to know that because of the gospel, "those who are with us are more than those who are with them" (2 Kings 6:16).

But the way of the gospel will always be strength in weakness, the transforming treasure of the gospel in fragile clay pots, like us. It was three hundred poorly armed soldiers, not thirty-four thousand fighting men, you sent with Gideon to defeat the Midianite army. Jesse's youngest son, David, a young shepherd, was your choice to be the king of Israel. Most profoundly, it was the crucifixion of Jesus, not an insurrection of zealots, that won our salvation.

Father, the odds are never really stacked against your covenant purposes and your transforming kingdom. You're not "trying" to do anything. You never have to resort to plan B. You never hedge your bets. You are God, and there is no other.

So help us, and your servants throughout the world, not to become weary in preaching the gospel and planting churches, in doing justice and loving mercy. We will reap a harvest at the proper time if we do not give up (Gal. 6:9), and the gospel is all the motivation, hope, and power we need to *not* give up.

Before Jesus returns, he will redeem his pan-national bride, and when Jesus returns, he will finish making all things new and will usher in the new heaven and new earth. Our labors in the Lord are often exhausting and discouraging, but they are never in vain (1 Cor. 15:58). We pray in Jesus' trustworthy and triumphant name. Amen.

A Prayer of Desperation for Peace

Do not be anxious about anything, but in everything by prayer and supplication with thanksgiving let your requests be made known to God. And the peace of God, which surpasses all understanding, will guard your hearts and your minds in Christ Jesus. (Phil. 4:6–7)

Dear Jesus, I've memorized this Scripture, taught it, preached it, and prayed it for many struggling friends. Today, however, I'm desperate to lay hold of it for myself. I am anxious, so I need grace to obey this command. I know you're not asking me to pretend and pose, for knowing you is the end to that way of life. And I know you're not asking me to be a stoic, for you are gentle and humble of heart.

Jesus, it was you who turned the chaos of an unformed world into the beauty of creation. Please do the same with all the chaos swirling around me and in me. Replace my angst and confusion with order and beauty.

For the things that grieve me, bring your tear-wiping hand. For the things that offend me, keep me from a critical and selfish spirit. For the things that alarm me, grant me the perspective of heaven and gospel sanity. Please don't let me get bitter.

For the things over which I have no control, give me a fresh vision of the occupied throne of heaven. For the things I do have control over, grant me wisdom and strength to act accordingly. Please help me steward my anger, my sadness, and my weariness to your glory. I don't want to waste this moment or these feelings.

Jesus, I have no reason to doubt either your mercy or your might. You gave your life for us upon the cross. You have risen to make all things new. You are unremittingly advocating and praying for us. No one loves us more than you do. I have seen you do astonishing things before. Do astonishing things again. I am weary and worn down.

Set the peace of God as a sentinel in my heart and mind. Great King of glory and grace, guard and protect my heart from the lies of Satan, the whisperings of gossip, and the cynicism of naysayers. I pray with hunger and hope, in your most trustworthy name. Amen.

A Prayer about American Politics and My Bad Attitude

Grace and peace to you from him who is, and who was, and who is to come, and from the seven spirits before his throne, and from Jesus Christ, who is the faithful witness, the firstborn from the dead, and the ruler of the kings of the earth. (Rev. 1:4–5 NIV)

Glorious Triune God, lately my attitude about the American political process has been brewing in me a cesspool of irritation and cynicism—a sure indication that I need the gospel to center me. So I begin this day reminding myself of exactly who you are and what you are up to in your world, as revealed in the Scriptures. Nothing has greater power to convict me of my sin and help me regain perspective.

Sovereign Father, I'm greatly encouraged to remember that you are timeless in your engagement with your creation and your people. You always have been, you presently are, and you always will be the God who is working all things together after the counsel of your will. You never need a holiday, you never suffer from ADD, and you always bring your "A game."

God the Holy Spirit, in your sevenfold perfection, you are constantly executing the will of the Father concerning all things—from feeding sparrows and clothing flowers; to revealing and applying the grace of Jesus; to raising up kings and putting kings down at the Father's bidding. Nothing and no one can resist you.

Lord Jesus, you are the faithful witness who reveals everything we need to know about all things. You've never lied, exaggerated, or withheld any revelation we need about anything. You are the firstborn from among the dead. Your death and resurrection are the guarantee and the firstfruits of the whole new creation order. Because you were raised from the dead, all who trust in you will be raised. The entire cosmos will be restored and brought to a grandeur of which the Garden of Eden was just a hint.

King Jesus, you are the ruler of the kings of the earth. Forgive me when I pine and whine about who's sitting in the biggest chair in the White House or the Kremlin, North Korea or China, Iran or Israel. The good news of your present and future reign should free us from all panic and paranoia. It should also free us from all passivity and presumption. Show us how to live as good citizens of heaven and America. May your kingdom come, your will be done, on earth as it is in heaven. We pray in your glorious and gracious name. Amen.

A Prayer about Waiting for Jesus' Return

Be dressed ready for service and keep your lamps burning, like servants waiting for their master to return from a wedding banquet, so that when he comes and knocks they can immediately open the door for him. It will be good for those servants whose master finds them watching when he comes. Truly I tell you, he will dress himself to serve, will have them recline at the table and will come and wait on them. (Luke 12:35–37 NIV)

King Jesus, through the years I've suffered through some horrible teaching about your second coming, most of which generated self-centered fear, gospelless speculation, and political sensationalism. That's hardly what you had in mind when you charged us to watch and wait for your return. But this morning, as I meditate on this passage, much of the rubbish and rubble is cleared away.

Jesus, I've never been less anxious and more ready for your return, but only because of a growing understanding of the gospel. I'm already wearing the right clothes—the wedding garment of your perfect righteousness. I'm no longer afraid of your return. I very much want you to come back—my loving bridegroom. The oil in my lamp will never run dry, for you've sealed me as your own and have sent the Spirit to dwell in my heart forever.

Because the gospel is true, I'm ready for service in two ways. First of all, I'm ready for you to serve me. According to the Scriptures, when you return, you will have us, your bride, "recline at the table," and you will come and wait on us. Jesus, this is simply overwhelming to ponder. I believe it, but help me believe it more.

What wondrous love is this, indeed! All you've ever done is serve your people, Jesus—in creation, by your incarnation, in your crucifixion, your resurrection, your ascension, and your heavenly intercession.

Secondly, as I consider all the ways you serve us, Jesus, I have a renewed passion to serve you and to serve with you as you gather your bride from among the nations and as you are busy making all things new. Whose feet do we wash today? Where are you setting prisoners free? Where are you bringing your kingdom of redemption? I pray with gratitude, in your loving name. Amen.

A Prayer about Patience, Pits, and Praise

> I waited patiently for the LORD;
>   he turned to me and heard my cry.
> He lifted me out of the slimy pit,
>   out of the mud and mire;
> he set my feet on a rock
>   and gave me a firm place to stand.
> He put a new song in my mouth,
>   a hymn of praise to our God.
> Many will see and fear the LORD
>   and put their trust in him. (Ps. 40:1–3 NIV)

Heavenly Father, my heart goes out today to those whose feet are in the mud and mire of various slimy pits—friends whose weariness is growing and whose patience is growing thin. The initial adrenaline rush that came after the flood is gone. Now there are long lines, red tape, looming decisions, limited resources, and short fuses. Breathe, O breath of God; send the winds of heaven. We need encouragement, wisdom, and strength.

Father, I pray both for those needing a lift from "the pit" and for the lifters, for those needing help and for the helpers. We're all in need of what you alone can give.

You've never commanded anything without supplying the grace to obey your commands, and you've never made an empty promise. So when you command us not to become weary in doing good, and when you promise us a guaranteed harvest at the proper time (Gal. 6:9), I take you at your Word. I will wait patiently for you, Lord—patiently, expectantly, and gratefully.

Bring great glory to yourself, Father. Cause many to see and to put their trust in you as you continue to write multiplied stories of redemption and restoration. I'm not asking you to make the mud and the mire go away; just make the Rock, Jesus, more evident and beautiful to all. Cause our feet to stand upon Jesus, the only firm foundation in this life and the life to come, in times of great adversity, in times of great prosperity, and in all the in-between times.

Fill our hearts and mouths with the new song of the gospel—hymns of praise to you, our loving and faithful Father. I pray in Jesus' trustworthy and triumphant name. Amen.

A Prayer about the Enjoyment of Little Things

So I commend the enjoyment of life, because there is nothing better for a person under the sun than to eat and drink and be glad. Then joy will accompany them in their toil all the days of the life God has given them under the sun. (Eccles. 8:15 NIV)

Gracious Father, the past few weeks have been incredibly demanding and depleting. I'm thankful you understand our frailties and our need for refreshment. If you never commanded Sabbath rest, I probably wouldn't take it. And if you never commended the enjoyment of life, I'd go to the extremes of either taking simple joys for granted or worshiping pleasure altogether.

So today, I'm slowing down enough just to say thank you—thank you for designing us for pleasure, for the experience of delight. Thank you for putting sensate responders and nerve endings in our bodies. You are glorified in our enjoyment.

Thank you for intending that joy would accompany us in our work (often exhausting, thankless, and seemingly fruitless work) all the days you have given us under the sun.

I praise you for the wet crunch of celery, the soothing texture of ice cream, the alluring aroma of baking bread. I praise you for my wife's gentle kisses and my grandson's infectious giggle. I praise you for the relaxing sound of ocean waves, the memory-connecting music of the sixties, the well-timed greeting of a friend, and how good it feels to finish a jog and start a new book. I praise you for the permanent smile on the face of a dolphin, the never-the-same array of sunrises and sunsets, the precise ways you show up when I need you the most.

Father, our ongoing work under the blazing sun has meaning because of the finished work of your beloved Son. Because the gospel is true, we can glorify you now and enjoy you forever. I pray in Jesus' holy name. Amen.

A Prayer about Anxiety Casting

Cast all your anxiety on him because he cares for you. (1 Pet. 5:7 NIV)

Gracious Father, I slept well last night but I awoke restless, fitful, and anxious. I know you tell me not to be anxious about anything (Phil. 4:6), but I am. Sunrise has yet to happen, yet I'm already looking forward to moonrise. Thank you for freeing me from the pressure of pretending otherwise. At least I'm not anxious about surprising, embarrassing, or disappointing you. The gospel has taken care of that old bondage and slavery.

What's going on inside of me? There's really nothing enormous looming on the horizon, no one major crisis staring me down, no boulder I'm assigned to push up a hill like Sisyphus. It's just one of those Mondays when I find myself looking at seventeen little backpacks of needs, issues, and hurting hearts lined up at my front door, waiting to be picked up as I head into the week.

So what will I do with my restless, fitful, anxious feelings? Father, I would surely despair if I didn't really believe you care for me. That would be the one unbearable burden. But please help me know what anxiety casting actually looks like today and this whole week.

Of these things I am certain: you're not calling me to be the fourth member of the Trinity; I'm not the whole body of Christ; you do promise sufficient grace; you will give wisdom to those who ask; and your strength is made perfect in weakness—in my weakness.

Show me which of the seventeen little backpacks I'm to pick up first. Which ones don't really have my name on them at all? Which ones will just have to wait, as you give me grace not to dread disappointing people? As you have promised, please send your transcendent peace to guard my heart and mind in Christ Jesus (Phil. 4:7). I pray in Jesus' trustworthy and treasured name. Amen.

A Prayer about the Pain of Broken Trust

The LORD is on my side; I will not fear.
What can man do to me?
The LORD is on my side as my helper;
I shall look in triumph on those who hate me.
It is better to take refuge in the LORD
than to trust in man.
It is better to take refuge in the LORD
than to trust in princes. (Ps. 118:6–9)

Lord Jesus, I'm just waking up, and though I'm yawning my way into your presence, you are fully alert and engaged. What a Savior you are! You never sleep or slumber; you never need a break or vacation; you're never moody; you never get bored with us; you never roll your eyes and say, "When will they ever get it?" You will never look for greener pastures or better sheep. I praise you for the constancy of your love.

Jesus, it's because your love is so unwavering that you're easy to trust. Only you can be fully trusted. I'm painfully aware of this truth as I lean into this day. I'd be lying if I didn't acknowledge to you my disappointment and hurt this morning. Thank you for caring.

As broken people, we fail one another. I get that. But the gospel's not supposed to make us immune to the pain of bruised trust, broken trust, or battered trust. Broken confidences and broken promises still hurt, no matter who they come from, but certainly more when they come from the very people we *should* be able to trust.

"What can man do to me?" the psalmist asks (Ps. 118:6). Plenty, Jesus, plenty. But with you as our refuge, with you as our very present help, with you as our advocate, intercessor, sovereign Lord, and gracious Redeemer—with you as the only prince who can be trusted, the Prince of Peace—I don't have to grow more angry, flint hard, and dangerously isolated.

I bring my pain to you, Jesus. Hold me and help me deal with the betrayals. I pray in your singularly trustworthy name. Amen.

A Prayer about Gospel Cover-Up

Whoever covers an offense seeks love,
but he who repeats a matter separates close friends. (Prov. 17:9)

Jesus, rarely does the phrase "cover-up" do anything but raise suspicion, eyebrows, and ire. We recoil when we experience the manipulation of facts, the minimization of harm, and the muting of our voices, especially in the face of blatant injustice. To be either an agent or victim of this kind of cover-up is never okay.

That being said, there's a stewardship of information—a way of handling one another's failures, sins, and weaknesses—that requires a gospel heart. There is such a thing as a "gospel cover-up," and I want to be much better at it. So as I meditate on this Scripture, hear my confession and my prayers.

Forgive me when I choose to uncover and use old offenses against my spouse, my children, or my friends just to win an argument, gain an advantage, or minimize my own sin. It's as though I never really forgave them the first time.

Forgive me when I repeat someone's offense to another friend or a number of friends under the guise of seeking prayer, when in reality I'm just gossiping or perhaps even slandering people I claim to care about. How insecure and insidious is that?

Forgive me when I keep uncovered and constantly rehearse the sins and offenses of others to myself—feeding my self-righteousness, fueling my anger, and fermenting my desire for revenge. That's really ugly.

Forgive me when I constantly repeat my own failures to myself—choosing to indulge my self-contempt and the accusations of Satan much more than I believe and relish the gospel. What a destructive way to do life, robbing you of much glory.

Jesus, you are the greatest promoter of love ever, for by your blood you have once and for all covered up, covered over, and carried away my sins forever. You'll never repeat my sinful matters to me or anyone else. How I praise you today for your great love for us! Continue to change my heart and channel my words, by your grace and for your glory and the good of others. I pray in your holy and kind name. Amen.

A Prayer about Praise Trumping Paranoia

When Daniel knew that the document had been signed, he went to his house where he had windows in his upper chamber open toward Jerusalem. He got down on his knees three times a day and prayed and gave thanks before his God, as he had done previously. Then these men came by agreement and found Daniel making petition and pleas before his God. (Dan. 6:10–11)

Heavenly Father, I am so drawn to the heart that beat in Daniel's breast—a heart filled with praise for you, not paranoia about his life. He just learned of a decree that anybody praying to any other god or man but King Darius would become lions' lunch. So what did he do? The same thing he'd been doing for decades in Babylon. The windows are open, his knees are bent, his gaze is set, and even before he asks you for help, he offers you thanks. He's neither paranoid nor presumptuous, but he's most definitely at peace.

What freedom, what beauty, what intimacy with you this aging son and servant of yours enjoyed. But why am I surprised? Haven't you promised, "The righteous will flourish like a palm tree, they will grow like a cedar of Lebanon; planted in the house of the LORD, they will flourish in the courts of our God. They will still bear fruit in old age, they will stay fresh and green" (Ps. 92:12–14 NIV)?

Father, you never demanded that Daniel get on his knees three times a day. You didn't have to—it was his delight. No government decree could keep him from praying to you, loving you, seeking you, worshiping you. He was much more committed to your eternal glory than to his personal survival.

How much more should this kind of peace and praise mark my life, no matter what spiritual warfare looks like in my day, no matter how intense the clash between the kingdom of darkness and the kingdom of God gets. For even as "the devil prowls around like a roaring lion, seeking someone to devour" (1 Pet. 5:8), he's a defeated foe. I live in the victorious day Daniel anticipated from afar. Indeed, your Son, "the Lion of the tribe of Judah, the Root of David, has triumphed" (Rev. 5:5 NIV). Jesus is the Lion with whom I want to be thoroughly preoccupied.

Father, as I get older, please keep me fresh and green and fruitful through the gospel. Fill my heart with your glory and grace, and use me however you choose, all the remaining days you give me in this your world. I pray in Jesus' magnificent and merciful name. Amen.

151

A Prayer about the Grossness of My Ingratitude

[The older brother] was angry and refused to go in. His father came out and entreated him, but he answered his father, "Look, these many years I have served you, and I never disobeyed your command, yet you never gave me a young goat, that I might celebrate with my friends. But when this son of yours came, who has devoured your property with prostitutes, you killed the fattened calf for him!" And he said to him, "Son, you are always with me, and all that is mine is yours." (Luke 15:28–31)

Forbearing Father, though I'd never boast about my many years of serving you and I'd never even think of boasting in my record of obedience to your commands, nevertheless, I do acknowledge that there are times when my ingratitude matches that of the older brother. This has become obvious to me lately, and I want to repent before it gets any worse. I do my best repenting not by groveling but by preaching the gospel to my own heart, so here goes.

Father, you are constantly running to me in the gospel—inviting me, imploring me, pleading with me to get on the dance floor of your grace, to enjoy the music of reconciliation, to sing the songs of redemption, to make merry to the glory of God. You are constantly saying to my grumbling, complaining, discontented, self-righteous face, "My son, you're always with me because I'm always with you. Nothing will ever separate you from the everlasting love I have for you and all my children. I greatly delight in you. I rejoice over you with singing. Everything I have is yours. All your sins are forgiven, including your gross ingratitude. I've declared you to be righteous in my beloved Son. I've hidden your life in his. I've begun a good work in you, and in my whole broken world, that I will bring to completion. I've made you a coheir of the new heaven and new earth. You are destined for an eternity of perfect relationships—perfect everything. Come, let us rejoice and be glad."

Father, I repent—but please don't relent. Keep beating down my ungratefulness with the love offensives of the gospel. I pray in Jesus' peerless and praiseworthy name. Amen.

A Prayer about Life in the Dead Places

The hand of the LORD was on me, and he brought me out by the Spirit of the LORD and set me in the middle of a valley. . . . I saw a great many bones on the floor of the valley, bones that were very dry. He asked me, "Son of man, can these bones live?" I said, "Sovereign LORD, you alone know." Then he said to me, "Prophesy to these bones and say to them, 'Dry bones, hear the word of the LORD! This is what the Sovereign LORD says to these bones: I will make breath enter you, and you will come to life. I will attach tendons to you and make flesh come upon you and cover you with skin; I will put breath in you, and you will come to life. Then you will know that I am the LORD.'" (Ezek. 37:1–6 NIV)

Heavenly Father, I would do well to meditate on this portion of your Word once a month—no, make that at least once a week. For it "calls out" my unbelief, it confronts my complacency, it deconstructs every excuse I offer for giving up on difficult situations and people.

So many churches, marriages, and hearts have become piles of dry, breathless bones. Vibrant green has become ashen gray. The music hasn't faded; it's gone. Selflessness has been supplanted with spite; desire got overgrown with weeds of disconnect, distrust, despair, and now, despisement.

But it's not Ezekiel who asks about the possibility of renewal, redemption, and restoration; it's you, Father. It's you! "Can these bones live?" you ask. The question is rhetorical, for you are the God of resurrection! I'll not presume on the process, but I'll trust in your promises.

Father, for your glory alone, I ask you to breathe on the near and already bone-dry marriages of a few dear friends. Where there's no hope left, bring a fresh outpouring of affection from and for the great Spouse, Jesus.

What but the love of Jesus can transform stubborn hearts into supple hearts, can replace mean with mercy, can supplant self-protective willfulness with gospel willingness? Who but Jesus can transform cold antipathy into kindhearted intimacy? Those are my rhetorical questions, Father, for I know of no other hope for cold marriages, dead churches, or hard hearts but Jesus and his great love lavished on us in the gospel.

Indeed, Jesus, you are the resurrection and life. Today as I pray for these marriages, churches, and friends, and for myself, I'm not going to be preoccupied with looking at dry bones but with you, a living Savior. Bring life, your life, to the places of death. Restore to all of us the joy of your salvation, the hope of your resurrection, and a passion for your glory above everything else, including our own happiness. I pray in the tender mercies of your name. Amen.

A Prayer about God Comforting the Downcast

For even when we came into Macedonia, our bodies had no rest, but we were afflicted at every turn—fighting without and fear within. But God, who comforts the downcast, comforted us by the coming of Titus. (2 Cor. 7:5–6)

Loving Father, this brief vignette from Paul's life comes to me today like a well-timed kiss from heaven, like a call from the right friend when you least expect it but most need it, like the first sign of daylight after a starless night.

First of all, Father, I praise you for chronicling Paul's experience of being restless, fearful, and downcast. Many times I suffer from "should-ness": if I really loved you, if I were more full of the Holy Spirit, if I truly got the gospel, I "should" never feel downcast. I should only feel upbeat, on top of my game, and happy.

It's comforting to know the gospel doesn't make me less human but simply more yours. Thank you for being a Father who doesn't shame the downcast. You pursue them, you provide for them, you comfort them—you comfort me.

As I begin this day, I feel like I'm swimming in a pool of baby piranha—no big sharks like Paul was dealing with, just small piranha nibbling at my spirit. I'm surrounded by a lot of little decisions, a lot of little needs, a lot of small conflicts, a lot of little unfinished projects, a lot of little things over which I have absolutely no control, and the combination of these things is weighing me down.

I'll not fight the piranha; I'll just look for you. Indeed, Father, it's so good to know you're running toward me in the gospel right now, not with a furrowed brow but with a compassionate, merciful heart. And as you comfort me, I will seek to be a Titus for others. What a privilege it is to comfort others with the very comfort you bring to us in all our troubles (2 Cor. 1:3–4). I pray in Jesus' name with great anticipation. Amen.

A Prayer of Intercession for Friends

As for me, far be it from me that I should sin against the LORD by ceasing to pray for you, and I will instruct you in the good and right way. Only fear the LORD and serve him faithfully with all your heart. For consider what great things he has done for you. (1 Sam. 12:23–24)

Lord Jesus, there's a lot more to friendship than praying for my friends, but I haven't really been a good friend unless I've prayed and continue to pray for them.

The fact that you call me friend is overwhelming. And knowing that you are always praying for me is all the motivation I need to repent of my prayerlessness. Indeed, how can I enjoy such a rich standing in grace and not "stand in the gap" for my friends?

For my friends with broken hearts, Jesus, I pray for the reach and touch of your tear-wiping hand. Spare them from those of us who would "heal their wounds lightly" (Jer. 6:14), not taking their pain seriously enough. Heal them in such a fashion that will leave them merciful toward others, not merely pain free.

For my friends with angry hearts, Jesus, I pray you will dialogue with them the way you entered Jonah's rage. "Do you have a right to be angry?" you asked the conflicted prophet. I'm not praying you will simply make my angry friends sweet. Help them see the sadness behind the mad, the pettiness in the petulance, and the real hurt being mishandled in more hurtful ways.

For my friends with fearful hearts, Jesus, I pray you will bring your centering, calming presence to bear. To be fearful is one thing, but to be fearful and alone is almost unbearable. Place your hand upon them in the gospel, the way you touched the apostle John. Speak deep into their hearts, "Do not be afraid. I am the First and the Last. I am the Living One" (Rev. 1:17–18 NIV).

For my friends with deceived hearts, Jesus, we're prone to wander and you're prone to come after us. For my friends with hearts en route to being hardened by the deceitfulness of sin, for those under Satanic spells, for those who are simply selfish, stubborn, and stupid—Jesus, rescue them before they bring any more harm to themselves and others, I pray.

Jesus, help all of us—starting with me—constantly remember what great things you have done for us, so that we might fear you with affectionate reverence and serve you faithfully with all our hearts. I pray in your grace-full name. Amen.

A Prayer about Being Subpoenaed to Hope

I pray that the eyes of your heart may be enlightened in order that you may know the hope to which he has called you. (Eph. 1:18 NIV)

Merciful Father, if a sheriff knocked at my door this morning with a subpoena, I'd be a bit unnerved. But today, like every day, the gospel is knocking at my door to subpoena me to hope. Nothing is more settling and centering.

Thanks for making hope a calling. You haven't just extended a general notification or given me a polite invitation. I am called to hope in Jesus, just as surely as you called me to a saving knowledge of his grace and will call me to an eternal celebration of your presence one day. I wouldn't think of ignoring a summons from the sheriff; I'd be crazy to ignore a summons from you.

This morning I'll gladly make myself a target of Paul's petition. Open the eyes of my heart right now. Wipe the morning crud from my eyes. Things seem a bit blurry. I'm having a hard time focusing. Help me to see Jesus clearly today. I'm glad to see more of heaven and all the amazing stuff you're got planned for us in the new heaven and new earth. But just show me more of Jesus as my righteousness, as my constant intercessor, as my bridegroom. That will be enough, more than enough.

Free me from fixing my gaze on circumstances and people. I tend to give them way too much power over my heart. Paul wrote these words of encouragement from a Roman prison, not from a Mediterranean condo. What do I have to complain about? I have real needs, but you give an even greater hope.

Bring enlightenment where there's been dullness and myopia of late. Throw the curtains all the way open; lift all the clouds; do more laser surgery on the eyes of my heart, if need be. Just show me more of Jesus—that's all I really need. I pray in his tender and triumphant name. Amen.

A Prayer about Snakes, Scorpions, and God's Spirit

What father among you, if his son asks for a fish, will instead of a fish give him a serpent; or if he asks for an egg, will give him a scorpion? If you then, who are evil, know how to give good gifts to your children, how much more will the heavenly Father give the Holy Spirit to those who ask him! (Luke 11:11–13)

Dear Father, it's been almost fifty days since Easter Sunday. That makes this upcoming Lord's Day Pentecost Sunday—the day when we celebrate the gift of the Holy Spirit. Like ignoring a houseguest, I can take this honored heart guest for granted. I repent, especially as I recall what a special Person he is.

Blessed Holy Spirit, it's because of you I believe the gospel. If you hadn't given life and faith in Jesus, I would still be dead in my sins and trespasses. You also sealed me forever as the Father's possession. You're the firstfruits of my final redemption—the guarantee that one day I will live with the whole family of God in the new heaven and new earth.

It's by you I hear the Father tell me I'm his beloved child. It's by you that I hear and learn more of the glory and grace of Jesus, for you are always drawing attention to him.

It's through your power I'm able to put to death everything in me that contradicts the gospel. It's through your work that good fruit is being produced. I'm becoming more and more like Jesus because of you.

I can pray and worship acceptably only because of you. In fact, you're praying inside of me right now, and you continue to do so even when I'm too undisciplined or too broken to pray. It's by you that I am gifted for service and empowered for mission. How I praise you for your multiple graces in my life!

Father, I take Jesus' promise seriously. Today, I ask for more of the Holy Spirit's work in my life. I love fish and eggs, but what I need and want is the gift of your Holy Spirit. Free me from my stereotypes. Free me from a mere correct-yet-notional theology of the Spirit. Free me from being held hostage to distortions of who the Holy Spirit is and fears of weird stuff. I am thirsty enough to be done with being cool and being in control. I pray in Jesus' exalted name. Amen.

A Prayer about the Generous Mystery of the Trinity

The grace of the Lord Jesus Christ and the love of God and the fellowship of the Holy Spirit be with you all. (2 Cor. 13:14)

Most glorious, Triune God, I'm finally at home in my finiteness. Mystery is now a good friend, not an intruder to figure out. It's no longer about explaining you as Trinity. It's about worshiping with wonder and surrendering with gratitude.

Dear Lord Jesus, what more could we possibly want or need than for your grace to be with us today? It was by your grace we received eternal life. It is by your grace we are being transformed to be like you. And by your grace one day we will enjoy the perfections of life in the new heaven and new earth. We praise you for your saving, sustaining, and sufficient grace.

Dear heavenly Father, what more could we possibly need today than the assurance and supply of your love? You've promised we will never be separated from your great love for us in Jesus. Because of what Jesus has accomplished, you will never love us more than you do today and you will never love us less.

Dear Holy Spirit, what more could we possibly long for today than fellowship with you? To fellowship with you is to enjoy the doxology and delights of the whole Godhead. I no more presume on such a privilege than I presume I have the ability to create a whole new universe.

Indeed, may your grace, Jesus; your love, Father; and your fellowship, Holy Spirit, be with us all day long. I pray in Jesus' trustworthy and triumphant name. Amen.

A Prayer about Working Hard to Rest Well

Therefore, while the promise of entering his rest still stands, let us fear lest any of you should seem to have failed to reach it. For good news came to us just as to them, but the message they heard did not benefit them, because they were not united by faith with those who listened. For we who have believed enter that rest. (Heb. 4:1–3)

So then, there remains a Sabbath rest for the people of God, for whoever has entered God's rest has also rested from his works as God did from his. Let us therefore strive to enter that rest. (Heb. 4:9–11)

Heavenly Father, what a glorious paradox. You're calling me to work diligently, to invest great effort, to strive with all my might to enter your rest. I know my performance-based heart well enough to appreciate the obvious irony. Work hard to rest well. Work hard to cease working.

The gospel contradicts the fundamental way I've been trained to approach every sphere of life—athletics, education, finances, career, reputation. "Do it the good ol' fashioned way—earn it!" "God helps those who help themselves." "You'll always get what's coming to you." These mantras have been my motivation and my madness.

Because the gospel is true, I didn't get what's coming to me, fortunately. You gave that to Jesus at the cross. And in exchange, you've given me what I never could've earned: complete forgiveness, the righteousness of Jesus, and your permanent favor resting on me. There's no greater rest than to know you are at peace with me, to be certain that you are resting and rejoicing in great love over me.

Jesus, you created the world in six days and then entered a Sabbath rest. Likewise, when you died on the cross, securing our salvation and the restoration of creation, you cried, "It is finished" (John 19:30). Your work was over and you rested, and now we enter your rest.

Our never-ending work is to hear and believe this gospel. What a most liberating vocation you have given us. In your gracious name I pray. Amen.

A Prayer about Not Relishing Revenge

Do not take revenge, my dear friends, but leave room for God's wrath, for it is written: "It is mine to avenge; I will repay," says the Lord. (Rom. 12:19 NIV)

Do not gloat when your enemy falls;
> when they stumble, do not let your heart rejoice.
(Prov. 24:17 NIV)

Merciful Father, I relish the taste of wasabi-kissed soft-shell crab sushi, of a seared-to-perfection rib eye steak, of fresh pistachio gelato dribbled with a few extra pistachios and a little hot fudge. But I also savor stories of revenge seasoned with spiteful retaliation and topped off with the gravy of extreme retribution—when the bad guy gets it even worse than he gave it. Alas, I am always in need of the gospel.

It's good to long for and to work for justice and to live for the day of ultimate justice. But I need and I must heed your warning to avoid a vengeful spirit like I would run from coiled rattlesnakes, toxic fumes, or E. coli–poisoned waters.

No matter what the provocation—from a personal "dissing" to evil parading its hatred of beauty—you are telling me I have no right to revenge, no right to gloat when an enemy falls, no right to get back at or to get even with anybody.

I'm so glad you didn't "get even" with me, Father, for all the ways I rebelled (and do rebel) against you, for all the ways I've chosen my gain over your glory, for all the ways I've misrepresented you to the world, even to my own heart. You didn't get even; you got generous. May the cross of Jesus keep me humble, patient, and expectant of the day of consummate justice. I don't want to waste one more self-absorbed moment relishing personal revenge. There are much better things to eat. I pray in Jesus' merciful and mighty name. Amen.

A Prayer about the Last Command in the Bible

The Spirit and the Bride say, "Come." And let the one who hears say, "Come." And let the one who is thirsty come; let the one who desires take the water of life without price. (Rev. 22:17)

Blessed Holy Spirit, it's Pentecost Sunday, and how appropriate to be meditating on the very last command in the Bible. "Come, thirsty ones! Come, desiring ones! Come and take the free gift of the water of life." I am thirsty . . . I do wish . . . I do come, gratefully and expectantly.

From the day you first convinced me of my need of Jesus and gave me faith to trust him, I've had an unquenchable thirst for the water of life. The bitter waters of sin only make me sick, fortunately. The deceiving waters of my broken cisterns satisfy ever so briefly. The illusionary waters of countless mirages are just that: illusions. I've paid for all of these waters, dearly. But the water Jesus gives is free!

So once again, I bring my thirst to you. I'm thirsty to know Jesus better and better. I'm thirsty to be quicker in my repentances and slower in my excuses. I'm thirsty to grow more of your fruit and less of my thorns. I'm thirsty to be freer to love others as Jesus loves me. Slake these thirsts by the water of the gospel.

I'm thirsty for the new heaven and new earth. I'm thirsty for the wedding feast of the Lamb, when the bride will no longer say, "Come!" but will say, "We are here, all of us!" I'm thirsty for the day when God's glory will cover the earth as the waters cover the sea. I'm thirsty for the day of no more thirst. I have no doubt you *will* satisfy all of these thirsts. I pray in the fullness and faithfulness of Jesus' name. Amen.

A Prayer about the War to End All Wars

Then I saw heaven opened, and behold, a white horse! The one sitting on it is called Faithful and True, and in righteousness he judges and makes war. His eyes are like a flame of fire, and on his head are many diadems, and he has a name written that no one knows but himself. He is clothed in a robe dipped in blood, and the name by which he is called is The Word of God. And the armies of heaven, arrayed in fine linen, white and pure, were following him on white horses. From his mouth comes a sharp sword with which to strike down the nations, and he will rule them with a rod of iron. He will tread the winepress of the fury of the wrath of God the Almighty. On his robe and on his thigh he has a name written: King of kings and Lord of lords. (Rev. 19:11–16)

Triumphant Jesus, on this Memorial Day I gladly stop to honor the men and women who have served our country in various branches of the armed forces. In a world filled with "wars and rumors of war," I don't take our servicemen and servicewomen for granted. There has never been more of a thankless, even despised job.

But on this particular Memorial Day, I want to stop and honor you as the ultimate servant-warrior—the quintessential man of service—the one who on the cross waged the war to end all wars.

No one hates warfare among vying nations more than you. No one is more offended even by the petty and pointless squabbles between spouses and friends (James 4:1–2). No one paid a greater price to bring the final and full peace for which we intensely long and hope.

Having secured the defeat of the prince of darkness on the cross, you're now the rider on the white horse—alone worthy of the name Faithful and True. You are faithful to fulfill every promise God made for the salvation of his people and the restoration of creation. And you are truly bringing to completion this good work of redemption, for your name is also the Word of God.

Though evil hates beauty, your love trumps all evil. Evil will not prevail. It has been defeated, and it will be eradicated. You are already the King of Kings and Lord of Lords. Your kingdom has come and your kingdom is coming. I pray in the memory and victory of your matchless name. Amen.

A Prayer about God's Ownership of Our Battles

The LORD saves not with sword and spear. For the battle is the LORD's.
(1 Sam. 17:47)

This is what the LORD says to you: "Do not be afraid or discouraged because of this vast army. For the battle is not yours, but God's." (2 Chron. 20:15 NIV)

Dear Father, I love it when you're selfish with things I don't really want anyway—especially when you claim ownership of any battle into which you place me. Though you call me into warfare and give me armor to wear (Eph. 6:10–18), it's you I must trust in as the Divine Warrior. I'm to be not a disengaged pacifist but a fully engaged worshiper, beholding the salvation of the Lord. I'm never more than David facing Goliath. But with you, I will not be afraid.

Whether it's a mere skirmish or an all-out assault, the battle belongs to you. Fear and discouragement are not the order of the day; faith and peace are.

When I'm afraid of events in world history—when it seems like evil and terror will triumph—let me hear the laughter of heaven. Let me see your installed King, the Lord Jesus. Show me the occupied throne of heaven, and it will shut up my fears (Ps. 2).

When I'm under attack by the seducer, accuser, and condemner of the brethren, once again let me see Jesus, the author and perfecter of my faith. He is my wisdom, righteousness, holiness, and redemption (1 Cor. 1:30–31). My boast is in Jesus, not in anything in me.

When I get pulled into petty fights with my brothers and sisters in Christ, slay us with the gospel and bring us back to faith expressing itself in love.

When I'm in the presence of evil and very broken people, keep me sane and centered by the gospel. When my divided heart wages war inside of me, come to me in the storm, Jesus, and make peace. I pray in your triumphant name. Amen.

A Prayer about Healing Words

The words of the reckless pierce like swords,
but the tongue of the wise brings healing. (Prov. 12:18 NIV)

Gracious Jesus, I love words. I especially love the way you use words to bring me healing, freedom, and hope. You never shame me with words. You never manipulate me with words. You never hurt me with words. You never flatter me, but you do bring great encouragement. You never repeat my failures to others; you only bring my sin and brokenness to the throne of grace. You never say too much or too little. You neither mince words nor waste words. You alone have the words of life.

My prayer is simple yet necessary: grant me greater stewardship of my words, Jesus. As you speak to me, please speak through me. I'm painfully aware that my words can bring great harm and death, even as they can be a source of hope and life (Prov. 18:21). If I'm not careful, my words can have the effect of gangrene (Eph. 4:29).

You tell me that my words are a sure reflection of what's filling my heart: "The good person out of the good treasure of his heart produces good, and the evil person out of his evil treasure produces evil, for out of the abundance of the heart his mouth speaks" (Luke 6:45). So no mere promise to avoid gossip, idle chatter, reckless words, or coarse jesting will be enough. I must constantly be preaching the gospel to my heart. May the overflow of your grace be obvious to all. I want my tongue to be a scalpel for healing, Jesus, not a hammer for harm. I pray in your merciful name. Amen.

A Prayer about the Blahs and the Blues

For even when we came into Macedonia, our bodies had no rest, but we were afflicted at every turn—fighting without and fear within. But God, who comforts the downcast, comforted us by the coming of Titus. (2 Cor. 7:5–6)

Gracious Father, the incidental pictures in the Scriptures are often as profound as the intentional promises. I'm thankful for this picture of a conflicted Paul being comforted by a good friend. For I begin today feeling very much on the blahs-and-blues side of things.

Thank you for reminding me that even your most faithful servants—those who know you so well, those who grasp the gospel a zillion times better than me—even these men and women experience restlessness, fear, and weariness.

At times I still labor under the myth of an omnicompetence. If I just prayed enough, believed enough, or was filled with the Spirit enough, I would never get discouraged or downcast. What a groundless lie. What a horrible burden. What a humorless joke.

Thank you for comforting us when we're downcast. You don't deride us, chide us, or hide from us. You comfort us. You're "the Father of mercies and the God of all comfort" (2 Cor. 1:3). And thank you for the comforters you send us. Though you're quite capable of sending ravens and rainbows and manna and miracles, more often than not you send a Titus to a Paul (2 Cor. 7:6) or a Phoebe to a Paul (Rom. 16:1). You love to show your kindness for your people through your people.

Father, on this gorgeous May morning, I'll wait for your grace as I bring you my weighed-down heart. Help me stay honest about my weariness, expectant of your comfort, and thankful for whomever you send.

And make me sensitive to the needs of others around me. I may be more helpful to them in this state of funk than when I feel "together" and "on top of my game." By the Holy Spirit, point me toward other weary travelers who need a gentle word of comfort, perspective, and hope. I pray with anticipation, in Jesus' compassionate name. Amen.

A Prayer for Quick, Engaged Listening

Know this, my beloved brothers: Let every person be quick to hear, slow to speak, slow to anger; for the anger of man does not produce the righteousness that God requires. (James 1:19–20)

Lord Jesus, I need this word today, a lot. People who love me have confronted me about being a poor listener, which is really more a case of hardly listening. You've given me two ears and one mouth, and the anatomical ratio is no mere accident. Help me become a much more engaged listener.

I'll take my cue from you, Jesus. There's no one more quick to listen. I never have to snap my fingers to get your attention. I never have to reel you back into focus. I never catch you looking away, as though you're bored with me. I never have to repeat myself several times to make sure you heard what I really said. You never interrupt me. You never spin what I'm saying. You never talk over me when I'm trying to tell you something. There's no one who listens as attentively, respectively, and compassionately as you.

I don't need healing for deafness but grace for listening—first and foremost to you, Jesus. You're always speaking, through the Scriptures, and you speak only words of life. What a foolish man I am not to hang on to every syllable you utter.

Help me give my wife, my children, and my friends the gift of being really heard. I find no joy in frustrating the very people who love me. Bring the gospel to bear in such a way that I will become more notorious for my good listening than for my frequent speaking.

It's a humbling joy to confess specific sin to you today, Jesus. I'm confident of your care and help. I pray in the riches of your great name. Amen.

A Prayer about the Singing of Redeemed Creation

I heard every creature in heaven and on earth and under the earth and in the sea, and all that is in them, saying, "To him who sits on the throne and to the Lamb be blessing and honor and glory and might forever and ever!" And the four living creatures said, "Amen!" and the elders fell down and worshiped. (Rev. 5:13–14)

Dear Jesus, I really need to connect with John's vision and promise today. Even as my heart breaks and my anger grows over the oil spill in the Gulf of Mexico and any of a number of environmental disasters, and even as I know that you order and use such hard providences in creation to humble the arrogant and grant repentance to the contrite (Rev. 8–9) . . . nevertheless I'm thankful that one day we'll enjoy the perfected and never-to-be-broken-again world of the new heaven and new earth. I'm filled with hope by your promise of the new creation world of inviolate beauty, goodness, and truth. I greatly long for the day when creation itself will be set free from its bondage to decay and will enjoy the glorious freedom of the children of God (Rom. 8:18–25).

By faith I can already hear the faint but sure singing of every creature "in heaven and on earth and under the earth and in the sea, and all that is in them" (Rev. 5:13) singing to you, Jesus. But what will that frustration-free (Rom. 8:20), fully engaged, full-throated, pan-creature symphony and chorus actually sound like? I'll gladly wait to see and hear.

Until that day, grant me the gospel sanity to want the conversion of your people more, much more, than I want an oil slick–free holiday by the sea. If by hurricane, earthquake, flood, tornado, oil spill, or whatever else your saving purposes are realized, I'll humbly submit, even as I'll also keep seeking to be a good steward of "the first heaven and the first earth" (Rev. 21:1) until the appearing of the new heaven and new earth. I pray with a conflicted yet hopeful heart, in Jesus' name. Amen.

A Prayer about the Gospel for Breakfast

Let me hear in the morning of your steadfast love,
for in you I trust.
Make me know the way I should go,
for to you I lift up my soul. (Ps. 143:8)

Heavenly Father, I cannot conceive of a better way to begin every day than feasting on the gospel. Lay the big breakfast buffet out before me, give me the choice of any and every delicacy imaginable, and I'll choose words of your unfailing love for me in Jesus, every time.

There's no nutrient I need more than the fresh manna of your grace. Nothing tastes as sweet as the assurance of your welcome, presence, and affection. I've never met a carbohydrate I didn't like, but just send me ample supplies of the Bread of Life and I'll be a happy camper—far better than that, I'll be a different man.

Indeed, Father, I'm not just looking to be a satisfied consumer of the gospel. I need your unfailing love for the challenges of the day—this day.

Apart from the gospel, I'll whine more than I'll worship. Apart from the gospel, I'll judge people more than I'll seek to understand them. Apart from the gospel, I'll get my feelings hurt quicker than being careful not to offend others. Apart from the gospel, I'll avoid people who want more from me than I want to give them.

Apart from the gospel, I'll react selfishly to irritants rather than responding graciously. Apart from the gospel, I'll talk more than I listen. Apart from the gospel, I'll think about me much more than I think about you. Apart from the gospel, I won't risk anything; I'll do just enough to get by. Apart from the banquet of the gospel, I'll be reaching for junk food all day long, literally and figuratively.

Father, because of your unfailing love for me in Jesus, I have put my trust in you. I do lift my soul up to you, right now. Show me the way I should go this very day. Show me what thinking, feeling, and choosing in line with the truth of the gospel requires of me, and then give me that supply. I pray in Jesus' beautiful and bountiful name. Amen.

A Prayer for Friends in Crisis

On one of those days, as he [Jesus] was teaching, Pharisees and teachers of the law were sitting there who had come from every village of Galilee and Judea and from Jerusalem. And the power of the Lord was with him to heal. And behold, some men were bringing on a bed a man who was paralyzed, and they were seeking to bring him in and lay him before Jesus, but finding no way to bring him in, because of the crowd, they went up on the roof and let him down with his bed through the tiles into the midst before Jesus. (Luke 5:17–19)

Most loving Jesus, I begin today with a sense of urgency for a few friends. Though I don't have to rip tiles off a roof to bring them to you, I would if need be. For you alone have the authority to forgive sins and the power to heal every disease.

You alone have the Spirit without measure. You alone care for the poor, bind broken hearts, free captives, release prisoners, bestow God's favor, comfort mourners, provide for grievers, and bring beauty, gladness, and praise (Isa. 61:1–3). What a Savior you are! And everything you do, you do with so much joy.

Jesus, for my brother who is absolutely paralyzed with fear, grant him your peace and heavenly wisdom. He has every right to be afraid because he is living in a vortex of great darkness. Important decisions have to be made and broken people well cared for. For your glory, show yourself as the God who is mighty to save.

Jesus, for my married friends who used to live face-to-face in kindness and affection but now live back-to-back with rancor and stubbornness, raise the dead, O God of resurrection. There is no hope unless you replace stony hearts with hearts of flesh. Both of them need to come to the cross, and soon, but at least soften one of my hardened friends. Bring somebody to gospel sanity so the other spouse will see beauty and dare to hope again.

Jesus, for my friend who lives with three hours of sleep a night, unrelenting depression, and haunting memories of inconceivable abuse, I simply cry for mercy, Jesus. With wet eyes, not clenched fists, I simply ask, "How long, O Lord? How long before my friend knows the freedom and healing you alone can give?"

This I know for sure, Jesus: you do all things well, even if you don't do some things the way I want you to. In your merciful and mighty name I pray. Amen.

A Prayer about Itchy Ears
and Loving the Word

Preach the word; be prepared in season and out of season; correct, rebuke and encourage—with great patience and careful instruction. For the time will come when people will not put up with sound doctrine. Instead, to suit their own desires, they will gather around them a great number of teachers to say what their itching ears want to hear. (2 Tim. 4:2–3 NIV)

Lord Jesus, many times when I read this Scripture, I immediately think of certain characters on TV whose perversions of the gospel raise my ire and dander like nothing else. In my heart I can become a serial killer of certain televangelists quicker than I can swat a mosquito. I confess this as sin, Jesus. I'm not boasting about or justifying my attitude.

But today, as I meditate on this Scripture, I'm looking in the mirror, not at the TV. What do I do when my ears get itchy—when my demand for pleasure, relief, or getting my way is stronger than my commitment to your glory? What do I do when the Scriptures say one thing and yet my wandering, bored, selfish heart yearns for something else?

Jesus, I know who to call when I want to hear what I want to hear: my codependent friends who are more afraid of disappointing me than they are committed to speaking the truth in love. I know what authors to read, what podcasts to listen to, what blogs to visit when I want a "second opinion"—that is, when I want to suit my own desires rather than serve the purposes of God.

Jesus, continue to prepare me for in-season and out-of-season living. Deepen my love for and submission to the Word. I ask you to correct, rebuke, and encourage me with the gospel every single day. Show me yourself in every portion of the Bible, for that's where the soundest doctrine will be found.

Lastly, Jesus, help me be a better friend to my friends. I don't want to be one of the very first people they call when they simply want to hear what they want to hear. I don't want to be an ear-scratching friend but a good friend—a gospel friend. I pray in your holy and loving name. Amen.

A Prayer about What It's All About

For us there is but one God, the Father, from whom all things came and for whom we live; and there is but one Lord, Jesus Christ, through whom all things came and through whom we live. (1 Cor. 8:6 NIV)

Dear Lord, I've always appreciated people who are able to "cut to the chase" no matter what the topic is. Just give me an accurate summation and comprehensive distillation of the issue, and I'm good to go. The apostle Paul has done precisely that for me in this one remarkable verse of Scripture.

Truly, there is no other God but you, and with immeasurable kindness, you've chosen to relate to us as the Father from whom all fatherhood derives its meaning (Eph. 3:14–15). You're not simply the best father there ever was, you are the quintessential Father. Everything comes from you—everything: my first breath, my next breath; my first heartbeat, my last heartbeat. You were a great Creator before you became a generous Redeemer. There's nothing that I have that I didn't receive from you (1 Cor. 4:7). It is for you that I live. I say this by faith, desiring an even greater manifestation in my life.

Truly, there is no other Lord but you, Jesus. You are the Christ, the promised and present Savior. Through you the Father created the world, through you he granted salvation, through you he's sustaining all things, and through you he'll complete his great story of redemption and restoration. It is through you that I live and move and have my being, Jesus (Acts 17:28). Autonomy is a pernicious myth, self-salvation a demonic lie. I have been justified, I am being sanctified, and I will be glorified by faith alone (the faith you give me) and by grace alone (the grace you give me).

And God the Holy Spirit, I see these things, understand these things, and believe these things because of your powerful and persistent work. Though you are the most silent member of the Godhead, you are so very present. I pray today in Jesus' peerless name, to the glory of the Triune God! Amen.

A Prayer about Singing in the Chaos

With harps of God in their hands . . . they sing the song of Moses, the servant of God, and the song of the Lamb, saying: "Great and amazing are your deeds, O Lord God the Almighty! Just and true are your ways, O King of the nations! Who will not fear, O Lord, and glorify your name? For you alone are holy. All nations will come and worship you, for your righteous acts have been revealed." (Rev. 15:2–4)

Sovereign Father, every single time I begin to get a little antsy, anxious, or angry about national and international politics, you center my heart with the music of heaven. What did followers of Jesus need in the crazy-making chaos of first-century Rome? The same thing we followers of Jesus need in the crazy-making chaos of our twenty-first-century global community. We need to sing your story. We need to sing our theology. We need to sing the gospel!

Hand me a harp today, Father. I'll gladly join the heavenly chorus singing the song of Moses—a song of your Exodus grace, deliverance from the bondage of Egypt, deliverance into a land of freedom. But I'll sing the song of the Lamb even *louder*! For Jesus has delivered us from sin and death, into the glorious freedom of the children of God, and Jesus will deliver us into the ultimate land of freedom—the new heaven and new earth!

Father, I choose to live and sing in light of the day when all nations will come and worship before you, for your righteous acts have been and are being revealed so clearly in the gospel. Great and marvelous are your deeds of mercy and grace in Jesus, Lord God Almighty.

All of your ways, in heaven and on earth, are just and true, for you are the King of the ages. Every other king gets the "fifteen minutes in the spotlight" you appoint them, but you alone are "the King eternal, immortal, invisible, the only God," and to you "be honor and glory for ever and ever. Amen" (1 Tim. 1:17 NIV).

I'll not be afraid of any human king, but I will fear you, Lord, for you alone are holy and you alone are good. As the gospel does its work in my heart, I pray my thoughts, words, and deeds will increasingly bring you glory. I pray in Jesus' sovereign and saving name. Amen.

A Prayer about the Boss of My Heart

Let the peace of Christ rule in your hearts, since as members of one body you were called to peace. And be thankful. (Col. 3:15 NIV)

Gracious Jesus, today, like every day, somebody or something is going to gain the upper hand on the attention and affection of my heart. My heart will be ruled—that's an indisputable fact. Some entity will be the boss of me. It could be my bitterness, pettiness, or cowardice. It could be the shaming power of darkness. It could be overbearing or aggravating people. It could be my greed to have a little more. It could be religion or my hatred of religion. It could be old regrets or new fantasies.

But by faith, right now, I choose your peace as the ruler of my heart, as the boss of me, as the centering and sending power for this one day. And who knows peace better than you, Jesus? You are the Prince of Peace! On the cross you secured God's peace with me and my peace with God. The enmity and hostility between us have been obliterated and eradicated. Peace with God is now a legal right of mine, a done deal, a settled issue. How can I not overflow with gratitude as this day begins and as it continues?

Jesus, please make this legal right a personal delight—an actual power mightily at work in my heart today and in all my relationships. Yours is a much better story than simply a tale of calming down my restless, wandering heart. Yours is a story of reconciling love. You make enemies friends. You humble stubborn people. You soften hard people. You make angry people gentle.

Because you have forgiven me, I will choose to forgive others. Because you have forgiven me, I will choose to ask forgiveness from others. Because you are at peace with me, I will do everything within my power to live at peace with others. I pray in your holy and persistent name. Amen.

A Prayer about Trusting Jesus in Transitions

Let the morning bring me word of your unfailing love,
　　for I have put my trust in you.
Show me the way I should go,
　　for to you I entrust my life. (Ps. 143:8 NIV)

Dear Jesus, in the morning, at midday, in the afternoon, and throughout the night, keep on bringing us word of your unfailing love. That's all we need; that's all we really need. By the Holy Spirit, incessantly gossip the gospel in our inmost ear. Wrap the good news of your boundless, endless affections around our hearts tighter and tighter and tighter. Permeate every bit of our being with your fresh mercies, steadfast love, and transforming grace, for we have put our trust in you.

Jesus, it's the assurance of your unfailing love that enables us to trust you with the transitions we go through in life and the uncertainties about the future. Change is never easy. Change makes us feel vulnerable, fearful, and insecure. We get tempted, once again, to be our own savior. Spare us that misery, Jesus; spare us and those we love. Don't let us go there, even for a moment. May your Word dwell in us richly, your peace rule in us powerfully, and your glory be our main passion and delight.

We've entrusted our lives to you, Jesus, because you alone are trustworthy. We've given you our sins, wounds, brokenness, and weakness. Now, in fresh surrender, we give you our planning for the next season of our lives. Show us the way we should go through our transitions—transitions of age and stage, career and calling, health and finances, relationships and ministries. Write stories of redemption beyond our wildest dreams and hopes. It's all about you, Jesus—not us, you.

We're not so arrogant as to expect all the details. Just take us by the hand and lead the way. Shepherd us, Jesus. Open doors we cannot shut and shut doors we cannot open. All we need to know is that you love us and that you're with us. You've promised us both, and you do not lie. We pray in your peerless and priceless name. Amen.

A Prayer for Seeing Much More of the Gospel

The god of this world has blinded the minds of the unbelievers, to keep them from seeing the light of the gospel of the glory of Christ, who is the image of God. (2 Cor. 4:4)

Jesus, I thank you for the gift of another day. Please fill my gaze with your beauty, my mind with your truth, and my heart with more of the gospel—much more of the gospel. If the main strategy of the kingdom of darkness is to keep unbelievers in the dark about the gospel of your glory and grace, why would I think evil would choose some other tactic for believers? So as I pray for my unbelieving friends today, I also pray for myself.

Jesus, reveal more and more of the gospel to me—more and more of who you really are; more and more of what you've already accomplished by your life, death, and resurrection; more and more of what you're continuing to do in your commitment to make all things new; more and more of what it's going to be like to live with you and the whole family of God in the new heaven and new earth. Show me, convince me, dazzle me, change me . . . and then show me more.

Don't let me frame any notion of God apart from you, for you are the very image of God—God incarnate. Don't let me read any part of the Bible without thinking about you—for everything written about you in the law of Moses, the Prophets, and the psalms must be fulfilled (Luke 24:44). Don't let me desert you by turning to some other gospel—which is really no gospel at all (Gal. 1:6–7). As the gospel is producing fruit and growing all over the world, so may it enlarge my heart and bring forth fruit to your glory (Col. 1:6).

Jesus, if you've moved me from total blindness to a 20/200 vision of the gospel, take me on to 20/100, then 20/50, then 20/20, then 20/15, until the day I see you with glorified eyes. In that day I will see you as you are, and I will be like you (1 John 3:2). Hallelujah! By the light of this hope, I surrender to your purposes for this day. I pray in your peerless name. Amen.

A Prayer about Evident Gentleness

Let your gentleness be evident to all. The Lord is near. (Phil. 4:5 NIV)

Dear Lord Jesus, there is no one more gentle with me than you. There is no one as welcoming of sinners, as kind to the broken, or as understanding of the struggling as you. You are gentle, yet persistent; gentle, yet firm; gentle, yet so very powerful.

You're like the perfect surgeon—the one I want working on me. You never get nervous, flustered, agitated, or hurried. You have a steady hand because of your steady heart. Oh, how I need you to do ongoing gospel surgery on me if I'm going to be a true gentle man—someone whose gentleness is evident to all, and not just evident to the people who are so easy for me to be with.

Gentle me when I'm behind slow drivers who stay in the fast lane. Gentle me when I face both fair and unfair criticism. Gentle me when I think things that are obvious to me ought to be obvious to everybody else. Gentle me when loud, boorish people invade "my" space—as though I have some inalienable right to an uninterrupted life.

Gentle me when I'm too tired to engage but my wife really needs me to listen. Gentle me when I need a nap but my grandson needs to play. Gentle me when someone gets the last cookie I was already planning on enjoying with a glass of milk. Gentle me when my plans are disrupted because it's too humid to run.

Gentle me when the vacation gets cut short by crises. Gentle me when friends keep making the same mistakes and foolish choices. Gentle me when the restaurant sends me home with the wrong take-out order. Gentle me when Satan starts condemning me for things I actually did but for which you already paid my debt.

Gentle me when I start debating theology rather than loving the people who see things differently. Gentle me when I cannot fix the very people you never gave me to fix.

Jesus, you are so near me in the gospel; in fact, you live in my heart. You're also near in terms of coming back to finish making all things new. May your nearness generate a much quicker repentance on my part. Make me a gentle man by the gospel and for your glory. I pray in your kind and loving name. Amen.

A Prayer about Being a Refreshing Friend

May the Lord grant mercy to the household of Onesiphorus, for he often refreshed me and was not ashamed of my chains, but when he arrived in Rome he searched for me earnestly and found me. (2 Tim. 1:16–17)

Dear Jesus, Onesiphorus is just one of many of my brothers and sisters I'll have to wait till heaven to meet. Being married to you has placed me in a most amazing family, and like every other family, it's a broken family filled with broken people. But like no other family, it's a family with a guaranteed future of whole people and perfect relationships beyond all imaginings (1 Cor. 2:9). I praise you for paying the supreme price of your life to secure such an unimaginable eternity for your bride.

But here's one of my brothers I'd like to be a lot more like before we meet. Though Onesiphorus's name literally means "bringing profit," he didn't have to live that way. He could have been self-absorbed, hypercritical, a record keeper of wrongs done, a quarrelsome type, real sensitive, taking everything way too personally. In short, he could have been a real drain to be around. But instead he was a source of refreshment, and according to Paul, he worked hard at it.

Jesus, make me a much more refreshing person. Fill my heart with your mercy. Give me gospel eyes to see others as you see them. Sensitize my spirit with your Spirit. Free me from working hard just to get my to-do list done, that I might work hard at bringing refreshment to others.

Jesus, please make me aware today of those who really need encouragement, some reason to hope, a concrete manifestation of care. It may be at the price of an airline ticket to find them. It may simply be a walk across the street, a drive across town, a face-to-face visit, a hug, a call, an email, a text—some small thing that will bring a profit beyond my imagining.

Jesus, you searched hard to find me and you did. You've broken my chains and you've borne my shame. May I offer a refreshing taste of your kindness to others today, no matter what their chains are. I pray in your loving and liberating name. Amen.

A Prayer about Our Stuff

Do not toil to acquire wealth;
  be discerning enough to desist.
When your eyes light on it, it is gone,
  for suddenly it sprouts wings,
  flying like an eagle toward heaven. (Prov. 23:4–5)

Loving Father, this has been a crazy and stressful season in our economy. Some of us who thought we'd be retired in a couple of years are now thinking it's ten, if at all. Some of us have lost jobs, even homes. Some of us are selling stuff, having stuff repossessed, having to move; some of our marriages are being stressed to the point of ending; and some of us are being tempted to steal for the first time. Others of us are holding tighter to our stuff than ever and are exerting great energy just to get more. Lord, we need wisdom for ourselves and for our friends.

Father, though the issues vary and we dare not generalize, bring the perspective of the gospel to bear as we think about our relationship to "stuff." Where have we assumed the right to excess? Why did we think only first-century disciples of Jesus would ever actually have to pray for daily bread? Where have we gotten used to a lifestyle of having so much stuff to the point that we actually call abundance "need"?

In our "iWorld" of new gadgets and cool widgets, help us to ponder the reality that over half of the population on the earth exists on three of our American dollars, or less, a day. Father, help us only to glance at riches rather than setting our gaze on them. Give us restraint, Lord Jesus. Holy Spirit, if we would wear ourselves out for anything, let it be to become rich toward God (Luke 12:20–21)—to have the gospel so penetrate our hearts that we cry out with spontaneous joy, "Who do I have in heaven but you, O Lord, and being with you I desire nothing on the earth . . . *You are my portion, sovereign Lord.*"

Lord Jesus, you who were outrageously rich in all things became incomprehensibly poor for us, so that we, who were desperately poor in sin, might be made immeasurably rich in grace. I pray in your most enriching and liberating name. Amen.

A Prayer about Interpreting Prophecy

As soon as you [Daniel] began to pray, a word went out, which I have come to tell you, for you are highly esteemed. Therefore, consider the word and understand the vision: "Seventy 'sevens' are decreed for your people and your holy city to finish transgression, to put an end to sin, to atone for wickedness, to bring in everlasting righteousness, to seal up vision and prophecy and to anoint the Most Holy Place." (Dan. 9:23–24 NIV)

And he said to them, "O foolish ones, and slow of heart to believe all that the prophets have spoken! Was it not necessary that the Christ should suffer these things and enter into his glory?" And beginning with Moses and all the Prophets, he interpreted to them in all the Scriptures the things concerning himself. (Luke 24:25–27)

Lord Jesus, every time I read certain prophetic sections of the Old Testament, like this one in Daniel, I get flashbacks of big charts, bombastic preachers, and a bevy of fears. As a young believer in the late 1960s to early 1970s, I was convinced ours was the terminal generation. Surely you were going to come back within a few years. The political climate was perfect for the last of the last antichrists to emerge. All things 666 were eschewed—credit cards, phone numbers, driver's licenses. The truth is, we gave the antichrist more credit than Satan himself. The egregious truth is, some of us spent more time fearing the antichrist than really getting to know you, the Christ!

Jesus, I grieve that I didn't know how to look for you in all the Scriptures, and therefore in all of history and life. You who've given me more than seventy times seven worth of forgiveness (Matt. 18:22) are best qualified to help me understand Daniel's seventy sevens and every other prophecy, simple or complex.

Whatever else is going on in this portion of Daniel, this I know for sure: Jesus, only you will one day put an end to all sin. Jesus, only in you can perfect and complete atonement for sin be found. Jesus, only you will one day usher in a world of everlasting righteousness—the new heaven and new earth (Rev. 21:1–5). Only you could seal up vision and prophecy, because you're the last Word from God the Father (Heb. 1:1–2) and the yes and amen to all of God's promises (2 Cor. 1:20). Only you could fulfill every symbol and stick of furniture in the Holy of Holies and make a way for us to enter there (Heb. 10:19–22).

Only you, Jesus, are worthy of our adoration, affection, attention, and allegiance—only you! I pray in your most glorious and gracious name. Amen.

A Prayer about Music in God's Ears

I hate, I despise your feasts, and I take no delight in your solemn assemblies. Even though you offer me your burnt offerings and grain offerings, I will not accept them; and the peace offerings of your fattened animals, I will not look upon them. Take away from me the noise of your songs; to the melody of your harps I will not listen. But let justice roll down like waters, and righteousness like an ever-flowing stream. (Amos 5:21–24)

Holy Father, these are some very strong words about worship and what really amounts to "music to your ears." But you never get "in my face" except to drive me into more of your grace. Such is the beauty of the relationship you've established with me in Jesus. Such is the purpose of your "life-giving correction" (Prov. 15:31 NIV).

Meditating on this Scripture leads me to these conclusions, convictions, and petitions. First and foremost, it's quite possible for me to thoroughly enjoy a service of worship—the liturgy, the Lord's Supper, the music—and yet the same service might truly grieve you. Conversely, there are probably services I exit bored, critical, and "uninspired," and yet in these services you find great delight and pleasure. Forgive me when I make my experience the measure of the acceptability of your worship. How arrogant of me.

Father, it's also obvious that "justice rolling like a river" and "righteousness flowing like a never-failing stream" is music in your ears—the kind of "praise songs" you really enjoy, a hymnody for which you long, the "new worship music" that's "new creation" new, and not just novel or noise in your ears.

Forgive me when the new song of the gospel does not lead me to a new life of caring for others. Forgive me when the satisfaction of being in your presence does not lead me to the sacrifice of serving in the community. Forgive me when I can be just as disconnected and merciless as the priest or the Levite in the parable of the Good Samaritan, who enjoyed your real presence and then proceeded to ignore real need (Luke 10:25–37).

Lord Jesus, you were the Good Samaritan to me, and you still are. But you didn't just find me beaten and broken alongside the road; you found me running as fast as I could from you. I know God and worship God only because you first cared for me, served me, loved me by giving your life for me. Make me a humble, grateful, joyful worship servant. I pray to your glory and by your grace. Amen.

A Prayer about Eggshell Walkin'

Therefore, as God's chosen people, holy and dearly loved, clothe yourselves with compassion, kindness, humility, gentleness and patience. Bear with each other and forgive one another if any of you has a grievance against someone. Forgive as the Lord forgave you. And over all these virtues put on love, which binds them all together in perfect unity. (Col. 3:12–14 NIV)

Merciful Jesus, I don't think there's any passage in any translation of the Bible that uses the image of "walking on eggshells" to describe one of the ways we broken sinners often relate to one another. But I'm glad there's repentance and grace for this and every other soul-sucking, crazy-making relational dance. We are people made for deep intimacy and selfless caring, but sin sure has done a number on our relationships.

Here's my prayer, Jesus: as someone chosen in you before the world began, holy in you, and dearly loved by you, help me realize when others experience me as a minefield of irritability, or a self-righteous porcupine, or a rigid control-meister. I don't want to be the kind of person who makes others feel the need to tiptoe around or avoid me. Through the resources of the gospel, help me to see, own, and deal with the things that make it easy for people not to feel at ease in my company.

My need doesn't stop there, Jesus. I'm also guilty of being on the other end of this broken style of relating—of treating others as too fragile or too dangerous to handle feedback or conflict. When I fall into this pattern, it simply reveals how little of your love I'm currently enjoying and how little of the power of the gospel is presently at work in my life.

Jesus, you've forgiven me everything. You forbear with me through all things. Never let me forget this for a nanosecond. Daily, sometimes hourly, remind me to put on the garments of your grace: kindness, humility, gentleness, and patience.

Along with a lot of my friends, I long for the day of complete wholeness and health, when every one of my relationships will reflect the joy, peace, and intimacy of the Trinity. Until that day, give more grace to these yet-to-be-glorified hearts of ours, Jesus. I pray in your kind and persistent name. Amen.

A Prayer about Jesus' Longing to Be Gracious to Us

This is what the Sovereign LORD, the Holy One of Israel, says:
"In repentance and rest is your salvation,
in quietness and trust is your strength,
but you would have none of it.
You said, 'No, we will flee on horses.'
Therefore you will flee!
You said, 'We will ride off on swift horses.'
Therefore your pursuers will be swift! . . .
till you are left
like a flagstaff on a mountaintop,
like a banner on a hill."
Yet the LORD longs to be gracious to you;
therefore he will rise up to show you compassion.
For the LORD is a God of justice.
Blessed are all who wait for him! (Isa. 30:15–18 NIV)

Dear Jesus, it's a great joy to begin this day knowing you long to be gracious to us. The way you care for your people is simply irresistible, and yet, foolishly, we do resist.

There are times when "riding off on swift horses" looks like a great option—when the demands upon us seem to far outweigh the resources with us; when we reach our emotional limits and exhaust our mental reserves; when tiredness gives way to "attitude" and patience gives way to pettiness. Even then, you woo us to yourself—especially then, we need you.

The call to repentance and rest, and quietness and trust, comes to us like a kiss from heaven. Jesus, we find great comfort in your pursuing love.

I need, again, to learn my limits. Help me say yes to the right things and no to the unnecessary things, Jesus. Help me reestablish the rhythms of a gospel-driven life.

I repent of letting needs dictate my pace. I repent of trying to be my own savior, yet again. I repent of doing more things for you than spending unrushed time with you. I repent of listening to the squawking voices of human parakeets more than the comforting voice of the blessed Paraclete—God the Holy Spirit.

Jesus, as you rise to show us compassion, we will sit down, shut up, be still, and let you. We pray with great anticipation, in your merciful and mighty name. Amen.

A Prayer about a Well-Used Mouth

Do not let any unwholesome talk come out of your mouths, but only what is helpful for building others up according to their needs, that it may benefit those who listen. And do not grieve the Holy Spirit of God, with whom you were sealed for the day of redemption. (Eph. 4:29–30 NIV)

Glorious Triune God—Father, Son, and Holy Spirit—I praise you for the incalculable riches of redemption you've lavished on us in the gospel. Father, for planning such a stunning salvation; Jesus, for accomplishing all things necessary for our complete salvation; Holy Spirit, for faithfully applying the work of Jesus to us. I wish I had adequate words to express my gratitude, but my words fail me.

That being said, I don't want my words to fail you, gracious God. You spoke the Word that gave life to my dead spirit—giving me both the will and the wherewithal to believe the gospel. Forgive me when I speak words, or even think words, that have the opposite effect on others, bringing discouragement, decay, even death.

Holy Spirit, you faithfully preach the gospel to my heart—incessantly telling me that I'm a beloved child of God. Continue to so fill my heart with the beauty of Jesus that, like Balaam's donkey, I cannot help but offer blessings to others. Train my heart and tongue in gospelspeak. Make me fluent in the vocabulary of heaven. Convict me quickly when my words are poorly chosen or intentionally hurtful or there are simply too many of them.

You've sealed me for the day of redemption. I don't want to sadden or grieve you by a foolish and hurtful misuse of words. I'm called to build up, not tear down. You study my needs and speak only helpful words to my heart. Educate me in the needs of my family and friends that I might likewise speak only words of encouragement and hope—even when that requires saying the hard things.

Lord Jesus, we praise you for taking the Father's word of final judgment on the cross, that we might hear him speak the words of complete welcome and acceptance in our hearts. I pray in your holy and loving name. Amen.

A Prayer about the Paradox of Weakness

"My grace is sufficient for you, for my power is made perfect in weakness."
Therefore I will boast all the more gladly of my weaknesses, so that the power
of Christ may rest upon me. For the sake of Christ, then, I am content with
weaknesses, insults, hardships, persecutions, and calamities. For when I
am weak, then I am strong. (2 Cor. 12:9–10)

Heavenly Father, as I meditate on these words of Paul, I vacillate
between feelings of anger and relief, for as a young follower of Jesus,
I wasn't taught to delight in weakness but rather to despise weakness, to
deny weakness, to demonize weakness, to dethrone weakness. That's why
I totally understand Martin Luther's statement that "bad theology is the
worst taskmaster of all." For I've suffered much under the merciless whip
of several gospel distortions.

It was all about "the victorious Christian life": overcoming and not
underachieving, kind of like having a type A personality on spiritual steroids. I didn't think in terms of sufficient grace, I wanted replacement
grace—getting rid of anything unpleasant in my life.

Thank you, Father, for rescuing me from this and other misrepresenta-
tions of life in Christ. Thank you for the godly men and women you've
brought into my life over the years, the humble and courageous servants
of Jesus who've helped me understand the true riches of the gospel and
the way of the cross. Increase their tribe, Lord; increase their tribe.

Father, I know I'm not to be defined by my weakness and brokenness,
but I realize more than ever, that's where Jesus meets me. I have no ability
to change my heart. I very much want your power to rest on me. I very
much *need* for your power to rest on me. I am desperate for all the sufficient grace you will give me.

As you continue to humble and gentle my heart, greatly increase my
compassion toward others in their weakness and brokenness. Forgive
my irritation, impatience, and avoidance of people whose need is much
greater than my supply.

What a wonderful, merciful Savior you are, Jesus. Indeed, it was because you embraced the weakness of the cross that I can gladly boast in
the weaknesses of my life and the more-than-sufficient supply of your
grace. What a most profound, liberating, and hope-filled paradox. I pray
in your holy and loving name. Amen.

A Prayer about Jesus' Transforming Love

If you have any encouragement from being united with Christ, if any comfort from his love, if any common sharing in the Spirit, if any tenderness and compassion, then make my joy complete by being like-minded, having the same love, being one in spirit and of one mind. Do nothing out of selfish ambition or vain conceit. Rather, in humility value others above yourselves, not looking to your own interests but each of you to the interests of the others. (Phil. 2:1–4 NIV)

Dear Lord Jesus, still sipping my first cup of coffee, I awake this day celebrating a great night's rest. Even as you gave me sleep last night, you gave to me in my sleep. You never sleep or slumber. You ever live to advocate and pray for your beloved bride. While we were catching z's, you were making us like yourself. There is no one like you, O Lord, no one.

How I long for the day when my heart will not even be tempted to share its adoration and affection with any other suitor or wannabe savior. Hasten that day, but until that day, keep changing me in ways that empower me to love well. Since the only thing that counts is faith expressing itself in love, I boldly ask for greater impressions of your love upon my heart. How else will I consider others better than myself? How else will I love my wife, my children, my friends, my church family, and strangers as you're calling me to love them?

So, Jesus, what encouragement do I have from being united to you, and what comfort do I find in your love? More than can be measured! It means that the Father loves me as much as he loves you, and there's nothing I can do about it. I can't add to it or take away from it. It means that all of my sins—past, present, and future—are forgiven. It means that I'm enveloped in your righteousness, already declared to have passed from judgment to life. It means I'm guaranteed, one day, to be as lovely and as loving as you are. It means all these things and many more.

It means I can love people and not expect them to give me what you alone can supply. It means I can serve people and not hold them hostage to my selfish ambition and vain conceit. It means I can become more intrigued than irritated with others, more restful than rigid in their presence, more caring than critical of them. Indeed, Jesus, I want to love to your glory, by your grace. I pray in your merciful and magnificent name. Amen.

A Prayer for Bringing Our Fears to Jesus

And I heard a loud voice in heaven, saying, "Now the salvation and the power and the kingdom of our God and the authority of his Christ have come, for the accuser of our brothers has been thrown down, who accuses them day and night before our God. And they have conquered him by the blood of the Lamb and by the word of their testimony, for they loved not their lives even unto death." (Rev. 12:10–11)

Dear Lord Jesus, even as these words first thundered from heaven by a loud voice, so shout this good news into my heart today. What a focusing and freeing perspective on spiritual warfare. We live in the "now" of your salvation, power, kingdom, and authority, Lord Jesus—not the "not-so-long-from-now" but the *now*. You're calling us to warfare, not war-fear.

I cannot help but wonder if Martin Luther was meditating on this passage when he wrote these remarkable words: "And though this world, with devils filled, should threaten to undo us, we will not fear, for God hath willed His truth to triumph through us. The Prince of Darkness grim, we tremble not for him. His rage we can endure, for lo, his doom is sure. One little word shall fell him." O sing, my heart, sing the praises of Jesus! The Prince of Peace has gloriously triumphed over the Prince of Darkness!

Indeed, Lord Jesus, though Satan is yet to be removed, you have already thoroughly routed him. The "accuser of our brothers" has been eternally defeated by you, the great Lover of your bride. It's because you loved us so much that you didn't "shrink from death" on the cross. Now, in light of your irrepressible love, empower us to love you more than we fear death. Empower us to show up rather than shrink back. Empower us for overcoming the darkness in our hearts, our communities, our culture.

We will overcome, not by our muscle but by your mercy—by the sacrifice of your blood and our grateful testimonies to your glory and grace. Indeed, Jesus, may the Spirit declare the gospel so loudly in our hearts that it literally drowns out Satan's constant protestations of our guilt. Indeed, how can I—how can we—keep from singing? "Did we in our own strength confide, our striving would be losing, were not the right man on our side, the man of God's own choosing. Dost ask who that may be? Christ Jesus, it is He. Lord Sabaoth, his name, from age to age the same, and He must win the battle."

Hallelujah! Hallelujah! Hallelujah! I pray in your holy and wholly trustworthy name. Amen.

A Prayer about Children and Childlikeness

People were also bringing babies to Jesus for him to place his hands on them. When the disciples saw this, they rebuked them. But Jesus called the children to him and said, "Let the little children come to me, and do not hinder them, for the kingdom of God belongs to such as these. Truly I tell you, anyone who will not receive the kingdom of God like a little child will never enter it." (Luke 18:15–17 NIV)

Dear Jesus, there's no more important or necessary gift we can give our children than to keep on bringing them to you. Whether they're babies, teenagers, or adults themselves, it makes no difference. At every stage of life, our kids need you, Jesus.

For our children who've yet to find life in you, have mercy on them and bring them to a saving knowledge of yourself, Jesus. They don't just need to "grow up." They don't need religion. They don't need moral reform. They need the gospel of your grace. Show them how much they need you, and show them how much you love them. Keep them restless until they rest in your complete forgiveness and perfect righteousness. More than we want Harvard for our children, we want heaven.

Jesus, some of us grieve the ways we've made the gospel less than beautiful and believable to our children. Forgive us, and show yourself to be the God who is limited by nothing, including parental self-righteousness. Transcend the ways we've blown it. But also grant us humility and grace to repent, first before you and then to them. Free us to give our children the gift of our repentance.

For our children who know you but currently seem to have waning or zero interest in you, or even ambivalence or antipathy toward you, hear our cry. Restore to them the joy of your salvation. Our confidence is in our Father's promise to bring to completion the good work he's begun in each of us, but Jesus, we cannot afford to be either presumptuous or passive. Work powerfully. Work presently. Work persistently, Jesus, we ask for your name's sake. Give us patience with their doubts. Give us forbearance in their struggles. Give us grace to welcome prodigals home.

Lastly, Jesus, we ask you to restore us to the childlikeness of our early days of knowing you. Free us from childishness, indeed, but renew our hearts in childlike joy, playfulness, gratefulness, and simplicity. Our bodies and minds are getting older, but cause our hearts to dance again in the utter and matchless delights of being loved by you. I pray in your glorious name. Amen.

A Prayer about the Stewardship of Woe

Woe to me if I do not preach the gospel! (1 Cor. 9:16)

*L*oving Jesus, I know that "to woe" is to express dread, distress, and despair—an orientation toward life with which I'm quite familiar, for I've certainly done my share of "woe-ing." "Woe is me, I've got pimples before my date." "Woe is me, I got cut from the team." "Woe is me, I didn't get into my school of choice." "Woe is me, I got left off the party list." "Woe is me, I didn't get the job I really wanted." I learned how to "woe" early in life. That's why this small portion of the Word is so convicting and refreshing.

"Woe to me if I do not preach the gospel!" Make us the kind of people, like Paul, who are so taken and captured with the gospel that all of life is measured in terms of the gospel—who you are and what you're up to, Jesus.

May our joys be defined by the incalculable riches of the gospel. May our thinking be shaped by the liberating truths of the gospel. May our dreams be fueled with the wondrous future of the gospel. May our hopes be bound up with the guaranteed advancing of the gospel. May our peace be strengthened by the resurrection power of the gospel. May our choices be regulated by the kingdom priorities of the gospel. May our satisfaction be intensified by the fruit-bearing presence of the gospel. May our woes be primarily determined by how little we "get" of the gospel.

We're not all gospel preachers, in terms of gifts and calling, but every follower of Jesus is to be a consumer and conduit of the gospel of your grace and kingdom. Forgive us, Jesus, when we waste our woes by feasting on our disappointments and criticizing others. I pray in your peerless name. Amen.

A Prayer for More Freedom in Worship

Praise the LORD! Praise God in his sanctuary;
  praise him in his mighty heavens!
Praise him for his mighty deeds;
  praise him according to his excellent greatness!
Praise him with trumpet sound;
  praise him with lute and harp!
Praise him with tambourine and dance;
  praise him with strings and pipe!
Praise him with sounding cymbals;
  praise him with loud clashing cymbals!
Let everything that has breath praise the LORD! Praise the LORD!
  (Ps. 150)

Most gracious Father, it occurs to me as I meditate on this psalm that I need a much bigger heart for the purposes of your praise. I need the gospel to expand my palate, multiply my taste buds, and increase my capacity to enjoy the rich diversity of worship that is offered by your pan-cultural beloved people.

My tendency is to treat this psalm, like many parts of your Word, as though it were a buffet line from which I pick and choose the items that I personally enjoy. What's worse, I find ways to marginalize or eliminate expressions that don't fit within my bandwidth of beauty. I love harps and lyres and strings and flutes, but trumpets make me cringe as I wait for a sour note, tambourines remind me of bad theology, clashing and resounding cymbals are simply too loud and nonmelodic for me, and there's no way I'm going to dance. Father, all of this I confess as sin. My heart is just too small, too turned in on me.

Oh, how I long for the day when the work of Jesus will be complete in my heart, when I will no longer be the measure of anything and I will no longer offer a measured response to your glory and grace. I long for the day when I will find great joy in celebrating your surpassing greatness with the whole family of God, with all of restored creation, with every single breath, instrument, sound, molecule, and nanoparticle.

Your greatest praiseworthy act of power was in sending, offering, and raising Jesus from the dead for us—for me. May the limits of my worship and praise be determined only by the riches and reach of the gospel. I pray in Jesus' magnificent and merciful name. Amen.

A Prayer about
a Most Glorious Appointment

For God has not destined us for wrath, but to obtain salvation through our Lord Jesus Christ, who died for us so that whether we are awake or asleep we might live with him. Therefore encourage one another and build one another up, just as you are doing. (1 Thess. 5:9–11)

Merciful Father, there are some appointments I dread like the black plague, others I tolerate like slow traffic, a few I simply forget, and others I celebrate as the highlight of my week. But there is one appointment on the books that I'm looking forward to with mounting joy and with exponential gratitude.

In your sovereign grace and quintessential kindness, you've booked me for the day of salvation in Jesus. You have counted me among those upon whom you have set your eternal affections in Christ. You've guaranteed that come "hell or high water," I am yours, now and forever. The salvation you generated within me, and in each of your children, will be brought to completion on the day of Christ Jesus. That's an inviolate appointment that you've made and signed with the indelible grace of the gospel—the blood of the Lamb.

Jesus, I praise you for your tender mercies and measureless sacrifice. For you gladly took the appointment of wrath on the cross—sustaining the judgment we deserve, enduring the suffering for our sins, paying the penalty we owe. And you did it all so that whether we are "awake or asleep"—alive or dead—we might be with you.

That you actually want us and want us to be with you is overwhelming. Indeed, this is love, not that we loved you, but that you first loved us and gave yourself as a sacrifice of atonement and propitiation for our sins (1 John 4:10).

In light of this good news and this unbreakable appointment, please use me as a source of encouragement in the lives of my brothers and sisters. By the quickening work of the Holy Spirit, make it obvious to me who needs a call today, a note, a face-to-face visit, a word of hope, earnest prayer for very present struggles, doubts, and fears. I pray in your kind and compassionate name. Amen.

A Prayer about Why We Love Jesus

But he [Jesus] has appeared once for all at the culmination of the ages to do away with sin by the sacrifice of himself. Just as people are destined to die once, and after that to face judgment, so Christ was sacrificed once to take away the sins of many; and he will appear a second time, not to bear sin, but to bring salvation to those who are waiting for him. (Heb. 9:26–28 NIV)

Dear Jesus, there are so many convincing reasons why you are singularly worthy of being loved, praised, trusted, and served. But as I begin this day, I want to rehearse some of those many reasons out loud—for any of a number of pseudogods, wannabe gods, and demigods will be clamoring for my heart's attention and affection today. Help me, my family, and my friends to love you with focused abandon and unwavering allegiance.

Jesus, you expressly came into the world of time zones and molecules, at the "end of the ages," at the appointed time in the history of redemption, to "do away with sin"—to take away the sins of your people, which includes my sins. The price was your life of perfect obedience, including obedience to death on the cross. Never let me think or speak of your offering glibly, mindlessly, presumptuously, or with a yawn, for the implications of your sacrifice are astounding.

Of these things we can be certain: Jesus, you've exhausted the penalty of our sins. Though I'm still destined to die, I've already been delivered from judgment because of your once-and-for-all sacrifice. You've broken the power of sin. Sin's dominion has been destroyed in my life. You're the boss, and the reign of grace is secure and is expanding. And when you "appear a second time," you'll rid my being and the entire cosmos of the very presence of sin.

Jesus, there is no other Savior like you. You've borne sin and you're bringing salvation; you've borne *our* sin and you're bringing *us* salvation; you've borne *my* sin and you're bringing *me* salvation! Love you? Indeed! Wait for you? Like a much-loved bride longing for her much-anticipated wedding day. Even so, Lord Jesus, come! We pray in your matchless name. Amen.

A Prayer for Freedom from Resentment

The godless in heart harbor resentment. (Job 36:13 NIV)

Dear heavenly Father, whether it's the annoying fly interrupting my needed nap, the thoughtless words spoken by a trusted friend, the new ding in my twelve-year-old car, or the old hurt that generates fresh pain, resentment never helps; it only hurts.

To harbor resentment is nothing short of harboring a criminal, for resentment is bent on criminal activity: stealing peace, vandalizing sleep, robbing relationship, killing kindness, murdering hope, infecting the innocent with deadly toxins, to name a few of resentment's crimes. Indeed, as much energy is being wasted as oil spills into the Gulf of Mexico. There's no greater waste of energy than resentment.

But worst of all, Father, resentment is a contradiction, a blatant misrepresentation of who you are and how you relate to us in Jesus. For if anyone has a right to hold a grudge, to keep a record of wrongs done, to rehearse and remember our sins against us, it is you.

Yet you do not treat us as our sins deserve or repay us according to our iniquities. For as high as the heavens are above the earth, so great is your love for those who fear you; as far as the east is from the west, that's how far you've removed our transgressions from us. You're the Father who has compassion on us as your children (Ps. 103:10–13). You show us neither vexation of spirit nor exasperation of heart, so great is your love for us in Jesus.

So Father, by the love that sent Jesus to the cross and by the power that raised him from the dead, continue to heal and change me. I don't want to be godless in heart but want to be grace-full in heart. I want to be free even from resenting other people's resentment. I pray in Jesus' wonderful and merciful name. Amen.

A Prayer about the Essence
of Eternal Life

And this is eternal life, that they know you the only true God, and Jesus
Christ whom you have sent. (John 17:3)

Jesus, meditating on this passage this morning has been like revisiting
an old friend, for I can remember the first time I memorized this verse
and you began writing it upon my heart. That was over forty years ago,
yet I feel like I'm just beginning to understand the true wonder of eternal
life—the life that is ours, that is mine, only because of who you are and
what you've accomplished for us. As you first uttered these words in a
prayer for your disciples, I find great joy in knowing that you continue to
pray them for us—for me.

How I praise you that eternal life is so much more than simply living
forever in your presence, though I so look forward to that. It's about knowing, in the most intimate sense imaginable, God as my Father and knowing
you, the "sent one," the Messiah, our Lord, my Savior, our righteousness,
my bridegroom. It's not merely knowing about you, though there is so
much more I do want to know about you, but knowing you now, better
and better and better.

Holy Spirit, I cannot know God better apart from your work. So my
prayer is simple: keep me hungry for the knowledge of God. Don't let
lesser breads satisfy this craving. Don't let lesser waters slake this thirst.
Keep revealing more and more of Jesus to me. Humble me with his glory.
Astonish me with his beauty. Mesmerize me with his mercy. Buckle my
knees with his affections. Change me by his grace. Free me for his purposes. For indeed, "the people who know their God shall stand firm and
take action" (Dan. 11:32). I pray in Jesus' all-consuming name. Amen.

A Prayer about Being
Too Easily Annoyed

Fools show their annoyance at once, but the prudent overlook an insult.
(Prov. 12:16 NIV)

Jesus, of all the prayerworthy things I can think of, "annoyance" has never made it onto my supplication list until now. Through the pastoral pestering of your Spirit, I see and grieve that I'm too easily annoyed. Have mercy on me, Prince of Peace. Free my foolish, fretful, fitful spirit. How can I possibly reveal the magnificence of the gospel when I'm showcasing the arrogance of my annoyance?

I'm annoyed by the guy who races me when two lanes are becoming one. I'm annoyed when the bar code reading machines in the self-checkout lanes can't read my items. I'm annoyed when the gas pump trickles way too slowly. I'm annoyed by waiters who fish for a bigger tip. I'm annoyed by fish that won't bite. I'm annoyed by humidity when I want to jog.

I'm annoyed by low talkers and loud talkers. I'm annoyed at people easily annoyed. I'm annoyed when there's not enough milk for a late-night bowl of cereal. I'm annoyed when I have to repeat myself. I'm annoyed at whiners, so much that I start whining. I'm annoyed at people preening in front of mirrors at the YMCA, as though I never peek. I'm annoyed when people use way too many words and way too big of words to say something way simple, as though that's not me.

I'm annoyed at ever having to wait in line for anything. I'm annoyed by the color orange. I'm annoyed at any box that has the words "requires some assembly" written on it. Oh, Jesus, if only those were the only things that annoyed me!

My prayer? Gentle my heart with your kindness and grace. Grant me much quicker repentances. Help me to slow . . . way . . . down. Help me to live in the moment and not simply live to get somewhere on time or get something done. Let me see people with your eyes and respond to them with your heart. There are no ordinary people around me. Everybody matters. Everybody has stories of heartache, foolishness, fear, and longing, just like me. Jesus, thank you that you died for all of my sins, including my "annoyability." I love being loved by you. I have no greater hope than knowing one day I will love like you love. I pray in your gracious and patient name. Amen.

A Prayer about Watermelon and Other Gifts

Every good and perfect gift is from above, coming down from the Father of the heavenly lights, who does not change like shifting shadows. He chose to give us birth through the word of truth, that we might be a kind of firstfruits of all he created. (James 1:17–18 NIV)

Heavenly Father, I awake today a grateful man, and I want to live that way all day long. Now, I'm sure that attitude will be challenged by life in this broken world and by the heart that beats in this broken man. But as someone who has every reason to overflow with thanksgiving, here are a few of your gifts for which I give you praise this morning.

First and foremost, I praise you for being the changeless Father of heavenly lights, as opposed to being the impetuous god of shifting shadows. I cannot predict you. I cannot control you. I cannot presume on your ways. But I can completely trust you to be impassible (without mood swings), yet passionately good and faithful. I know this through Jesus, who is the same "yesterday and today and forever" (Heb. 13:8).

I'm also thankful that twice you've chosen to give me birth. I can claim responsibility for neither the first time I breathed in oxygen nor the second time you breathed the life of Jesus into my spirit, giving me the new birth.

And I'm also thankful for all kinds of gifts you bestow—perfect ones and otherwise. Most recently, I'd include these: the watermelon I ate yesterday that was sweeter, crunchier, and more refreshing than any I've ever tasted in my life; the dancing bend of my pole and the tug-of-war the big red snapper gave me a couple of weeks back; the call from a friend that came at the perfect time with the perfect life-giving rebuke; the color blue with its many hues; the understanding look my wife gave me yesterday; the assurance that you will finish making me like Jesus one day; and the hope (many hopes) of the new heaven and new earth.

Father, these are just a few of the many, many gifts that come down from you all the time. What do I have that I have not received from you? Nothing. What gift have you given me that you don't intend me to enjoy? None. How can I live as a "kind of firstfruits of all you've created"? Show me! I pray in Jesus' most glorious name. Amen.

A Prayer about Marriage to Jesus

As a bridegroom rejoices over his bride,
so will your God rejoice over you. (Isa. 62:5 NIV)

Then I heard what seemed to be the voice of a great multitude, like the roar
of many waters and like the sound of mighty peals of thunder, crying out:
"Hallelujah! For the Lord our God the Almighty reigns. Let us rejoice and
exult and give him the glory, for the marriage of the Lamb has come, and
his Bride has made herself ready." (Rev. 19:6–7)

Dear Jesus, today as every day, I need the gospel, and I need the power of the gospel *even to believe the gospel.* For sometimes the Good News seems just too good to be true. So I pray for grasping power today—power to grasp the multidimensional love that is ours in you, a love that surpasses knowledge but will never diminish through eternity (Eph. 3:14–21).

Jesus, you are the bridegroom who rejoices over your bride. You're not just committed to us; you're not just faithful to us; you're not just a great provider; you actually love and enjoy us. You're glad to be married to us. You have no doubts or regrets. You haven't discovered something recently that makes you wonder what you were thinking when you chose us. You're not bored with us. You were never just infatuated with us. You don't look longingly at some other spouse and think, "If only . . ."

If your great affection for us wasn't written down so clearly in your Word, I'd never believe it was true or even possible. Continue to free me from my unbelief and under-belief.

As I meditate on John's startling vision of our wedding day, I totally understand the thunderous sounds of heaven extolling the wonder of it all. Where can a greater reason for unfettered rejoicing be found? What other hope could possibly generate such unabated gladness? Come, Holy Spirit, come and stun my heart afresh with this good and true news! Renew, refresh, restore to me and my friends the joy of this glorious salvation!

Jesus, I'm ready for that day for only one reason: you died to make us yours. We wear the wedding garments of your grace—your perfect righteousness freely given to us because of your costly sacrifice for us. That is our only hope and our only boast. May your marriage to us and great love for us profoundly alter and affect every other relationship in which you've placed us—every one of them, I pray in your glorious name. Amen.

A Prayer about Accepting One Another

Accept one another, then, just as Christ accepted you, in order to bring
praise to God. (Rom. 15:7 NIV)

Dear Jesus, it's both settling and centering to begin this day with the assurance of your acceptance. You know everything about me, and still I'm fully and eternally accepted by God in you. You know my failures, fickleness, foolishness, faithlessness . . . and yet you totally accept me. When I confess my sins, I don't inform you of anything you don't already know. In fact, I'm probably aware of only 3 or 4 percent of my actual sins. It's absolutely overwhelming to be this known and this accepted by you.

I'm the immature younger brother you welcomed home. I'm the self-righteous elder brother you constantly pursue. I'm the one lying at your feet whom others would stone, but you have loved. I've been up in the tree with Zacchaeus and down in the depths with Peter, and you have accepted me.

But here comes the difficult part, Jesus. As you've accepted me, you're calling me to accept others. I'll need all the grace you promise to love like that, for there are a lot of my brothers and sisters in Christ with whom I disagree about many things, including theology, politics, dress, issues of Christian liberty, how to spend money, worship styles, what to do on Sunday, educating children, drinking alcohol, entertainment . . . and that's just for starters.

Jesus, I need a bigger gospel heart and more gospel wisdom if I'm going to make headway in this calling. Please help me show kindness without compromising my convictions. Please teach me the difference between essential and nonessential matters. Please show me the difference between acceptance and acquiescence. Please free me from the limitations of my perspective, the prejudices of my heritage, and the insecurities of my comfort zone. Please free me from insincere niceness and the need to be right.

Let me remember that your promise to bring to completion the good work you began in me also applies to each of your children. Burn the conviction indelibly into my heart: it brings *you* praise when I work hard at accepting others as you accept me. I pray in your matchless and merciful name. Amen.

A Prayer about Satan's Main Strategy

I hope you will put up with me in a little foolishness. Yes, please put up with me! I am jealous for you with a godly jealousy. I promised you to one husband, to Christ, so that I might present you as a pure virgin to him. But I am afraid that just as Eve was deceived by the serpent's cunning, your minds may somehow be led astray from your sincere and pure devotion to Christ. (2 Cor. 11:1–3 NIV)

Gracious Lord Jesus, as I pray my way through this Scripture this morning, two things stand out with flashing neon brilliance. First of all, we already belong to you as a washed, cherished, and betrothed bride. This is our defining identity as your church—your called-out, beloved people. Our organization doesn't define us. Our work doesn't define us. Our ministries don't define us. Your relationship with us and your love for us define us.

We are the people upon whom you have set your heart, for whom you gave your life, and to whom you are returning as a great bridegroom. There's no other relationship that comes close to offering the peace and hope as your relationship with us—no other.

This underscores the second thing that stands out in this Scripture: the intensity of Satan's hatred for the "first thing"—your great love for us, bridegroom to bride. He'll do anything possible to lead us astray from our sincere and pure devotion to you.

Satan hates your love for us. Satan hates our love for you. He'll let us be anything other than a church filled with deep affection and devotion to you. Whether overtly through condemnation and persecution or covertly through seduction and prosperity, his strategy is the same—to steal our hearts away from you.

Jesus, he will not succeed, for you have crushed his head and you have won our hearts forever. But send your Spirit with fresh convicting and invigorating power. Wake us from our slumber. Restore to us the bridal affections we had for you at first. Rekindle the fire and passion we experienced when it first dawned upon us that you chose us to be your bride.

We are counted as pure virgins only because you have clothed our nakedness and sin with your blood and righteousness. We are devoted to you, Jesus, only because of your love and devotion to us. Fill our hearts and churches with the sights and sounds of the great wedding feast to come. We make our prayer in your most loving name. Amen.

A Prayer about Consummate Freedom

It is for freedom that Christ has set us free. Stand firm, then, and do not let yourselves be burdened again by a yoke of slavery. (Gal. 5:1 NIV)

Dear Jesus, it's the Fourth of July—a holiday set aside to remember and revel in the freedom we enjoy as citizens of America. Two things immediately come to mind as I think of the Fourth. I thank you for our country, as broken as she is, and for the liberties and privileges I have as a citizen of the United States. And I thank you that I escaped childhood with all my fingers, given how many fireworks I abused on and around this holiday!

But that for which I'm most grateful as I think of the Fourth is the consummate freedom I enjoy as a citizen of heaven—as a member of the "chosen people, a royal priesthood, a holy nation, God's special possession, that you may declare the praises of him who called you out of darkness into his wonderful light" (1 Pet. 2:9 NIV).

To be set free by you, Jesus, is to be free indeed (John 8:36). I will certainly enjoy the pageantry, food, and fun of the Fourth of July this week. But I will resolutely stand firm, for the rest of my life, in the freedom for which you have set us free.

I praise you, Jesus, that I am free from the guilt of my sin, for you took my place on the cross, exhausting the judgment I deserve. I praise you for freedom over the power of sin, for you have broken its dominion in my life. I praise you for freedom from the fear of death, for you removed its sting and robbed the grave of its victory.

I praise you that I can now obey God from my heart, and not out of pride, pragmatics, or pretense. I praise you for the freedom to come boldly to the throne of grace, into the very Holy of Holies, for you have secured this "new and living way" for us. I praise you for the freedom of repentance, for you have borne my shame and I don't have to pretend or pose anymore. I praise you for the freedom to risk, instead of rusting the rest of my life, for life is no longer about performance but about your praise.

Jesus, by the power of the gospel, I will seek to stand firm in these and many more freedoms you've won for us, and I will seek to resist all slaveries until the day you return to finish this magnificent "liberation suite." Hallelujah, what a Savior you are! Hallelujah, what a salvation you freely give us! I pray in your liberating and lovely name. Amen.

A Prayer about the Glory to be Revealed

I consider that our present sufferings are not worth comparing with the glory that will be revealed in us. For the creation waits in eager expectation for children of God to be revealed. For the creation was subjected to frustration, not by its own choice, but by the will of the one who subjected it, in hope that the creation itself will be liberated from its bondage to decay and brought into the freedom and glory of the children of God. (Rom. 8:18–21 NIV)

Heavenly Father, first of all, please know that I do not presume on the privilege of calling you Abba, Father. What a sacred and joyful honor. It's only because of the work of Jesus that I dare refer to you by such an intimate and comforting name. How I praise you for adopting me into your family and into your future.

Indeed, Father, I'm stunned and stirred as I think about the future you've secured for us, your beloved children, and for the whole of creation—a future that puts all suffering, decay, and bondage into perspective. Oh, that I might know more of the "eager expectation" for "glorious freedom" that marked Paul's life and groans within creation.

"Glorious freedom"—may those two words be tattooed on my heart, an irrepressible melody in my spirit, the lens through which I see all things and participate in your work in the world. Not just "freedom" but "glorious freedom"—freedom filled with your glory!

Please, Father, open the eyes of my heart wider to behold the "glory to be revealed" in us and in creation. Heal me of spiritual myopia. Get the morning gunk out of my eyes. Do gospel laser surgery so that I can behold these things more clearly, and live and love accordingly.

I don't want just to quote Paul but to join Paul in proclaiming, "I consider that the present sufferings are not worth comparing with the glory that will be revealed."

In the midst of decay, I want to be for your delight. In the frustrations of creation, let me savor the firstfruits of your salvation. Rather than being weighed down by present sufferings, I want to be hope-filled by future liberations. I pray in Jesus' strong and saving name. Amen.

A Prayer about New Heart Softness

I will sprinkle clean water on you, and you shall be clean from all your uncleanness, and from all your idols I will cleanse you. And I will give you a new heart, and a new spirit I will put within you. And I will remove the heart of stone from your flesh and give you a heart of flesh. And I will put my Spirit within you, and cause you to walk in my statutes and be careful to obey my rules. (Ezek. 36:25–27)

Gracious Father, your promise of a new heart beating within my breast shouts of your mercy and might. There are few things I need or want more, and I praise you for how much of this great new covenant promise you've already fulfilled in your children.

Already I've experienced the greatest of all sprinklings—the once and for all cleansing by the blood of Jesus. Though I'm still sucker punched by the accusing and condemning work of Satan, you've forgiven me of all of my sins: past, present, and future; sins of word, thought, and deed. May this grand affirmation never fall glibly from my lips. May this good news never be blasé or cliché to me.

Father, you've already declared your children to be perfectly righteous in your sight forever—a status that makes me yearn for the complete healing of my yet-to-be perfected heart. How I long for the day when my heart will beat only for Jesus' glory, be enamored of his beauty, feel with his passion, think with his wisdom, and love with his affection.

Indeed, that's what I'm most earnestly desiring today. By the work of your indwelling Spirit, change my heart, Father. The image of a heart of stone being replaced with a heart of flesh is no mere metaphor to me; it's a gospel miracle. I want a kind heart, a tender heart, a sweet heart, a compassionate heart, a caring heart, a servant's heart, a soft heart—the heart of Jesus.

I long to be more restful and less resentful, more merciful and less mercenary, quicker to listen than to speak, quicker to be flexible than rigid, more likely to be consoling than controlling, more often saying yes than no.

I want to forgive from my heart and not just avoid the pain of conflict. I want to encourage people for their good, not flatter them for my benefit. I want to see what you see in others and not obsess over what I want for others. I want to feel joy and hope every time I hear your name and not feel rejection and self-pity when I don't hear my name. Like John the Baptist, I want Jesus to increase and me to decrease.

I praise you, Father, for promising just such a heart through the resources of the gospel. My longings, hopes, and prayers are not in vain. I pray with fresh gratitude, in Jesus' matchless name. Amen.

A Prayer of Thanks
for Long-Standing Friends

For I have derived much joy and comfort from your love, my brother, because the hearts of the saints have been refreshed through you. (Philem. 1:7)

Two are better than one, because they have a good reward for their toil. For if they fall, one will lift up his fellow. But woe to him who is alone when he falls and has not another to lift him up! Again, if two lie together, they keep warm, but how can one keep warm alone? And though a man might prevail against one who is alone, two will withstand him—a threefold cord is not quickly broken. (Eccles. 4:9–12)

Heavenly Father, I cannot imagine how storms can be navigated, burdens borne, and hardships handled without the company of a few good friends. I praise you today for the gift of friendship—for the joy, encouragement, and refreshment you've just given me through a special band of brothers. It could not have come at a better time.

When we walk through difficult seasons we're sometimes inclined to think, "No one can possibly understand what I'm going through; no one can begin to relate to my feelings and confusion; no one is a mess like me." Those are the times when it's easy to withdraw into isolation, fall into the pit of condemnation, and reach for some ill-chosen medication. That's when the gift of long-standing friends becomes especially precious.

Father, I praise you for the gift of hearing my friends say these two words: "Me too." I praise you for brothers who know how to "refresh the hearts of the saints"—including this saint. I praise you for friends who remind me of the truth and power of the gospel, of the love of Jesus, and of the bigger story you are always writing.

I praise you for friends who share their lives and not just their gospel. I praise you for friends who offer tears and not just their answers. I praise you for friends who give life-giving wisdom and not just mess-fixing formulas.

Father, these cherished friendships turn my heart heavenward. They simply remind me that the foundation and fountain of all good friendship is found in you. I praise you for befriending us in the gospel. It is overwhelming, settling, and centering to hear Jesus say to us, "I no longer call you servants. . . . I call you friends" (John 15:15 NIV). What wondrous love is this, indeed? "Greater love has no one than this: to lay down one's life for one's friends" (John 15:13 NIV). Hallelujah, what a salvation! Hallelujah, what a Savior! I pray in Jesus' most glorious and gracious name. Amen.

A Prayer about the Joy of Becoming Less

They came to John and said to him, "Rabbi, that man who was with you on the other side of the Jordan—the one you testified about—look, he is baptizing, and everyone is going to him." To this John replied, "A person can receive only what is given them from heaven. You yourselves can testify that I said, 'I am not the Messiah but am sent ahead of him.' The bride belongs to the bridegroom. The friend who attends the bridegroom waits and listens for him, and is full of joy when he hears the bridegroom's voice. That joy is mine, and it is now complete. He must become greater; I must become less." (John 3:26–30 NIV)

Dear Jesus, I'm not sure about a wardrobe of camel's hair clothing and a diet of locusts and wild honey (Matt. 3:4), but I am sure I want more of John the Baptist's joy—the joy of you becoming greater while I become less. Indeed, John leaped for joy at the very thought of you even before he was born (Luke 1:39–41). Could you, would you do the same in my heart?

Jesus, when I try to imagine this kind of joy and freedom, I get really excited . . . and a bit quiet. What would it be like to have a joy largely defined by people making much about you—so much, in fact, that I wouldn't really notice them not making much about me? That would bring greater freedom from the insecurities of my pride and from my desire for the approval of others.

Jesus, what would it be like to want your name to be loved and vindicated a zillion times over mine? What would it be like to wait and listen for your voice a whole lot more than impatiently clamoring for my voice to be heard? That would bring more freedom from my need to be understood and to be in control of my reputation.

Jesus, what would it be like to experience greater grief when people don't "get" you than when they don't "get" me? What would it be like to say with John, "A person can receive only what is given them from heaven" (John 3:27 NIV) and really, really mean it—to accept the giving and the taking away in life equally as sovereign appointments from your throne of grace? That would bring freedom to love and serve you no matter what.

Jesus, most kind and beautiful bridegroom, bring more of this joy and freedom to my expectant heart. I pray in your priceless and peerless name. Amen.

A Prayer about Jesus' Shameless Love for Us

For he who sanctifies and those who are sanctified all have one source. That is why he is not ashamed to call them brothers, saying, "I will tell of your name to my brothers; in the midst of the congregation I will sing your praise." And again, "I will put my trust in him." And again, "Behold, I and the children God has given me." (Heb. 2:11–13)

Dear Lord Jesus, I've thought, said, and done a lot of things about which I am truly ashamed. I've been painfully shamed, and I've inexcusably shamed people I dearly love. Shame is a pillaging thief, one that robs us of dignity, freedom, and joy. So when I hear you say you're not ashamed of us—that you're not ashamed to call me your brother—it humbles and gladdens me like nothing else.

Indeed, Jesus, you're the only one who can break the binding power of our shame because you have completely broken the condemning power of our guilt. How we praise you for doing everything necessary to deal with the ways we've been both agents and victims of sin—sin that has led to multiple layers of shame.

We freely cry, "Abba, Father," because you first cried out, "My God, my God, why have you forsaken me?" (Mark 15:34). You took all the guilt and all the shame of our sin on the cross. I really do believe this. I really want to experience it more fully.

Because God has placed us in you, we are now "of the same family." What more could we possibly want in this life and the life to come? And you're the only one who can make us holy, for you are our wisdom from God—that is, our righteousness, our holiness, and our redemption (1 Cor. 1:30). What peace, what transcendent and everlasting peace this brings to our hearts.

Jesus, now you constantly sing to us of the Father's love—you declare his praises to our hearts every time we hear the gospel; every time we gather with our brothers and sisters to worship the Triune God; every time we take the bread and cup of holy communion; every time we read the Scriptures; every time we listen to your voice in creation proclaiming the majesty and mercy of God.

Jesus, you're not ashamed of us—you're not ashamed of me. This is the theology I passionately defend. Make it the doxology in which I fully delight. I pray with joy, in your most holy and compassionate name. Amen.

A Prayer for Regaining Perspective

When my heart was grieved
and my spirit embittered,
I was senseless and ignorant;
I was a brute beast before you.
Yet I am always with you;
you hold me by my right hand.
You guide me with your counsel,
and afterward you will take me into glory.
Whom have I in heaven but you?
And earth has nothing I desire besides you.
My flesh and my heart may fail,
but God is the strength of my heart
and my portion forever. (Ps. 73:21–26 NIV)

Gracious Father, the older I've gotten, the more I've come to appreciate the many characters and voices you've recorded for us in your Word. There's no moment or scenario I'll experience in life that you haven't anticipated. Such is the reach and riches of the Scriptures. Today I praise you for writing into Israel's hymnal a song for the bitter and the beastly.

There are times when I forget that I'm living in a fallen world, with a fragile heart, among people just as foolish as me. When my fellowship with you gets broken, I'm capable of acting out in very harmful ways. I lose perspective and love poorly. My expectations of you and of others become more connected to la-la land than to reality. I become just like the psalmist Asaph—an envious, angry, senseless mess.

That you tolerate me in those times of disconnect is extraordinary. That you still treasure me when I lose touch with gospel sanity is astonishing. When I shake my fist at you, your grasp of grace is all the tighter. When I complain about a stony silent heaven, you're actively, quietly guiding my every footstep. When I try to ignore, spite, or run away from you, you're just as resolved to end my journey in the full presence of your glory. The gospel really is this big and this good.

Such love melts my icy heart. Continue the thaw. I'm not just the biggest loser when I pitch my tent in the land of disconnected heart. I'm also a thief, robbing a lot of people who are dear to me. Rescue me from my self-centeredness and demandingness. Amen.

A Prayer about Revealing Jesus in the Hard Times

But we have this treasure in jars of clay, to show that the surpassing power belongs to God and not to us. We are afflicted in every way, but not crushed; perplexed, but not driven to despair; persecuted, but not forsaken; struck down, but not destroyed; always carrying in the body the death of Jesus, so that the life of Jesus may also be manifested in our bodies.

(2 Cor. 4:7–10)

Dear Jesus, to compare my season of stress with the apostle Paul's would be like comparing my guitar playing with Phil Keaggy's, or my photography with Ansel Adams's, or my cooking with Bobby Flay's. There is simply no comparison. When I consider everything he experienced as your servant, honestly, I have nothing to bemoan or groan about.

Nonetheless, Paul's honesty is a great gift to me this morning. His freedom to acknowledge both his anguish and his joy in the same paragraph gives me tremendous encouragement and focus. Posing and pretending were crucified at Calvary. Despair and hopelessness were sabotaged by your resurrection.

Jesus, help me to be far more preoccupied with the treasure within than with the pressures without. If your all-surpassing power will be shown most dramatically through my weakness, I surrender to your will. If your incomparable beauty will be most clearly revealed through my hardships, I surrender to your ways. If your redeeming purposes will be most fully realized through my brokenness, I surrender to you.

With my palms up, I offer you praise for the treasure of the gospel. The gospel will win the day, my heart, the nations, and the cosmos. Though there are seasons when throwing in the towel, finding another story, or just flat running away are incredibly attractive, where else would I go but to you? You alone give the words of life, the sufficient grace, and the hope of glory. May your voice be ten times louder than the murmurings around me and the grumblings inside me.

Jesus, in the coming hours and days and weeks, prove the wonders of your love in our midst. I pray with hungry expectancy, in your powerful name. Amen.

A Prayer of Hope
in God's Unfailing Love

The king is not saved by his great army;
  a warrior is not delivered by his great strength.
The war horse is a false hope for salvation,
  and by its great might it cannot rescue.
Behold, the eye of the Lord is on those who fear him,
  on those who hope in his steadfast love. (Ps. 33:16–18)

Dear Jesus, though it's not fun, it is a good thing to come to the end of ourselves—to be in situations where all of our resources, all of our strength, all of our wisdom are simply not enough. Indeed, it is a gospel thing to feel the pain of realizing that whatever worked in the past is not working in the present moment; to feel the confusion of not knowing what to do next; to feel the helplessness of being out of control.

For only in those times do we fully abandon ourselves to the God who alone can part Red Seas; overthrow whole Midianite armies with three hundred gunless soldiers; take down Goliaths with a pebble; feed multitudes with a few fish and pieces of bread; raise a dead man for the salvation of his people and the transformation of the cosmos.

Jesus, we abandon ourselves to you today, for you are that dead man who now lives. You are the One who is redeeming his bride and making all things new. It is your unfailing love that we can and must hope in. There is no other supply sufficient to the need. There is no other strength sufficient for the task. There is no other balm sufficient for the pain. There is no other rest sufficient for the exhaustion. There is no other hope sufficient for the crisis.

We bring our broken hearts to you. We bring our struggling marriages to you. We bring our divided churches to you. We bring our conflicted relationships to you. We bring our wayward children to you. We bring our unbelieving friends to you. We bring the needs of our community to you. We bring it all to you, Jesus. We will trust in you and your unfailing love. Astonish us by bringing much glory to yourself. We pray in your merciful and mighty name. Amen.

A Prayer about a Heavy-Laden Heart

Come to me, all who labor and are heavy laden, and I will give you rest.
Take my yoke upon you, and learn from me, for I am gentle and lowly in
heart, and you will find rest for your souls. For my yoke is easy, and my
burden is light. (Matt. 11:28–30)

Most gracious Jesus, I'm lacing up my running shoes this morning to come to you as fast as I can. Your gentle, lowly heart is simply irresistible to me. Your easy yoke and light burden beckon me, and I will gladly shoulder up. Your promise of soul rest has never been more timely or needed, for I am restless as I begin this day. Thank you for being so welcoming, understanding, and kind.

The burden and confusion I'm feeling are clearly connected to old wounds with lingering pain. Sometimes fresh hurts become like a magnifying glass or a megaphone by which you remind us of unfinished business in our souls. Like a broken bone that wasn't set properly, broken hearts that weren't healed the first time are susceptible to new pain.

Jesus, I need you. Flood my heart with your presence. Kiss my soul with the assurance that you are enough. Confirm the promise that we can—that I can—do all things through you as you give us strength. Give me the sufficient grace you have pledged.

Be the great Warrior of our hearts as you rebuke the devil on our behalf. Don't let the dark one seize this current situation for spewing his toxins. I don't have a thousand tongues to praise you, but let my one tongue speak with the wisdom of the gospel, rather than wag with the poison of gossip.

As the day unfolds, help me separate the issues at hand. I need wisdom to deal with the pressing concerns right before me. I cannot afford to drag the stockpile of old pain into this day. If I do that, I will get defensive and will be on the offensive. As usual, this isn't about me, but about your glory.

Jesus, help me walk today as a man of faith, hope, and love with the people I greatly care about. Give us the wisdom and power you promise. Bring much glory to yourself. Write stories of repentance and restoration by the grace and truth of the gospel. I pray in your most worthy and gracious name. Amen.

A Prayer for Strength in the Face of Temptation

I can do all things through him who strengthens me. (Phil. 4:13)

Jesus, this verse has been underlined in my Bible, pasted on my refrigerator, even stitched in needlepoint by my grandmother. But today I need to believe this promise and see your faithfulness at work. I'm desperate for the strength you alone can give, Jesus. There are powerful temptations blasting away at my heart relentlessly. You've promised that I will never be in any circumstance that will not also find you providing a way of escape. Show me the way, dear Jesus.

There are people who have more functional power over my heart than you, Jesus. That's *my* issue, not theirs. Their praise can "complete me," and their rejection can ruin a perfectly good day or week. Give me your strength to take back my heart from the influence of such people. I cannot love anyone to whom I have given such idolatrous power.

There are people in my life who are choosing to live very destructively. Marriages, health, and your glory are on the line. I need strength, Jesus, to get involved where, frankly, I'd rather not. It would be much easier just to "pray from afar" than to run after a prodigal or two. Strengthen me so that I will not wimp out. You pursued me, and you pursue me still. Be such a persistent lover through me in these messy situations.

Lastly, Jesus, I need strength even to seek you, and I am embarrassed to confess it. Lately it's much easier to watch TV than to read the Scriptures. It's a higher priority to exercise my body for vanity than my heart for godliness. I gossip quicker than pray. I make all kinds of excuses why I am not in rich fellowship with my brothers and sisters in Jesus. The truth is, I have a lazy heart, exhausted from lesser things. Give me strength to return to my first love, Jesus, for you alone are worthy of my heart's affection, adoration, and allegiance. I pray in your gracious name. Amen.

A Prayer about My Whining

Why do you complain, Jacob?
    Why do you say, Israel,
"My way is hidden from the LORD;
    my cause is disregarded by my God"?
Do you not know?
    Have you not heard?
The LORD is the everlasting God,
    the Creator of the ends of the earth.
He will not grow tired or weary,
    and his understanding no one can fathom.
He gives strength to the weary
    and increases the power of the weak. (Isa. 40:27–29 NIV)

Gracious Father, I remember my parents' "get over it" body language when I would whine as a child. I forgave them once I became a parent. Nobody likes to be on the other end of a whine.

Today I find great delight in knowing that I am your child, but you will never be disgusted with me. You will never roll your eyes at me. You will never slam a door in my face. You will never be irritated with me or shame me. The only look you give me reminds me of your welcoming heart. Though you find no pleasure in my whining, you find great pleasure in your Son. And because you have hidden my life in Jesus, you find great delight and pleasure in me.

Though it presently *feels* as though heaven isn't paying attention to some very important things in my heart and story, I hear you say to me in the gospel, "Come to me, all of you who are weary and burdened, and you will find rest, because I will give you rest."

Jesus, you took the ultimate abandonment of the cross that I might be assured I will never be disregarded or abandoned. Though I'm tired and weary, you're not. Though you may not answer me the way I want you to answer, you promise to give me all the power and strength I need for my present weakness. Turn my whining into worship this day, O gracious and ever-present Lord. I pray in your loving name. Amen.

A Prayer about Being Overtaken by Gladness and Joy

Those the LORD has rescued will return.
They will enter Zion with singing;
everlasting joy will crown their heads.
Gladness and joy will overtake them,
and sorrow and sighing will flee away.
"I, even I, am he who comforts you." (Isa. 51:11–12 NIV)

Father, words cannot capture my gratitude for the hope these promises bring today. I believe your Word, but free me even more from the unbelief that dogs and dulls my heart. As this day begins, I choose to remember I've *already* been ransomed, redeemed, purchased by Jesus for you. I was bought out of sin, condemnation, and death and brought into your eternal embrace. Thankfully, I'm no longer my own. I'm yours, and you love me because you love me . . . period.

All captivities—the ones I've generated and those brought upon me by others—all of them are broken in Jesus. No imprisonment, no bondage, no stronghold will keep me from arriving safely home in the New Jerusalem.

Jesus, you are my Jubilee, my eternal year of the Lord's favor. I will enjoy this freedom more fully when the new heaven and new earth arrives, but I am already fully and eternally accepted in you. The saints in heaven are more happy than I am, but they're not more secure. This standing in grace is just a preview of coming attractions. You are so generous and faithful.

What will it be like when we're crowned with everlasting joy? What will it sound like when my voice blends in with the entire family of God as we enter the New Jerusalem together? I know what it feels like to be overtaken by guilt and shame, but what will it be like to be overtaken by gladness and joy? Jesus, bring the blessed day when all sorrow and sighing will flee away forever.

Indeed, Jesus, you comfort us like no one else. Forgive me for seeking my comfort from anyone or anything else. Give me enough comfort in the gospel today that I might freely share with others the very comfort I find in you. I pray in Jesus' merciful name. Amen.

211

A Prayer for the Discouraged

> As a deer pants for flowing streams,
>   so pants my soul for you, O God.
> My soul thirsts for God,
>   for the living God.
> When shall I come and appear before God?
> My tears have been my food
>   day and night,
> while they say to me continually,
>   "Where is your God?" (Ps. 42:1–3)

Gracious Father, your Word gives voice to every season, circumstance, and emotion we experience in the journey to gospel wholeness. In our joy and in our despair, and in everything in between, you are with us and you are for us.

You don't love us more when we have a dancing heart. You don't love us less when we have a doubting heart. Indeed, with kindness you drew us, and with an everlasting, unwavering love, you hold us.

Today I bring my discouraged, weary heart to you, and I bring some of my deeply hurting friends with me. Lord, sometimes it feels like life is just too much: the hard providences, the difficult people, the aches and pains of this tent I live in called "my body," cars and plumbing that break down, friends who bury their wives way too early, children who seem allergic to the gospel, mounting bills and decreasing resources, and a world and even family members who say, "Where is your God in all this?"

Tears in my coffee, in my beer, on my sandwiches, in my cereal, and dry tears when there is no heart water left. Lord Jesus, you know what this is like, you better than anyone else. For you took the ultimate combination of assaults, somersaults, and insults on the cross, for me and my friends. Your cry, "My God, my God, why have you forsaken me?" (Matt. 27:46) assures me I will never be forsaken—*never*, even when life mocks my assurance. It's your thirst on the cross that assures me that my thirst is only fleeting, though at times it feels fatal. Indeed, as I pant for you, Jesus, you are running to me with the living water of the gospel. Thank you on behalf of myself and that of my very thirsty friends. I pray in your faithful and tender name. Amen.

A Prayer for Taking Off Graveclothes

Jesus called in a loud voice, "Lazarus, come out!" The dead man came out, his hands and feet wrapped with strips of linen, and a cloth around his face. Jesus said to them, "Take off the grave clothes and let him go."
(John 11:43–44 NIV)

Dear Jesus, as surely as you spoke and Lazarus walked out of his tomb fully alive, so when you spoke the gospel to my heart, I too was raised from the dead and was made fully alive in you! With all of my brothers and sisters in Christ, I have passed from death to life. For the sovereign grace and the resurrection power of the gospel, I praise you today. Indeed, salvation is of the Lord!

Yet as surely as Lazarus needed to be freed from his graveclothes, so do I. The smell and signs of death still haunt me and stalk me. There are many areas of my life for which I long for greater freedom.

Jesus, I want greater freedom from living for people's approval. I want to be able to respond to trying situations and people with grace and wisdom rather than reacting with irritation and fear. I want freedom to value and see in others what you value and see in them. I want to be quicker to pray and slower to worry.

I want indifference to be replaced with good listening. I want passivity to be replaced with passion. I want to be free from the toxic shame that often paralyzes my heart. I want to know what stuff from my past still needs to be dealt with and what stuff simply needs to be left till the day of final resurrection. I want to be much bolder in sharing the gospel and much slower to share gossip.

I want to be able to sit still longer and laugh louder. I want to age gracefully, not regret-fully. I want to stay more fully alive to the only love that will never let me go—your love, Lord Jesus, the only love that is better than life. You've made me alive in you, Jesus; make me much, much freer, all for your glory. I pray in your priceless name. Amen.

A Prayer of Assured Triumph

The God of peace will soon crush Satan under your feet. The grace of our
Lord Jesus Christ be with you. (Rom. 16:20)

O Father, this promise holds so much hope and timely encouragement for me. Though not always readily apparent to our eyes, the
crushing defeat Satan was given under the feet of Jesus is being applied to
all the chaos and evil that threatens our peace, joy, and sanity. We will live
to see the day of Jesus' triumph over evil played out under our very feet!
Though at times it feels like we are being walked on by a gloating devil, it
is he who is actually getting ready to know our dancing feet on his head.
And according to your Word, this will happen "soon"! Lord, our weary
yet joyful cry is, "Make soon, *real* soon!"

Jesus, the reason you came into this world was to destroy him who
holds the power of death (that is, the devil) and free those who all their
lives were held in slavery by their fear of death. Indeed, you have come
to destroy the devil and all his works. You faithfully and fully fulfilled the
first gospel promise: indeed, your "bruised heel" on the cross secured the
"crushed head" of the serpent (Gen. 3:15). Our foe is defeated and waiting
to be utterly destroyed. His present flurry of fury is actually a sign he knows
his time is short. Lord, our weary yet joyful cry is, "Make short, *real* short!"

O God of peace, grant us your peace that passes all understanding when
the battle rages most fiercely and the schemes of Satan seem to be winning
the day. O triumphant Lord Jesus, we boldly ask not just for surviving
grace but for thriving grace, until the day you return to finish making all
things new. I pray in Jesus' triumphant name. Amen.

A Prayer for Repentance, Refreshment, and Restoration

Repent therefore, and turn again, that your sins may be blotted out, that times of refreshing may come from the presence of the Lord, and that he may send the Christ appointed for you, Jesus, whom heaven must receive until the time for restoring all the things about which God spoke by the mouth of his holy prophets long ago. (Acts 3:19–21)

Dear Jesus, we continue in the Christian life the same way we began this journey with you—through repentant faith leading to times of refreshing, leading to more repentant faith and more times of refreshing. This cycle of repentance and refreshment will only be finished when you return to restore everything broken and make all things new, in us and in this world. Therefore, we cry out collectively, "Hasten that day, Lord Jesus! Hasten that glad and glorious day!"

Until then, deepen our repentance and multiply our times of refreshment. Why would we have it any other way? Who of us could improve upon such a glorious gospel state of affairs? How many different ways do you have to say it, Jesus? How often do we need to hear it? You resist the proud but give grace to the humble. Seriously, who wants to try to resist you? Who doesn't want more grace? Who would prefer times of self-righteousness over times of refreshing?

Jesus, by your life and by your cross, you've clearly shown us that the way up is down. You have never sinned, but you humbled yourself and became sin for us at Calvary. We have never been righteous, though we have pretended to be. In fact, all of our so-called righteousness is like filthy rags, yet we have been declared righteous in you. How can this good news not move us to a greater humility, softer hearts, and quicker repentances?

We "get" the gospel the best when we are face down and palms up before you in repentant faith—not in groveling despair, nor in face-saving penance, but in the beauty of repentant faith. Forgive us when we make excuses, offer explanations, shift the blame, or try to dodge the convicting work of your Spirit. All such madness simply demonstrates the insanity of sin. You promise times of refreshing. Why are we so afraid to repent? Why am I so slow to repent?

As I begin this day, Jesus, please show me the ways I love poorly. May your kindness lead me to repentant faith all day long. I pray in your tender and tenacious name. Amen.

A Prayer about the Greening of Our Hearts

Will you not revive us again,
    that your people may rejoice in you?
Show us your unfailing love, LORD,
    and grant us your salvation. (Ps. 85:6–7 NIV)

Dear Lord Jesus, it's amazing what one really good rain can do to transform my brown, crispy yard into a garden of fresh, green life. I begin this day grateful for the showers of the last couple of days. I can run my sprinkler endlessly, but there's just something about the water that falls from the sky that brings restoration and renewal like nothing else.

Jesus, our hearts are no different. When we grow brown and crispy on the inside—when our rejoicing in you is displaced with complaining about you (and others and anything), when our delighting in you fades into detachment from you (and from others, and eventually from our own heart), when our love for you atrophies into fading memories of you (and then into all kinds of hideous thoughts about you)—we are powerless and shut up to your provision. There's no hose, fire hydrant, or reservoir of our own making that can even begin to make a brown heart green.

So we cry out with the Sons of Korah, "Show us your unfailing love, LORD, and grant us your salvation" (Ps. 85:7 NIV). Jesus, just as it was your unfailing love that first brought life to our deadness, so it will be your unfailing love that brings fresh green to our current brown. You have promised to "satisfy our needs in a sun-scorched land" and "strengthen our frame." You have promised that we will be "like a well-watered garden, like a spring whose waters never fail" (Isa. 58:11 NIV).

So we boldly come before you praying the promises of the gospel. You've never lied to us, Jesus, never. You suffered the ultimate thirst of the cross so that we will never thirst again. So revive us that we might rejoice in you. Restore to us the joy of your salvation, that we might offer fresh fruit, grace fruit, to our family, friends, the community, and the nations. In your verdant and vital name we pray. Amen.

A Prayer about Disconnected Hearts

But to Jonah this seemed very wrong, and he became angry. He prayed to the LORD, "Isn't this what I said, LORD, when I was still at home? That is what I tried to forestall by fleeing to Tarshish. I knew that you are a gracious and compassionate God, slow to anger and abounding in love, a God who relents from sending calamity. Now, LORD, take away my life, for it is better for me to die than to live." (Jon. 4:1–3 NIV)

Father, I used to stand in self-righteous judgment of Jonah and other believers like him who got angry and distanced themselves from you, but no longer. Like Jonah, I know the right answers, I've got Scriptures underlined in my Bible—how you're a "gracious and compassionate God . . . slow to anger and abounding in love," and all that stuff. But right now, those words hold little charm or power for me. I still believe I'll go to heaven when I die, but it's living that's got me most concerned. I've known you well enough that I don't want to disown you, but I've also known you well enough that your ways sometimes leave me feeling confused and angry.

So today I bring my disconnected heart and the hearts of some of my friends before you. Lord, help me understand; show us what happened: Where did we lose connection with you, or did we simply choose disconnection from you?

Jonah didn't want to go to Nineveh and preach. Where am I afraid of going or staying? I do know that some of my friends so want to run away from their marriages. Help them, Lord. I don't understand all the issues, but please intervene, if for no other reason than for their children. When I look at some of my friends' stories, I see new chapters of loss, reversals, trials, and heartaches being written weekly. I understand why they look at the sky and cry, "Where are you, God, in all this?"

Lord, my resources are low, so I have so little to offer them. I feel like such a hypocrite, so I simply cry out from my dryness and weakness, "Jesus, Son of God, have mercy on these I love."

And in my case, please show me in the coming hours and days what I've done with my heart. What's broken about me that I've yet to see? What is my sin in all of this? What am I afraid of that I don't want to admit?

So far, every time I have bought a one-way ticket away from your presence, it hasn't worked very well for me. I find myself saying with the disciples, "Where can we go, Jesus? You alone have the words of eternal life." Jesus, Son of God, have mercy on me, a sinner. I pray in your glorious name. Amen.

A Prayer about God's Goodness
and Nearness in the Storm

But now thus says the LORD, he who created you, O Jacob,
    he who formed you, O Israel:
"Fear not, for I have redeemed you;
    I have called you by name, you are mine.
When you pass through the waters, I will be with you;
    and through the rivers, they shall not overwhelm you;
when you walk through fire you shall not be burned,
    and the flame shall not consume you.
For I am the LORD your God,
    the Holy One of Israel, your Savior." (Isa. 43:1–3)

Heavenly Father, your Word is a balm for the broken, ballast for the bewildered, and bread for the hungry. This is not theory. It's not even just good theology. It's my reality and I praise you. You've promised to show up, and you have. Thank you for being the Father from whom all fatherhood derives its name and meaning. No god is as near as you and no god is as good, in every season and storm. The aroma of fresh gospel bread is wafting through the air.

You've created us and you are redeeming us, all for your glory. You've summoned us by name, calling us to life in the gospel. You've given us a new name, "Mine." There's no sweeter name.

Father, you don't promise we won't experience floods and torrents and fires and flames. But you do promise you will be with us. To know you are near and to know you are good is all we really need. We will go anywhere and do anything as long as we are convinced that you will never leave us, forsake us, abandon us, shame us, or reject us.

Father, we know ourselves to be precious and honored in your sight, and greatly loved, because you gave Jesus in exchange for us. Though Jesus was rich, yet for our sakes he became poor, so that through his poverty we might become rich (2 Cor. 8:9). We praise you for the one and only truly indescribable gift (2 Cor. 9:15)! And since you didn't spare your own Son, we can trust you graciously to give us everything else we need (Rom. 8:32), for every season and storm ahead. We don't have to be afraid of anything or anyone. You are with us and you are for us.

Continue to write bigger and better stories of reconciliation and restoration than we ourselves would ever choose to pen. We pray to the glory of the true Peacemaker, Jesus. Amen.

A Prayer for Gospel Sanity

> I, Nebuchadnezzar, lifted my eyes to heaven, and my reason returned to me, and I blessed the Most High, and praised and honored him who lives forever, for his dominion is an everlasting dominion, and his kingdom endures from generation to generation; all the inhabitants of the earth are accounted as nothing, and he does according to his will among the host of heaven and among the inhabitants of the earth; and none can stay his hand or say to him, "What have you done?" . . . Now I, Nebuchadnezzar, praise and extol and honor the King of heaven, for all his works are right and his ways are just; and those who walk in pride he is able to humble. (Dan. 4:34–37)

King Jesus, once again I find myself needing a vision of your sovereignty and your goodness. There are two places of insanity, or "crazy," I tend to fall into. Sometimes, like King Nebuchadnezzar, I arrogantly think I'm in control. I disregard you and act like a sovereign over a little fiefdom called "self." If I'm successful, I take the credit. If I'm not, I blame others and usually find a way to get what I want anyway. After all, I *am* the point.

Other times I act like the consummate orphan. I get afraid and panicky, and I blame you for not answering my prayers the way you're "supposed to." I fall into a navel-gazing negativity, and I trust the national news media more than I trust the good news of the gospel. Have mercy! Have mercy on *me*, King Jesus!

Indeed, help me to live more of my hours, days, weeks, and months in gospel sanity, Jesus. For it is *your* kingdom that endures from generation to generation. There has never been a time when you were not King of Kings and Lord of Lords. You're not a cheerleader, just pulling for us from afar. You're not a coach, just telling us what to do. You are the King of glory, beauty, compassion, mercy, and grace! You are the King who died for us, was raised for us, is praying for us, and is returning for us!

Right now, you are working all things together after the counsel of your will. Right now, you are working in all things for the good of those who love you, and we love you because you first loved us. Right now, you not only have the heart of every king in your hand, you have my heart in your hand. Right now, you do as you please with all the powers of heaven and the peoples of the earth, and with me. Right now, everything you do is right and just. Right now, you are the King who has made us your beloved bride. Right now, it is so awesome and comforting to be yours—an object of your affection and a subject in your kingdom! I pray in your peerless name. Amen.

A Prayer about My Fears

He placed his right hand on me and said: "Do not be afraid. I am the First and the Last. I am the Living One; I was dead, and now look, I am alive for ever and ever! And I hold the keys of death and Hades." (Rev. 1:17–18 NIV)

Jesus, it's timely, stunning, and encouraging to know the most repeated command throughout the whole Bible is "Do not be afraid." The angels spoke these words to startled shepherds at your birth, and you repeated the command to a devastated Mary on the morning of your resurrection. Now you speak these liberating words to my heart and conscience: "Do not be afraid!"

Because you are the First and the Last, Jesus, I don't have to be afraid of anything in between. You are God, and I am not. You will never say "oops" about anything in world history or in my own life. You never "try" to do anything. You never have to scratch your head in confusion. You never have to resort to plan B. You are perfectly executing your sovereign will, from naming the stars to numbering my hairs. Glory!

Because you are the Living One, who was dead and who is now alive forever, I don't have to be afraid of judgment day or this day, for your death on the cross is my judgment day and your resurrection from the dead is my assurance of being eternally and fully accepted by God. Constantly sung over me by my Father, and all my brothers and sisters in you, is the most liberating of all lyrics: "There is now and forevermore no condemnation for those who are in Christ!" Not only is there no condemnation, there is only full delight! Oh my goodness!

Jesus, because you hold the keys of death and Hades, and to everything else, I don't have to be afraid to die or to live. You have robbed the grave of its victory, you have removed the sting of death, and you have defeated the devil and all the powers of darkness! I don't have to be afraid of people. I don't have to be afraid of failing. I don't have to be afraid of getting old. Yes, yes, yes!

I know you will never leave or forsake us. I know I'm in the palm of your hand. Free me more fully from my fears that I might live more fully to the praise of your glory. I pray in your loving and powerful name. Amen.

A Prayer about a Full Harvest
and Few Workers

After this the Lord appointed seventy-two others and sent them on ahead of him, two by two, into every town and place where he himself was about to go. And he said to them, "The harvest is plentiful, but the laborers are few. Therefore pray earnestly to the Lord of the harvest to send out laborers into his harvest. Go your way; behold, I am sending you out as lambs in the midst of wolves." (Luke 10:1–3)

Dear Lord Jesus, it's really not all that complicated. All of history—every millennium, century, year, and nanosecond—is determined by your outrageously generous commitment to redeem: to "harvest" your beloved bride from every nation, tribe, people, and language. You've done everything necessary to guarantee this magnificent nuptial story will end perfectly.

You bought us with your life and death. You love us with more passion and delight than we can possibly imagine. You've secured our safe arrival in the new heaven and new earth. There's no chance the wedding feast of the Lamb will not take place. Yet even as you've determined the glorious end of all things, so you've appointed the means to that end. We're to be not just the bride in waiting but workers in the harvest—the plentiful, ripe harvest.

As the church, your greatly loved bride, we're not supposed to be hanging out in the spa reading glamour magazines and getting our nails done. We're supposed to be getting dirt under our nails as we do the hard and heart work of evangelism and missions. You send us out like lambs among wolves. It's a costly, messy, much-resisted work you've given us to do. But it's worth all the sacrifice, tears, and conflict. For you came to us as the Lamb among sinners and the Lamb for sinners. The price you paid "to have and to hold" your bride makes our most agonizing work a kingdom joy.

Jesus, gracious Lord of the harvest, send us into the harvest you've secured for yourself. What more could we possibly want for our church family? What other story would we choose for the rest of our days in this world than to be the means by which you gather your bride from the nations and prepare her for a future beyond our wildest dreams? Forgive us, focus us, and free us. We pray in your loving and triumphant name. Amen.

A Prayer about Friendly Wounding

Better is open rebuke
  than hidden love.
Faithful are the wounds of a friend;
  profuse are the kisses of an enemy. (Prov. 27:5–6)

Merciful Jesus, I need courage today for loving in sticky, broken, messy relationships. Sometimes the fear of making an even bigger mess makes it easier just to ignore certain people and issues. But that's kind of like trying to avoid a broken bone or cancer. The matter will only get worse. To say I'm conflict avoidant is a confession of sin but not an excuse.

Thank you for the stark frankness of your Word. When I multiply kisses but withhold life-giving rebukes from my friends, I'm living as their enemy. When I'm not willing to offer a redemptive wounding, I'm a bad friend, not just too busy of a man. Have mercy on me, Jesus. Grant me the grace, words, and courage that I need.

I bring to you my fear of man, which I know to be a snare. I confess it as sin and repent. I also acknowledge that I need the power of the gospel for change. It's because you clearly revealed my need of your grace that I now rest in your love. It's because of your open rebuke that my life is now hidden safely in you. It's because you cared enough to confront me that I will eternally enjoy your comfort.

Jesus, you took the ultimate unfriendly wounding of sin and evil on the cross that I might know your kisses to be those of a Savior-Bridegroom. Help me now, I pray, with the resources of your great love, to love well in the very situations that I dread. I pray in your compassionate name. Amen.

A Prayer about Feeling Conflicted

This is what the LORD Almighty says: "Many peoples and the inhabitants of many cities will yet come, and the inhabitants of one city will go to another and say, 'Let us go at once to entreat the LORD and seek the LORD Almighty. I myself am going.' And many peoples and powerful nations will come to Jerusalem to seek the LORD Almighty and to entreat him." This is what the LORD Almighty says: "In those days ten men from all languages and nations will take firm hold of one Jew by the hem of his robe and say, 'Let us go with you, because we have heard that God is with you.'" (Zech. 8:20–23 NIV)

Jesus, I went to bed feeling conflicted, and I awake with the same divided heart. I need the wisdom you alone can give and the peace you graciously promise. I need to know how to serve you faithfully and love my neighbors well when the two seem to be on a collision course.

Here's what's going on: I live with the great hope of Zechariah's vision being fulfilled. People from many cities and nations are coming, and will continue to come, to receive the salvation God alone can give. People from all kinds of religious backgrounds and worldviews will continue to discover that you, Jesus, are the "one Jew" we need to "take firm hold of" for the knowledge of God.

For you are the way, the truth, and the life, and no one comes to know God as Father apart from you, Jesus (John 14:6). Salvation can't be found anywhere else, for God hasn't given any other Savior but you (Acts 4:12). Your life of perfect obedience and your death on the cross have earned salvation for us. You have done for us what we could never do for ourselves. This is the best news ever. There is simply no better news than the news of God's grace. You have secured the salvation of the "many peoples" and the "powerful nations" of Zechariah's vision. So why am I feeling conflicted on the inside?

Jesus, not only in foreign countries or distant cities but in my community, there are plans for mosques to be built. I acknowledge my unrest; I own my prejudices; I name my fears; I grieve my stereotypes. Jesus, I want to love my new neighbors to your glory. I want to be a good citizen of heaven and a good citizen in my community. Show me and my friends what that looks like in this very situation, Jesus.

Zechariah's vision describes something very attractive going on in the lives of your people—your church, your bride. He envisions the presence of God having a magnetic appeal to people from all kinds of backgrounds. May this be true of my family and our church family. Give us your wisdom and give us your peace, but please, make the gospel beautiful and believable through us. We pray in your glorious name. Amen.

A Prayer for Renewed First Love

The word of the LORD came to me, saying, "Go and proclaim in the hearing of Jerusalem, Thus says the LORD, 'I remember the devotion of your youth, your love as a bride, how you followed me in the wilderness, in a land not sown.'" (Jer. 2:1–2)

Loving Jesus, that you are jealous for my love is as humbling as it is astonishing. What greater compliment could you possibly give me? That you miss my affection tests the limits of my imagination. That you ever made me a part of your bride in the first place continues to move me to cry out, "I believe—help my unbelief!"

When I slow down enough to remember, when I allow myself enough quiet to reflect, when I rid myself of defensiveness and excuse making, of course I have to agree with you. There was a time, early in your relationship with me in the gospel, when I loved you with the passion, delight, and devotion of a young bride. Wherever you led me, even through the desert and barren places, I went with joy, because you were my oasis, nourishment, and utter satisfaction.

In time, I began to depend on other things and other people to supplement the joy of being your beloved bride. You weren't quite enough for my foolish, longing heart. I thought my earthly spouse, or my children, or more money, or a different appearance, or the approval of people, or ministry success, or stolen kisses were also necessary. And though it grieves me to say it, at times these other things and other people have actually replaced you as the source of my deepest joy, contentment, meaning, peace, and hope.

Jesus, I confess and repent. It would be one thing if you were a harsh, disengaged, demanding bridegroom. But you love me as none other. You lived and died to make me your own. You have robed me in the bridal gown of your own righteousness. You care for my heart and my whole being as no one else. You enjoy me, delight in me, and rejoice over me, and your entire bride, with irrepressible singing!

Indeed, Lord Jesus, restore to me the joy of your salvation and the first love of bridal affection. I have no power to change me, but you have all power. I love you now in light of the day I will love you fully. I pray in your all-sufficient name. Amen.

A Prayer about Being Re-Parented by God

For this reason I bow my knees before the Father, from whom every family in heaven and on earth is named, that according to the riches of his glory he may grant you to be strengthened with power through his Spirit in your inner being, so that Christ may dwell in your hearts through faith—that you, being rooted and grounded in love, may have strength to comprehend with all the saints what is the breadth and length and height and depth, and to know the love of Christ that surpasses knowledge, that you may be filled with all the fullness of God. (Eph. 3:14–19)

Heavenly Father, I bow before you today, not floundering in my fears but marinating in your mercies, not groveling in my guilt but growing in your grace. For you're the Father from whom all fatherhood derives its name and meaning. You come to us in the gospel, adopting us to be your beloved sons and daughters and growing us to become like your most beloved Son, Jesus. What wondrous love is this, indeed!

Father, I'm in constant need of your re-parenting. I need to know you better and better as Abba, Father, the most caring, engaged, and loving parent ever. I need you to continue to free me from the illusion that my earthly parents could have ever been enough. For the wounds and holes in my childhood, bring the gospel to bear with healing and liberating power. Free me from believing I need any other parent but you in order to become a whole and healthy person.

Father, I also need you to re-parent me as a parent. You've already forgiven me for the years I spent parenting by fear and control and out of guilt and pride. Now I pray for the redeeming of those years. Indeed, Father, teach me what it means to parent by grace, in every season of our relationship. Write stories of restoration and renewal.

Grant me humility and vulnerability with my children. What failures do I need to own? What stories do we need to share with each other? There's no condemnation, but there must be conviction. What will the fruit of my repentance look like? Father, be pleased to do well beyond all I can ask or imagine. I pray in Jesus' loving name. Amen.

A Prayer about the Disruptive Comfort of God's Sovereignty

Remember this, keep it in mind,
    take it to heart, you rebels.
Remember the former things, those of long ago;
    I am God, and there is no other;
    I am God, and there is none like me.
I make known the end from the beginning,
    from ancient times, what is still to come.
I say, "My purpose will stand,
    and I will do all that I please." (Isa. 46:8–10 NIV)

Holy and gracious Father, I offer you no push back this morning for addressing me as a rebel. I not only rebel against your commandments, I also rebel against your gospel. My only hope is in knowing that you will complete the good work of salvation you began in me. You do all that you please, and it pleases you to justify and transform rebels like me. Hallelujah!

I also find great hope today in knowing that your purposes for everything else will stand. This truth is both disruptive and comforting. There are some things I'm desperate for you to do, Father—some things that make all the sense in the world to me but are not going to happen.

There are other things I don't have the faith for which to trust you—things that I cannot imagine coming to pass. Yet like a lush garden blossoming in the arid desert, those very things will come to pass.

Father, help me "fix it in mind and take it to heart." You are God and you do as you please. No one can ultimately resist your will, and we're foolish when we try. You're not a manageable deity; you're not predictable; you're not programmable. You are mysterious—good, but mysterious.

As I head into a week of difficult decisions, I'm so thankful that you are a sovereign Father, having equal care for each of your children. I can trust you. I don't have to panic. I don't have to worry. I don't have to take matters into my own hands. I don't have to fear outcomes, "what ifs," or "if only's." Second-guessing must surrender to gospel sanity.

Father, help me to want your purposes to stand more than I want life not to be messy. Help me to glory in your pleasure more than I finagle for fewer hassles. Help me to accept disruption as a necessary part of transformation. There is no comfort like the comfort that comes from knowing you and calling you Abba, Father. I pray in Jesus' trustworthy name. Amen.

A Prayer about My Heart's Destination

May the Lord direct your hearts to the love of God and to the steadfastness of Christ. (2 Thess. 3:5)

Holy Father, the hymn writer must have been thinking about me when he penned the words, "Prone to wander, Lord, I feel it, prone to leave the God I love. Take my heart, O take and seal it, seal it for thy courts above." There are days when my heart instinctively races in so many unhealthy, even destructive directions.

Some days I wake up with my heart running to self-pity, when my disappointments loom larger than your delights. Some days the GPS of my heart seems to be programmed for a need to be appreciated and approved by people, when my insecurities are shouting down your name and praise. Some days I lace up my running shoes for a quick jog to unforgiveness and bitterness, when I've been rehearsing the failures of others more than the riches of the gospel. Still other "unguarded heart days" I take little side trips into lust, greed, envy, resentment, whining, self-righteousness, fear, and a whole host of other fruitless destinations.

So today, Father, I want you to answer the apostle Paul's prayer on my behalf, and also on behalf of my friends and family. Please direct our hearts into the lavish resources of your love and the much-needed perseverance of Jesus. I'm not at all affronted when you limit the assumed freedom of my will. By the power of your sovereign goodness, reel in my wandering heart once again and send it into the glorious refuge of your love. I will only persevere to the end as Jesus perseveres in me and for me.

Jesus, I praise you with humility that you have already given me a new heart. Holy Spirit, I praise you with joy that you have already sealed my heart, once and for all. Father, I praise you with peace that I really can say, "Signed, sealed, delivered, I'm yours!" I pray in Jesus' trustworthy name. Amen.

A Prayer about Gospel Astonishment

To those who have been called, who are loved in God the Father and kept for Jesus Christ: Mercy, peace and love be yours in abundance. (Jude 1–2 NIV)

Glorious Triune God, on this Lord's Day I'm overwhelmed as I ponder the immeasurable and irrepressible goodness of the life we have in Jesus. Gospel astonishment pretty well describes what I'm feeling. I want to shout and shut up at the same time.

You didn't just invite me to become a Christian; you called me and adopted me as your own child. Now I call you Abba, Father, as the Holy Spirit continues to free my heart from acting like a homeless, fatherless orphan. Thank you, Father, that because of the work of Jesus, you will never love me more than you do today and you will never love me less! What wondrous love is this indeed!

Lord Jesus, help me to grasp your grasp of me. I am both kept by you and kept for you. Nothing can pull me from your hand or tear me from your heart. Many times this seems too good to be true, but it is all the assurance I need to face the rest of my life, even the next hour.

Indeed, Holy Spirit, bring from the throne of grace into my heart and story an abundance of mercy, for I am a foolish man; peace, for I am a broken man; and love, for I am a selfish man. Be praised on this Lord's Day and every day, O glorious and grace-full God! I pray in Jesus' exalted name. Amen.

A Prayer about Finishing Well

To him who is able to keep you from stumbling and to present you before his glorious presence without fault and with great joy—to the only God our Savior be glory, majesty, power and authority, through Jesus Christ our Lord, before all ages, now and forevermore! Amen. (Jude 24–25 NIV)

Heavenly Father, the older I get the more I care about finishing this life well. I wish less temptation came with more years. I wish diminishment of physical strength brought an automatic increase in spiritual strength. But that's not the way it works.

I need Jesus' mercy and grace today just as much as the first day you placed me safely in Christ. Thus I abandon myself to the promises that overflow in this passage. They are a balm to my whole being.

I praise you, Father, that the most important grasp in the gospel is yours, not mine. You will keep me from ultimately falling away from you. And when I do falter, fall, and fail to love you and others as I am commanded in the gospel, you will pick me up.

As hard as it is to imagine, especially in my times of weakness, one day you will present me before your glorious presence without fault and with great joy. How many times do I have to say that for my heart to really believe it? Without fault and with great joy . . . without fault and with great joy . . . without fault and with great joy!

Indeed, may my heart passionately proclaim with myriads of angels and countless believers: to the only God our Savior be glory, majesty, power, and authority, in this life and in the life to come!

Jesus, trusting in the life you lived for me as the second Adam, the life you gave for me as the Lamb of God, and the life you now live through me as my hope of glory, I will finish well—without fault and with great joy . . . without fault and with great joy . . . without fault and with great joy! I pray in your glorious name. Amen.

A Prayer for Those We Love

This is what the LORD says—
>   he who made you, who formed you in the womb,
>   and who will help you:
> Do not be afraid, Jacob, my servant,
>   Jeshurun, whom I have chosen.
> For I will pour water on the thirsty land,
>   and streams on the dry ground;
> I will pour out my Spirit on your offspring,
>   and my blessing on your descendants.
> They will spring up like grass in a meadow,
>   like poplar trees by flowing streams.
> Some will say, "I belong to the LORD";
>   others will call themselves by the name of Jacob;
> still others will write on their hand, "The LORD's,"
>   and will take the name Israel. (Isa. 44:2–5 NIV)

Compassionate Father, today we bring before you those we love, especially members of our families. How we long for you to be gracious on behalf of our children, our parents, our siblings, our extended families, and our friends. O Lord, there are so many for whom we carry heartbreaking concerns and heavy burdens.

Gracious Father, thank you not only for forming us in our mother's womb but also for revealing Jesus in our inner hearts. This gives us great courage in asking you to pour out your Spirit on a vast array of people we know: for our children, siblings, and parents who don't know you, Father, bring them to a saving knowledge of Jesus. Above all, we are praying that a very real knowledge and experience of the grace and truth of the gospel will capture their hearts. More than anything else, we long to hear those we love say, "I belong to the Lord."

Holy Spirit, for our family members and friends who are living like destructive idiots and senseless morons, do whatever it takes to save them from themselves. Arrest them in their foolishness and spare them with the fullness of your grace. To the meadows of their madness, bring the grandeur of your goodness.

Jesus, for those we know who love you deeply but are living in hard stories of failing health, financial stress, emotional and mental illness, marital meltdown, and spiritual disconnect, pour forth your life-giving Spirit. Where there is floundering, bring flourishing; where there is despair, bring delight; where there is hopelessness, bring fruitfulness—all for your glory.

We forsake our fears in light of the pledge of your help. We pray in your matchless name. Amen.

A Prayer about the Compassion of Jesus

And Jesus went throughout all the cities and villages, teaching in their synagogues and proclaiming the gospel of the kingdom and healing every disease and every affliction. When he saw the crowds, he had compassion for them, because they were harassed and helpless, like sheep without a shepherd. (Matt. 9:35–36)

Lord Jesus, there are so many reasons to love you, so many reasons to risk being completely honest and vulnerable with you. Today I'm particularly thankful for your compassion.

Compassion presupposes merciful feelings. When you look at crowds of harassed and helpless people, you don't ignore them, you're not irritated by them, you don't despise them. Sympathy beats within your breast; kindness overflows. I see this everywhere in the Scriptures. Help me know this is what you feel *for me* in my den this morning and not just what you felt for the multitudes in Galilee.

At times my theology far outstrips my experience, Jesus—my doctrine being more certain than my doxology. I need your Holy Spirit to convince me afresh that as you look at me right now, it's mercy you feel. I can't say I'm either harassed or helpless, but I need to be certain of your compassion nevertheless.

Compassion requires actual presence. Jesus, when I pray, I'm still inclined to think you're "up there" somewhere, sitting on a big chair beside the Father, surrounded by a multitude of angels and a lot of singing. But I know better. I know you live in the hearts of every one of us who believe the gospel. I know you've promised to never leave us or forsake us. I know that and I really believe it, but would you make it more current and real? Would you come and shepherd my heart today?

Compassion shares the suffering of another. Jesus, it really is enough to know that you suffered *for us* on the cross. I stake my life and my certain death on this gospel—this good news that you were "pierced for our transgressions . . . crushed for our iniquities" (Isa. 53:5 NIV), that by your blood "you ransomed people for God from every tribe and language and people and nation" (Rev. 5:9). What you suffered on the cross, you suffered once and for all (Heb. 10:1–18), and we worship you now and will worship you forever because of your matchless sacrifice.

But it's also as overwhelming as it is comforting to know that you share in our sufferings right now. You suffered *for us*, once and for all, and you suffer *with us* now. During the times when you feel so far away, so removed, so disengaged, *you could not be nearer than you actually are*, Jesus. I pray with gratitude, in your compassionate name. Amen.

231

A Prayer about Shame

And the man and his wife were both naked and were unashamed. (Gen. 2:25)

Gracious Father, it's nearly impossible for me to imagine the day when there was no need for the emotion of shame. In their innocence, our first parents were absolutely free of any need to turn away from your gaze, or that of one another. There was no need to fear, cover up, hide, pose, pretend, get defensive, feel guilty, make excuses, blame the other, want to disappear, do penance, numb out, medicate, or try any other broken attempt to deal with the disintegrating effects of shame.

It is only in you, Jesus, that we now find hope to deal with both our guilt and our shame. For in light of the joy set before you by the Father, you endured the agony of the cross for us, scorning its shame—the shame of being made sin for us—that in you we might become the righteousness of God (2 Cor. 5:21; Heb. 12:2). Indeed, Jesus, those who trust in you will never be put to shame, for you took our shame and made it yours (1 Pet. 2:6) so that we might know the present and eternal favor of God. How can we ever praise you enough for such love?

Therefore, Jesus, we cry out for freedom today—freedom in our on-going struggles with shame, both the shame we feel and the shame we give. Though our guilt has been completely taken care of by your work on the cross, Jesus, we still feel varying degrees of shame, and we act out in a variety of destructive ways. We vacillate between self-contempt and other-centered contempt, and both of these contradict and sabotage the very love by which, and for which, we were saved. Indeed, we need the freedom you alone can provide, Jesus. Bring the grace and truth of the gospel to bear in profoundly healing and liberating ways, Lord Jesus. All for your glory, we ask this in Jesus' freeing name. Amen.

A Prayer about God's Goodness

And they shall be my people, and I will be their God. I will give them one heart and one way, that they may fear me forever, for their own good and the good of their children after them. I will make with them an everlasting covenant, that I will not turn away from doing good to them. And I will put the fear of me in their hearts, that they may not turn from me. I will rejoice in doing them good, and I will plant them in this land in faithfulness, with all my heart and all my soul. (Jer. 32:38–41)

Generous Father, I know you don't lie, but this portion of your Word exposes the depths of my unbelief and my small notions about you. It also invites me to see that the gospel is so much bigger and better than I could ever hope or imagine.

The first thing I notice is all the "I will's" connecting this extraordinary catalog of promises. Indeed, Father, you make promises you alone can keep. I praise you for your inviolate commitment to be such an outrageously, immeasurably generous God.

I praise you for promising never to stop doing good to us and for finding so much joy in doing us good. This is truly overwhelming, almost too good to be true. However, you've already "made good" on your promise to make an everlasting covenant with us, and this fuels the fire of our faith.

Lord Jesus, well beyond Jeremiah's day, you came and you accomplished everything necessary to prove our Father wasn't exaggerating. Your life, death, and resurrection, on our behalf, guarantee God is *this good*, all the time . . . and all the time, God is *this good* to us!

Because of you, Jesus, we are already perfectly forgiven and have already been declared to be righteous in God's sight. Because of you, one day we will be made completely whole and the whole creation will be made new. On that day our Father will plant us in the land of the new heaven and new earth. We believe; help us in our unbelief, dear Lord.

Until that day, Holy Spirit, continue your transforming and liberating work in our lives. Free us to love and serve our God with singleness of heart, affectionate reverence, and gospel-driven obedience.

Hallelujah, what a salvation! Hallelujah, what a Savior! We pray in Jesus' triumphant name. Amen.

A Prayer about Christmas in August

For to us a child is born,
>to us a son is given,
>and the government will be on his shoulders.
And he will be called
>Wonderful Counselor, Mighty God,
>Everlasting Father, Prince of Peace.
Of the greatness of his government and peace
>there will be no end.
He will reign on David's throne
>and over his kingdom,
establishing and upholding it
>with justice and righteousness
>from that time on and forever.
The zeal of the LORD Almighty
>will accomplish this. (Isa. 9:6–7 NIV)

Gracious Jesus, it won't surprise me one bit if we begin to see Christmas decorations beside Halloween candy on store shelves before September starts. It gets earlier and earlier each year. That being said, it's never too early to remember why you came into the world. In fact, there's nothing seasonal about any portion of Scripture.

There aren't "Christmas verses" that are the private domain of Advent. There's just you, and your glory, and your magnificent story of redemption and restoration. Today, on this hot August morning, I'm glad to remember—I need to remember—why you came and what you're up to right now.

Jesus, the government of the entire cosmos is already sitting squarely upon your shoulders. Nothing happens apart from your sovereign doings and delight. I don't have to be vexed over a nuclear-armed Iran any more than I have to be defined by a lousy golf game. It may not be apparent to my naked eye, but everything is subject to you. You were before all things, and in you all things are held together (Col. 1:17). Everything in heaven and on earth is being summed up in you (Eph. 1:10).

You are Wonderful Counselor—that is, our wisdom from God, our righteousness, holiness, and redemption (1 Cor. 1:30). There is no salvation apart from you. It's the gospel or despair. You are Mighty God—eternally one with the Father, coequal, coglorious, along with the Holy Spirit. There is nothing you can't do. You never "try" to do anything. You simply execute your pleasure at your discretion.

You are Everlasting Father—the Son who perfectly reveals the Father's image and riches to us. It's because of you, Jesus, that we've been adopted into God's family and given all the rights and delights of the children of God. You are Prince of Peace—by your life and death, you made peace between God and us. You yourself are our peace, Jesus; you destroyed the hostile barrier that stood between us (Eph. 2:14–15).

Right now, on this early August morning, you are extending your glorious kingdom of peace. You are "shaloming" all things, making all things new, putting all things right. Justice and righteousness are coming to every place where sin and death have done their worst. All of this is happening because you are the zealous Lord, jealous for his bride, who accomplishes everything he has promised. Suddenly I feel like putting on some Christmas CDs, Jesus! I pray in your peerless name. Amen.

A Prayer about My Heart's Worship

Shadrach, Meshach and Abednego replied to him, "King Nebuchadnezzar, we do not need to defend ourselves before you in this matter. If we are thrown into the blazing furnace, the God we serve is able to deliver us from it, and he will deliver us from Your Majesty's hand. But even if he does not, we want you to know, Your Majesty, that we will not serve your gods or worship the image of gold you have set up." (Dan. 3:16–18 NIV)

Heavenly Father, I'm intrigued, convicted, and encouraged by the faith of Shadrach, Meshach, and Abednego. How refreshing to behold such a nonutilitarian love for you. These three friends worshiped you not because of the gifts you give but because of the God that you are. They were firmly convinced that you could rescue them from the fiery furnace, but even if you didn't rescue them, it would have no effect on their worship of you. They would rather be delivered into your presence through the fire than worship some other false god just to escape the fire.

Father, forgive me when my worship varies in response to my perceptions of how well and quick you answer my prayers. As cynical as I am about the "name it and claim it" and prosperity theologies, I'm quite capable of doubting your love when life gets complicated and painful. I want to worship you before there's a fire, when I'm in the fire, when the fire's extinguished, or if you should choose to take me home through the fire.

Lord Jesus, you alone can give me such freedom and love for God. You were the fourth man King Nebuchadnezzar saw walking around in the fiery furnace, and you're the only one who endured the fiery trial of the cross. Even as you purchased your bride, you never leave or forsake us, at any time or in any trial.

Because of you, Jesus, we don't have to be afraid to die, and we don't have to be afraid to live. May your beauty and grace be so compelling that at the very moment we're tempted to turn to some false god or idol for temporal deliverance or instant relief, *we won't*. We pray in your peerless name. Amen.

A Prayer about the Sufferings
of Jesus and the Victory of Justice

And many followed him [Jesus], and he healed them all and ordered them not to make him known. This was to fulfill what was spoken by the prophet Isaiah: "Behold, my servant whom I have chosen, my beloved with whom my soul is well pleased. I will put my Spirit upon him, and he will proclaim justice to the Gentiles. He will not quarrel or cry aloud, nor will anyone hear his voice in the streets; a bruised reed he will not break, and a smoldering wick he will not quench, until he brings justice to victory; and in his name the Gentiles will hope." (Matt. 12:15–21)

Dear Lord Jesus, I'm greatly moved today as I ponder your compassionate heart for the broken and suffering. Surely there's no Savior like you: entering, not running from our chaos; taking, not despising our shame; shouldering, not ignoring our burdens. "Bruised reeds" and "smoldering wicks" love your appearing. Justice will be fully victorious because you have been the willing sufferer.

For sure, for gloriously sure, your sufferings as our sin-bearer are over. As the Lamb of God, you offered yourself once and for all upon the cross. No additional sacrifice for our sin remains to be offered. None. I no longer fear being judged by God for my sin. Your perfect love has driven away all fear of punishment, anxiety about judgment day, and uncertainty about eternity. I boast and rest in your sufferings for me, Lord Jesus, and I also shout a hearty "Hallelujah!" But I also cry out, "Help me, Lord Jesus . . . help me."

Help me go with you into the sufferings of friends and family, further into the groans of my own heart, and into the injustices and brokenness of my community. Like most, I have an aversion to pain and suffering. Like many, I'd love for the Christian life to be an antidote for all discomfort and distress. Like some, I get overwhelmed and overtaxed by the sufferings of others.

Here's my peace, my consolation, my ballast, Jesus: you're not calling us to suffer for you but to suffer with you, and that makes all the difference in the world. We're called into the fellowship of your sufferings, not into the isolation of our sufferings.

You'll never lead us into hard places where you're not present. You'll never ask us to do anything all by ourselves. You'll never leave us or forsake us, Jesus. You will lead justice to victory, and in your name all the nations will put their hope. I pray in your kind and compassionate name. Amen.

A Prayer about the Renewal of Joy

Will you not revive us again,
   that your people may rejoice in you?
Show us your unfailing love, LORD,
   and grant us your salvation. (Ps. 85:6–7 NIV)

Gracious Father, I begin my day thankful for the honesty and candor of your Word, for when you diagnose a problem, you always resource your children with more grace. Today I'm thinking about my need for gospel renewal and restored joy. I join the chorus of many who cry, "Revive us again."

When I hear the apostle Paul ask believers in Galatia, "What then has become of the blessing you felt?" (Gal. 4:15), I'm not sure how I'd answer. Have I fallen back into legalism? Am I struggling with unbelief? Am I looking for joy somewhere else? Have I hoarded my hurts and wounds to keep them from you? Am I angry at you and don't want to admit it? I'm not sure how or where my heart began to leak joy, but I don't want to get used to this condition. Show me, Lord.

Since your joy is my strength, Father (Neh. 8:10), cause my heart muscle to beat afresh with your joy, the joy that fills the courts of heaven. Holy Spirit, since joy is one of the fruits you grow in the lives of the children of God, please weed, prune, and fertilize my heart for a fresh crop.

Jesus, since you are praying for the fullness of your joy to be in us (John 17:13), I will live with anticipation and hope, for your prayers never fail. Though I've never seen you, I do love you, and I love you because you first loved me and gave yourself for me on the cross. Fill me afresh with the inexpressible and glorious joy of the salvation you have won for us (1 Pet. 1:8–9). I pray in your trustworthy name. Amen.

A Prayer about Being Desired by Jesus

I am my beloved's, and his desire is for me. (Song of Sol. 7:10)

Dear Jesus, the Song of Solomon has never been one of the most underlined books in my Bible, but the more I look for you in all the Scriptures (Luke 24:25–27), the more I'm drawn to its startling, scintillating, sensual imagery. To read the Song of Solomon is to tap into our deepest longings for intimacy, playfulness, passion, and delight—knowing and being known by you.

Indeed, you are the great lover of whom this book speaks. In our best moments, our love for one another is a mere hint and whisper of the way you love us. And we are the beloved, the bride upon whom you've set your deepest affections and for whom you've given your very life.

This isn't the gospel I grew up with, but this is the gospel. To be desired is to be wanted, pursued, enjoyed, seen and accepted, known and nourished, remembered and cherished. All of this is promised and provided in the gospel.

Only the Holy Spirit can enable us to believe and experience the liberating truths, the unparalleled beauty, and the oceans of delight revealed in this book and held out in the gospel. So I cry out today: come, Holy Spirit, come. Rescue me and my friends from our unbelief; dethrone my false notions of God and the gospel; soften my hard heart. It's one thing to rest in Jesus' finished work, but it's another thing to be alive to his present desire. Do a great work in our hearts, Holy Spirit. Do a fresh work in my heart.

Forgive me, Jesus, for believing that any human being could possibly satisfy the very longings you created in me. Forgive me, Jesus, for assuming I could ever be to someone else what you alone can be. Help all of us—the unmarried, the happily married, and the miserably married—to realize that you, Jesus, are the spouse we always wanted and the one to whom we belong. And more importantly, Jesus, help us to believe that you are the spouse who always wanted *us*. We pray in your peerless name. Amen.

A Prayer for Hearing the Voice
of the Holy Spirit

For you did not receive the spirit of slavery to fall back into fear, but you have received the Spirit of adoption as sons, by whom we cry, "Abba! Father!" The Spirit himself bears witness with our spirit that we are children of God. (Rom. 8:15–16)

Gracious Father, on any given day a number of voices contend for our attention. There are the voices of the past, sometimes yammering loudly, sometimes just nickeling-and-diming our peace away with the refrain "You still don't have a clue, do you? You haven't changed one bit. Why would God ever love someone like you? Didn't I tell you you'd never amount to much? If people really knew who you are . . ."

Then there are the voices of the present, often hijacked by our defeated enemy, Satan. His incessant scheme is to tempt, seduce, then accuse us—doing everything possible to rob us of our enjoyment of the gospel. Sometimes he shouts; more often he whispers; always he's conniving and always he's condemning.

Then there are the voices from the future, usually fueling our fears with suggestions like "You're not as sharp as you used to be, are you? You'll probably be forgotten, won't you? You'll eventually end up alone, right? Why do you think God would let someone like you into heaven?"

But then there's the voice of the Holy Spirit. Oh, how we praise you for that one voice that transcends and trumps every other voice—the gossiper of the gospel, the herald of our healing, the bearer of beauty, the messenger of mercy, the singer of sanity, the cantor of Christ—God the Holy Spirit testifying with our spirits that we are your bought, belonging, and beloved children. How we praise you for the ministry of the Holy Spirit.

Abba, Father, by the Spirit of sonship, continue to free us from all of our slavish fears—past, present, and future. May the Spirit speak so loudly that every dark voice is muted. May he speak so clearly that every deceiving lie is silenced. May he speak so convincingly that every paralyzing doubt is routed. We pray expectantly, in Jesus' tender and triumphant name. Amen.

A Prayer about Loving Well

And so we know and rely on the love God has for us. God is love. Whoever lives in love lives in God, and God in them. This is how love is made complete among us so that we will have confidence on the day of judgment: In this world we are like Jesus. There is no fear in love. But perfect love drives out fear, because fear has to do with punishment. The one who fears is not made perfect in love. We love because he first loved us. (1 John 4:16–19 NIV)

Gracious Jesus, today I'm remembering the call to love well all kinds of people in all kinds of situations. I'm recognizable as one of your disciples by the way I love others (John 13:34). This would be an unbearable burden if you didn't love us as you do. We love you, and anybody, only because you first loved us.

Because of your great love for us, Jesus, we don't have to fear judgment day. Your cross is judgment day for all who trust in you. You took the punishment I deserve for all the ways I love so poorly. I now rely on the love you have for me. In that assurance, here's my plea, Jesus.

Help me love well the members of my immediate family. They are at the same time the easiest and the hardest people to love, day in and day out. Sometimes I think I have the greatest family on the earth; sometimes I think we'd trade one another in for a Diet Coke. Bring your kindness, compassion, patience, and perseverance to bear. Help us to provoke one another to love and good deeds, and not just provoke one another.

Jesus, help me to love my friends well. Help me not to take them for granted. Help me know how to give my friends feedback lovingly and receive feedback from them without being defensive. Forgive me when I want friendship to be simply a mutual admiration society rather than a community of groaning, grace, and growth.

Help me to know how to love the irritating people in my life, those I try hard to avoid. Help me know how to love the foolish people in my life, the ones making destructive choices, the ones I'm mad at right now.

Help me know how to love the depressed and sad people in my life. I instinctively try to fix them and make them happy, but I know that's not really what they need from me. Help me to love the poor, the orphans and widows, the marginalized, "the least and the lost," for among them I will surely find you, Jesus. I pray in your compassionate name. Amen.

A Prayer about the Full Extent of Jesus' Love

Having loved his own who were in the world, he [Jesus] loved them to the end. (John 13:1 NIV)

Dear Jesus, this story always grabs my heart, but today it's rekindling awe. It's the night of your betrayal—the night you would be denied and abandoned not just by Peter but by all of the disciples. You knew this and yet you persisted in disrobing yourself, bending low, and washing the dirty feet of these broken, bungling men.

The beauty and truth revealed in this scene is what keeps me sane—gospel sane. It anchors me when I lose my moorings, centers me when I feel crazy, quiets me when I'm restless, reels my heart in when I am in a wandering mode.

This is how you love each of your followers, all of your disciples, your whole bride. You've made us your own. You bought us with the very price of your blood. We were redeemed from sin and death and placed into your righteousness and embrace. Absolutely nothing can separate us from your love.

While we're in this world, you're constantly loving us. You're loving us when we're alive to your presence and affections, and you're loving us when it feels like you're ignoring our prayers, indifferent to our pain, or displeased with our lives. In fact, whether we perceive it or not, the most constant can-be-counted-upon reality in our lives is not death and taxes but your loving-kindness.

Jesus, it's the last line in this little verse that nearly does me in. As with the men in the upper room, so with those of us in any of a number of rooms right now: you're still committed to showing us the full extent of your love—its height, depth, width, and breadth.

This turns our gaze to your cross, for it's in your death, Jesus, that we realize that there's no greater love to be found anywhere. On the cross, you laid down your life for others: for the rebel other, the foolish other, the sinful other—for me.

Though you died for a huge pan-national bride, I declare today that the Son of God loved *me* and gave himself for me (Gal. 2:20). This isn't narcissism; it is necessity. It's not selfish; it's sacred. It's not Western individualism; it's deeply personal. I'm once again in awe, Jesus. Intensify my awe even more on this hot August day. I pray in your truly astonishing name. Amen.

A Prayer for Renewal in Our Hearts and Churches

You are the salt of the earth, but if salt has lost its taste, how shall its saltiness be restored? It is no longer good for anything except to be thrown out and trampled under people's feet. You are the light of the world. A city set on a hill cannot be hidden. Nor do people light a lamp and put it under a basket, but on a stand, and it gives light to all in the house. In the same way, let your light shine before others, so that they may see your good works and give glory to your Father who is in heaven. (Matt. 5:13–16)

Gracious Jesus, at times I fantasize about running off to Switzerland with my family; living in a community of chalets with several other "healthy" families; escaping the craziness of church life; disengaging from the chaos of my culture; eating good food; "enjoying" the Christian life; and waiting for your second coming. That's a confession of sin, not a prayer request.

For starters, I know I couldn't afford to pay for such a selfish fantasy. More importantly, I realize this isn't the lifestyle for which you've redeemed us. The church belongs to you, Jesus; she's your beloved bride. Yet, as with everything else, we often take the church into the idol factory of our hearts and retool her to be an ingrown club for our own satisfaction. Forgive us, Jesus. Forgive me.

You've called and commissioned us to live as the "salt of the earth." We're not garlic, paprika, or sugar; we're salt. Salt preserves and fends off decay. Salt heals and soothes—it has medicinal value. Salt brings flavor and enhances other flavors. And salt only "works" when it's out of the saltshaker. Alas, my own prayer convicts me.

Jesus, how does a believer lose their saltiness, or for that matter, how does a whole church family lose their vision and passion? What's involved in flavor loss? More importantly, what does renewal look like?

Come, Holy Spirit, come. We need you to stir our hearts. Only you are powerful enough to resalt the desalted; to bring us back to gospel sanity; to restore in us the joy of God's salvation; to reengage the disengaged with God's plan for our communities, the cities, and the nations.

How we praise you that our cry is your pleasure. Before we ask you know our need. Do exceedingly beyond all we ask and can imagine. We pray gratefully, in Jesus' merciful and mighty name. Amen.

A Prayer for Broken Hearts and Crushed Spirits

The LORD is near to the brokenhearted
and saves the crushed in spirit. (Ps. 34:18)

Dear Lord Jesus, there's no Savior like you—none so kind, so compassionate, so merciful, so very close. The brokenhearted don't need to "buck up" and be brave when they see you coming. The crushed in spirit don't need to pull themselves together, as though you would be greatly disappointed to find us less than conquerors.

We praise you that the gospel is heaven's declared end to all pretense and pretending. Jesus, you have no need for us to be anything other than we actually are. It's the proud you know from afar. It's those who need your grace to whom you are nearer than the next breath. This gives us incalculable comfort as we bring ourselves and a wide array of weary friends before you today.

Jesus, we pray for our friends struggling with infertility. They don't need any more words; they simply want a baby to love to your glory. The tragedy of abortion on demand, the growing population of neglected children, and the ever-increasing cost of adoption has strained their sensibilities and faith. Bring glory to yourself in this and similar stories, Jesus. And show us how to love well beyond our usual pat answers.

Jesus, we pray for weary friends serving on church staffs or in vocational ministry. Many of them wake up today disillusioned, depleted, and despondent. We naively assume some jobs should be beyond the gamesmanship and brokenness we find in other vocational settings. But sinners saved by grace are still sinners, no matter where they work. Grant wisdom, humility, and grace for hard decisions to be made and implemented to your glory. And where the world, rather than the gospel, seems to be winning the day, grant quick and sure repentances.

Jesus, for those of us who don't feel crushed in spirit but rather feel discombobulated in spirit, help us to sort through the issues. Show us what is repentable and what is repairable, and help us quiet our noisy hearts so we can hear you speak. We need your presence much, much more than we need circumstances and people to change.

Jesus, today and every day, we declare that our hope is built on nothing else, nothing less, and nothing more than you and what you've done for us on the cross. We pray in your near and compassionate name. Amen.

A Prayer about Paralyzed Friends

They gathered in such large numbers that there was no room left, not even outside the door, and he preached the word to them. Some men came, bringing to him a paralyzed man, carried by four of them. Since they could not get him to Jesus because of the crowd, they made an opening in the roof above Jesus by digging through it and then lowered the mat the man was lying on. (Mark 2:2–4 NIV)

Merciful Jesus, all of us have friends who are paralyzed by a variety of conditions. We lift them up to your throne of grace today, thankful we don't have to fight crowds or remove any roof tiles to get to you.

We bring you our friends still paralyzed by sin and death. You healed the paralytic to demonstrate your authority on earth to forgive sins (Mark 2:5–12). There's no greater or more necessary healing than to be raised from spiritual death. So, Jesus, for the praise of your glory, we bring you our friends who have yet to receive the righteousness that comes only by faith. Save them from both religion and nonreligion. Give them faith that they might receive your grace.

Jesus, we bring you our friends paralyzed by shame, guilt, and contempt. Breathe gospel healing into our friends who are being constantly assaulted by "the accuser of the brethren" about real and imaginary failures. Let them experientially know there is now no condemnation for those who are in Christ (Rom. 8:1). Without this knowledge they won't be able to repent, heal, and get their eyes off themselves.

Jesus, we bring you our friends paralyzed by old wounds, still raw with pain and grief. For our friends who have suffered various degrees of abuse and trauma, please bring the gospel to bear with great power and healing hope. And give us wisdom about how to love and be patient with them.

Jesus, we bring you our friends paralyzed by various obsessions and addictions. Before your throne of grace, we bring those who are hooked into pornography and other sexual entanglements, chemical and drug abuse, eating disorders, self-righteousness and legalism, greed, gossip, preoccupation with physical beauty, and so many other conditions for which the gospel alone provides sufficient power and grace.

Lastly, Jesus, we bring you our friends paralyzed by the demands of caregiving. On behalf of those called to love heroically in situations that have depleted them emotionally, financially, spiritually, and physically, we cry for great mercy, Jesus.

Thank you for the privilege of both praying for our friends and being sent as a part of the answer to these prayers. We pray in your faithful name. Amen.

A Prayer about Bringing Encouragement

Let us hold fast the confession of our hope without wavering, for he who promised is faithful. And let us consider how to stir up one another on to love and good works, not neglecting to meet together, as is the habit of some, but encouraging one another, and all the more as you see the Day drawing near. (Heb. 10:23–25)

Jesus, as I meditate my way through this "let us" patch of gospel admonitions today, a couple of things stand out. On one hand, I'm convicted about the importance of holding on to the hope you've won for us—a living hope, an anchor of hope, a glorious hope. Our hope is certain, but I certainly need to "hold it" like I hold a treasured fly rod or one of my cameras. We're meant to enjoy hope, not fear losing it.

It's also so good to remember that I'm not called to "hope against hope" or to hope in hope, but *to hope in you*. For you've made promises you alone can keep, and you are not a man, that you should lie. You're faithful and you're loving, and that's all I need to know. Not hoping is not an option.

Jesus, this Scripture also convicts me about the importance of being a lot more intentional and regular in bringing encouragement to my friends, my family members, and those you put in my way. As the great day of your return approaches—the day when all hoping in part will give way to the fullness of hope—help me to speak your words of life and hope and healing to those who need them the most. Help me to bring your hands of mercy and grace to bear in very tangible and timely ways.

Very specifically, just as we celebrate your coming to us in the person of Jesus, to whom would you send me today? Put names and faces before me who need the encouragement you alone can bring, Jesus. May the glory of that day bring the grace of encouragement to this day. I pray in your loving name. Amen.

A Prayer about Prayer

Do not be anxious about anything, but in everything by prayer and supplication with thanksgiving let your requests be made known to God. And the peace of God, which surpasses all understanding, will guard your hearts and your minds in Christ Jesus. (Phil. 4:6–7)

Heavenly Father, as I read these words from Paul, I'm convicted about my prayer life. In some ways I'm more certain of what I *don't* believe about prayer than I'm settled on what I do believe. So I'm praying about prayer today, and I humbly own my need for the Spirit to teach me and free me. Give me a renewed love for spending much time with you in vital, expectant prayer.

I praise you for the promise of peace through prayer. Irrespective of how you might choose to answer my prayers, you promise a transcendent peace to those who bring their petitions, thanksgiving, and requests to you. The promise of your peace "guarding my heart and mind" is so encouraging. That's where the most critical battles of life are waged—right there in the arena of my thinking, feeling, and choosing.

Father, please teach me more about the relationship between your sovereignty and my praying. I know you to be the God who works all things together after the counsel of your will (hallelujah!), so how does my praying fit into the outworking of your perfect and irrepressible plan for all things? Send me to the Scriptures that will help me understand this mystery. How do persistence and surrender work hand in hand?

Father, help me understand some of the mechanics of prayer. The teaching I had on prayer as a young believer led me to believe that the likelihood of an affirmative answer to prayer was directly related to how many people were praying. But that's how pagans pray—stirring a begrudging god to action by more commotion. So what is the value of corporate prayer? You commend it, even command it. What really happens when we gather together to cry out to our great and gracious God in Jesus' name? Teach me.

Forgive me and help me, Father. I know I have overcorrected in the direction of being a generalist in prayer. I don't tend to ask for very much specifically *in prayer*, and therefore I don't tend to expect very much specifically *from prayer*. Teach me to be more bold in my asking and trusting of your answering. I pray in Jesus' gracious name. Amen.

A Prayer about Good Grief over Sin

You became sorrowful as God intended and so were not harmed in any way by us. Godly sorrow brings repentance that leads to salvation and leaves no regret, but worldly sorrow brings death. (2 Cor. 7:9–10 NIV)

Holy and loving Jesus, today I'm praying about my heart, in particular my heart's *convictability*. It would be impossible for me to overstate the joy and peace I have in being able to affirm, "There is now [and forever] no condemnation for those who are in Christ Jesus" (Rom. 8:1 NIV). How I praise you for completely exhausting the judgment I deserve for the multiple ways I fail to love God and my neighbors as commanded.

But I'm seeing a disconnect between the good news of no condemnation for my sin and the very important news of *deep conviction* about my sin. Through recent circumstances and in certain relationships, I can see that I haven't been taking my sin as seriously as I should. I know this isn't right, so I need your help. If anything, the gospel of grace should make for quicker and more repentances, not fewer.

To be specific, I'm seeing how I indulge a critical spirit toward some people, and at the same time I work so hard to maintain the approval of others. I'm also aware of the fresh enticements of sexual lust and greed for more "stuff." Left to myself, I am capable of acting out in very foolish and destructive ways.

Jesus, bring me to a fresh place of godly sorrow for my sin—the kind of good grief that will lead me to repent more quickly and yet not get weighed down with vain regrets. I know you don't want me to put my conscience back under the law, but I'm equally sure you *do* want me to live with my conscience under the gospel. For there is no power like grace that can possibly convict me, humble me, gentle me, and strengthen me for a life of loving well to the glory of God.

Great is your faithfulness, kind are your ways, and sufficient is your grace. I pray in the wonders of your name. Amen.

A Prayer about God's
Unparalleled Kindness

But God, being rich in mercy, because of the great love with which he loved us, even when we were dead in our trespasses, made us alive together with Christ—by grace you have been saved—and raised us up with him and seated us with him in the heavenly places in Christ Jesus, so that in the coming ages he might show the immeasurable riches of his grace in kindness toward us in Christ Jesus. (Eph. 2:4–7)

Gracious Father, reading these words from Paul is like standing under Niagara Falls with my mouth wide open. I'm capable of taking in only a tiny portion of the mighty waterfall of all this gospel goodness. You inundate us with your great love, multiplied blessings, and incomparable grace. It's actually fun to repent since repentance opens the floodgate to more of your mercies.

But today, what really arrests my attention the most is the image of being raised from the dead and seated in Christ so that throughout eternity you might demonstrate your kindness to us in Jesus. That absolutely fries the circuit board of my imagination, throws fuel on the fire of my longings, and reveals the paucity of my faith.

Father, the revelation of your kindness touches something very deep inside of me in this season of life. Maybe it's because of how little kindness I see in the world today. Maybe it's because of how much I long to be a genuinely kind man. Maybe it's because it contradicts so many wrong images I've had of you so much of my life. By the power of the gospel, continue to rid my heart of all the false notions I've entertained about you.

There is no other God who would raise up dead sinners for an eternity of lavishing on them more and more of his kindness. I'm left speechless, breathless, and ever so grateful. I pray in Jesus' glorious name. Amen.

A Prayer for Those Who Want to Be Great and First

Whoever wants to become great among you must be your servant, and whoever wants to be first must be slave of all. For even the Son of Man did not come to be served, but to serve, and to give his life as a ransom for many.
(Mark 10:43–45 NIV)

Dear Lord Jesus, as I meditate on your Word this morning, once again I realize the gospel is the most counterintuitive, paradigm-shattering, worldview-transforming force in history. Because of you, true greatness is now measured in terms of being a servant rather than owning the estate. Being first is no longer calculated by how many slaves we own but rather by how many people we serve. You have changed the value and price tags for everything.

"The Son of Man did not come to be served, but to serve, and to give his life as a ransom for many" (Mark 10:45 NIV). Jesus, tattoo these words on our hearts with indelible ink; make them the most replayed song in the iPod of our soul; keep them before our eyes with neon-flashing brilliance.

This revolutionary truth contradicts our most basic instincts about everything, including salvation. We don't want to be ransomed, as guilty rebels; we want to be coddled, as misunderstood victims. We want a second chance, not a second birth. Forgive us, Lord Jesus.

In our marriages, too often we come not to serve but to be served and to give our criticisms about many things. As leaders in your church, we tend to associate greatness with exercising power and authority rather than washing feet and nurturing your lambs. Forgive us, Lord Jesus.

What a powerful Lord you are, redeeming the huge mess we've made of your world. What a gracious Savior you are, giving your life as the price for making all things new. We fall down before you, in awe of your humility and sacrifice for us. We rise to dance before you, as those upon whom you have lavished such great love, and so joyfully.

Lord Jesus, only you can change our hearts, and grace always runs downhill—always. We tremble to ask this, but expose our pride, humble our attitudes, and soften our hearts. Make us prefer the hidden place of service over the public place of being noticed. Make us glad to be your servants, wherever you place us. We pray in your tender and powerful name. Amen.

A Prayer about Normal Trials

Blessed be the God and Father of our Lord Jesus Christ! According to his great mercy, he has caused us to be born again to a living hope through the resurrection of Jesus Christ from the dead, to an inheritance that is imperishable, undefiled, and unfading, kept in heaven for you, who by God's power are being guarded through faith for a salvation ready to be revealed in the last time. In this you rejoice, though now for a little while, as was necessary, you have been grieved by various trials, so that the tested genuineness of your faith—more precious than gold that perishes though it is tested by fire—may be found to result in praise and glory and honor at the revelation of Jesus Christ. (1 Pet. 1:3–7)

Heavenly Father, today I need a fresh supply of persevering grace, for the "all kinds of trials" of life are sapping my spirit and weighing me down. I need to be reassured that you are refining my faith and not just ignoring me. I feel tired, weary, disillusioned, and a simmering anger is emerging in my spirit. A part of me just says, "Buck up, you woozy whiner!" But I think the gospel offers a better way.

Honestly, I'm embarrassed to even speak of my trials, because I didn't go to sleep hungry or thirsty last night, I didn't hear gunfire echoing through my neighborhood, there's no plague pillaging my community, I don't live with the fear of my children being sold into slavery, and my government isn't threatening the exercise of my faith. These are realities with which many of my brothers and sisters in Christ live on a daily basis.

For me, it's more like swimming in a pool of tiny piranha just nibbling away at my joy, energy, and peace. Please give me grace perfectly suited for the demands and the dailiness of normal life—in this body with aging joints and a leaking memory; among fellow sinner-saints who, like me, love inconsistently; in unresolved stories from the past and present of brokenness and weakness; in the face of minor injustices and a lack of common mercies; when cars, plumbing, air conditioners, and other stuff just break; when people don't say "thank you," people drive like maniacs, and pets pee on the carpet.

Lord, in all these things, I want your hand and heart to be at work. I want to know what a man of faith looks like, not just when I am praying for daily bread or facing a firing squad but when I'm living out the implications of the gospel in the daily messiness of normal life. I pray in Jesus' tender name. Amen.

A Prayer about Teachability

Whoever heeds life-giving correction
will be at home among the wise.
Those who disregard discipline despise themselves,
but the one who heeds correction gains understanding.
(Prov. 15:31–32 NIV)

Lord Jesus, scanning through the book of Proverbs recently, I noticed how many verses about staying teachable, receiving correction, and loving discipline I've underlined over the course of the years. I wish the sheer number of highlighted verses was an indication of how humble and nondefensive a man I am. But that's simply not the case. I still shift blame, make excuses, and sew fig leaves with the best of them.

So here's my prayer: I want to own, grieve, and repent of my defensiveness, Jesus. I'm not sure why, but I've become a little more touchy of late, a little more likely to bristle when confronted. I'm sure it's my pride, insecurities, and self-righteousness, but I'm equally sure you've got grace for that.

Jesus, help me anticipate and welcome feedback from my spouse about my attitude, choices, and excesses. Help me to hear your voice in things my children may want to or need to share with me about the past and the present. Help me to cultivate friendships in which growing in grace is just as important as the fun stuff we choose to do. Don't let me ignore concerns and corrections from mentors, "underlings," neighbors, even angels you send.

Help me not just to read the Bible but to have the Bible constantly reading me—exposing my sin and brokenness and revealing more and more and more of the riches of the gospel. There's no way I'll make "my home among the wise" without having my heart at home in your mercy, grace, and peace.

Jesus, it's because you made yourself of no reputation, becoming sin for me on the cross, that I don't have to live for my own reputation. Because I'm no longer guilty or condemned for my sin, I can live in the freedom of convictability, teachability, and humility. Help me, Jesus, help me. I pray in your gracious name. Amen.

A Prayer for Friends Weighed Down with Various Burdens

Moreover, as for me, far be it from me that I should sin against the LORD by ceasing to pray for you. (1 Sam. 12:23)

Dear Jesus, your intercession for us is one of our most prized gifts. And it's because of your great care and love for us that we bring our friends before you today—friends who are weighed down with various burdens and cares. There are enough stories of stress and struggles all around us to keep us on our knees for a long time. Where else can we go but to you? Hear our prayers for those we love.

Jesus, we pray for friends dealing with health issues. All along the continuum of common colds to uncommon cancers, we ask you to bring your mercy and healing, Jesus. Whether by the special grace of divine intervention or the common grace of good medicine and health care, it makes no difference. Mete out sufficient grace in each situation. Bring great glory to yourself. Make your presence clearly felt even if your ways cannot be easily discerned.

We pray for friends struggling financially and in their careers. You don't promise us abundance or surplus, Jesus, but you do promise to meet all our needs. We especially think of friends who are closer to mental and emotional bankruptcy than financial collapse. By the power of your resurrection and for your name's sake, open doors that seem locked and bolted. From your storehouse of everlasting goodness, bring forth the right provision at the right time. It's most likely you will use us as a part of the answer to our prayers. May we be generous and gracious in serving our friends.

We pray for friends who are burdened relationally. Marriage will always be a center of unrelenting spiritual warfare, for this relationship is meant to tell the story of your great love for your bride. Pour out your Spirit, Jesus. Humble the proud and bring hope to the despairing. Defuse the anger and clarify the issues. Supply the right counsel, and grant ample supplies of forbearance, forgiveness, and reconciliation.

We ask the same for whole families, long-standing friendships, and local churches under the siege of broken relationships and battered trust. Do far beyond what we can ask or imagine, for the only thing that counts is faith expressing itself in love. Help us, Jesus, for your glory and fame. We pray in your peerless and priceless name. Amen.

A Prayer about Quarrelsomeness

It is better to live in a corner of the housetop
than in a house shared with a quarrelsome wife. (Prov. 21:9)

Gracious Jesus, how often have I read this proverb with the image of a group of "good" men sitting around a Judean campfire complaining about their nagging, "drippy faucet" wives. How arrogant and male of me to act as though only women and wives can be quarrelsome! Yikes! I well know this verse could just as accurately describe a husband, friend, or parent.

Today I want to own my quarrelsomeness and to ask you to free me for far more healthy and redemptive ways of expressing disappointment, making a point, and engaging in conflict.

Jesus, when I lose sight of the real issue and simply get argumentative with my spouse, friends, kids, or even strangers, arrest my proud heart. I'm very aware that sometimes my need to win sabotages my commitment to love well. The result is never good.

When I keep festering and pestering, rather than resting in you, expose my insecure ways for what they really are: I'm assuming the role of the fourth member of the Trinity. Lord, there's no joy in driving the people I love onto the corner of a roof.

Jesus, when I protest more than I pray; when I launch more than I listen; when I'm more grouchy than grace-full; when I'm more self-righteous than either right or righteous; when I repay nag for nag, petty for petty, immaturity for immaturity—convict me, forgive me, help me, change me.

Because the gospel is true, I have hope. Because the gospel is true, I repent. I pray in your compassionate name. Amen.

A Prayer about Soul Satisfaction

Because your love is better than life,
    my lips will glorify you.
I will praise you as long as I live,
    and in your name I will lift up my hands.
I will be fully satisfied as with the richest of foods;
    with singing lips my mouth will praise you. (Ps. 63:3–5 NIV)

Dear Jesus, King David's words of unbridled adoration are a rebuke to my measured heart. I spend a lot of time and energy trying to make a "better" life for myself, and yet David speaks of your love as being *better than life itself*! What a holy paradox. Oh, to know your love in such a sensate, soul-satisfying way.

Jesus, what would it be like to be so alive to the width, length, height, and depth of your love that I lose control? David danced with shameless nakedness before the returned ark of the covenant. Why can't I be as free before the finished cross of glory?

I have no trouble singing to you or lifting my hands in the assembly of your people. But I want to be free to love out loud in contexts not so safe and predictable. I want your love to free me for loving one woman well the rest of my life, no matter what that involves. Oh, that my wife would taste your delight by the way I care for her. I want to be free to use fewer words in relationships so there's more space for listening, sitting still, and savoring other people's stories and struggles. I want to be a friend who offers a taste of how you love us—how you love me.

I want your love to be so compelling that I don't think of "witnessing" to people, just loving and serving them. I want your love to be so satisfying that I find it hard to make excuses for my brokenness and much easier to live transparently and authentically before others. I want your love to bring forth hot tears of compassion and loud guffaws of joy. You've set me free for eternity. Jesus, please set me free for today. I pray in your loving name. Amen.

A Prayer about No More Death

"He will wipe every tear from their eyes. There will be no more death or mourning or crying or pain, for the old order of things has passed away." He who was seated on the throne said, "I am making everything new!" Then he said, "Write this down, for these words are trustworthy and true." (Rev. 21:4–5 NIV)

Dear Jesus, I've never longed for the day of "no more death" more so than today. It's a source of immeasurable comfort to know this promise is trustworthy and true, for your death was the death of death, Jesus. Indeed, Jesus, you are making all things new. Your resurrection is the guarantee and firstfruits of a whole new order. Decay and death, in every form, will be gone forever. Hasten that day, Jesus; hasten that day.

No more picking out caskets for loved ones. No more compost piles of yesterday's bouquets. No more walking to divorce court with broken friends. No more death of innocence. No more life-robbing cancers. No more burying of unrealized dreams. No more environmental disasters. No longer the heartache of "putting down" a beloved pet.

Jesus, this is the first day in nearly sixteen years I wake up minus a faithful friend. The void is great and the tears are many. Luther had it right: some of the greatest companions you give us in life are our pets. I never dreamed a Yorkshire terrier could have been such a declaration of your glory.

A part of me is embarrassed for feeling so sad. The other part says, "Go for it. Let yourself go. Grieve the loss; grieve the ugliness of death that you might advocate for the promise of life—resurrection life—eternal life." Surely that's the way of the gospel, Jesus.

So as you wipe my tears, please fuel my hope and focus my gaze. Death is defeated but not yet annihilated. Decay will be no more, but not yet. Send us forth as your people, Jesus, into the valley of the shadow of death with a glimpse of the first sunrise in the new heaven and new earth. It's supposed to feel like hurt and hope at the same time.

You will make the written saying true: "Death has been swallowed up in victory." "Where, O death, is your victory? Where, O death, is your sting?" (1 Cor. 15:54–55 NIV). You are the grave robber, Jesus. Our labors in you are not in vain. In your trustworthy and triumphant name I pray. Amen.

A Prayer about a Third Kind of Son

And he arose and came to his father. But while he was still a long way off,
his father saw him and felt compassion, and ran and embraced him and
kissed him. (Luke 15:20)

Heavenly Father, I'm not beginning my day in a faraway country,
derelict and destitute. Though I'm capable of anything, I'm not
sitting here filled with shame for squandering an inheritance, and neither
am I out in a field feeding somebody else's pigs.

I'm in a comfortable chair, sipping a fresh cup of coffee, surrounded by
more than my share of creature comforts. And yet I'm just as much in need
of fellowship with you as *any* of your broken children . . . so here I come.

Because the gospel is true, I bring you my busy, bland, somewhat disconnected heart. I feel like a third son right now. I'm not struggling with the
extremes of either of your boys in Luke 15. I'm not acting out in destructive "fleshy" ways, and I'm not presently wallowing in the ugliness of my
self-righteousness. I'm just somewhere in between. I still hear and love the
wonderful music of the gospel, but I just don't feel like dancing right now.

So, Father, as I come to you today, I take great comfort in knowing that
I'll *always* find you filled with compassion for me, even when my feelings
are not fully engaged with you. As I saunter toward you, you're always
running toward me in Jesus. As I'm glad to see you, you see me from afar
and are *thrilled* at the sighting.

When I'm not as inclined to lift my arms in praise to you, your embrace
is the most predictable element in my day. You don't just put your hand on
my shoulder; you throw your arms around me in the gospel. And though
my affection for you wavers, you will shower me with multiple kisses all
day long, for you love your children with an everlasting, unwavering love.

Because the gospel is true, I'll seek to live to your glory today, neither
by sight nor by my feelings but by the faith you've given me to trust and
love you. It's not my grasp of you but your grasp of me in the gospel that
matters the most. It's not the enjoyment of my peace with you but the
assurance that you are at peace with me that is the anchor for my soul. I
pray in Jesus' wonderful and merciful name. Amen.

A Prayer about the Impossible

But he [Jesus] said, "What is impossible with men is possible with God."
(Luke 18:27)

Gracious Jesus, you offered these words of hope to disciples trying to picture a camel squeezing through the eye of a needle. You speak the same words to me in light of many situations for which I need to accept my limitations and lay hold of your sufficiency.

I begin this day remembering that your commitment is to make all things new, *not* make all new things. There is an enormous difference between the two. Indeed, Jesus, you've placed us in a story of restoration, not replacement. You are actively at work in the broken places and among broken people, including me. Through your resurrection, we've been given great assurance and hope for a redeemed universe. This is incredibly good news—the best news ever.

The hard news is that I have to accept that many things are impossible for me. My best intentions, efforts, and resources are simply not enough. I see this especially in my relationships. This requires a humility and faith the gospel alone can provide. Grant me both, Jesus; grant me both.

I cannot change me, so why do I assume the omnipotence to fix others? As much as I long to see friends freed from addictions, marriages brought back from the brink of death, and stubborn people made gentle and kind, Jesus, you alone have the power of resurrection. Maybe the greater challenge will be for you to make me a patient, caring, present friend. Please show me the first nose hair of this camel poking through a needle's eye. Hasten the day of perfect newness in my heart. I pray in your majestic name. Amen.

A Prayer about Death by Resentment

Resentment kills a fool. (Job 5:2 NIV)

Gracious Jesus, it's been entirely too hot in our city this summer, and I've been registering that complaint entirely too many times—so much, in fact, that I can now see how my complaining has been morphing into resenting. It came to a head yesterday when I walked out my front door for a jog, only to find myself cursing the humidity, the temperature, even the sun.

I came back inside and inaugurated a thirty-minute pout. That's when you convicted me, when you let me know the weather's not the only thing I've been resenting lately.

I resent having to explain and repeat myself. Why can't everybody instantly intuit what I'm thinking? I resent grocery stores running out of my favorite cereal. Who does their stocking, anyway? I resent gossips, so much that I gossip to others about their gossip. I resent change and transition. Why can't everything stay the same, or at least disrupt my plans and "groove" minimally?

I resent resentful people. Why can't they stop their whining and be more content with what they have? I resent roads that are always being repaired, drivers that delay moving four seconds after the red light turns green, birds that do their business on my windshield. I resent good grass dying and crabgrass thriving. I especially resent that people I love suffer too much, too soon in life. It just doesn't seem right or fair.

Jesus, my resentment will either kill me as a fool or drive me to you for life. I choose the second option. Forgive me for fertilizing a spirit of entitlement. Forgive me for not pulling up the roots of bitterness sooner. Forgive me for being better at resenting than repenting of late. Forgive me for demanding life in the "not yet" before the "already" is over. Forgive me for preaching the gospel to others but not to myself. Forgive me for telling others of the sufficiency of your grace while looking for some other balm for myself.

I make no excuses or promises. Today, right now, I simply collapse upon you afresh as my wisdom, my righteousness, my holiness, and my redemption (1 Cor. 1:30). I praise you that I'm not feeling condemnation, for there is none. I praise you that I am feeling conviction, for there is plenty. I pray in your patient and loving name. Amen.

A Prayer about Jesus' Joyful Kingship

But of the Son he says, "Your throne, O God, is forever and ever, the scepter of uprightness is the scepter of your kingdom. You have loved righteousness and hated wickedness; therefore God, your God, has anointed you with the oil of gladness beyond your companions." (Heb. 1:8–9)

Lord Jesus, there's really nothing that affects my life more than how I think about you. The more I see you everywhere in the Scriptures, the more I understand why you alone are worthy of our adoration, affection, and allegiance. I expect to say the same thing ten thousand years from now.

Today I'm marveling at your joyful kingship. It's stunning to see the relationship between your joy and your hatred of wickedness and love of righteousness. Jesus, you delight to crush evil and you rejoice in making all things new. Indeed, your kingdom is a kingdom of righteousness, peace, and joy in the Holy Spirit (Rom. 14:7). The Father has placed the government of the entire cosmos on your shoulders, and your reign of grace and peace is expanding all the time. You are the joyful King of the ages.

But I also marvel at your request for the Father to fill your church with this very same joy—the fullness of your joy—the joy you have eternally enjoyed within the Godhead (John 17:13).

May an increase in our joy propel us into expanded servanthood. May it be the fire we need for doing justice, loving mercy, and walking humbly with our God. May the oil of your joy encourage and refresh us lest we grow weary in the battle.

Jesus, Satan was crushed under your feet on the cross, and he will soon be crushed under *our* feet at your return (Rom. 16:20). Your throne will last forever and ever, and your kingdom will never end. We pray with joy, in your triumphant name. Amen.

A Prayer about Sex

For this is the will of God, your sanctification: that you abstain from sexual immorality; that each one of you know how to control his own body in holiness and honor, not in the passion of lust like the Gentiles who do not know God; that no one transgress and wrong his brother in this matter.
(1 Thess. 4:3–6)

Jesus, a part of me is blushing and squirming as I pray through this text. The word *sex* engenders the widest range of thoughts and emotions. There is no part of our being that carries a greater capacity to reveal beauty and evil.

Grant us grace and wisdom to steward the precious gift of sex. In our marriages, may your servant love be revealed in the way we honor and care for one another. In the ebb and flow of sexual desire, give us kindness to be for the other.

In our singleness, give grace shaped for each situation. When good desire gets hijacked by sinful choices, forgive us and strengthen us. In our struggles, grant us a loving and holy commitment not to exploit anyone else's heart or body to satisfy ourselves.

For those of us engaged in sinful indulgence—pornography, prostitution, infidelity, and other expressions of broken sexuality—have mercy on us. Give us convicted hearts, repentant faith, and a willingness to get help. For those of us married to someone sinfully entrapped or addicted to sex, grant exponential grace, wisdom, safety, and more grace. May the pain of betrayal not preclude the desire and hope of redemption.

For those of us wounded and broken by stories of sexual abuse or sexual misuse, bring your healing heart and hand to bear, Jesus. Take us on the path to safety, beauty, and restoration. For those of us married to a husband or wife wounded and broken through sexual sin, grant us kindness, mercy, patience, and hope.

Lord Jesus, in all of these situations and stories, convince us that what we need more than anything else is to connect with you intimately. Even the best marriage and most fulfilling sex life is no substitute for the wonders of marriage to you. You are the spouse we always wanted and needed. That is not hype, Jesus; it is our hope. We humbly pray in your great and tender name. Amen.

A Prayer about Fear and Trusting God

When I am afraid, I put my trust in you.
In God, whose word I praise—
in God I trust and am not afraid.
What can mere mortals do to me? (Ps. 56:3–4 NIV)

Heavenly Father, as the reach of the internet keeps getting bigger, my world keeps getting smaller. More so than ever, I'm aware of my brothers and sisters all around the world who are clinging to you and to this Scripture today. Be praised, O trustworthy Father, even as we bring our family before you.

I pray for the Christian community in Pakistan. The recent flood has been inconceivably devastating for the whole nation, and yet even more so for the 2 or 3 percent of the population who are followers of Jesus. They're already persecuted, and now they're being neglected in this time of crisis. For the glory of Jesus, I pray for enough clean water and food to meet their needs *and* enough to share with their Muslim neighbors. May the gospel advance in Pakistan by way of this horrible crisis, through your faithfulness and the servant love of your people.

I also pray for our brothers and sisters in North Korea, Saudi Arabia, Iran, Somalia, Maldives, Bhutan, Yemen, Vietnam, Laos, and China—the ten places in the world where Christians are most likely to be singled out for persecution. Father, may your perfect love drive out their fears and strengthen their trust in you.

What can mortals do to us? Plenty, Father, but in view of who you are and what really matters, very little. Grant us all the same grace and courage you gave Justin Martyr. When facing those who would take his life, he responded, "You may kill us, but you cannot harm us." What but the gospel can create such a people?

Lastly, gracious Father, for friends on our streets and in our churches facing hard medical reports, dwindling financial resources, and other hard providences, bring the gospel to bear in tangible and faith-producing ways. And use us, Father, as answers to the very prayers we pray. We pray in Jesus' most glorious name. Amen.

A Prayer about Temptation

No temptation has overtaken you that is not common to man. God is faithful, and he will not let you be tempted beyond your ability, but with the temptation he will also provide the way of escape, that you may be able to endure it. (1 Cor. 10:13)

Faithful Jesus, as you know, this was one of the very first verses I memorized back in the summer of 1968 as someone who had known you only a few months. It was timely and encouraging then, and a little over four decades later, it's still the same. The seizing power of temptation is just as real to a sixty-year-old as to an eighteen-year-old.

It would be one thing if temptation came like junk mail, quite easy to recognize, ignore, and discard. But at times temptation comes with such enticing, alluring, and promissory power that "standing up under it" doesn't appear possible. I would despair and question the reality of my faith if I didn't have the assurance that temptation itself is not sin (James 1:13–15). Jesus, the very fact that you suffered the full fury of temptation also gives me hope and keeps me sane.

The encouraging and timely parts of this verse, Jesus, are the commonality of every temptation and the promise of a way out of any temptation. This assures me that no matter how dark, foolish, or destructive are the things that enter my mind, such temptations are not unique to me. Such temptations are common to other believers, just like me. I'm not terrible because I'm tempted, but I am tempted to do terrible things.

Jesus, I ask for myself and for a host of friends, bring the hope and resources of the gospel to bear at the very places we feel the seducing power of temptation the most. Whether our temptations are sexual, financial, relational, or alcohol or drug related, it makes no difference—show us the way of escape, and give us strength to choose that way. Jesus, give us enough grace in this very day to prove your faithfulness and to keep ourselves free from acting out in ways we will surely regret. We pray, Jesus, in your all-sufficient name. Amen.

A Prayer about the God Who Encourages

May our Lord Jesus Christ himself and God our Father, who loved us and by his grace gave us eternal encouragement and good hope, encourage your hearts and strengthen you in every good deed and word.
(2 Thess. 2:16–17 NIV)

Gracious Father, just reading your Word encourages me. You could delegate a legion of angels, you could send a bird to sit on my shoulder, you could have a few friends call me—any of which would be nice—but you, yourself, come to us in the Bible. I'm humbled and I'm very grateful.

The Scriptures are such a gift to us. They are a treasure trove of hope, an artesian spring of well-timed refreshment, a perpetual supply of redemptive surprises and return trips to gospel sanity.

Father, because of the "eternal encouragement and good hope" of your grace for us in Jesus, I can risk making myself vulnerable today and cry out to heaven without muting or masking my weariness. Lord, I'm more than a bit weary as the day begins. I feel tired, discouraged, listless, on edge, and uptight.

I don't know if I've tried to get too much done in too little time. I'm not sure about the spiritual warfare issues swirling about me; it could be the accuser whispering lies and condemnation. Perhaps it's just that I'm getting older and I don't have the same energy I used to have. It could just be the tension of life in the "already and not yet," or maybe I'm trying to do life with too little sleep. Then again, possibly it's just the groaning of birth pangs in my heart, so wanting to be much more like Jesus than I already am. Probably it's all of the above.

In any case, and every case, I look to you to encourage my heart and strengthen me for gospel deeds and words all this day long. I cast my care on you because I know you care for me. I pray in Jesus' name, with thanksgiving and glad anticipation. Amen.

264

A Prayer about the Process of Forgiving

Bear with each other and forgive one another if any of you has a grievance against someone. Forgive as the Lord forgave you. (Col. 3:13 NIV)

Gracious Jesus, every time I pray the Lord's Prayer, I'm confronted with the dailiness of the call to forgiveness. Usually that's not a big deal. Maybe it's because I'm conflict avoidant and would rather wave off an offense than deal with the chaos and mess. But you've been forcing the issue over the past few weeks. There's brokenness all around me and in me.

My conflict avoidance is a thin veil for the serial killer that lives within. Even as I write and pray this prayer, two names and faces come before me that I *know* I haven't forgiven. I've so enjoyed holding them hostage emotionally by my critical spirit and self-righteous smugness. Help me, Jesus, and others like me. Though I'm convicted, I can't say that I relish the idea of letting go of my pain. Have mercy on me, Jesus.

I praise you for already forgiving all of my sins—past, present, and future; every sin of word, thought, and deed. I praise you for not merely waving off my sins but wading into the mess and paying the supreme price of your life and death. As I ponder the riches of your grace, I realize that unforgiveness is the greatest non sequitur of all. I purpose to begin forgiving these two people and anyone else you bring to mind. I repent, but I do not promise anything. You must help me, Jesus. I cannot and I will not do this on my own. I pray in your holy and loving name. Amen.

A Prayer about Freedom and Christian Cannibalism

For you were called to freedom, brothers. Only do not use your freedom as an opportunity for the flesh, but through love serve one another. For the whole law is fulfilled in one word: "You shall love your neighbor as yourself." But if you bite and devour one another, watch out that you are not consumed by one another. (Gal. 5:13–15)

Dear Jesus, I'm thankful the gospel is more like a subpoena than a mere invitation. Our need is so great that we could not respond apart from such a strong summons. Indeed, the gospel is a life-giving subpoena—the means by which you call us from death to life, from slavery to freedom. We were just as dead and bound in graveclothes as Lazarus was when you spoke the words "Come out" (John 11:43), and you raised us from spiritual death.

I praise you for the sovereign, death-defeating, liberty-giving power of the gospel. Those you set free are free indeed! And the freedom to which you've called us is to define the rest of our days and permeate every area of our lives.

This is nowhere more necessary than in the world of our relationships. We're to love one another as you love us, Jesus. According to you, this is a confirming mark of true discipleship (John 13:34–35). But as in Galatia, so in our churches, marriages, and friendships; it's a blatant and ugly contradiction of the gospel when we fall into "Christian cannibalism"—biting and devouring one another. Worse, it's a sabotaging of your glory and a veiling of your beauty. It's lying about who you are and what it means to be in relationship with you. Forgive us; forgive me.

Please show me where I'm living like a relational piranha—nibbling on others' brokenness and inconsistencies more than I'm feasting on the gospel; holding on to unforgiveness just to gain advantage in a relationship; rehearsing the sins of others more than I'm remembering the way you've forgiven me; being petty rather than patient, critical rather than compassionate, mean rather than merciful. Help me know when overlooking the failures of others would be not cowardice but courage. Help me learn how to go through conflict redemptively, rather than destructively.

Lord Jesus, we're free only because of you. Help me to steward this costly freedom today in a world of broken people and broken relationships. I pray in your glorious and graceful name. Amen.

A Prayer about Wisdom

If any of you lacks wisdom, let him ask God, who gives generously to all
without reproach, and it will be given him. (James 1:5)

Heavenly Father, how I praise you for free and full access into your
presence, all the time, all because you have declared all your children to be perfectly righteous in your Son, Jesus. And I praise you that as
I come today seeking wisdom, I'm kissed by your welcome and inundated
with your generosity.

Indeed, I really need your wisdom, Father, about a few matters that
currently confuse me, all of them centering on who I am as a relational
person. However you wish to inform my heart, the peace I have is that
you will always do so in concert with the gift of your Word.

Father, I need you to show me the difference between a healthy costly
investment in people's lives versus an unhealthy entanglement and enmesh-
ment. I know the gospel is *always* calling me and giving me the resources
to love as Jesus loves me, but sometimes I don't really know what that
looks like. Help me, Father; help me.

I need wisdom to discern the difference between rightly validating the
emotions of those I love versus wrongly taking responsibility for their
emotions. My broken default mode will probably always be to try to "fix"
people, but I confess yet again that you are not calling me to fix anyone
but to love everyone. Grant me wisdom, dear Father; grant me wisdom.

I need wisdom, Father, about my own emotional world. The emotion
of anger has always confused and threatened me. Help me to know when
the anger I feel is nothing more than the response of a little boy not getting
his way. Help me to know when the anger I swallow should be expressed
appropriately, not swallowed. Help me to get angry in the face of injustice,
that I might love redemptively in the face of evil. Help me to listen and
seek to understand the emotion of anger in others and not rush to judgment or rush out of their story too fast.

Father, just praying this prayer stirs up so many other thoughts and
feelings inside my heart. My joy is in knowing that we can keep this
conversation going throughout the day. My great joy is in knowing that
you will give me and my friends the wisdom we need, and you will do so
generously. You gave *all* our fault to Jesus on the cross that we might live
in your permanent world of *all* your favor. We cry hallelujah as in your
name we pray. Amen.

A Prayer for Bringing Conflicting Friends to Jesus

I therefore, a prisoner for the Lord, urge you to walk in a manner worthy of the calling to which you have been called, with all humility and gentleness, with patience, bearing with one another in love, eager to maintain the unity of the Spirit in the bond of peace. (Eph. 4:1–3)

Gracious Jesus, there are times when your faithful servants don't see eye to eye on very important matters. Our best efforts at keeping "the unity of the Spirit in the bond of peace" (Eph. 4:3) get stressed and tested. Differing perspectives lead to sharp disagreements, and sharp disagreements can lead to the parting of ways. This happens in marriages, among good friends, on the mission field, in local churches, and in seminary boardrooms.

This morning I'm bringing three current expressions of this very scenario before your throne of grace. My heart's heavy, but not as heavy as it would be if I didn't believe you to be the Prince of Peace; if I didn't believe in the power of the gospel; if I didn't believe that your name is Redeemer and Restorer. Here's my prayer for friends in the throes of turmoil.

Lord Jesus, may seeking first your kingdom and your righteousness far outweigh any other seeking—seeking to win, seeking to be right, seeking to avoid pain, seeking to get our own way. It's your glory and story that matter the most, Jesus, not ours.

Help us to recognize and resist the schemes of Satan in these conflicts. He hates you, your followers, your church—he is passionately committed to destroying all expressions of beauty among your people. Help my friends keep the main issues in view and not get drawn into biting and devouring one another (Gal. 5:13–15).

May friends who see the issues so differently still honor one another as family and beloved servants of Jesus. How we handle our conflicts is just as important as the issues that generate our conflicts—maybe even more important at times.

Even as you redeemed the painful story between Paul and Barnabas (Acts 15:36–40; 2 Tim. 4), so bring redemption in these broken stories that are breaking my heart. I pray with sadness but trusting in your powerful name. Amen.

A Prayer about Peace

Peacemakers who sow in peace raise a harvest of righteousness.
(James 3:18 NIV)

Dear Jesus, it's the day on our calendar that now has its own dark branding, "9/11." There have been many days in history that stand out as graphic reminders of the pervasive brokenness of the world—of just how far we have fallen and just how fully the peace of creation has been violated by sin and death. But in my lifetime, no day in American history tells that story more clearly than September 11.

I'll never forget how it felt watching the Twin Towers of the World Trade Center crumble to the earth. It was chilling, frightful, and surreal. But as I remember that day of extreme terror and trauma, I also choose to remember you, Jesus. Otherwise I would stew in despair or simply be driven to rage.

Lord Jesus, you are the Prince of Peace—the archetypal Peacemaker. You are the one who has come to make all things new, to restore broken things, to bring new creation delight from old creation decay.

Your death on the cross was the ultimate sowing of peace. As you died, taking the judgment we deserve, you were planted as the very seed that has secured an eternal harvest of righteousness. Your death was the death of death itself and the promise of eternal shalom.

Because of you, terror is terrified. Indeed, because of you, one day there will be no terror or tears. There will be no more brokenness or barrenness, no more heartaches or even heartburn, no more human trafficking or even human tooth decay, no more war or even aggravation, no more evil or even envy, no more poverty or even pouting, and no more "not yet," "not enough," or "not now."

Our labors in you, King Jesus, are not in vain. Because of you we can, and must, live as peacemakers, sowing the peace of the gospel of the kingdom, with the absolute assurance that a harvest of righteousness is being raised and will be reaped.

We praise you that your name is Redeemer, Reconciler, and Restorer. We cry out loud, "Maranatha!" Come, Lord Jesus, come! Until that day, give us all the mercy, grace, and peace we need for this day. We pray with joy and hope. Amen.

A Prayer about Soul Rest

Yes, my soul, find rest in God;
    my hope comes from him.
Truly he is my rock and my salvation;
    he is my fortress, I will not be shaken.
My salvation and my honor depend on God;
    he is my mighty rock, my refuge.
Trust in him at all times, you people;
    pour out your hearts to him,
    for God is our refuge. (Ps. 62:5–8 NIV)

Gracious Father, nothing compares with being certain of your love for me. The peace I have knowing I no longer have to perform or pretend with you about anything is incomparable. Today, in particular, I'm thankful for the freedom to pour out my heart to you. Because the gospel is true, I don't have to measure or monitor my words with you. You don't judge my prayers. You purify them as they meet you at the throne of grace. How I praise you for such a standing in grace!

Here's what's going on inside of me today. I feel a restlessness that I cannot really attach to any one thing. There's a floating disquiet, a nibbling anxiousness, a low rumble of dread that's just hanging there. It could easily morph into something much bigger if I'm not connected to you in a fresh and vital way.

So today I echo back to you King David's longing for soul rest, and I make his prayer mine. "Soul, find your rest in God alone! Don't medicate with anything else. Don't minimize or supersize your restlessness. Just go to Jesus. Go to Jesus right now!"

Indeed, Jesus, I don't want to waste energy on the "paralysis of analysis." I don't want to spend time navel-gazing today. I don't want to treat my soul like an onion to be peeled, layer by layer. Whatever is repentable or repairable, I'm sure you'll show me. *I just want you*, Lord Jesus. I ask you to bring your centering presence, your stabilizing mercy, and your calming peace to my soul. Kiss my heart with the gospel, and it will be enough.

I do trust you, Jesus, at this time, even as I want to trust you at all times. You are my rock, my salvation, my fortress, my honor, my refuge, and a whole, whole lot more King David didn't mention in this psalm! I pray today with hope and anticipation. Amen.

A Prayer about Triumph

But thanks be to God, who in Christ always leads us in triumphal procession,
and through us spreads the fragrance of the knowledge of him everywhere.
(2 Cor. 2:14)

King Jesus, I greet and praise you this day for being a most merciful and mighty Savior. You completely save those who come to you in faith, and the very faith we need for coming to you, you freely give us in the gospel. You're the great warrior of the heart. You've come to overthrow the reign of sin by the reign of grace. You are the victorious King.

Jesus, I gladly take my place in the triumphant procession Paul described in this passage. I humbly assume the posture of both the conquered and the conqueror. I praise you for rescuing me from the dominion of darkness, a kingdom in which I was both a willing citizen and a desperate slave. Only the gospel was powerful enough to set me free. Thank you for triumphing over me and in me.

I'm also grateful to be among those released for a life of announcing your triumph of mercy and grace. What more could I want for the rest of my life than to be someone through whom the fragrance of the gospel is released—the aroma of forgiveness and freedom, the incense announcing a kingdom of reconciliation and restoration?

Jesus, how I praise you that life in the gospel is not a preoccupation with the "victorious Christian life" but a preoccupation with you, the victorious Christ! You are my loving master, not my private masseuse. Forgive me when my prayers reflect a greater commitment to my comfort than to your kingdom. Free me from "claiming" things you never promised. Give me much more joy in living for your glory than in living for my personal gain.

Wherever you take me in the triumphant procession of the gospel is the best place to be. However you want to spread the fragrance of knowing you is the best way to live. I pray in your glorious name. Amen.

A Prayer about Completion

And I am sure of this, that he who began a good work in you will bring it to completion at the day of Jesus Christ. (Phil. 1:6)

Gracious Father, today is a great day to be reminded that "salvation is of the Lord." You're the one who begins the "good work" of redemption in our lives. You're the one who is carrying it on, even when you're not working according to our timetable and agenda. And you're the one who will complete our redemption on the day Jesus returns to finish making all things new.

This is incredibly good news, I recognize as I ponder my story and the lives of other people you've placed in my life. I can't be my own savior, and neither can I be anyone else's savior. The pressure is off! What a great relief, but also what a critical truth to remember. This good news, this best of all news, leads me to offer these earnest prayers . . .

Father, give me the same confidence for my friends you gave Paul for the Philippians. Sometimes irritation, worry, and fear loom larger in my life than patience, trust, and hope. When this happens, I'm pretty worthless as a friend.

Teach me how to wrestle in confident prayer for others, like Epaphras, who wrestled in prayer for the believers in Colossae (Col. 4:12). My tendency is to wrangle emotionally rather than wrestle believingly. This leaves me worn out, and it simply frustrates others. They feel pressure from me to change, rather than encouragement in their journey.

Keep me tender enough to engage in my friends' broken stories but tough enough not to give in to the pulls I often feel from them. Help me not to get entangled in things that have nothing to do with me, but give me the tenacity to stay present. Teach me how to wait on you without falling into self-protective passivity or self-validating activity.

Only the gospel is sufficient for the demands of loving well, so I abandon myself to you and your resources. Help me see others as you see them, Father, and help me to love them as Jesus loves me. I pray in Jesus' compassionate name. Amen.

A Prayer about Jesus
Opening Our Minds

"Everything written about me in the Law of Moses and the Prophets and the Psalms must be fulfilled." Then he [Jesus] opened their minds to understand the Scriptures, and said to them, "Thus it is written, that the Christ should suffer and on the third day rise from the dead, and that repentance and forgiveness of sins should be proclaimed in his name to all nations, beginning from Jerusalem." (Luke 24:44–47)

Lord Jesus, I've always considered myself to be pretty open-minded. Yet as I meditate on this remarkable scene in Luke's Gospel, I realize I'm not nearly as open-minded as you intend. For myself and for my friends, I ask, help us to see you *everywhere* in the Bible, Jesus. Enable us to read the law of Moses, the Prophets, and the psalms with you clearly in view.

For years I thought of the law only as a bunch of rules and principles by which I could earn God's favor and blessings, or at least micromanage my life for greater success. Now I understand that the law was given to drive us to you, Jesus. It was never given as a basis of my acceptance with God. You've fulfilled the law for us by your perfect obedience, and you've exhausted its judgment by your death on the cross. I wish I'd understood this earlier in my walk with you.

I used to read the Prophets with a fear of judgment and great intrigue about the future of Israel. Now I realize that all of God's promises point to you, Jesus. You are the "Yes" and "Amen" to every promise God has made. The gospel of your kingdom claims the entire cosmos, not just the Middle East—not just Jerusalem but the New Jerusalem as well.

I've always loved the Psalms, but until recent years, I read them more with an appreciation for David than with adoration for you, Jesus. But you are the King installed by your Father, the one who inherits the nations and the ends of the earth (Ps. 2). Indeed, Jesus, continue to open our minds to understand how the entire Bible is a revelation of the gospel—the story of God's commitment to redeem his people and restore the world by you . . . and through us. Show us more of you and our place in your story. We pray in your peerless name. Amen.

A Prayer for Perfectionists

There is no fear in love, but perfect love casts out fear. For fear has to do with punishment, and whoever fears has not been perfected in love. We love because he first loved us. (1 John 4:18–19)

Gracious Father, I begin this day with a desire to live much less of a driven life and much more of a called life. In essence, I want to live with less fear and more freedom, less by frenzy and more by faith, with fewer obsessions and with much more adoration of you, the God of all peace.

As I get older I just don't have as much energy to juggle as many balls or spin as many plates as I used to. This is simultaneously a humbling thing and a good thing. For if greater grace comes to the humble, then accepting my limitations is essential for my liberation. Lord, I believe; help my unbelief!

It's not difficult to see that my drivenness and busyness are rooted in fear—the fear of not being enough and having enough, the fear of losing face and losing control, the fear of missing the mark and missing out.

Come, Lord Jesus, come. Your perfect love alone can liberate this poser, performer, and perfectionist. Drive out my fears by a greater grasp of your grace. You lived a life of perfect obedience for me as the second Adam, fulfilling everything God requires of me. You died a death of perfect love for me as the Lamb of God, exhausting God's judgment against my sin. Your resurrection from the dead on the third day is the firstfruits and guarantee that one day I will be as lovely as you and as loving as you, Jesus.

Indeed, one day I will be made perfect in love, all because of you, Lord Jesus, for perfection can only be found in you. I love you because you first loved me and continue to love me. May your perfect love continue to drive all pernicious fear from my life. I pray in your glorious name. Amen.

A Prayer for Treasuring Jesus

For in Scripture it says: "See, I lay a stone in Zion, a chosen and precious cornerstone, and the one who trusts in him [Jesus] will never be put to shame." Now to you who believe, this stone is precious. (1 Pet. 2:6–7 NIV)

Jesus, when I hear the word *precious*, I immediately think about silver, gold, and platinum, all called "precious metals." Or I think about "precious gemstones" like diamonds, sapphires, rubies, and emeralds.

But if anything or anyone deserves the appellation "precious," it's you, Jesus—God's chosen cornerstone and precious capstone of our redemption. For the combined worth of all precious metals and gemstones that have ever existed does not compare with the unsearchable riches that are found in you. To trust in you, Jesus, is to be free from the burden of our guilt and the paralyzing power of our shame.

To trust in you, Jesus—to boast in the gift of your righteousness, to rest in the constancy of your love, to wake up each day to your endless mercies, to hear you sing to us in the gospel—is to feel the stranglehold of shame lose its grip over our hearts.

Jesus, I praise you for taking the guilt of our sin and the shame of our brokenness on the cross. You became sin *for us* that *in you* we might become the righteousness of God. Because of you, judgment day holds no terror. The cross was our judgment day. We no longer fear the gaze of God because of the grace of God we have in you.

May you become more and more precious to us, Jesus. May the gospel continue to change the price tags on everything in our world. May yesterday's values be considered today's loss compared to the surpassing greatness of knowing you. We pray in your glorious name. Amen.

A Prayer about a Fresh Encounter with God's Favor

The Spirit of the Lord is on me, because he has anointed me to proclaim good news to the poor. He has sent me to proclaim freedom for the prisoners and recovery of sight for the blind, to set the oppressed free, to proclaim the year of the Lord's favor. (Luke 4:18–19 NIV)

Jesus, I know this passage very well, but today I feel my need for these truths in a desperate way. I'm zeroing in on the promise of God's favor, which you proclaim. Several things have converged in the past few days that make me feel like the banner flying over my head isn't *love* (Song of Sol. 2:4) but *disfavor . . . failure . . . unwanted*.

You've taught me in the past about the importance of stewarding my emotions—that is, about not reacting to difficult people with fear and anger but responding to them with listening and grace. Jesus, all of that just flew out the window yesterday, and I'm coming to you now in brokenness and sadness. I'm not proud of the way I acted, but I don't want to settle down into a pity party or a blamefest.

I'm a poor man in need of the Good News today, Jesus. I need you to proclaim freedom for my worn down, weary heart. I need you to open my eyes to see the gospel today as though I were seeing it for the very first time. I need release from the oppression of my introspection and the condemnation of Satan.

Jesus, by the power of the Holy Spirit, proclaim the year of the Lord's favor to my heart today, in this moment. I can explain this great truth to others, but right now I need to know it for myself. My theology is not in doubt, but my doxology is sucking wind. Wrap the good news of my justification around my heart all over again. The favor of people was never enough, and it never will be. Bring me the peace of knowing God's favor is resting on me, only because of you. I pray in your most loving name. Amen.

A Prayer about the Longing to Belong

And you also are among those Gentiles who are called to belong to Jesus
Christ. (Rom. 1:6 NIV)

Gracious Jesus, so much of life is about the desire and delights of belonging. From the day we offered our first cry as a newborn baby, our deep longing for attention, attachment, and affection have been patently obvious.

We were born into families, and our quest to find our place in our family has been a source of incredible joy for many of us and multiplied heartbreaks for others. This same story has played out in every other relationship context: friendships, work, romance. Wanting to belong is a constant theme.

And yet "the belonging of all belongings" is found only in relationship with you, Jesus. I praise you today that the gospel is a calling to belong to you.

The healthiest relationships we enjoy are good gifts to be treasured, but they are only a scent and symbol of what it means to belong to you. And our most painful and disconnected relationships don't have to define us. We can grieve the loss and bring the wounds to you.

We are "called" to belong—not merely invited, but subpoenaed into an eternal life of being wanted, desired, known, loved, celebrated, and enjoyed. We are "called" to belong—not owned like a new car but connected like a new bride. Lord Jesus, you have purchased us with the price of your life, and your love for us, alone, is better than life. We belong, now and forever, to you! Help me, help us, to come more fully alive to our "belongingness" in you, Jesus. We pray in your gracious name. Amen.

A Prayer about Praying
for God's Servants

Continue steadfastly in prayer, being watchful in it with thanksgiving. At the
same time, pray also for us, that God may open to us a door for the word,
to declare the mystery of Christ, on account of which I am in prison—that
I may make it clear, which is how I ought to speak. (Col. 4:2–4)

Most loving Jesus, I stand convicted about how sporadic my prayer
life has been of late on behalf of servants of the gospel. Unfortunately, it's often a case of "out of sight, out of mind," and therefore off the
radar screen of prayer. That's not an excuse but a lament and confession of sin.

My great consolation is in knowing that no one is more watchful and
devoted to prayer than you, Jesus. You're always praying for us; indeed,
you never stop. Because you pray, we can pray with great boldness, joy,
and confidence. I'm so grateful for your steadfast, vigilant intercession,
Jesus, especially in light of my own context and circumstances. Sometimes
our weakness and needs become the best motivation and fuel for praying
for others. Here's who I'm thinking about today, in particular.

Jesus, for missionaries seeking to bring the gospel to unreached people
groups or in situations long resistant to the Good News of who you are,
open doors no one can shut. You've bought a bride from every nation, so
we pray with anticipation, not with doubt. Give your servants patience,
provision, and enough fruit to keep them encouraged. May the gospel be
clear not only through them but to them. Keep their hearts alive to your
great affection and mercies. Shower their marriages and friendships with
the gift of your real presence and gospel nourishment.

Jesus, for your servants seeking to bring the liberating power of the
gospel to places of systemic brokenness and evil, grant them protection
and success. I'm thinking about the women and men who labor in arenas
like human trafficking, AIDS, hunger and poverty, and other places of
cruel injustice. When your servants feel most weary in doing good, give
them fresh manna of gospel encouragement. Grant them favor with local
authorities. Grant them good working relationships with other agencies
and missions organizations. Let them know for certain that a harvest of
righteousness and peace is coming.

Indeed, we praise you, Jesus, that our labors in you are never in vain,
for we don't minister for you but with you. You're the one who is making
all things right and new. Your kingdom of justice and mercy will prevail.
The government of the world is already on your shoulders, and there will
be no end to the increase of your redeeming reign and your healing peace.
We pray in your name, with hope and encouragement. Amen.

A Prayer for Those of Us Who Still Need a Doctor

Jesus said to them, "It is not the healthy who need a doctor, but the sick. I have not come to call the righteous, but sinners." (Mark 2:17 NIV)

Gracious Jesus, we often read this text looking in the rearview mirror, as though we no longer need your medicinal care—as though we only used to be big sinners needing the Great Physician to heal us. How we wish that were the whole diagnosis.

We're thrilled you've already given us the perfect and permanent "health" of justification. We cannot and will not ever be more justified than we already are in you, Jesus. We've been completely healed of our cancerous and condemning guilt. The gospel is our declaration of a clean bill of righteousness health. In that sense, we're no longer a sick sinner—but only in that sense.

For the more of your beauty we behold in the Scriptures, Jesus, the more fully the gravity of our condition is revealed. We need you today as much as the first moment you called us from death to life. You're the only doctor with the mercy and might sufficient for our many, many needs.

Jesus, as you've freed us from the guilt of our sin, please heal us more fully from its shame. Few maladies in this fallen world hold greater debilitating power than shame. We cannot love others well if we're living with the dark paralysis of shame. We're not asking for greater self-esteem. We've not victims making excuses but your beloved bride crying out for greater gospel health.

Jesus, as you've totally freed us from the penalty of our sin, please heal us more fully of its pillaging power. For our mind, emotions, and will have been pervasively infected with sin.

Heal our thinking from the ever-present disease of unbelief—a congenital condition that affects everything we do. Transform us by the renewing of our minds, Jesus. Grant us a greater measure of gospel sanity. We want to think your thoughts. We want your mind to be in us (Phil. 2:1–11).

Heal our emotions from the malignancy of self-interest. We want godly anger, not destructive pouting. We want gospel joy, not circumstantial happiness. We want sadness born from a heart of mercy, not melancholy born from simply not getting our way.

Heal our choosing of selfishness, stubbornness, and demandingness. Jesus, may your will be our bread and your glory be our portion.

Jesus, we are so thankful for the coming day of our completed healing (Rev. 21:1–22:5). Until that day, continue to make us healthier by your grace and Spirit. We pray in your holy and healing name. Amen.

A Prayer about Tarshish Looking Good

The word of the LORD came to Jonah son of Amittai: "Go to the great city of Nineveh and preach against it, because its wickedness has come up before me." But Jonah ran away from the LORD and headed for Tarshish. He went down to Joppa, where he found a ship bound for that port. After paying the fare, he went aboard and sailed for Tarshish to flee from the LORD.
(Jon. 1:1–3 NIV)

Jesus, Tarshish is looking pretty good to me today, and it wouldn't be very hard to buy a ticket to start sailing in that direction. As I start my day, I'm more aware of the demands of the gospel than the delights of the gospel. That's not news to you, but it's good for me just to "get it out there." If I could offer you only selective obedience, there'd be no problem. But you are asking me to go to some places and some people I'd just as soon not see till heaven.

I understand Jonah's struggle, but more importantly, *you understand mine*. No one has wrestled with doing the will of God more than you, Jesus. No one has been more honest about the price of obedience. No one counted the cost more carefully than you. You sweat blood; I sweat only water. You were thinking about the great needs of others; I'm thinking primarily about me and how much I want a hassle-free, mess-free, conflict-free life.

This is why it's so easy for me to come to you today without editing my feelings, repackaging my angst, or spinning my thoughts: because I'm one of those people you were thinking about as you prepared to go to the cross. As you cried out, "Father, forgive them, for they don't know what they're doing," you had me in view. As you crushed the head of the serpent, you had me in mind. As you were raised from the dead, you had me in your heart. When you spoke the words to Mary, "Don't be afraid," it wasn't just for her benefit but for mine as well.

Just talking to you this morning, I'm feeling better, Jesus. It's not that all of a sudden I now want to go to Nineveh. But I am feeling a little less inclined to break in line at the ticket counter to pay my fare to Tarshish. Thank you for being so welcoming, patient, and understanding.

Jesus, you paid our fare for a life in the new heaven and new earth, and you'll walk with us every step of the way and be with us every moment of the day until then. Even as I'm not thrilled about my current and future assignments to Nineveh, to know that you are with us and for us should be enough. Surprise me with the power of the gospel. Make my resigned heart into a willing and glad heart. I pray in your loving name. Amen.

A Prayer for Wrestling with the Sovereignty of God

Who are you, a human being, to talk back to God? "Shall what is formed say to him who formed it, 'Why did you make me like this?'" Does not the potter have the right to make out of the same lump of clay some pottery for noble purposes and some for common use? (Rom. 9:20–21 NIV)

Gracious Father, this morning I'm pondering the mystery and mercy of your sovereignty, especially as I consider everything you did to redeem rebels and broken people like me. The cross was no accident. It was you who handed over Jesus to wicked men, who put him to death by nailing him to the cross, all according to your set purpose and foreknowledge (Acts 2:23–24).

Indeed, Jesus' death for us on the cross was no accident, afterthought, plan B, or redeeming of a good story gone kaput. The comfort and peace I enjoy from this supreme demonstration of your sovereignty is incomparable and immeasurable.

Lord Jesus, no one could've put you on the cross apart from your will, and though your own disciples tried, no one could have kept you from the cross. Because of the forthcoming joy, you endured the cross for us—scorning its shame and exhausting our guilt (Heb. 12:1–3). We praise you for your incomparable gift.

So Father, as much as I celebrate and find comfort in your sovereignty seen in Jesus' cross, why do I struggle with it anywhere else? Why do I want to reverse roles to make me the potter and treat you like malleable clay? Why do I prefer at times to have a Play-Doh or Gumby God instead of a sovereign Father?

I don't have any problem with you setting up and sitting down presidents, premiers, and potentates. But when it comes to things that are limiting, inconvenient, or a contradiction of my sensibilities, I often question your goodness. Free me from such foolishness. You're always at work for your glory and our good.

Father, give me joy in simply being gospel pottery. You've placed the incredible treasure of Jesus in this jar of clay to prove your all-surpassing power in making all things new. You are the Potter who is redeeming a pan-national family to inhabit the new heaven and new earth. Let me be humble, grateful, and content with my place in that story. You truly do all things well. I pray in Jesus' most glorious and sovereign name. Amen.

A Prayer about Remembering
God's Forgetfulness

"Their sins and lawless acts I will remember no more." And where these have been forgiven, sacrifice for sin is no longer necessary. (Heb. 10:17–18 NIV)

Heavenly Father, what a heart-pounding joy it is to begin this day by remembering your forgetfulness. You promise never again to remember our sins and lawless acts against us. You will never again deal with us according to our sins or reward us according to our iniquities. For on the cross, you dealt with Jesus according to our sins and rewarded him according to our iniquities.

But that's not all, gracious Father. Because the gospel is true, you now deal with us according to Jesus' righteousness and reward us according to his obedience. What an exchange! What a salvation! What a God!

This is why I can pray back to you today these amazing words of hope and peace, written by German Christians in the sixteenth century:

Question: How are you right with God?

Answer: Only by true faith in Jesus Christ. Even though my conscience accuses me of having grievously sinned against all God's commandments and of never having kept any of them, and even though I am still inclined toward all evil, nevertheless, without my deserving it at all, out of sheer grace, God grants and credits to me the perfect satisfaction, righteousness, and holiness of Christ, as if I had never sinned nor been a sinner, as if I had been as perfectly obedient as Christ was obedient for me. All I need to do is to accept this gift of God with a believing heart. (Heidelberg Catechism, Question and Answer 60)

Father, thank you for such a legal, lavish, and lively salvation. Rescue us in those delusional moments when we forget your forgetfulness, when we act as though Jesus' sacrifice for our sins wasn't enough, when we think there is something more we can do to gain your acceptance and enjoy your favor. We pray in Jesus' exalted name. Amen.

A Prayer about Guaranteed Glory

In him you also, when you heard the word of truth, the gospel of your salvation, and believed in him, were sealed with the promised Holy Spirit, who is the guarantee of our inheritance until we acquire possession of it, to the praise of his glory. (Eph. 1:13–14)

Gracious Father, sometimes reading Paul's letters is like standing in front of a gushing fire hydrant. It's hard to stand up to the rush of so much glory and grace. It's simply overwhelming.

For instance, as I read through Ephesians I'm confronted with being loved before the foundation of the world, being chosen in Christ and called in life, being justified by faith and declared to be righteous, and being adopted by Abba, Father, betrothed to Jesus, and indwelt by the Holy Spirit. I'm shown that I have a completely forgiven past, a present standing in grace, and a future of unimaginable wonder. You've given us staggering riches in Jesus.

But what really encourages me today is knowing that all of this is *guaranteed*. You've "sealed the deal" by the Holy Spirit. You've guaranteed our inheritance in Christ. You've given us the down payment, the firstfruits, the promise of a future beyond our wildest dreams and asking.

There's no possibility of "bait and switch" or "revoking the warranty." There are no factory recalls, no fine print or doublespeak, no possibility of bankruptcy or legal maneuverings. Nothing will sabotage your bringing to completion of the good work you've begun in us and in your entire cosmos!

Father, rip and grip our hearts with the gospel of your grace. Let us be a people who live to the praise of your glorious grace. What else is there? What else could we possibly want to do with the rest of our lives and throughout eternity? We pray in Jesus' glorious name. Amen.

A Prayer about Nature-Speak

The heavens declare the glory of God,
  and the sky above proclaims his handiwork.
Day to day pours out speech,
  and night to night reveals knowledge.
There is no speech, nor are there words,
  whose voice is not heard. (Ps. 19:1–3)

Glorious and gracious Father, as I pray this early morning, lightning is dancing across the skyline of the still-dark dawn. Thunder is rumbling as the welcomed late summer showers fall. Soon you will start to paint our trees with the kaleidoscopic glory of the next season.

Slow me down, Father. Slow me down in the coming days to savor nature's declaration of your glory. I've been way too busy this summer, and I don't want to waste the upcoming fall. Tune my ears to hear what you want to teach me about yourself through the things you have made.

The pouring forth of nature-speak is endless, wondrous, and sumptuous—a visual, auditory, aromatic smorgasbord of delights. How can anyone with any degree of sensual awareness ponder creation and not worship you, the Creator of all things?

Father, you invented the sonic wonder of waves crashing on the shoreline. You created the mesmerizing sparkle in my grandson's eyes. It was you who designed the Swiss Alps—irrepressible in their power to draw forth awe from my soul. You hand paint every trout in the world. You're responsible for the permanent smile on the face of a dolphin. It's you who put the crunch in toffee and the aroma in coffee. You gave the gift of melody to The Beatles and the gift of symphony to Beethoven. You are the envy of every artist who studies sunrises and sunsets, some of your best and most daily work.

Topping everything you have done, it was you, Father, who gave Jesus for us. Not content just to be a magnificent Creator, you choose to be a merciful Redeemer. Oh, how we praise you . . . oh, how we *praise* you! We pray in Jesus' peerless name. Amen.

A Prayer about Asking for Forgiveness, without "Buts"

Have mercy on me, O God,
   according to your steadfast love;
according to your abundant mercy
   blot out my transgressions.
Wash me thoroughly from my iniquity,
   and cleanse me from my sin! (Ps. 51:1–2)

Loving Father, few things are as attractive as genuine humility. It's like a five-course meal in a five-star bistro. When someone offers a contrite heart, takes responsibility for their failure, acknowledges the impact of their choice, asks to be forgiven, and seeks to make restitution—there's no restaurant on the face of the earth that can offer up more exquisite cuisine.

Yet, Lord, when it comes to asking for forgiveness, too often I'm like a short-order cook in a fast-food drive-through. I hear myself saying things like, "I'm sorry, *but* you took what I said all wrong." "I'm sorry, *but* if you weren't so sensitive, it wouldn't be that big of a deal." "I'm sorry, *but* if you understood what my last couple of weeks were like, you'd cut me some slack." "I'm sorry, *but* you know what kind of home I grew up in. I didn't get the 'relationship chip.'" "I'm sorry, but that's just *your* reality."

Father, as I pore over your Word, I don't see a single place where the phrase "I'm sorry, *but*" is celebrated as the vocabulary of genuine humility and loving well. Have mercy on me, indeed. May your unfailing love and great compassion free me from all "I'm sorry, buts." Instead, I want to offer many more of these: "Will you forgive me?" "I can see I really hurt you. What do you need from me?" "Tell me more about how my words and actions made you feel." "I'm genuinely sorry and I offer no qualifiers, just an apology."

I know that in Jesus, all of my sins have already been forgiven—past, present, and future; sins of thought, word, and deed. May such good make it increasingly easier for me to humble myself and ask forgiveness of others and increasingly difficult for me to remain oblivious to how I impact others. I pray in Jesus' merciful and mighty name. Amen.

A Prayer about the Obedience of Love

As the Father has loved me, so have I loved you. Abide in my love. If you keep my commandments, you will abide in my love, just as I have kept my Father's commandments and abide in his love. (John 15:9–10)

Jesus, there are times when just the right Scripture comes into view at just the right time. Today is just such a day. These words, *your* words, cut through my confusion and cut to the chase. Because you love me, I'm to obey you.

In my zeal to guard the gospel of grace—the good news that all our efforts, works, and obedience could never gain or maintain a relationship with you—I've been less clear about the place of obedience in the life of your children. But it's really not complicated at all.

The hardest part is to believe you actually love us as much as the Father loves you. How can you possibly love us with the same passion and delight you've enjoyed from the Father throughout eternity? Every time I ask you that question, you direct my gaze to the cross. Because you were obedient to death upon the cross, I can be certain of God's love for me.

Here's where *my* obedience comes in. I'm to remain in your love by my obedience in the same way you remained in the Father's love by your obedience. Obviously this doesn't mean you earned his love, any more than I can earn your love. I can see how your obedience to the Father's commands was a primary way of communing with him—of enjoying your relationship with him and bringing him great glory. You spoke of his will being your bread, and bread is a life-sustaining gift.

May the same be true in my life, Jesus. Deepen my awareness of your love for me, even as you draw forth a more consuming and consistent obedience to your commands. Because the gospel is true, your commands are not burdensome to me. They are beautiful. They are bread. They are life. I have been saved by your obedience; be glorified by mine. I pray in Jesus' name. Amen.

A Prayer about My Critical Spirit

Do not judge, or you too will be judged. For in the same way you judge others, you will be judged, and with the measure you use, it will be measured to you. (Matt. 7:1–2 NIV)

Forbearing Jesus, I should've seen it coming. Just when I was starting to feel pretty self-righteous about not being self-righteous, the serial killer inside of me woke up. My irritability factor has gone from a 3 to what feels like an 8 on a scale of 1 to 10. The telltale knots inside of me aren't about nervousness, they're about *judgmentalism*. It's been easier catching people doing the wrong thing than affirming the many more things they do right. Once again, I've taken on the role of an Olympic judge with scorecards in hand, and I'm not giving out any 10s.

God, have mercy on *me*, the sinner. I really mean that, Jesus. You have exhausted God's judgment against all my sins upon the cross—the 4 percent I am aware of and the other 96 percent I am oblivious to as well. Who am I to judge your servants, your beloved? To you they answer, not to me. Jesus, you have called me to love others as you love me, not judge others with the judgment that has been entrusted to you alone.

Soften my heart today, Holy Spirit. Gentle my heart with your love, heavenly Father. Tenderize my heart with your grace, Lord Jesus. Indeed, it will take the whole Trinity to change someone like me. Bring the resources of the gospel to bear upon my grumpy heart. Bring the power that raised Jesus from the dead to bear upon my untamed tongue. Bring the hope of the new heaven and new earth to bear upon my impatient attitude. I pray in Jesus' powerful name, with gratitude and expectancy. Amen.

A Prayer for Grace to Accept Change

Jesus Christ is the same yesterday and today and forever. (Heb. 13:8)

Dear Jesus, I really don't like change. I like newness, excitement, and adventure, but when it's all said and done, I love to come home to the normal and the predictable. My nostalgia for the known runs so deep—maybe teetering toward obsession at times. Grant me grace to accept change, because there's so much change going on everywhere I look.

Another freshly planted "For Sale" sign confirms old friends are moving away. A favorite tree, whose leaves gave the relief of shade and a vibrant tapestry of fall color, is taken down by a storm. The restaurant that served great food, rich conversation, and the ambiance of perpetual welcome had to close. I don't like it, Jesus. Change is disruptive. Precious things don't become vintage things overnight.

How thankful we are that there's one part of our lives that will never change, and that's you, Jesus. You are the same yesterday, today, and forever. That certainly doesn't make you predictable, and even less so manageable. But it does mean that we can trust you without any reservations whatsoever. In fact, it's only in knowing you that change is put into perspective.

The most fundamental change we need is to become like you, Jesus, and that process is the most disruptive and painful change we will ever go through. Yet with the knowledge that one day we'll be as lovely and as loving as you, we gladly surrender to the work of the gospel in our lives. We learn to pray, "Lord, may it hurt so good, if growth will reveal your grace and glory in my life."

Likewise, Jesus, the better we know you, the more we come alive to your promise to make all things new. Change has no sovereignty. Only you are Lord. Nothing is random in this world. Nothing catches you off guard. The scary becomes the sacred when we're wearing the lens of the gospel.

Jesus, help each of us see and accept changes as part of a far better story than we could ever hope to write. You are making all things new, right now—right before our very eyes, if we have eyes to see and a heart to accept. Because of your life, death, and resurrection, we're heading toward a place, family, and eternity in which it will all make sense and everything will be the way it's supposed to be. Hasten that magnificent day!

Until then, Jesus, may we love you with abandon, serve you without question, and order our lives after your transforming purposes. We pray in your merciful and matchless name. Amen.

A Prayer about the Orphan in Me

I will not leave you as orphans; I will come to you. (John 14:18)

But when the set time had fully come, God sent his Son, born of a woman, born under the law, to redeem those under the law, that we might receive adoption to sonship. Because you are his sons, God sent the Spirit of his Son into our hearts, the Spirit who calls out, "Abba, Father." So you are no longer a slave, but God's child; and since you are his child, God has made you also an heir. (Gal. 4:4–7 NIV)

Lord Jesus, thank you for this incredible promise, your pledge to love us with filial affection, far beyond our imaging. There are moments, days, even much longer stretches when I begin to think, feel, and live as though I am an orphan—as though I don't really have a heavenly Father who loves me deeply and is involved in every detail of my life.

When I get sucked back into this downward spiral, my spirit shrinks and my fears enlarge. My peace says, "Bye-bye," and my control issues say, "We're back!" I get defensive and I go on the offensive. In short, I'm no fun to be around. Instead of the aroma of the gospel, I start exuding the smell of a waif.

Jesus, enough of my generalities: I repent. I smell like a dirty orphan *this morning*. I wish there was a button I could push or a switch I could throw and all of a sudden "snap out of it." There is no such shortcut, but there is repentant faith, which is better by far.

Jesus, you haven't left me as an orphan. You came to us through the gift of the Holy Spirit—the Spirit of Adoption—the very Spirit by which we now cry, "Abba, Father!" You never have and never will abandon me. Right now, I *abandon myself to you* and to the resources of the gospel. And as one hour gives way to the next, may the aroma of the gospel override the smell of a waif. I pray in your loving name, with longing expectancy. Amen.

A Prayer about the Normalcy
of Suffering

Dear friends, do not be surprised at the fiery ordeal that has come on you to test you, as though something strange were happening to you. But rejoice inasmuch as you participate in the sufferings of Christ, so that you may be overjoyed when his glory is revealed. (1 Pet. 4:12–13 NIV)

Dear Lord Jesus, this portion of your Word comes like a kiss from heaven. To know that suffering is a normal part of the Christian life actually brings me, and many of my friends, a great deal of relief today. For many of us have endured the destructive consequences of bad theology—various teachings that make Christians feel like spiritual pygmies for suffering any degree of illness, lack, loss, defeat, doubt, economic struggle, emotional duress, and the list goes on. But you tell us painful trials and suffering are not strange at all.

It's not that I want to suffer more, and I know I can suffer much simply from my own foolishness. But no one wants to suffer in vain or with a sense of being a disappointment to you, or feeling abandoned by you, or being punished by you. The gospel tells us we are not, but pain is an accomplished and effective liar.

In reality, most of our brothers and sisters in Jesus live in conditions that would make me wilt with whining, given my creature comfort–laden life. Indeed, Jesus, help me realize the aberration of the American "good life." I thank you for the many things you allow me to enjoy where I live, but I don't want to presume on them as a right. Rather, help us receive these good gifts as stewards and share them as servants.

Jesus, please help us understand how our suffering can be understood as participating in your sufferings. Your death on the cross was a once-and-for-all suffering—perfectly securing the salvation of your people. However, you're not a distant, disconnected, dispassionate Savior. You're presently making all things new, and this involves showing up in the messes and madness of life. Where there is injustice, disease, brokenness, and suffering, you are present. How do we join you there and fellowship with you there (Phil. 3:10)?

A day of no more suffering is coming (Rev. 21:1–5)—the day when your glory will be fully revealed—and what a day of rejoicing that will be. Until then, give us all the sufficient, sustaining, serving grace we need now to suffer with you and for you. We pray in your wonderful and merciful name. Amen.

A Prayer about Being with Jesus

Now when they saw the boldness of Peter and John, and perceived that they were uneducated, common men, they were astonished. And they recognized that they had been with Jesus. (Acts 4:13)

Dear Lord Jesus, this simple story confronts and corrals my wandering heart this morning. Two unschooled, ordinary fishermen named Peter and John were radically changed because "these men had been with Jesus"—with you, the same Lord who lives in my heart and rules all things from heaven.

Oh, to be a man about whom others would be inclined to say, "He's obviously been with Jesus. What else could explain his merciful heart for the broken, his courage in the face of injustice, and his calm in the presence of chaos? What other motivation and reason would he have for loving so boldly, forgiving so quickly, and sharing so generously? What else could account for his patience when provoked, his loud laugh and his ready tears, the way he treats his wife and looks a stranger in the eye? Yeah, he's been with Jesus, all right, because that's not the same guy we remember from a while back."

Lord Jesus, doing noble things for you is not the same thing as spending life-giving time with you. Thinking great thoughts about you is not the same thing as vital communion with you. Helping others understand the gospel is not the same thing as drinking presently and deeply from the wellspring of grace for myself. In all honesty, I'm not really concerned about others being able to say, "He's been with Jesus." I want my own heart to know that I've been with you.

Because who or what do I have in heaven but you, Jesus? You make heaven heavenly. And being with you, I desire nothing on earth, because absolutely nothing else satisfies my soul like you do. My flesh and my heart may fail, but you, Jesus, are the strength of my heart and my portion, my banquet, my inheritance, forever. It is good, and it is enough, for me to be near you, my sovereign Savior and my loving refuge. I pray in your holy and compassionate name. Amen.

A Prayer about Old Hurts
and Fresh Forgiveness

Then Peter came up and said to him [Jesus], "Lord, how often will my brother sin against me, and I forgive him? As many as seven times?" Jesus said to him, "I do not say to you seven times, but seventy times seven."
(Matt. 18:21–22)

Jesus, I'm running to you this morning with joy in my heart and knots in my gut. The joy is about the exhaustive forgiveness I have in you. The knots are about the costly implications of that same forgiveness. As I pray for myself, I pray for others with the same struggle to love well in broken stories that just won't seem to go away.

As you well know, Jesus, I ran into an old friend recently with whom I've shared a lot of life and no small heartache. That run-in was kind of like bumping a previously broken shin into the corner of a low-sitting coffee table. I winced with pain and wanted to scream. Even worse, I did harm to him in my heart. And that's just as stupid as kicking the low-sitting coffee table.

Jesus, I thought I was over the hurt. I thought I'd already forgiven him from my heart. I thought I was already healed. I thought I'd dealt with this thing a long time ago. That's just not the case. Out of sight might be out of mind, but it's not out of the memory band of betrayal and loss.

So I come to you today for seventy-times-seven grace. I'm being held hostage by my own unforgiveness. Certainly the gospel is big enough and powerful enough to set me free. So I humble myself before you, Jesus. I may never enjoy the gift of my brother's repentance, at least this side of heaven, but there's no justification for me tying my repentance to his.

I'm to forgive him as you've forgiven me. It's as simple and as costly as that. No, I'm not to be a doormat, but I am to be a doorway to the miracle of reconciliation. By the work of the Holy Spirit, I ask you to show me what that will entail in these next several weeks. Some broken relationships are less complex than this one. Some are no-brainers in terms of applying the gospel. But this one's different.

Jesus, you've promised me all the wisdom I need, and I'll take it. But I also ask you for a great measure of determination, strength, and follow-through. Low-sitting coffee tables can morph into coiled rattlesnakes in time, and the venom of unforgiveness is just too toxic to ignore. Untie the knots in my gut with your liberating hands. I pray in your redeeming and restoring name. Amen.

A Prayer about Ultimate Insanity

Do you show contempt for the riches of his kindness, forbearance and patience, not realizing that God's kindness is intended to lead you to repentance? (Rom. 2:4 NIV)

Heavenly Father, I've seen many crazy things in my life. I've encountered a few crazy people. And I've certainly done my share of crazy things. But the most certifiably insane thing I do is to show contempt for the riches of your kindness, tolerance, and patience toward me in Jesus. I do this when I dig my heels in and refuse to follow your kindness into fresh repentance.

The GPS of the gospel will never direct me to a destination of harm but only to a place of greater freedom. When I refuse to humble myself, when I refuse to acknowledge the ways I love poorly and act out immaturely, when I refuse to repent of attitudes and actions that rob me and others and most tragically rob you of glory, that is insanity. Showing contempt for your kindness is true craziness!

Father, I praise you today for being outrageously affluent in the currency of kindness, tolerance, and patience. There's no economic downturn in heaven—never has been, never will be. But there's nothing in me that assumes the right to any of your loving ways. It's only because Jesus willingly endured the judgment I deserve that I'm in a position to be dealt with so mercifully and graciously.

Father, thank you that you're leading me to humility, not to humiliation; to shelter, not to shame; to repentance, not to penance. For when I repent, I'm not the one making promises for change—you are. Only you can change me, and you are changing me, for you have covenanted to do so. That's what the gospel is all about. When I repent I simply collapse upon Jesus, once again, as my righteousness, my holiness, and my sure hope of a new and changed heart.

So this morning, kind Father, I repent. I repent of not trusting that you are at work in my current irritating circumstances. I've looked at the weaknesses of others more than I've kept my eyes fixed on Jesus. It's been easier (and more fun) to gossip than to pray. I've been moping and plotting like an orphan rather than rejoicing and trusting as a beloved son.

I've been more preoccupied with the ways of broken men than thrilled with the occupied throne of heaven. I've acted as though I care more about Jesus' church than he does. That is certifiably insane! I repent. Because the gospel is true and you are so kind, I repent. I pray in Jesus' merciful and mighty name. Amen.

A Prayer about Unparalleled Privilege

As a bridegroom rejoices over his bride,
so will your God rejoice over you. (Isa. 62:5 NIV)

Gracious Jesus, I know I'm not the point. I realize and rejoice in the fact that all of history is pointing toward the day when your redeemed people and the restored creation will make much of you. For indeed, you alone are worthy of such honor, praise, and glory. And I long for the day when you will finally receive the every-nation, all-creation worship you deserve.

That being said, it is profoundly humbling and encouraging to realize how much you make of us. Knowing you've forgiven all of our sins is more than enough reason to praise you for all eternity. Knowing you've covered us with your own righteousness is reason to praise you for ten eternities. But to realize that the righteousness with which you've already clothed us in the gospel is actually a wedding garment is staggering.

You've made a most unlikely people your bride and queen. This isn't the story of Cinderella we're in. There was nothing about us, or in us, that made us attractive to you. We're the mean stepmother and the two conniving stepsisters, so ill-deserving of ever knowing the unparalleled privilege of being your bride. But you've made us your own. You died for us, and now you live for us. You actually cherish us.

You're preparing us for yourself through the riches of the gospel. One day we will be radiant with your beauty, for we will see you as you are and we will be made like you. But on that day, our wedding day, you will not rejoice in us one bit more than you rejoice in us today. I believe this because you do not lie. But I want to believe it with all of my heart, so that with unfettered abandon I might love and serve you so much more, well before that day. I pray in your matchless name. Amen.

A Prayer in Praise of the Unity
of Believers

Behold, how good and pleasant it is
  when brothers dwell in unity!
It is like the precious oil on the head,
  running down on the beard,
on the beard of Aaron,
  running down on the collar of his robes!
It is like the dew of Hermon,
  which falls on the mountains of Zion!
For there the Lord has commanded the blessing,
  life forevermore. (Ps. 133)

Dear Jesus, it was wonderful to fall asleep last night having just witnessed a small but real outpouring of "the oil and dew of unity" among weary friends. "Good and pleasant" seems to be an egregious understatement—a woefully inadequate description of what happens when you show up and begin to thaw the tensions, deconstruct the divisions, and enable your people to move forward together in unity.

It's obvious that where there's unity, you bestow your presence and blessing. It's equally obvious that where there's disunity, Satan bestows his darkness and evil.

Boldly and shamelessly, I ask you for an even greater outpouring of your Spirit, leading to "the unity of the Spirit in the bond of peace" (Eph. 4:3). Drench us with the humbling and unifying dew of the gospel. We want to be sopping wet, not merely damp. Saturate and satiate us with the fullness of the Holy Spirit.

We don't look to Aaron and his beard but to you, Jesus, and your enthronement at the right hand of the Father. You are our great High Priest who has received the Spirit without measure, so you can deploy him without reservation.

As I think of our own church family, I pray for new church plants meeting resistance and older church families needing renewal; for missionary teams under fire and in duress; and gospel ministries of various and sundry sorts. Jesus, bring the grace and truth of the gospel to bear in observable and transforming ways.

No one has done more to secure our unity than you, Jesus (Eph. 2:14–22). No one is praying more for our unity than you (John 17:20–21). No one is more glorified by our unity than you (John 17:22–26).

Continue to heal us, reconcile us, and deploy us into your ripened harvest and broken creation together. We pray in your glorious and gracious name. Amen.

A Prayer about Gospel Gardening

And a harvest of righteousness is sown in peace by those who make peace.
(James 3:18)

Jesus, you know my less than stellar history of being a backyard gardener. Like the time I planted the cucumbers and the cantaloupe too close to one another and, through the wonder of cross-pollination, grew either "catacumbers" or "cuculoupes"—an interesting sight but worthless to eat.

However, I praise you that there's at least one kind of farming for which there's no possibility of failed crops. When we sow in peace—when we choose to live as gospel gardeners—there's great assurance of luscious, delectable, righteous fruit.

Jesus, you are the ultimate Peacemaker. Our only hope for a good crop of reconciliation and restoration is entirely bound up with you. I've borne the worthless fruit of both my peace-breaking and my peace-faking in the past.

Jesus, keep me alive to the peacemaking you have already accomplished between yourself and me. While I was your enemy, you died for me, destroying the hostility, deconstructing the enmity, and displacing my insanity through the gospel of peace. You have reconciled me to yourself through the price of your blood. You have secured the ultimate reconstruction and "shaloming" of my whole being. The coming harvest of glorification is not the least bit in doubt. You will bring to completion the good work you have begun in each of us and your universe. There's no chance of crop failure, none! Don't let me forget this hope for one nanosecond.

Give me your patience when gospel gardening takes much longer than I want. Give me courage when you send me to people and situations I want to avoid like canned asparagus. Give me love, your love, for you have called me to people, not to a project. I pray in your peacemaking name, Lord Jesus. Amen.

A Prayer about Godly Jealousy

I am jealous for you with a godly jealousy. I promised you to one husband, to Christ, so that I might present you as a pure virgin to him. But I am afraid that just as Eve was deceived by the serpent's cunning, your minds may somehow be led astray from your sincere and pure devotion to Christ.
(2 Cor. 11:2–3 NIV)

Dear Jesus, nothing good has ever come out of my jealousy—my insecure possessiveness. But nothing *but* good arises from *godly* jealousy—your intensely committed love, your determination "to have and to hold" your bride for yourself and to enjoy her forever.

What could be a greater compliment to any of us than to know that you are jealous for us—jealous for *me*—jealous and zealous for the affection of our hearts, the pleasure of our company, the intimacy of our communion? I believe this, Lord Jesus. I want to believe it more. Heal and free me from my unbelief.

That you really want us, desire us, and enjoy us is almost too much to take in. That you are actually saying today in the gospel, in this very moment, "Come away, my beloved . . . my desire is for you, my banner over you is love . . ." seems impossible and, tragically, at times not enough.

I can certainly understand why Paul was so concerned about the heart drift of the Corinthian believers. For surely Satan is always seeking to lead us away from the simplicity and purity of devotion to you, Jesus, our great lover and Lord. When he distracts, deceives, and draws me away from the wonders of your love, *everything* else is affected.

I begin to look to people, "stuff," and circumstances more than I look to you for life, satisfaction, joy, and a genuine sense of completion. Oh, foolish man that I am. Oh, how I long for the day of no more illusions or delusions, no more deceived thinking or divided heart, no more ungodly jealousy or ungodly anything. Hasten that day, Jesus; hasten that day.

But in this day, give me enough gospel manna, enough sanity, and enough gospel freedom to live and to love as yours—delightfully yours, belovedly yours. I pray in Jesus' name. Amen.

A Prayer about Heart Strength

It is good for our hearts to be strengthened by grace. (Heb. 13:9 NIV)

Lord Jesus, as you know, I've lost friends and family members to heart disease of the congenital and life-choice varieties. I've also had many other friends suffer heart attacks, both young and old alike. So the theme of heart care is personal to me, and the issue of stewarding my health is of great importance to me and indeed a part of living to your glory.

However, what will it profit me if I eat only foods from Whole Foods, can still run an eight-minute mile at age sixty, have a cholesterol level of 125 and a resting heart rate of 59, and yet have a heart that is weak in grace? I remember the apostle Paul weighing in on this topic too when he said that physical training definitely has some value, but godliness has value for all things, for both this life and the life to come (1 Tim. 4:8).

So my prayer today, Jesus, is about heart strength through grace. Lead me to the gym, the training table, the sauna, the spa, the regimen that will cause my heart to grow stronger and stronger and stronger in your grace. For surely the more my heart is strengthened by grace, the more it will beat for your glory, be healed of heartbreaks and heartaches, and have less room for idols.

As my heart is strengthened by grace, I will repent quicker, forgive deeper, and love louder. I will throw more gospel parties and fewer pity parties. I will not think less of me; I will just think about me less of the time. I think I'll stop right there, Jesus, and enter this day with that thought, that longing, and that great hope. Indeed, it is good, it is *very* good for our hearts to be strengthened by grace. I pray in your name and for your glory. Amen.

A Prayer of Longing for an Outpouring of the Holy Spirit

The hand of the LORD was upon me, and he brought me out in the Spirit of the LORD and set me down in the middle of the valley; it was full of bones. And he led me around among them, and behold, there were very many on the surface of the valley, and behold, they were very dry. And he said to me, "Son of man, can these bones live?" And I answered, "O Lord GOD, you know." Then he said to me, "Prophesy over these bones, and say to them, O dry bones, hear the word of the LORD. Thus says the Lord GOD to these bones: Behold, I will cause breath to enter you, and you shall live. And I will lay sinews upon you, and will cause flesh to come upon you, and cover you with skin, and put breath in you, and you shall live, and you shall know that I am the LORD." (Ezek. 37:1–6)

Gracious heavenly Father, I've always prayed that I'd get to experience one significant revival before you choose to take me to the revival of all revivals, heaven itself. I renew that prayer today, and I'm going to be quite specific.

For the glory of Jesus alone, I ask you to demonstrate the truth, beauty, and power of the gospel by pouring out the Holy Spirit on our church family in a most tangible and transforming way. My hope is in knowing that you are a far more generous God than we are a desperate people, and we are desperate. We need what you alone can give, Father. Make yourself unmistakably known as the Lord in our midst.

Prophesy the gospel to our dry, scattered bones. Drench our drought with the dew of heaven. Breathe your life-giving breath into our empty lungs. Reattach brothers and sisters to one another as one body, for we are in great relational distress. The only "skin" we need is the covering you've already given us—the righteousness of Jesus. May our glorious standing in grace humble us, quiet our racing hearts, bridle our wagging tongues, and send us to our faces before you, prostrate and repentant.

You are a God who gives grace to the humble, but also one who resists and knows the proud from afar. Have mercy on us; have mercy on me. I cannot imagine a better story to be a part of than for our repentance and transformation to become far more notorious than our sin and brokenness. Spirit of the living God, fall afresh on us. I pray in Jesus' merciful and mighty name. Amen.

A Prayer about Grace Allergies

There came a woman of Samaria to draw water. Jesus said to her, "Give me a drink." (For his disciples had gone away into the city to buy food.) The Samaritan woman said to him, "How is it that you, a Jew, ask for a drink from me, a woman of Samaria?" (For Jews have no dealings with Samaritans.) Jesus answered her, "If you knew the gift of God, and who it is that is saying to you, 'Give me a drink,' you would have asked him, and he would have given you living water." (John 4:7–10)

Dear Lord Jesus, you spoke these inviting words of hope to a broken woman trying her very best to keep her distance from you. She'd been on a quest to find life in the arms of men—many men—and it obviously wasn't working for her very well. The more she tried to evade your gaze, the more you simply applied your grace. She ran; you pursued. She danced around; you stopped the music. How I praise you that you came to seek and save the lost, not just broadcast an offer from the distance.

Though the details of my story are different from this nameless Samaritan woman's, the same foolish strategy is there: playing games with you, like hide-and-seek, only I do all the hiding and you do all the seeking. I wish this were just true of me a long, long time ago, but I still default to this insanity.

Jesus, deliver us from grace allergies—living with an aversion to the gospel. Why we choose broken cisterns, dumb idols, and self-help over your love is sheer madness. Grace is for sinners, not for pretenders, posers, and performers. You mean to heal us, not harm us; embrace us, not embarrass us; succor us with compassion, not shame us with contempt.

So, Jesus, once again I bring real thirst to you today. I bring my penchant to avoid you. I bring my allergic reactions to the gospel. I bring my excuse making, my unbelief, my pride, my self-righteousness. I bring that part of me that would rather help others discover your grace than partake of it for myself.

I ask you for a fresh imbibing of living water, sufficient for the needs of my heart and the demands of this day. May this be a twenty-four-hour period in which I spontaneously join the chorus of many others who are singing, "Come see the man who told me everything I ever did, and he *still* loves me and is bent on my freedom. Certainly this is the Messiah, the Savior, the Lord. . . . He is Jesus!" I pray in your pursuing and all-satisfying name. Amen.

A Prayer about Thick Skin
and a Big Heart

Repay no one evil for evil, but give thought to do what is honorable in the sight of all. If possible, so far as it depends on you, live peaceably with all. Beloved, never avenge yourselves, but leave it to the wrath of God, for it is written: "Vengeance is mine, I will repay, says the Lord." To the contrary, "if your enemy is hungry, feed him; if he is thirsty, give him something to drink; for by so doing you will heap burning coals on his head." Do not be overcome by evil, but overcome evil with good. (Rom. 12:17–21)

Lord Jesus, apart from your presence and your grace, the admonitions in this one passage mock our sensibilities. We cannot and we will not live this way without you, Jesus. Everything within us instinctively wants to get even when we are hurt by others.

Whether it's a "lighthearted" insult or an outright assault, whether it's our forgotten birthday or a remembered failure, whether we're excluded from a party or included in someone's madness, relationships hurt like nothing else. And so often, too often, the pain we feel gets recycled and redistributed to others.

Jesus, we ask you for thick skin and a big heart. We want to love well—to love to your glory—when we experience everything from unintended slights to fully intended harm. Where evil has already deeply wounded us or is presently stalking, remind us that you will repay, you will avenge. Make this real to us and not just a vague spiritual maxim.

Indeed, more clearly than we see the enemies of beauty, let us see the wonders of your cross. More than we desire to see burning coals heaped on their heads, let us see you, Jesus. The only way we can even imagine overcoming evil with good is by remembering you've already secured the utter annihilation of all evil and darkness.

But we confess, Jesus, we're clueless about feeding hungry, thirsty enemies. Take our hand and show us the way. No one does this better than you.

And Jesus, where we're just too sensitive, too easily offended, too quick to keep a record of wrongs done to us, too slow to overlook what can and what should be overlooked, have mercy on us, but also be at work within us. Free us to do the right thing, the gospel thing. As far as we are able, as far as it depends on us, show us how to make peace, guard peace, nurture peace with everyone. All of this is simply impossible apart from you, Jesus. We pray in your holy and sufficient name. Amen.

301

A Prayer in Praise of God's Care

Casting all your anxieties on him, because he cares for you. (1 Pet. 5:7)

Loving Father, it's incredibly comforting to begin this day remembering how much you care for your children. This is always good news to me, but especially this week. The combination of what I've taken on plus the burdens that have been laid at my feet are way too much for me to carry. I need your kind heart and broad shoulders.

So by faith, right now, with palms up, I cast my cares upon you, gracious Father. Carry my burdens for the people I love—dear friends I so wish I could change. Sometimes I foolishly think if you'd only let me be the fourth member of the Trinity for fifteen minutes, I could do a lot of good in the lives of a lot of people. What arrogance! You haven't called me to fix anyone but to love as Jesus loves me. You haven't called me to live with indifference but to live with deference to you. You are God and I am so very not.

Receive my anxieties about living in a world with a broken economy, the ongoing threat of terror, and the increase of diseases, even things like the swine flu. Father, I cannot add one minute to my life through worry. In fact, I can take a lot away from my life through trying to carry burdens you alone can carry. Turn my "What ifs?" into "Now thats"—now that Jesus has risen from the dead, everything has changed.

You've numbered my hairs and my days. You have the hearts of every king in your hand. Nothing catches you off guard or by surprise. There are no wrinkles in your brow and there's no second-guessing in your courts. You give and you take away—blessed be your name, O Lord.

Whenever I am tempted to doubt your burden-bearing care, may Jesus' cross loom large in my gaze. For it was there, Lord, where you bore the greatest of all my burdens—my sin—and demonstrated the incomparable extent of your care. I pray in Jesus' matchless name. Amen.

A Prayer about Jesus as a Mother Hen

O Jerusalem, Jerusalem, the city that kills the prophets and stones those who are sent to it! How often would I have gathered your children together as a hen gathers her brood under her wings, but you would not! (Luke 13:34)

Dear Jesus, of all the pictures you painted and metaphors you used to help us understand who you are and how you love, I have to admit, "mother hen" never made its way into my top five. And yet as I ponder this image, it profoundly endears you to my heart. It makes me want to know and worship you all the more.

That you chose such a metaphor says much about the depths of your affection and the intensity of your engagement in our lives. It also reveals how fragile, vulnerable, and foolish we are as your chicks.

Jesus, I praise you today for your ongoing commitment to gather me, because I am "prone to wander, Lord, I feel it; prone to leave the God I love." Keep running after me, Jesus, when I drift naively and when I roam wantonly to places I have no business exploring.

Jesus, I praise you today that like a mother hen, you gather me and place me under your wings, next to your heart. You are such a compassionate, kind, tender Savior. How foolish I am to think otherwise. How foolish I am to think there's any better place to be than under your "wings," in the embrace of your grace.

Though a nursing mother may even forget her suckling child (Isa. 49:15), you will never forget or forsake one of your chicks. Because the gospel is true and powerful, I am willing to be gathered today. I pray in your gracious name. Amen.

A Prayer about the Gift of Affliction

It was good for me to be afflicted
so that I might learn your decrees. (Ps. 119:71 NIV)

*P*atient Father, only a humble certainty about your love could have moved King David to praise you for the "gift" of affliction. The same is just as true for me. I well remember all the years I spent trying to spiritually finagle my way out of harm's way—believing that if I just claimed the right verses, prayed the right prayers, did the right things, then I'd have an "abundant life" filled with "blessings" and marked by a scarcity of difficulties.

I wanted you to be a "sugar daddy" rather than "Abba, Father." I wasn't thinking about learning your decrees but about escaping discomfort.

Lord Jesus, because you took all the afflictions I deserved as a sinful rebel, I'm now afflicted only as a beloved son. Because of you, Jesus, I'm not afraid of God as my judge, but I revere and love him as my Father. Only because of you, Jesus, I no longer despise or dread the decrees of God, but I delight in them. Indeed, Father, your decrees are not rules by which I earn anything from you; they are the wisdom by which I learn about everything from you.

Holy Spirit, I gratefully and expectantly ask you to keep me in this journey and joy of gospel freedom, even this one day. I pray in Jesus' name. Amen.

A Prayer about God at Work in the Pain

For I know the plans I have for you, declares the LORD, plans for welfare and not for evil, to give you a future and a hope. (Jer. 29:11)

Heavenly Father, there's simply no other god as merciful, gracious, and engaged as you. Your forbearance is immeasurable; your kindness is inexhaustible; your plans are irrepressible.

When your people received this letter of encouragement from Jeremiah, they were in exile in Babylon. How could they not feel bereft, bewildered, even betrayed by you? Yet we know by your own testimony, Father, that when you lead us into difficult seasons, it's not to punish us but to prosper us. When you send hardships, it's not to bring us harm but to give us hope. When you discipline us, it's not to send us into the "doghouse" of your displeasure but to guarantee our good future.

It's so comforting to remember that you always know exactly what you are doing with your people and everything else in the world. You know the plans you have for us, individually and corporately. There's no happenstance in heaven. You don't make up things as you go along. You're not a God who reacts out of irritation, but one who always acts out of great affection. There are no coincidences, just providences. "Stuff" doesn't just happen; sovereignty is always happening.

Father, this way of thinking would be utter madness if you never sent Jesus—a big-time spitting into the wind; the spin of all spins; delusional at best, demonic at worst. But Jesus is the "yes" to every promise you have made. His life, death, and resurrection are the guarantee of our gospel prosperity, living hope, and glorious future. Apart from Jesus there is only unimaginable hopelessness. Because of Jesus there is joy unspeakable.

So bring the truth, grace, and power of this gospel into our current situations, into our personal stories of pain, into the brokenness in our local churches, and into the needs of our communities.

Turn our sighs into songs, our cynicism into servanthood, and our grumblings into the rumblings of a coming visitation of the Holy Spirit. We pray in Jesus' triumphant and compassionate name. Amen.

A Prayer for Fresh Endurance and Encouragement

May the God of endurance and encouragement grant you to live in such harmony with one another, in accord with Christ Jesus, that together you may with one voice glorify the God and Father of our Lord Jesus Christ. Therefore welcome one another as Christ has welcomed you, for the glory of God. (Rom. 15:5–7)

Heavenly Father, I'm like a hungry little bird with my mouth wide open this morning. I'm glad you're the God who gives endurance and encouragement, for I'm starving for both. Bring an abundance of both, Father—"good measure, pressed down, shaken together, running over" (Luke 6:38)!

I praise you for these twin sisters of grace. One without the other would simply not be enough. Endurance without encouragement can atrophy into heartless stoicism. Encouragement without endurance can wither into short-lived enthusiasm. Give us both, bunches of both.

Father, I'm not just praying for me but for the whole family of believers with whom I'm so privileged to walk. Along with endurance and encouragement, I ask you to give us a fresh supersized order of unity. How else will we be able to glorify you with one heart and one mouth? How else will we even want your glory above our own preferences and priorities?

Our church family is so much like the churches Paul was addressing in Rome. We come from many different backgrounds. We've been rescued from nonreligion and gospelless religion. We have different perspectives and varying passions. We are at different stages in knowing how to follow Jesus and knowing what following Jesus actually means. All in all, we are prime candidates for a fresh visitation of the Holy Spirit, for he is the true Spirit of Unity.

Father, whether or not we actually get to experience a full-bore revival, help us to accept one another just as Jesus has already accepted each of us. This brings you great praise. The gospel we already have is all the gospel we actually need. Our city and the nations of the world are desperate to see Christ-followers who know how to love one another when it's easy and when it's not. Let us be just such a people. We pray expectantly, in Jesus' mighty and merciful name. Amen.

A Prayer about Brokenhearted Friends

He has sent me to bind up the brokenhearted. (Isa. 61:1)

Dear Jesus, I'm numb with sadness for a few friends this morning. I'm not sure what to do for them, but I do know I haven't done enough until I've prayed. The Father sent you to bind up the brokenhearted, and that's why I come to you. You are meek and gentle of heart, and yet you have the power to keep the planets in orbit and the authority to command sea creatures to dance. Your mercy and your might are my great hope.

I pray for my friend who just lost a job. She's sixty-four, a widow, and undone. The betrayal she feels is so deep. The uncertainty of where to go next is paralyzing. Her family offers no solace. She loves you so much, Jesus, yet this has rocked her world. By your Spirit, bring the peace you alone can give. Help us, as a community, to know how to come around her. Far more than I worry for her financial needs, I'm concerned about the pain of betrayal. Help us to know what to say and what not to say, Jesus. Bring your tear-wiping hand to bear through us.

I pray for the couple who just miscarried for the third time. This story is one of the hard ones to accept in this broken world of ours, Jesus. It just doesn't make sense. With all the abortions and abandoned children, it's hard to understand this heart-crushing providence. Jesus, I cannot imagine a better home for children to grown up in—help me know how to pray and to love well in the confusion. I've got theological categories, but I don't have much emotional currency right now. Help me love my friends with the kindness you alone can give. Help me resist trying to explain anything.

In such heartbreaking situations, give freedom for tears, space for grief, room for anger. I praise you that the gospel alone offers such gifts when we walk through these things together. You give and you take away—blessed is your name, O Lord Jesus. Amen.

A Prayer about Feeling Scattered

He made known to us the mystery of his will according to his good pleasure, which he purposed in Christ, to be put into effect when the times reach their fulfillment—to bring unity to all things in heaven and on earth under Christ. (Eph. 1:9–10 NIV)

Dear Jesus, there are times when I am, as one of my favorites hymns says, "prone to wander . . . prone to leave the God I love." When I get lulled and dulled into that place, it's usually because I haven't been spending unrushed time with you—gazing upon your beauty and bounty, reflecting upon your glory and grace, listening for your singing and rejoicing over me in the gospel. That's when I get enamored, then hammered, with the illusion that you're not enough—that someone or something else might make my life more complete. What a maniacal myth.

But that's not at all what I'm feeling today. I see your beauty in the gospel, and I do not doubt your love for me one bit. Right now I'm just feeling scattered, splintered, discombobulated, pulled in a myriad of directions with a big school of little piranha nibbling away at my soul. I'm not feeling tempted to do something crazy; I'm just feeling a little crazed.

I so long for the day when "all things in heaven and on earth" will be brought together in you—that is, "summed up," integrated, reunited. No more discombobulation, just combobulation! In light of that day, please meet me in this day. Center and settle me, Jesus. Help me to take my thoughts captive; help me to reel in my fluctuating emotions; help me to still the clatter and remove some of the clutter from my spirit.

You are my head and I am in your heart, and that is enough. I love being loved by you, Lord Jesus. I love you only because you first loved me and gave yourself as a sacrifice of atonement and propitiation for my sins. I am presently and eternally grateful. I pray in your name, and for your glory. Amen.

A Prayer about Toasting Jesus

To him who loves us and has freed us from our sins by his blood, and has
made us to be a kingdom and priests to serve his God and Father—to him
be glory and power for ever and ever! Amen. (Rev. 1:5–6 NIV)

Dear Jesus, John's words have the feel of a toast to them, as though
we've just finished a great banquet and have risen to our feet with
glasses hoisted to honor you, "To him who loves us . . ." That's really not
very farfetched.

Indeed, there's no date on the calendar of my heart more anticipated
and longed for than the wedding feast of the Lamb—the banquet of all
banquets, the mercy meal by which we will celebrate your marriage to us
and the inauguration of our shared life together in the new heaven and
new earth. Even so, hasten that day, O great bridegroom; hasten that day.

Until then, please help me grasp the implications of that one enormous
little phrase, "To him who loves us. " Though every page of Scripture either
shadows, suggests, or shouts it, to my knowledge this is the only verse in
the whole Bible that actually says that you love us. How fitting that this kiss
of grace would be found in the opening words to the concluding book of
your whole revelation. What a glorious summation of your work on our
behalf, and what a magnificent affirmation of the central theme in the history of redemption: "Jesus loves me, this I know, for the Bible tells me so."

Keep me from taking your love for granted. Humble me over the cost
of your love—the cross. Rescue me when other loves seem more appealing
or satisfying. Open my heart to the immeasurable dimensions of your love.
Focus and free my heart for living out the radical implications of your love.

To you be the glory and power forever and ever, Lord Jesus! Your bride
awaits your return. I pray in your matchless name. Amen.

A Prayer about Wholly Holy

Now may the God of peace himself sanctify you completely, and may your whole spirit and soul and body be kept blameless at the coming of our Lord Jesus Christ. (1 Thess. 5:23)

Gracious Father, it's a source of incredible comfort to know that you are tenaciously at work in changing us—in making us more like Jesus. For you've promised to bring to completion the good work you began in your children.

I'd despair if this wasn't the case, for the disparity between Jesus' beauty and my brokenness is overwhelming to me at times. The thoughts I think, the things I feel, the choices I make are so unlike Jesus. I could never be my own savior, and only a great Savior like Jesus is sufficient for someone like me.

But as the God of peace, you're making me wholly holy, changing me through and through. You're freeing every part of my being—spirit, soul, and body—from the effects and affects of sin. You're not anxious about the process. You're at peace, even when I'm not. You don't roll your eyes, furrow your brow, clear your throat, or show any signs of a nervous twitch when you think about me. O kind Father, you rest in your love toward me in Jesus.

I will be wholly blameless and shameless at your second coming, Lord Jesus, only because you took my blame upon the cross and despised its shame for me. Even now, my life is hidden safely in you, and when you do return, I will appear with you in glory, for you are my life—my righteousness, holiness, and redemption (1 Cor. 1:31; Col. 3:4). I boast in you, for I have nothing in myself in which to boast. My hope is built on nothing less, nothing more, and nothing other than your blood and righteousness, Lord Jesus!

So I will actively trust in the righteousness I have passively received in you, Jesus. And I will actively surrender to the very active ministry of the Holy Spirit, by whom I'm sealed, with whom I'm indwelt, and through whom I will be safely delivered into your presence. I pray in your faithful name. Amen.

A Prayer about Good Food and Glad Hearts

They broke bread in their homes and ate together with glad and sincere
hearts, praising God and enjoying the favor of all the people.
(Acts 2:46–47 NIV)

Jesus, I just got home from a feast. The food was amazing and the fellowship was priceless. I'm not sure when I've been as glad to belong to you and your people. The music almost made even *me* want to dance. Deep-dish apple pie never tasted so good. Multiply these precious, holy, joyful moments. Surely it's to your praise when we can put aside the busyness and madness of our schedules and simply enjoy enjoyment and enjoy one another.

And to think, I almost didn't go. Forgive me, Lord. I repent of not wanting to go before we went. I repent of being such a stick-in-the-mud toward my wife. I repent of thinking about the three people I was most dreading being there. I repent of being so small hearted. Grow me up in the gospel, Jesus. Expand the chambers of my heart to take in more of your grace. Free me to be genuinely intrigued with other people. Jesus, that kind of freedom was a sure evidence of your Spirit's work in the early church.

Indeed, Jesus, this little taste of rich community tonight has me thinking about our church. We've become so good at talking about and defending the gospel, but we don't really seem to be enjoying it right now. We've run off the legalists and moralists, but have we simply become "grace legalists"—self-righteous about the gospel? How could that be?

Restore to us the joy of your salvation, Jesus. Bring us back to the childlike wonder of our early days of knowing you. May your welcoming heart once again be extended to stranger and friend alike. Oh, to enjoy the favor of those around us simply because you are so clearly in our midst. I pray in your welcoming and renewing name. Amen.

311

A Prayer about the Teaching Ministry of Grace

For the grace of God has appeared, bringing salvation for all people, training us to renounce ungodliness and worldly passions, and to live self-controlled, upright, and godly lives in the present age, waiting for our blessed hope, the appearing of the glory of our great God and Savior Jesus Christ, who gave himself for us to redeem us from all lawlessness and to purify for himself a people for his own possession who are zealous for good works.

(Titus 2:11–14)

Jesus, if there's one teacher I want to excel under, if there's one curriculum I need to master, if there's one school I want to do well in, it's the academy of grace. In the past I've either taken education too seriously, turning grades into idols, or I've not taken learning very seriously at all, doing only enough to get by. Please help me to become a student of grace, to your glory and for my transformation.

Your grace first appeared to me like a longed-for sunrise after the bleakest night of darkness. It came quite literally bringing salvation to me, for I could never find it on my own, earn it through my efforts, or even desire it, left to my own sin and foolishness.

And this is the grace of your gospel, Lord Jesus: you gave yourself for us on the cross to redeem us from sin, to purify us for yourself, to make us eager to do good.

Anything less is not the gospel. Anything more is not the gospel. Anything other is not the gospel. If I'm not being challenged and changed by the power of your grace, then how can I say I have ever been sought and saved by the riches of your grace?

So as one under the pedagogy of your grace, Lord Jesus, help me learn to say an emphatic "No!" to everything that robs you of your glory and an enthusiastic "Yes!" to everything that promotes your honor and reveals your beauty.

May my repentances be more notorious than my sins. May the blessed hope of your future return motivate me toward a greater obedience in the present moment. Jesus, continue to teach me the difference between an uptight life of rigidity and an upright life of holiness. Continue to free me from my unrighteousness and my self-righteousness. I pray in your loving name. Amen.

A Prayer about Those Who Wrestle Wild Beasts

And as for us, why do we endanger ourselves every hour? I face death every day—yes, just as surely as I boast about you in Christ Jesus our Lord. If I fought wild beasts in Ephesus with no more than human hopes, what have I gained? If the dead are not raised, "Let us eat and drink, for tomorrow we die." (1 Cor. 15:30–32 NIV)

Dear Jesus, I have no clue what kind of wild beasts Paul wrestled with in Ephesus, whether they were of the four-legged or two-legged variety or if they were simply demons. It makes absolutely no difference. For Paul, all of life became a journey and adventure of living out the radical implications of the gospel. Because of your resurrection, he would be resurrected; therefore death held no threat. Because of your resurrection, all "beastliness" will be ultimately eradicated; therefore, he would wrestle anything for your glory.

Jesus, this moves me to pray today for friends who have taken on various "beastly" callings. I praise you for my friends who have gone to work for the International Justice Mission—for their willingness to work in the seedy, dark world of human trafficking. I thank you for these servants, many of whom endanger themselves every hour. I bless you, Jesus, for the women and children they have already rescued, and I pray for thousands more. Keep them resourced, wise, and filled with the hope of the gospel.

I pray for my friends living in AIDS colonies in the mountains of Uganda. Jesus, it is so encouraging to know that the percentage of those infected with HIV has decreased in Uganda. Much of this progress has come through the care of your people: good scientists, health care personnel, politicians, and missionaries. Bless their efforts even more. They often get weary in well doing, so bring the grace and truth of the gospel to bear in supernatural ways. Refresh them with your grace. Renew their heart affections for you. Keep their relationships oiled with the Holy Spirit, as sometimes it gets very hard to love one another in such demanding and draining circumstances.

Jesus, don't let us sin against these by failing to pray for them. We don't understand all the mysteries of prayer; we just know you have taught us to pray. Shut the mouths of the beasts by the power of the gospel, for the glory of your name. Amen.

313

A Prayer about Refreshment

I will refresh the weary and satisfy the faint. (Jer. 31:25 NIV)

racious Father, I am like a baby bird in a nest before this promise, with my mouth wide open. I *am* weary. I haven't fainted yet, but I am weary.

It's heartening to know that I don't have to pretend around you. I don't have to feel guilty, feign strength, or make excuses. You meet me in my weariness to refresh me as a loving Father, not reprimand me as a disgruntled coach. You meet me with the gospel, not a scorecard.

So what am I weary about, Lord? I'm not really sure. I need you to help me sort all that out. It's probably a combination of things. Though I hate to admit it, I am getting older, and my energy level's not exactly what it used to be. I know I must make more time to relax, rest, and replenish. And then there's the "wars and rumors of wars" thing. I never saw the day coming when walking people rather than flying planes would be the delivery system for bombs.

My weariness probably also has something to do with the energy it takes to stay connected to family and friends. Relationships are so complex, Father. No one knows that better than you. How I long for the day when all brokenness will give way to the perfect blessedness of loving well in the new heaven and new earth. That day cannot come a day too soon.

We look forward to an eternity of no more pettiness or petulance; no more hard-heartedness or fragile-heartedness; no more hurt feelings or bullying egos; no more communicating in part or conflicting to win; no more passive-aggressiveness or active indifference; no more innuendo or bravado or anything else that hides the beauty of Jesus.

Indeed, Jesus, there's no refreshment apart from you. You still cry out in a loud voice for the thirsty ones to come to you and drink. You still call to the weary and heavy laden to come to you for rest. Kiss my heart today with the Good News, the fresh news of the gospel, and it will be enough. Not for a month, or a week, but just for this one day, help me to love others as you love me. I pray in your faithful name. Amen.

A Prayer about True Blessedness

Blessed are those whose transgressions are forgiven, whose sins are covered.
Blessed is the one whose sin the Lord will never count against them.
(Rom. 4:7–8 NIV)

*L*oving Father, I'm thinking about the word *blessings* today and how this perfectly good word seems to have been taken hostage. There are all kinds of books, DVDs, blogs, broadcasts, podcasts, tweets, and chirps calculated to help me know how to get more "blessings" from you—telling me how to live a life that you reward, decorate, and "bless" or giving me formulas for gaining more of your favor and getting more "favors" from you.

Though I feel the cynic in me rising, I confess that I'm just as selfish as anyone, and just as committed to a life of personal peace and affluence. Have mercy on me, dear Lord; have mercy on me.

Like all words, categories, and concepts, true "blessedness" is defined only by you, heavenly Father. You alone have the right to define blessing, and you've done so. In the words of a broken king, David (Ps. 32:1–2), and a humbled Pharisee, Paul (Rom. 4:7–8), you've made abundantly clear what a "blessed life" is all about.

I am a most blessed man, for you have *completely* forgiven all my transgressions, once and for all. You have *thoroughly* covered my sins by the blood of Jesus. You will *never* count my sin against me because you counted my sin against Jesus and you now count me righteous in him!

Abba, Father, whether I live in a penthouse or an outhouse, drive a BMW or pedal a bicycle, feast on caviar or munch on a crust of bread, have a retirement fund or live from paycheck to paycheck, wear updated fashion or hand-me-downs—I am a blessed man, *a truly blessed man*. There is no greater state of blessedness than simply to be in Christ. And in those moments of insanity when I'm tempted to think otherwise, bring me back to gospel sanity. I pray in Jesus' merciful and mighty name. Amen.

315

A Prayer about Nonstop Good

And they shall be my people, and I will be their God. I will give them one heart and one way, that they may fear me forever, for their own good and the good of their children after them. I will make with them an everlasting covenant, that I will not turn away from doing good to them. (Jer. 32:38–40)

Gracious Father, here you go again, exposing the brokenness of my heart and the bounty of your mercies. Don't stop, please, until the day you bring to completion the good gospel work you've begun in us and even in the whole cosmos.

I want what you've promised—a singleness of heart—for much of the time my heart feels rather divided. It is parceled to lesser gods, too easily charmed by foolishness, fickle and fragile rather than faithful. You alone are worthy of my heart's affection and adoration.

I want singleness of action, seeking first the kingdom of redemption, restoration, and righteousness—the kingdom of your beloved Son, Jesus. Too many of my thoughts and too much of my energy is spent on the little fiefdom of me; it is squandered, frittered, wasted.

I want to fear you, Father, now that I no longer have to be afraid of you. Through the work of Jesus, you have eternally freed me from the fear of death and judgment. Now give me awe and reverence consistent with the measure of your mercies and grace that are mine in the gospel. Give me astonishment and wonder worthy of your great love and endless compassion for me in Jesus.

Lastly, Father, I want and I need you to convince me, over and over and over, of your commitment to never stop doing good to me. Such a promise is simply overwhelming, almost too much to wrap my heart around, and would be groundless apart from Jesus.

You've forgiven my unbelief; now free me even more from its pillaging presence. You are good, all the time, and all the time, you are good. Even when you discipline me, it is a kiss from heaven. Everything you do is for your glory and therefore good for me. I do believe this, but I long to believe it more. I pray in Jesus' glorious name. Amen.

A Prayer about Restored Sanity

At the end of the days I, Nebuchadnezzar, lifted my eyes to heaven, and my reason returned to me, and I blessed the Most High, and praised and honored him who lives forever, for his dominion is an everlasting dominion, and his kingdom endures from generation to generation; all the inhabitants of the earth are accounted as nothing, and he does according to his will among the host of heaven and among the inhabitants of the earth; and none can stay his hand or say to him, "What have you done?" (Dan. 4:34–35)

*L*ord Jesus, it's one of those seasons again when I need to be reminded of which kingdom and which King is actually in control. This world feels so out of control. All the suicide bombings, all the covert attempts to develop nuclear weapons, and all the overt rhetoric of political evil and global domination—it's a recipe for fear-mongering, Bible-twisting, and crazy-making.

But I flat-out refuse to capitulate to the earlier days when I used to allow the newscasters, pundits, and prophecy pirates to interpret world history for me. You are God, and there is no other god. You've spoken in your Word, and you haven't stuttered.

You have no rivals, contingencies, or concerns. There's no sweat on your palms, vacancy in your eyes, or vexation in your heart. You set up kings and you sit them down at your discretion. You live forever, your dominion is eternal, your kingdom endures, and you do as you please . . . *period*!

Even as you brought King Nebuchadnezzar of Babylon to his theological and political senses, so keep me in gospel sanity as you show me more and more of the occupied throne of heaven.

Today, right now, I affirm that you, Lord Jesus, are already the King of Kings and the Lord of Lords. I'm not waiting for the day you will become the true King, for you are already reigning over all things at the right hand of God the Father. The government of all things is on your shoulders. Your kingdom of redemption and restoration is the only unshakable kingdom. Of the increase of your government and peace there will be no end, for you will reign forever and ever!

You play no national favorites, for you are the pan-national Savior and the pan-universal Lord. So I bow down, I humble myself, and I honor you as my King, my Sovereign, my Lord. And I raise my hands and heart in adoration of you, for though you are the true King, you have made me a part of your beloved bride. What wondrous love is this, indeed, that you would conquer, capture, and enrapture the dark nation of my heart! I pray with astonishment and surrender. Amen.

A Prayer about Losing and Regaining the Gospel

But now the righteousness of God has been manifested apart from the law, although the Law and the Prophets bear witness to it—the righteousness of God through faith in Jesus Christ for all who believe. For there is no distinction: for all have sinned and fall short of the glory of God, and are justified by his grace as a gift, through the redemption that is in Christ Jesus, whom God put forward as a propitiation by his blood, to be received by faith. This was to show God's righteousness, because in his divine forbearance he had passed over former sins. It was to show his righteousness at the present time, so that he might be just and the justifier of the one who has faith in Jesus. (Rom. 3:21–26)

Dear Jesus, how did it ever come to pass that there was even a need for the Reformation? What circumstances created the necessity for Martin Luther to nail his Ninety-Five Theses to the front door of the Castle Church at Wittenberg on October 31, 1517?

All my questions are rhetorical, Jesus, for I know quite well why we needed the Reformation and why we'll always need to be rediscovering and reaffirming the gospel of your sovereign and saving grace. I know this because I know my own proud and foolish heart.

Jesus, the gospel declares me to be a whole lot worse off than I can imagine, and certainly a whole lot worse than I want to acknowledge. Jesus, I never needed you merely to be a moral model for me to follow. I never needed a religious experience or rules to obey. I needed you to live a life of perfect obedience for me. I needed you to fulfill all the demands of the law for me. Thank you for doing this perfectly, Jesus.

And I needed you to take my place upon the cross, receiving the punishment I deserve for all the ways I fall short of God's glory: breaking, ignoring, and going way beyond his law, and worst of all, worshiping other gods. I needed you to exhaust God's just and holy wrath against me and my sin—lest I despair of my guilt or foolishly try to curry God's favor by anything of my own. Thank you for doing this perfectly, Jesus.

Jesus, I even needed you to give me the very faith I needed to receive this free and full justification. This you have done perfectly as well. I praise you. I worship you. I once again affirm today that my hope is built on nothing less, nothing more, and nothing other than your blood and your righteousness. On you, Lord Jesus, the solid and saving Rock, I stand. All other ground is sinking sand. Keep bringing me back to the gospel, Jesus; keep bringing me back to the gospel plus nothing. I pray in your most holy and gracious name. Amen.

A Prayer about Gospel Heroes

Therefore, since we are surrounded by so great a cloud of witnesses, let us also lay aside every weight, and sin which clings so closely, and let us run with endurance the race that is set before us, looking to Jesus, the founder and perfecter of our faith. (Heb. 12:1–2)

*L*ord Jesus, on the ancient church calendar, this is the weekend we celebrate All Saints' Day—a time for remembering our faithful brothers and sisters who have gone on before us into heaven, leaving us examples of commendable spirituality. It's also Halloween—a celebration of hideous attire, doorbell ringing, and tooth decay. I never really thought about how much these two seemingly antithetical dates have in common until now.

For a good part of my life I thought the "cloud of witnesses" referred to in this passage was to be understood as a huge crowd of spiritual giants peering down from heaven onto the earthly playing field of Christianity, cheering me on in the righteousness race, pulling for me to make it across the finish line. Noah, Abraham, Moses, King David, the apostle Paul . . . all winners now motivating me to do well, persevere, and finish strong.

Jesus, all that led to was pride in my performance or despairing of my failures, depending on the day. I got the "treat" if I performed well. I got the "trick" if I performed poorly. I now understand that there's no more ghoulish or ghastly costume to wear than my own efforts to appease and please you. The one thing Noah, Abraham, Moses, David, and Paul all had in common was their abject brokenness and consuming need of your grace—which you freely gave them.

So this weekend, Jesus, I purpose yet again *to fix my gaze on you*, the author and finisher of my faith. I'm only a saint because the Father has hidden my life in yours. My only "dress" is your righteousness, plus nothing. I will run and finish the race because in you, Jesus, I live, move, and have my being. I will make it to heaven not because of my efforts but because of yours. I'll not busy myself with tricks or treats, because everything that is yours is now mine, Lord Jesus. What wondrous love and eternal inheritance is this, indeed!

And I will remember, with great joy, the gospel heroes you have given me: the men and women who have turned away from unrighteousness and self-righteousness to *Christ-righteousness*, those dear saints who make me hunger and thirst for more gospel astonishment and gospel righteousness. I pray in your name, Jesus. Amen.

A Prayer about Gospel Words and Gospel Works

We give thanks to God always for all of you, constantly mentioning you in our prayers, remembering before our God and Father your work of faith and labor of love and steadfastness of hope in our Lord Jesus Christ. For we know, brothers loved by God, that he has chosen you, because our gospel came to you not only in word, but also in power and in the Holy Spirit and with full conviction. (1 Thess. 1:2–5)

Heavenly Father, it's a great time to be alive, for even as there's growing turmoil in the world, there's unruffled triumph in heaven, a peaceful certainty that the gospel *will* win the day, the nations, and the cosmos. I am overjoyed today as I consider the gospel of your grace, the gospel of the kingdom, the great story of redemption and restoration.

In fact, I don't remember a time when there's been a greater proliferation of gospelspeak. Everywhere I look I find an openness and earnestness to reexamine and rethink what the gospel is all about. All the public discourse about the gospel, by believers and nonbelievers alike, is a very good thing.

But as I look at my life, the body of believers with whom I walk, and the community in which I live, I'm praying that the gospel will increasingly impact us the way it impacted the men and women of Thessalonica. What a stirring image: "Not simply with words but also with power, with the Holy Spirit and deep conviction" (1 Thess. 1:5 NIV).

Dear Father, may gospel *words* lead to gospel *works* in my heart. In particular, I'm praying for the power of the gospel to be at work in my marriage and other relationships. It's still easier for me to live in the world of words than to really invest in the complexities of heart-to-heart engagement. I'm committed to loving one spouse well for the rest of my life, but I need the power of the gospel to do so to your glory.

May the love you've lavished on me in Jesus, and the love you have given me for Jesus, really work in me. May the gospel prove its resurrection power in turning me further from my idols to serve you, the only true and loving God. To be specific, I acknowledge and repent of the idols of control and self-protection.

Lastly, Father, may the great hope you've given us in Jesus, including the hope of the new heaven and new earth, deepen and lengthen my endurance. I pray in Jesus' matchless name. Amen.

A Prayer about My Plank-Filled Eye

Do not judge, or you too will be judged. For in the same way you judge others, you will be judged, and with the measure you use, it will be measured to you. Why do you look at the speck of sawdust in your brother's eye and pay no attention to the plank in your own eye? How can you say to your brother, "Let me take the speck out of your eye," when all the time there is a plank in your own eye? You hypocrite, first take the plank out of your own eye, and then you will see clearly to remove the speck from your brother's eye. (Matt. 7:1–5 NIV)

Heavenly Father, when I rubbed my irritated eyes this morning, I soon realized it was not a speck of dust but a rough-hewn board stuck there. I didn't realize it till now, but I went to bed last night having made myself the chief prosecuting attorney in the supreme court—the judge and jury and executioner. Just because I don't throw things or scream and yell doesn't mean I'm not a critical person. Condescending smugness is just a synonym for *clanging cymbals* (1 Cor. 13:1).

Have mercy on me, Lord Jesus. You are so forbearing, kind, and gracious. Have mercy on me, the self-righteous sinner.

My self-righteousness usually shows up not in trying to merit more of your love but in withholding your love from others. The dark irony is that the sins that offend me most in others are the very sins most pronounced in my own life—a lack of mercy, unbelief, a critical spirit . . . I wish those were the only ones.

Lord Jesus, as cardiologist and ophthalmologist, bring your grace and truth to bear in my heart and my eyes. I want to love as you love and see as you see. I do not want people to feel pressure to change who they are around me, nor do I want them to feel my indifference and disengagement. Teach me and lead me in the third way—the way of the gospel.

Since you do call us to help one another with our "specks of sawdust," help me be a first responder to the life-giving rebukes of friends; a humble recipient of the feedback and reproof of those who long for my freedom; and someone who anticipates, welcomes, and acts on the daily, evenly hourly call to repentance. I pray in Jesus' gracious name. Amen.

A Prayer about a Gospel Tattoo

But when the kindness and love of God our Savior appeared, he saved us, not because of righteous things we had done, but because of his mercy. He saved us through the washing of rebirth and renewal by the Holy Spirit, whom he poured out on us generously through Jesus Christ our Savior, so that, having been justified by his grace, we might become heirs having the hope of eternal life. (Titus 3:4–7 NIV)

Heavenly Father, if I were into tattoos and this Scripture weren't so long, I might consider having it inked onto my body. I need to have this amazing summary of the gospel ever before my eyes. I just too easily forget. Much better than getting a tattoo, however, is knowing you've already written this truth on my heart with indelible ink.

You're such an outrageously generous God. Your kindness and love appeared to me out of nowhere, like a giant full moon on the horizon of a very dreary night. I wasn't seeking you, Father, but you were seeking me—running to me, running after me, not to harm me but to rescue me from both paralyzing guilt and foolish pride. I praise you for your multiplied mercies.

And what a "bath" in the gospel you gave me—washing me, once and for all, through the new birth. Now you continue to renew, revive, and refresh me through the ministry of the Holy Spirit, poured forth like a healing waterfall. All of these blessings come so freely because you've given Jesus so fully.

Now that you've justified me by your grace, the rest of my life is defined by *heirship* and *hope*. Though I sometimes feel and act like a fatherless, futureless orphan, nothing could be further from the truth. The saints in heaven are happier but no more secure than I am. You *will* bring to completion the good work you've begun in us and in the entire universe. I pray in Jesus' glorious name. Amen.

A Prayer about Being Needed Yet Empty

But he [Jesus] said, "What is impossible with men is possible with God."
(Luke 18:27)

Dear Jesus, thanks for the freedom to acknowledge when life feels like it's just too much. It's so good to remember today that the gospel calls us to hope, not to hype; to believe, not to make believe; to intercession, not to presumption.

Sarah laughed at the thought of having a baby in her nineties. Mary was shocked at the thought of giving birth to you, as a virgin. Though overwhelmed, she believed, and I want her cry to be mine: "I am the servant of the Lord; let it be to me according to your word" (Luke 1:38).

Jesus, I need the resources you've promised and you alone can give. I haven't had a good night's sleep in a few weeks. I'm irritated, I'm scared, and I'm out of gas. I've got friends who are on the equivalent of a spiritual life-support system, and they're looking to me for life. Breathe enough grace into my heart that I might have something to give my friends who are knocking on my door at midnight. They're desperate, and I don't want to turn them away.

For my friend so destructively hooked into a pornography addiction, give me wisdom, Jesus. I want to strangle him—not literally, but I'm worn out by his madness. Where do I take him for the best care? What do I say to his wife and kids?

Jesus, O God of the possible, I also bring to you three marriages that "have spent everything they have on a multitude of doctors and cures" but are no better. Have mercy . . . have mercy, dear Lord.

Though I want to run away, I choose to run to you. There's a whole lot that is impossible with me, Jesus. So however you choose to bring glory to yourself in these situations, you will most definitely get all the credit. I pray in your merciful and mighty name. Amen.

A Prayer about Enemy Love

If you love those who love you, what benefit is that to you? For even sinners love those who love them. And if you do good to those who do good to you, what benefit is that to you? For even sinners do the same. And if you lend to those from whom you expect to receive, what credit is that to you? Even sinners lend to sinners, to get back the same amount. But love your enemies, and do good, and lend, expecting nothing in return, and your reward will be great, and you will be sons of the Most High, for he is kind to the ungrateful and the evil. Be merciful, even as your Father is merciful. (Luke 6:32–36)

Dear Father, if I were ever in doubt about the power of your law to drive me to Jesus, all doubt is removed by this one Scripture. I *cannot* and I *will not* love like this apart from union and communion with Jesus. So as I pray through this passage today, I do so convinced of your love for me in Jesus and comforted to know that you have hidden my life in his.

Father, I'm the ungrateful and wicked one to whom your kindness has been wondrously expressed in the gospel. Indeed, it was while I was your enemy that you reconciled me to yourself through the death of your beloved Son, Jesus (Rom. 5:10). Every time I try to excuse myself from loving difficult people, remind me of these truths. I've never been "choice," just chosen by your sovereign grace.

Who *are* my enemies, real or imagined? Forgive me for labeling some people "the enemy" simply out of my bruised pride, hurt feelings, and fragile self. Bring the power of the gospel to bear. Gentle me in those relationships. Simply avoiding them will do no good, and rehearsing their failures will only fertilize my bitterness.

Father, for real enemies—those who've been instruments of great harm in my life, by their words or with their own hands—for these situations, give me wisdom and courage. I'll seek to revoke all revenge as I wait on you, gracious Father.

Lastly, in the situations where I've been labeled an enemy, help me to care more about your glory than my reputation. I don't want to obsess over their gossip. I don't want to be paralyzed by their distance and disdain. Where I need to own my sin and repent, please make it clear to me, loving Father. Where their anger has very little or nothing to do with me at all, sustain me in the chaos while you do your work of redemption.

I praise you for not rewarding me according to my sins, Father, and I praise you for fully rewarding me according to Jesus' righteousness. I pray in Jesus' strong name. Amen.

A Prayer about the Gospel and Dancing

You turned my wailing into dancing;
    you removed my sackcloth and clothed me with joy,
that my heart may sing your praises and not be silent.
    LORD my God, I will praise you forever. (Ps. 30:11–12 NIV)

Jesus, how could there ever have been a king more into dancing than King David? His victory over Goliath was the inspiration for singing and dancing by many in Israel (1 Sam. 21:11). When the ark was returned to Jerusalem, he danced before the Lord with all his might and very little modesty (2 Sam. 6:14). It's obvious he wrote this psalm as a dancer, for other dancers, whose joy at the dedication of the temple was uncontainable.

But King Jesus, you're the *real* Lord of the Dance. Though David didn't realize it, his work and joy simply prefigured yours. Only you can turn the wails of our sin and brokenness into the dance of hope and joy. By your cross, you've removed the filthy garments of unrighteousness that we might be clothed with the white robe of your own righteousness. Astounding . . . astonishing . . . and so very true.

How can we *not* sing and make music to you in our hearts? How can we possibly remain silent and still in response to who you are and everything you've done for us? Cause us to hear the Father speaking to us right now: "Son, you are always with me, and all that is mine is yours" (Luke 15:31). Forgive us when we, like the elder brother, remain smugly on the outside, off the dance floor (Luke 15:25).

Forgive us for confusing reverence with rigor mortis. Forgive us for living more by our temperament tests, Myers-Briggs profiles, and personality types than by the lyric, music, and dance of the gospel.

One day, King Jesus, we *will* give thanks to you with all our might. All personal inhibitions, cultural limitations, and sinful prohibitions will be gone. May that coming day have much greater impact on *this* day. We pray in Jesus' gladsome name. Amen.

A Prayer about Heart Guarding

Dear children, keep yourselves from idols. (1 John 5:21 NIV)

Gracious Father, how I long for the day when I will no longer be temptable, deceivable, or capable of worshiping any other god but you. I so look forward to an eternity of giving you the adoration, affection, attention, and allegiance of which you alone are worthy. No one redeems us like you. No one loves us like you do. No one cares for us like you. No one understands us like you. There is no God but *you*.

In Jesus, you've already given us a new heart and have placed your Spirit inside us. In Jesus, you've already turned our heart of stone into a heart of flesh (Ezek. 36:25–27). In Jesus, you've already given us a heart to know and love you (Jer. 24:7). In Jesus, you've already written your law upon our hearts (Jer. 31:33).

Indeed, Father, you've already given me a perfectly forgiven heart—yet it is far from being a fully perfected heart. The battle for my heart's worship continues, daily and relentlessly. This conflict will persist until the day Jesus returns to finish making all things new. Thus the warning to keep myself from idols is not going away.

Father, there are some idols I run from like the plague, but others I don't even recognize as idols. It's easier to see the idols outside of me, but help me to discern the "idols of the heart" (see Ezek. 14:4). Help me to know when I've made a good thing an ultimate thing. When I don't think you are "enough," where do I take the trust and worship you deserve—where do I go for life, deliverance, and salvation?

I praise you for the assurance that I am already one of your "beloved children." You cannot love me more than you already do, and you will never love me less. Surely the gospel, *this* gospel, will win the day, my heart, and the entire cosmos. I pray in Jesus' name. Amen.

A Prayer about God's Laugh

A little while, and the wicked will be no more;
    though you look for them, they will not be found.
But the meek will inherit the land
    and enjoy peace and prosperity.
The wicked plot against the righteous
    and gnash their teeth at them;
but the Lord laughs at the wicked,
    for he knows their day is coming. (Ps. 37:10–13 NIV)

Dear Father, laughter is not one of the things I grew up associating with you. Austerity, rigidity, sobriety, yes—but not laughter. I praise you that the gospel continues to expose, deconstruct, and replace all kinds of groundless notions I've had about you. There's really nothing more important about us than the image of *you* we have in our hearts.

I so look forward to the day when I will actually hear you laugh, for that will be the day when all evil, wickedness, and injustice will be eradicated. It's hard to conceive of a universe, a nation, a city, a relationship—even one heart, my heart—in which every semblance of sin and brokenness is completely gone.

That day is coming, and we praise you for this great hope that "the meek will inherit the land and enjoy peace" (Ps. 37:11). Because of Jesus we have an inheritance "that can never perish, spoil or fade . . . kept in heaven" for us (1 Pet. 1:4 NIV). I only wish the little while longer we have to wait would be a little less long.

But you are the God who does all things well. I know this to be true, and whenever I doubt it, one look at the cross tends to bring me back to gospel sanity—back to the meekness that is appropriate for those who are destined to inherit the new heaven and new earth.

So when wicked plots and gnashing teeth seem to be on the increase and righteousness seems to be on the decrease, please, Father, allow me and all of your children to hear your laughter in the gospel of the kingdom. May your joy be our strength, your promise be our confidence, and your timing be our schedule.

May the hope of great peace compel us and propel us into greater expressions of missional living and loving. Give us eyes to see and hearts to believe that even right now, Jesus is making all things new. We pray in Jesus' triumphant name. Amen.

A Prayer about the "How Much More" of the Gospel

For if many died through one man's trespass, much more have the grace of God and the free gift by the grace of that one man Jesus Christ abounded for many. And the free gift is not like the result of that one man's sin. For the judgment following one trespass brought condemnation, but the free gift following many trespasses brought justification. If, because of one man's trespass, death reigned through that one man, much more will those who receive the abundance of grace and the free gift of righteousness reign in life through the one man Jesus Christ. (Rom. 5:15–17)

Most holy and gracious Father, today my heart is filled with praise for the hyperabundance of grace you've given us in your Son, Jesus. Through the failure of the first Adam, we were born spiritually dead—willing subjects, coconspirators, members in good standing in the reign of sin and death. But now, through the work of the second Adam, Jesus, we've been made alive and now live as objects of your affection and subjects in Jesus' kingdom—the reign of righteousness, peace, and joy—the reign of grace.

As dead as we were in our sins and trespasses, we are much, much more alive in Jesus' forgiveness and righteousness. As distant and disconnected as we were from you because of Adam's sin and our own sin, we are much, much more at peace and intimate with you through the perfect work of Jesus on our behalf. As narcissistic and navel gazing as we were through our connection to the first Adam, we are becoming much, much more others-centered, loving, and caring through our union with Jesus.

Most generous and loving Father, you are most definitely for us. You didn't spare your own Son, but gave him up for us all—how will you not also, along with Jesus, graciously give us all things? You've justified us, and there is now no condemnation. Jesus, you died for us and you now perpetually live to pray for us and advocate for us. *Nothing* will ever separate us from your love (Rom. 8:31–35)!

Indeed, as grave and great as our condition was through sin and death, the "how much more" of the gospel has trumped it a million times over! We pray with astonishment, wonder, and gratitude, in Jesus' name. Amen.

A Prayer about Loving
as the Dearly Loved

And do not grieve the Holy Spirit of God, by whom you were sealed for the day of redemption. Let all bitterness and wrath and anger and clamor and slander be put away from you, along with all malice. Be kind to one another, tenderhearted, forgiving one another, as God in Christ forgave you. Therefore be imitators of God, as beloved children. And walk in love, as Christ loved us and gave himself up for us, a fragrant offering and sacrifice to God. (Eph. 4:30–5:2)

Merciful Father, mighty Holy Spirit, most compassionate Lord Jesus, I praise you today for the love with which you love us, in which you have rooted us, and by which you are transforming us.

It took the whole Trinity to redeem me, and it takes the whole Trinity for me to live this life of love to which you have called us. There's no other way I will even begin to be an "imitator of God." So hear my cry.

Father, I don't want to live today just with a theoretical or theological awareness of being your dearly loved child. Let it be deeply *experiential and existential*—very real, very encouraging, and very humbling. Your great love for me is the greatest convicting power this side of the new heaven and new earth.

All day long, let me hear you serenading me in the gospel, that I might grieve the ways I grieve the Holy Spirit—with my thoughts, with my words, and with my actions. Otherwise, I might try to justify the ways I love so poorly.

Lord Jesus, you are so kind, compassionate, and forgiving of me. I want the fragrant aroma of the sacrifice you made for me on the cross to permeate all my relationships. You're not calling me to change anybody. You're calling me to live as a broken perfume bottle through which the aroma of grace will bring your disruptive and gentling presence. Let me live more out of brokenness than out of my woundedness and self-righteousness.

God the Holy Spirit, you who raised Jesus from the dead, give me the power I will need today to rid myself of—not to nurse, tolerate, or justify—my bitterness, anger, rage, brawling, slander, and malice and all the other ways I love poorly. Indeed, Triune God, the life of love you live for me, please live through me. I pray in Jesus' peerless name. Amen.

A Prayer about Loving the Wrong Thing

I have written something to the church, but Diotrephes, who likes to put himself first, does not acknowledge our authority. So if I come, I will bring up what he is doing, talking wicked nonsense against us. And not content with that, he refuses to welcome the brothers, and also stops those who want to and puts them out of the church. (3 John 9–10)

Dear Jesus, being chronicled, by name, in the Scriptures as someone who loved being first isn't a very attractive proposition. I have no clue what was going on in Diotrephes's life and heart that made him so distrusting of the apostle John and so insecure and divisive, but his story certainly invites me to look at mine. Jesus, please convict me and free me from the ways I too love to be first.

In my marriage—when my zeal to be right and win the argument is more notorious than my commitment to listen and understand my spouse; when I pout more than I pursue my spouse.

In my friendships—when my need to be remembered and appreciated is more pronounced than my commitment to stay in touch with and serve my friends.

In my vocation—when the people who work with me feel like I'm far more taken up with my reputation and success than I'm committed to love and serve as a member of a team.

In the general population—when I navigate through life with little eye contact and don't work hard to remember names.

In the grocery store—when I push my shopping cart around like I'm driving in the Daytona 500, racing up and down the aisles, grabbing items, and speeding up to get to the shortest checkout line first.

Lord Jesus Christ, Son of God, have mercy on me, a sinner. You didn't consider your equality with God something to be held on to selfishly. You didn't love to be first. Rather, you emptied yourself by taking the very nature of a man—a servant man, a man who served me by fulfilling all the demands of the law for me and by exhausting God's judgment against all my sin on the cross. Now you ever live to serve me as my advocate, intercessor, and bridegroom.

I am convicted and humbled afresh by your lavish and selfless love. Restore my first love for you, that my love for being first will decrease and die a thousand deaths. I pray in your matchless name. Amen.

A Prayer about Eating Soul Food

Come, all you who are thirsty,
   come to the waters;
and you who have no money,
   come, buy and eat!
Come, buy wine and milk
   without money and without cost.
Why spend money on what is not bread,
   and your labor on what does not satisfy?
Listen, listen to me, and eat what is good,
   and you will delight in the richest of fare.
Give ear and come to me;
   listen, that you may live. (Isa. 55:1–3 NIV)

Most gracious Father, I praise you today for the simple pleasure of eating. Right now I'm thinking about pan-seared pompano, a well-chosen white wine, a fresh mango salad, sweet potato fries, grilled asparagus, and some fresh pistachio gelato to finish off the banquet. Thank you, Father, for the utter joy of eating. But alas, like all of your good gifts, even our eating is broken, and we are such poor stewards of our thirst and hunger.

Too much of the time, Father, I'm a hungry man demanding instant gratification. I'll grab whatever drink I think will slake my thirst, and I'll eat whatever bread will make me full in the moment. Like Esau, I let a bowl of steaming oatmeal in my hand hold more power than the promise of a sumptuous feast.

Yet, Father, you're always beckoning me to the only feast that will satisfy the insatiable hunger and thirst of my soul. You've spread before me the gospel feast of your Son, Jesus, and the whole bountiful banquet has already been paid for in full. You designed me for delights you alone can satisfy through your grace.

Indeed, Lord Jesus, you are the Bread of Life and the giver of living water. You're the richest fare the Father has promised. You so generously nourish us through the means of grace: the Scriptures, prayer, fellowship, private and corporate worship, service, the Eucharist. Yet all of these are just a foretaste of the meal from which all banqueting derives its meaning: the wedding feast of the Lamb (Rev. 19). Hasten that blessed day and eternal feast. In your gracious name we pray. Amen.

A Prayer about Seduceability

With much seductive speech she persuades him;
    with her smooth talk she compels him.
All at once he follows her,
    as an ox goes to the slaughter,
or as a stag is caught fast
    till an arrow pierces its liver;
as a bird rushes into a snare;
    he does not know that it will cost him his life.
And now, O sons, listen to me,
    and be attentive to the words of my mouth.
Let not your heart turn aside to her ways;
    do not stray into her paths,
for many a victim has she laid low,
    and all her slain are a mighty throng.
Her house is the way to Sheol,
    going down to the chambers of death. (Prov. 7:21–27)

Dear Lord Jesus, we've been created and re-created to connect with you deeply—to enjoy an intimacy, union, and communion of which our best relationships are only a hint, a whisper, a symbol. But alas, like all good things, our longings get hijacked and sabotaged by sin and death.

Samson and King David do not stand alone. There are many lonely husbands, many lonely wives, many lonely single people who are primed for a fling, targets for an affair—aching, yearning, reaching for a few minutes of pleasure to medicate months, years, even a lifetime of disconnect and emptiness. It may never become physically sexual, but sometimes just the emotional connection can bring an exhilaration bordering on intoxication, and it is an intoxication that can lead to addiction, then destruction.

Jesus, even when we're connecting well, even when our marriages are at a good place, or even when we're quite content and fulfilled in our singleness, our seduceability is ever present. Help us, Lord Jesus. How we long for our life in the new heaven and new earth—when we will never be capable of ever sinning again, or even of being tempted.

The way of the gospel is neither paranoia nor presumption but rather wisdom, care, and freedom. So, Lord Jesus, give us—give me—more gospel sanity. We turn our hearts toward you. You are constantly wooing us in the gospel, saying, "Come away, my beloved." Who do we have in heaven but you, Lord Jesus, and being with you, who or what could we possibly desire more on this earth? Only your love is better than life. We believe; help our unbelief. We humbly pray in your loving name. Amen.

A Prayer about Church
as a Gospel Garden

If you do away with the yoke of oppression,
    with the pointing finger and malicious talk,
and if you spend yourselves in behalf of the hungry
    and satisfy the needs of the oppressed,
then your light will rise in the darkness,
    and your night will become like the noonday.
The LORD will guide you always;
    he will satisfy your needs in a sun-scorched land
    and will strengthen your frame.
You will be like a well-watered garden,
    like a spring whose waters never fail.
Your people will rebuild the ancient ruins
    and will raise up the age-old foundations;
you will be called Repairer of Broken Walls,
    Restorer of Streets with Dwellings. (Isa. 58:9–12 NIV)

Heavenly Father, you seem to have a recurring penchant for gardens. Our first home was the garden paradise of Eden, and our future home, the new heaven and new earth, sounds like it's going to be the Garden of Eden on steroids (Rev. 21:1–22:6).

It shouldn't surprise us, then, that you'd choose the image of a garden to describe our shared life as your redeemed people. The more we're alive to the life-giving resources of the gospel, the more we'll become like well-watered gardens—gospel gardens. You plant us in broken cities to bring your beauty and share your bounty, for a garden exists not for its own benefit but for the benefit of others.

Lord, forgive us when we turn our churches into private orchards or gated estates. You've called us to love and to serve the least and the lost, to care for the poor, the oppressed, and the hungry in our communities. To love them well is to love you well.

Jesus, you are the true seed that was sown that death itself would die. You are the firstfruits of a whole new people and a whole new creation order—raised from the dead to bring forth the living waters that alone will never fail, that alone truly satisfy, and which alone will eradicate all evil and injustice one day.

Jesus, you are the ultimate rebuilder of ancient ruins, the "Repairer of Broken Walls," and the "Restorer of Streets with Dwellings." Continue your gospel gardening work in us and through us, until the day you return to finish making all things new and all things a garden once again. I pray in your bountiful and beautiful name. Amen.

A Prayer about Beloved Thornbushes

I will block her path with thornbushes;
  I will wall her in so that she cannot find her way.
She will chase after her lovers but not catch them;
  she will look for them but not find them.
Then she will say,
  "I will go back to my husband as at first,
  for then I was better off than now." (Hosea 2:6–7 NIV)

Dear Jesus, I've praised you for the fall foliage of western North Carolina; the panoramic wonder of Cape Town, South Africa; everything about Switzerland; the Eden-like echoes in Butchart Gardens on Victoria Island; and the azure blue waters kissing the sugar white beaches of Destin, Florida. But today, I praise you for the gift of thornbushes.

Jesus, you love us so much that when we love you less, you come after us with tenacity and uncomfortable providences. You are unrelenting in your commitment to rescue our hearts from illusions, mirages, broken cisterns, idols, and wannabe lovers. I wish you didn't have to be, but I am grateful you are so doggedly committed to us.

O blessed and beloved thornbushes, ever block my path when I begin chasing after lesser gods and other lovers. Hedge me in like a formidable fortress. When I set my GPS for an affair of any kind, cause me to lose my bearings and my way. Frustrate my every attempt to look for more, or settle for less, than Jesus.

Jesus, that you are jealous for us and the affection of our hearts is the greatest compliment you could ever pay us. Who are we that the Lord of glory would make us his bride? Who am I that you would rejoice over me with the festive joy, the impassioned delight, and the desire-filled gaze of a bridegroom?

How I long for the day when I will never again have to say, "I will go back to my husband as at first." Until that day, Lord Jesus, that consummate wedding day, keep me sane, centered, and settled through the gospel. I pray in your holy and loving name. Amen.

A Prayer about Being Oblivious

Then the mother of the sons of Zebedee came up to him [Jesus] with her sons, and kneeling before him she asked him for something. And he said to her, "What do you want?" She said to him, "Say that these two sons of mine are to sit, one at your right hand and one at your left, in your kingdom." Jesus answered, "You do not know what you are asking. Are you able to drink the cup that I am to drink?" They said to him, "We are able." (Matt. 20:20–22)

Lord Jesus, every time I read this story about two of your apostles and their mother asking for a position of privilege and power in your kingdom, I find my incredulity meter going berserk. How in the world could James and John possibly think this request would ever be appropriate, especially given the three years of mentoring and modeling to which you exposed them? Everything you taught and how you lived life absolutely contradicted their request. How dare they, how could they be so oblivious to the obvious?

But just as I climb onto my hobbyhorse of disgust and judgmentalism, the gospel dismounts me. I have to ask these questions of myself: How am I just like James and John? How do my words, attitudes, and choices contradict the very gospel that I love and defend? Whose incredulity meter am I forcing into overdrive?

Is it those who live with me or those who work with me? Those who taste my impatience when I'm behind a steering wheel? Those who overhear my idle chatter and self-indulgent banter in any of a number of settings? Those most exposed to my unbelief, my fears, my rudeness, my driven-ness, my insincerity, my irritability?

Jesus, I praise you for your patience and forbearance with me. Sit on your right or left? I'm just grateful to be in your kingdom, covered in your righteousness, secure in your heart. I could *never* drink the cup you alone drank for us on the cross.

The cup I now drink and the bread I now eat remind me of your death, unite me to your life, and call me to your likeness. Jesus, I don't want to be incredulous over anyone's sin but my own. Through the gospel, please make me less and less oblivious to my patently obvious need for your transforming grace. I pray in your patient and forbearing name. Amen.

A Prayer about Hope Setting

Therefore, prepare your minds for action, and being sober-minded; set your hope fully on the grace that will be brought to you at the revelation of Jesus Christ. (1 Pet. 1:13)

Heavenly Father, you won't let us get away from thinking about your grace for even one minute, will you? And let me hasten to say thank you, thank you, thank you.

I praise you for the day you finally convinced the legalist and leper in me that salvation is by grace alone through faith alone. I praise you for the ongoing schooling in the sufficiency of your grace for all the broken things in my life: broken relationships, broken health, broken promises, broken church . . . broken me.

And now I praise you for commanding me to set my hope on *yet-to-be-received grace*—the unleashed fullness, the unfettered wonder, the undiminished glory of your contraconditional love for us in Jesus. There is no God like you. There is no God so immeasurably generous with such ill-deserving people like me.

Help me to remember that this hope-setting command is just as much a command to be obeyed as "Do not lie, do not steal, and do not covet." You are serious about where we set our hope.

Father, you are so wise, for you know if we don't intentionally and fully set our hope on your present and future grace, we'll set it somewhere else: on saviors that cannot save, on people who are not God, on gospels that are not gospels, and on idols that will ultimately fail us.

Lord Jesus, I've never so looked forward to the day when you will be *fully* revealed—when the firstfruits of grace will give way to the full harvest of grace, your gathered bride and renewed world. Until that day, keep us engaged in your story of redemption and restoration. Where do we work for justice? Where do we show your mercy? How shall we walk humbly with our God? We ask and pray in your trustworthy name. Amen.

A Prayer about the Triumph of Mercy

So speak and so act as those who are to be judged under the law of liberty.
For judgment is without mercy to one who has shown no mercy. Mercy
triumphs over judgment. (James 2:12–13)

Jesus, my heart is stunned today with a fresh awareness of your mercy.
You are, indeed, a most wonderful, merciful Savior. Because of what
you've done for us, I'm no longer afraid to die; I don't have fears about
the life to come. And I'm not afraid to live, for I'm not at all uncertain
about what God thinks about me, for by your life and death, you did
everything necessary not just to reconcile me to God but also to place me
in his eternal favor and delight. Mercy trumped judgment, on my behalf!

Now, all day long, every minute of every day, Jesus, you constantly show
me mercy. You do not give me what I deserve, but instead you give me more
grace. In the gospel you are incessantly speaking words of encouragement,
hope, and kindness to me. Even when you have to correct me, which is
quite often, you give me life-giving rebukes, not shame-inducing stares or
guilt-inflicting words. Mercy continually trumps judgment on my behalf.

Jesus, you've completely reoriented my relationship to the Scriptures
as well. The law that used to condemn me now consoles me; that which
used to be a source of fear in me has become a source of freedom for me.
Because the gospel is true, I can now honestly say, "the law of the Lord is
perfect, reviving the soul"—*my soul.*

Jesus, in view of so much mercy, your mercy for me, I have no excuses.
I cannot justify allowing my judgmental attitude to trump your mercy in
any of the difficult relationships and situations I now find myself. Help me
to speak and act today as someone for whom the triumph of mercy over
judgment is complete. Help me to speak and act as someone the Son of
God has set free, free indeed.

I need wisdom, gospel wisdom, to live and love this radical way. I fear
being exploited, but my greater fear is being coldhearted. Have mercy
on me, Jesus; continue to have mercy on me. I pray in your loving and
strong name. Amen.

A Prayer about the Stewardship of Hatred

We know that we have passed out of death into life, because we love the brothers. Whoever does not love abides in death. Everyone who hates his brother is a murderer, and you know that no murderer has eternal life abiding in him. (1 John 3:14–15)

Merciful Father, there are a lot of things I rather casually express hatred for. I hate stringy canned asparagus. I hate bumper-to-bumper traffic going in my direction. I hate high humidity days when I want to jog. I hate pulling out a nearly empty milk carton from the refrigerator when I'm primed for a big bowl of cereal. I hate loud talking in a quiet restaurant when I'm already peopled out. I hate having to engage in deep conversation after 9:00 p.m.

But this portion of your Word puts all of my hating into perspective. I'm sobered by the warning concerning the hatred of people—especially hating my brothers and sisters in Christ. Holy Spirit, I ask you to examine my heart and quicken my memory. Who are the people toward whom I have feelings of hatred? Though I may have never spoken the violent words "I hate you!" to their face, nevertheless I've committed murder in my heart. I've relished their reversals, dreamed of their demise, and longed for their languishing.

Big disappointments and painful betrayals are common in life, even by the hands of those with whom we share life in Christ. Some of us have been egregiously violated and seriously abused, too often by those we were trained to trust. But when our real hurt grows to retaliatory anger and our anger morphs into spiteful hatred, arrest our hearts, Lord. Let me see the ways I become the very thing I hate. Bring us back to gospel sanity, sooner rather than later.

Vengeance belongs to you, not us, Father. Even as you are a God of mercy, you are also a God of justice. We can trust you for both. You do all things well, in your timing, for your glory and for our good.

Receive our praise, O God, for bringing us from death to life in Jesus. Receive our praise, Lord Jesus, for becoming the hater and the hated on the cross for us, for me. May the gospel compel me to hate evil and to hate my sin more than I hate anything or anyone else in the world. Receive our praise, Holy Spirit, for constantly gossiping the gospel to our hearts. I pray in the holy and compassionate name of our Triune God. Amen.

A Prayer about Grace for Grumpiness

But he said to me, "My grace is sufficient for you, for my power is made perfect in weakness." Therefore I will boast all the more gladly of my weaknesses, so that the power of Christ may rest upon me. (2 Cor. 12:9)

Heavenly Father, I'm waking up humbled and repentant. I need some of your manifold sufficient grace today—just like every day. Not only do I need your grace for owning and boasting in my weaknesses, but I need your grace so that I will stop despising weaknesses in others. I've had the attitude of a grumpy toddler, indulged my impatience, and been a serial killer in my heart. I need the gospel today.

Though I'd love to justify myself, there is no such justification. I'm a selfish man who would love for everything and everyone to make my life tolerable, predictable, and manageable. I assume the right to green lights at every intersection. I assume there will be an open cash register when I'm ready to check out. I assume the fish will be biting.

What is worse, there are times when I don't want people to fear the stuff they should fear, struggle with the same things I struggle with, or simply be the normal sinners that we all are. God, have mercy on me, the sinner . . .

Abba, Father, I'm so thankful that your love for me is steadfast and that I can count on new mercies every morning, including this morning, and all day long. I not only grieve my attitude, I do repent and abandon myself to the resources of the gospel.

Lord Jesus, I want and I need your power to rest on me and to settle my restless heart. I'll not pray about next week or even tomorrow. Just give me the manna of gospel kindness for this one day. Help me to respond gently and not react rigidly to the weaknesses of others. Help me to roll up my sleeves and not roll my eyes when I meet brokenness in others. Help me to love as you love me, for that is the bottom line and the top priority. I pray in your powerful name. Amen.

A Prayer about My Dad's Welcome Home

I desire to depart and be with Christ, which is better by far. (Phil. 1:23 NIV)

We are confident, I say, and would prefer to be away from the body and at home with the Lord. (2 Cor. 5:8 NIV)

Dear Jesus, I already had so much to be thankful for this Thanksgiving season, but now you've upped the ante considerably; you've fueled the furnace of my gratitude; you've added grace upon grace. I praise you that my dad finally knows the "better by far" of being with you. As of last night, he's gone from that ninety-one-year-old, Alzheimer's-invaded body and is free at last. He's at home with you. What more could I possibly want for my dad? Hallelujah, the gospel is true!

No more of my dad looking at me with kind eyes but with a clueless expression about who I am or even what the word *son* means. No more loss of dignity and no more limits on delight; no more grabbing for a thought or gasping for a breath; no more confinements, confusion, or cares about anything; no more wandering around, just the wonder of your glory and the fullness of your grace. Hallelujah, the gospel is true!

Jesus, though my dad and I were never able to carry on deep conversations about you or engage in meaty biblical and theological discussions, right now he knows more about you than I ever dreamed was knowable. He's experiencing the promised "more than all we ask or imagine" (Eph. 3:20 NIV), while I still have to ask and try to imagine. Everything I know about your beauty and bounty can fit into a thimble, with room left over, compared to what my dad now knows to be true about you. Hallelujah, the gospel is true!

Jesus, knowing he's with you also thrills me to think about the company he's now keeping—the fellowship dad is enjoying. I love the thought of my dad and mom seeing each other again after forty-nine years. Indeed, to be present with you is to be present with everybody else in heaven. My dad is in heaven not because he was a good man (though he was) but because you are a great Savior. Hallelujah, the gospel is true!

I make my prayer with great thanks, in your merciful and mighty name. Amen.

A Prayer about Gospelicious Friends

I thank my God every time I remember you. In all my prayers for all of you, I always pray with joy because of your partnership in the gospel from the first day until now, being confident of this, that he who began a good work in you will carry it on to completion until the day of Christ Jesus.
(Phil. 1:3–6 NIV)

Heavenly Father, it's Thanksgiving, and of all the things I'm grateful for, I'm especially thankful today for the women and men you've used over the years to bring me into a greater understanding and experience of the gospel.

I praise you for friends who've helped me understand *the lyric of the gospel*—theology. As a young convert my arrogant mantra was, "Don't give me theology, just give me Jesus." My sentiments were good, but my sensibilities were shoddy. To speak the name Jesus is to do theology. Thank you for patient teachers who have opened the Scriptures and have shown me the real Jesus—the one who lived and died in my place and who is making all things new.

I praise you for friends who've helped me hear and experience *the music of the gospel*. For those broken and beautiful saints who have helped me get a taste of the radical goodness of the gospel—its life-giving liberty, its healing melody, its soul-engaging joy—I praise you, Father. Now I know you to be a God who greatly delights in your people, who quiets us with his love, who rejoices over us with singing. This is astonishing, even shocking, and it's all because of what Jesus has done for us.

I praise you for friends who've been modeling *the missional dance of the gospel* for me. It's encouraging and challenging to discover the whole world as the dance floor of grace. Father, you created all things and you are redeeming all things, and when you get wild prodigals and stuffy elder brothers into your dance of the gospel, you take the dance outside of the house into our neighborhoods and among the nations. Thank you for my dance instructors.

Lord Jesus, you crushed the head of the serpent for us, and you will soon crush him under our own feet (Rom. 16:20). The gospel of the kingdom is infiltrating and transforming every sphere of life, and our future is so far beyond all that we can ask or imagine. On this Thanksgiving morning, I am *most of all thankful for you*, for you *are* the gospel. I pray in your glorious name. Amen.

A Prayer about Running
after the Wrong Things

So do not worry, saying, "What shall we eat?" or "What shall we drink?" or
"What shall we wear?" For the pagans run after all these things, and your
heavenly Father knows that you need them. But seek first his kingdom and
his righteousness, and all these things will be given to you as well.
(Matt. 6:31–33 NIV)

Lord Jesus, this is one early morning I don't feel alone at all. From where
I'm seated, I can already see streams of cars heading for the stores
and malls, and it's only 4:00 in the morning! They call it Black Friday, the
day after Thanksgiving—a day when your words about "running after all
these things" really come to life.

People will be pushing against doors, running up aisles, and grabbing
for items. They'll act like famished people who haven't eaten in weeks with
manners that would usually embarrass most grandmothers—except today,
because the grandmothers are right there with them.

Jesus, I'm not sitting here smugly judging anyone, for there's no one,
by nature, more greedy or grabby than me. I thank you that I live in a
time and place of abundance. I thank you I've never had to be concerned
about what I'll eat, drink, or wear. I even thank you that many people will
enjoy fine savings and get real bargains today.

But on this Black Friday, I'm especially grateful for *Good Friday* and what
you accomplished on the cross. It's only because of you, Jesus, that I know
God as Abba, Father—who knows my every need, who answers before I
ask, who gives me all things richly to enjoy, who satisfies my hunger, slakes
my thirst, and clothes me. Lord Jesus, to be clothed in your righteousness,
to feast upon you as the Bread of Life, to drink the living water you alone
can give—I am a wealthy man beyond all accounting.

In this next season of our lives, show us, Jesus, how to seek your
kingdom first, above everything else. Rather than spending more money
on ourselves, where would you have us invest our time, talent, and treasure; our energy, tears, and laughter? What new chapters of your story of
redemption and restoration would you write through us? We pray with
gratitude and anticipation, in your loving name. Amen.

A Prayer about
"Seventy Times Seven" Forgiveness

Then Peter came up and said to him [Jesus], "Lord, how often will my brother sin against me, and I forgive him? As many as seven times?" Jesus said to him, "I do not say seven times, but seventy times seven." (Matt. 18:21–22)

Jesus, I'm sure I've read this story at least seventy-seven times since the day you rescued me from the dominion of darkness and planted me in your kingdom of grace. But I need to keep on reading it, because forgiveness is as daily as breathing, eating, and sleeping.

I know I sin against you in thought, word, and deed, every hour of every day. Jesus, I also know that you've already forgiven all of my sins, past, present, and future. Such is the wonder of the gospel.

When I confess my sins and ask your forgiveness, I don't get more or new forgiveness. I humble myself and appropriate the forgiveness that you've already given me. Jesus, you're not informed by my confession of sin. You know it's a lot worse than I realize. You also know that your grace and forgiveness are far more abounding and thorough than I realize.

Where can greater riches be found? That's the most rhetorical question I can imagine. *Nothing* compares with the treasures we've received in the gospel.

Jesus, right now I confess how much I take your forgiveness for granted. I recognize this because there are a few "seventy times seven" forgiveness scenarios that are gnawing away at my peace and nibbling on my joy like tiny piranha.

I've forgiven seven times, but now I want them to pay; I want to be smug; I want to retreat into self-righteousness; I want to gossip and tell others not to trust those who have hurt me. In short, Jesus, I am a mess. I needed to write these feelings out so I could see just how ugly my heart can be.

Here's my cry: come, Holy Spirit, come; apply the power of the gospel to my heart today. Slay the wicked servant in me. Humble me, gentle me, settle me, focus me, free me. Love in me and through me, for the glory of God. I pray in Jesus' perfectly holy and forgiving name. Amen.

A Prayer about My Restless, Antsy Heart

Be still, and know that I am God.
  I will be exalted among the nations,
  I will be exalted in the earth! (Ps. 46:10)

Heavenly Father, I don't have "ants in my pants," but I am antsy. I don't have "restless leg syndrome," but I do have a restless heart. That's why the command to be still and know that you are God comes like a kiss from heaven. Please bring the settling and centering power of the gospel to bear, for my sake and the benefit of those around me.

I'm not sure what all's going on inside of me. I haven't been able to identify all the issues, but I know I'm not as peaceful, quiet, or trusting as I want to be or as you intend.

When I get in this anxious, edgy, squirmy place, I usually run to my control idols. I try to micromanage the chaos—and whoever and whatever else is in sight. I start acting either like an orphan or like the fourth member of the Trinity, vacillating between fear and arrogance. I cannot remember a time when that *ever* led to anything good. Usually it just makes other people wary and weary of being around me, especially members of my family.

So I humble myself before you, loving Father. I come boldly to an occupied throne of grace, throwing down my plastic scepter and presumption about being in control. You who will be exalted among the nations, be exalted in my heart, my day, my circumstances.

Lord Jesus, take captive my roaming thoughts. As you spoke and stilled the tossing waves for nervous disciples, speak and still my disquieted emotions—even if nothing or no one around me changes. As you harnessed the power of the wind, harness the passions of my will, that I might obey the gospel of grace. I pray in your mighty and merciful name. Amen.

A Prayer about Overflowing Gratitude

So then, just as you received Christ Jesus as Lord, continue to live your lives in him, rooted and built up in him, strengthened in the faith as you were taught, and overflowing with thankfulness. (Col. 2:6–7 NIV)

Lord Jesus, I want to be a man who gives you the quality and quantity of thanks of which you are so absolutely worthy. Not like a slow drip, a babbling brook, or a meandering stream, but like a geyser—a gospel geyser. I want to overflow with thankfulness, to the praise of your glory and grace!

I have every reason to be like the healed Samaritan leper, who with a stunned heart and irrepressible gratitude returned to give you heartfelt thanks (Luke 17:11–17). I return today, and I want to return every day, to express my profound thankfulness.

From the first nanosecond I was given faith to receive you as Savior and Lord, I was fully and firmly rooted in your righteousness and love. Now, completely forgiven, I have no other righteousness than yours. Just as I cannot add one iota to your righteousness, I can never, ever be separated from your love, and your love alone is better than life. You have already set me free from the penalty of sin, you are continually setting me free from the power of sin, and one day you will set me free from the very presence of sin.

Jesus, I want to *live in you*, reflecting upon your glory with an unveiled face and marinating in the riches of your unfailing grace. I want to *be built up in you*, maturing by the same grace that saved me, being liberated for the race that you've set before me. I want to *be strengthened in you*, forgiving others as you have forgiven me, forbearing with others as you forbear with me, accepting others as you accept me.

Lord Jesus, I would love to be done with all carping and droning, with all whining and complaining, with all boo-hooing and Eeyore-ing, and with every other expression of ingratitude. So rise up in me, O living water, unto eternal life. Artesian spring of grace, come forth with such compelling and propelling force that my thanks will be not miserly but geyserly. I pray in Jesus' name. Amen.

A Prayer about Crouching, Pouncing Sin

The LORD said to Cain, "Why are you angry, and why has your face fallen? If you do well, will you not be accepted? And if you do not do well, sin is crouching at the door. Its desire is for you, but you must rule over it."
(Gen. 4:6–7)

Lord Jesus, I'm always vulnerable to the destructive power of sin, but it seems like I'm especially vulnerable when there's some kind of emotional upheaval in my heart. Like Cain, when I'm angry and sulking about something or someone, I can be easily "had" by sin, giving in to its desire—its seductive and destructive ways. I wish there was no such thing as "the fleeting pleasures of sin" (Heb. 11:25).

Jesus, thank you for pursuing me today and asking me questions like, "Why are you angry?" "Why are you so sad?" "What are you afraid of?" and "Why are you so quiet and distant?" Though you know the answers to these and every question you ask, I need to think about these things. Show me my heart, Jesus.

I wish I had to think about only the sin that's crouching just outside my door—the tempter and temptress without, just waiting to pounce. But the truth is, Jesus, until you return to finish making all things new, I've got to be wise to the sin that's crouching *inside* of me as well. Like Paul, the very things I don't want to do, I still do, and the very things I want to do, they're not easily done (Rom. 7). I long for more freedom to live and to love as I am loved by you, Jesus.

How I praise you that there's no condemnation hanging over me for my sin, for you hung on the cross in my place. How I praise you that to be tempted is not an act of sin, for even you, Jesus, were tempted. I would despair if this were not the case. You've mastered sin for us, Jesus. You've exhausted its penalty and broken its power. Sin *will not* have dominion over us ever again.

In this good news, in this gospel, I trust today. As you show me my vulnerable heart, Jesus, show me your compassionate and loving heart ten times over. That will more than meet my need. I pray in your strong, present, and redeeming name. Amen.

A Prayer about Second-Coming Loving

The end of all things is at hand; therefore be self-controlled and sober-minded for the sake of your prayers. Above all, keep loving one another earnestly, since love covers a multitude of sins. Show hospitality to one another without grumbling. As each has received a gift, use it to serve one another, as good stewards of God's varied grace. (1 Pet. 4:7–10)

Dear Jesus, may Peter's words sink and settle deep into my heart. If I really believed "the end of all things is at hand," if I *really* believed your return could happen within my lifetime, it seems it would make a significant difference in how I live and love.

Whenever I attend a funeral, I always go away with a sense of my mortality and the fragility of life. At least for a few days, I hug loved ones a little tighter and linger a little longer in conversations. But then it's "back to normal," and the same old harried pace takes over and the same old broken patterns in relationships resume.

Normal sinners go on loving as normal sinners do: rather than covering sins, we get irritated with one another's sins; rather than welcoming one another without grumbling, we guard our own space with complaining; rather than using your gifts to serve each other, we hoard your gifts to satisfy ourselves; rather than administering your multifaceted grace to one another, we withhold it from one another. Yet "the end of all things is at hand." God, have mercy on me, the sinner.

Jesus, please bring the gospel to bear in fresh and powerful ways in my way of relating to others. I don't want to love by guilt but by grace. I don't want to love by fear but by faith. I don't want to love with a heart of manipulation but with a heart of ministry. I don't want to love with a view to another funeral but with a view of your second coming. I don't want to love to get anything but because I've received everything in you.

Jesus, you're the one who loves us deeply. You're the one who has covered not just a multitude but *all* of our sins. You're the one who always offers us hospitality without grumbling. You're the one who's always serving us and giving us more grace in all its forms. Live in us and love through us, whether you return in fifteen minutes or fifteen hundred years. We pray in your faithful name. Amen.

A Prayer for Marriages

For no one ever hated his own flesh, but nourishes and cherishes it, just as Christ does the church, because we are members of his body. "Therefore a man shall leave his father and mother and hold fast to his wife, and the two shall become one flesh." This mystery is profound, and I am saying that it refers to Christ and the church. (Eph. 5:29–32)

Lord Jesus, I'm greatly saddened about the growing number of my friends who are disconnected, despairing, or dying in their marriages. I'm saddened, but not shocked, for two reasons.

It makes complete sense that the powers of darkness would assault the one relationship meant to tell the story of your great love for your bride. Of course marriage is going to be a war zone—the front lines of spiritual warfare until the day you return. Satan hates you, he hates the gospel, and therefore he hates your bride and he hates marriage.

But knowing my own heart also decreases the shock factor. Like most of us, I came into marriage with a little gospel and big naïveté. I had no clue about the depths of my brokenness, the degree of my selfishness, or the devices of my sinfulness. I had no clue about what it would take to love one person well the rest of my life—a person who needs the gospel just as much as I do.

And I certainly had no clue that your love alone is better than life; that your love alone can slake the deepest thirst of my heart; that your love alone can provide the depths of intimacy I crave and for which I've been made; that your love alone can free me to love another sinful spouse the way you love me as your spouse—for better or for worse, for richer or for poorer, in sickness and in health, to love and to cherish, forgiving and forbearing, accepting without acquiescing, doing the hard and heart work of the gospel.

Jesus, I pray for my friends, and I pray for myself. Protect us from the evil one, and rescue us from ourselves. Give hope to the hopeless, conviction to the foolish, nourishment to the famished, grace to the betrayed, and godly sorrow to the betrayers. I pray sobered yet expectant, in your loving and powerful name. Amen.

A Prayer about the Radical Generosity of Grace

We want you to know, brothers, about the grace of God that has been given among the churches of Macedonia, for in a severe test of affliction, their abundance of joy and their extreme poverty have overflowed in a wealth of generosity on their part. For they gave according to their means, as I can testify, and beyond their means, of their own accord, begging us earnestly for the favor of taking part in the relief of the saints—and this, not as we expected, but they gave themselves first to the Lord and then by the will of God to us. (2 Cor. 8:1–5)

Heavenly Father, we come before you today challenged by this picture of radical grace. This one story alone underscores why we can never emphasize your grace too much. Grace is never to be counterbalanced with law, only multiplied with more grace. Indeed, through Jesus you continue to give us grace upon grace (John 1:16).

What an amazing story—the severely afflicted and extremely poor Christians of Macedonia became a model of radical generosity to the much wealthier believers in Corinth. And according to you, their motivation wasn't fear and guilt; it was multiplied grace. For you love cheerful giving, not reluctant giving compelled by pressure from without (2 Cor. 9:7).

Father, only your grace is powerful enough to give us abundant joy in the absence of affluence, coupled with hearts that beg to give sacrificially beyond our means for the benefit of strangers! The law cannot produce that kind of people—not even grace plus law, but only grace upon grace.

For the glory of Jesus and the advancing of your kingdom, we ask you to give us the same grace you gave the churches of Macedonia. The needs all around us are exponential, but your resources are endless. Indeed, help us to excel in the grace of giving. For you are "able to make all grace abound to [us], so that having all sufficiency in all things at all times, [we] can abound in every good work" (2 Cor. 9:8). Enrich us in every way that we might be generous in every way (2 Cor. 9:11)—with our time, talents, and treasures, and with great forbearance and extravagant forgiveness.

Jesus, you are the ultimate cheerful giver. That is what the gospel is all about. Though you were rich, you gladly became poor for us, that by your poverty we might become joyfully rich through you (2 Cor. 8:9). Make your gladness ours. Make your generosity ours. We pray in your great and gracious name. Amen.

A Prayer about Burying My Dad

"Where, O death, is your victory? Where, O death, is your sting?" The sting of death is sin, and the power of sin is the law. But thanks be to God! He gives us the victory through our Lord Jesus Christ. Therefore, my dear brothers and sisters, stand firm. Let nothing move you. Always give yourselves fully to the work of the Lord, because you know that your labor in the Lord is not in vain. (1 Cor. 15:55–58)

Dear Jesus, on the calendar, Thanksgiving has just passed and Advent is about to begin. But in my heart, it's the day I'll bury my dad next to my mom. The promise of sufficient grace is one I'll selfishly grab all this day long.

As I pray, I'm sitting in Dad's favorite chair—the one in which he worked thousands of crossword puzzles to keep his mind sharp and subtle. The same chair from which he began to look at me with confusion until the day he simply couldn't connect my face and name any longer.

I praise you that though we may forget one another's names, you'll never forget us—never. Alzheimer's robbed Dad of a lot, but you robbed the grave of its fear-holding, heart-ripping victory. You've turned death's sting into a harmless noodle, a fangless threat, even a portal to heaven. Your death on the cross was the death of death. The comfort and joy I have in knowing dad is with you is simply immeasurable.

But I also have great comfort and joy in remembering what took place before you took Dad home. Jesus, I praise you for working in our relationship way beyond what I could've asked or imagined. For decades Mom's death had more power over us than your life. Jesus, thank you for bringing healing to that wound before Dad disappeared into Alzheimer's. Thank you that Dad and I were finally able to weep together over the loss that ripped us apart. Thank you that we were finally able to return to her grave together ten years ago for the first time. Thank you that your name is Redeemer, not only of the grave but before the grave.

And thank you that as we return to Mom's grave together again today, it will not be a day of grieving as those who have no hope, but as those with a living hope and an unspeakable joy. I treasure knowing Dad and Mom are with you. Hallelujah, what a Savior! Hallelujah, what a salvation! I pray with great joy, in your gracious name, with wet eyes and a full heart. Amen.

A Prayer about the Advent Arms of God

You who bring good news to Jerusalem,
　　lift up your voice with a shout,
lift it up, do not be afraid;
　　say to the towns of Judah,
　　"Here is your God!"
See, the Sovereign LORD comes with power,
　　and he rules with a mighty arm.
See, his reward is with him,
　　and his recompense accompanies him.
He tends his flock like a shepherd:
　　He gathers the lambs in his arms
and carries them close to his heart;
　　he gently leads those that have young. (Isa. 40:9–11 NIV)

Gracious Father, Advent is upon us—the cherished season when we remember and celebrate the coming of Jesus, the promised Messiah, your beloved Son, our gracious Savior. Grant that it will prove to be much more than Advent-as-usual.

Surprise us, Father. Let us engage with the story of Jesus' birth as though for the very first time. Rescue us from the sentimental and the predictable. Bring familiar Scriptures alive in fresh ways. Reshape how we do Christmas this year by the power of the gospel.

Already this morning I've been arrested with Isaiah's picture of your "Advent arms." The promise of the Messiah carries with it the promise of the embrace we all need but scarcely believe. In Jesus, you come near to us as the sovereign Lord, with your sleeves rolled up as the great ruler. Your arm rules over all history, all nations, all kings, all circumstances. Nothing and no one can alter, subvert, or change the story you are telling through Jesus and the kingdom you are advancing through Jesus.

In Jesus, you come near to us as the most compassionate Shepherd, gathering and carrying your lambs in your arms. The image and hope are staggering. To be tended as a dumb sheep, to be held close to your heart, to be gently led—what more could we possibly long for?

These aren't mere metaphors, Father. Metaphors cannot save us, only inspire us. You *really are* this kind of God and you *really are this kind*. The coming of Jesus puts all nations on notice: there is only one true King. And the coming of Jesus puts all your people facedown in adoring love, for Jesus is a most wonderful, merciful Savior, Immanuel, the God who is with us and the God who is for us. I pray with Advent wonder, in Jesus' matchless name. Amen.

A Prayer about Loving from the Heart

Having purified your souls by your obedience to the truth for a sincere brotherly love, love one another earnestly from a pure heart, since you have been born again, not of perishable seed but of imperishable, through the living and abiding word of God. (1 Pet. 1:22–23)

Dear Jesus, this is an awesome morning: good coffee, a fire in the fireplace, Christmas music playing, and a Scripture about loving well. It's only because you came into the world for me that I have the slightest clue about what loving well—having a "sincere love"—looks like. Jesus, it's only because you lived for me and died for me that I have any experience of being loved deeply from the heart—your heart.

I need to sit still and marinate in this good news as my day begins: O joy beyond all delightings, O peace beyond all understandings, O hope beyond all imaginings—Jesus loves you deeply from his heart . . . and there's nothing you can do about it. You can't add to his love for you and you can't diminish his love for you. You can simply enjoy it, be changed by it, and share it with others.

Jesus, I never could have "purified myself." I never could have gained a relationship with God through purgings, penance, and promises of doing more and trying harder. What religion could never do for me, you've done for me. That's what we celebrate at Advent: your coming to do for us what we could never do for ourselves. "Born that man no more may die, born to raise the sons of earth, born to give them second birth—Hark! The herald angels sing, 'Glory to the newborn King!'"

It's only because I was given the "second birth," only because I was born again of the "imperishable seed" of grace, that I discovered my need of the gospel and was able to obey the truth of the gospel by believing it. You get all the credit, Jesus, from beginning to end.

So as I celebrate your incarnation this early morning, I surrender to its implications. Love in me and love through me, Jesus. There's no other way I will love anybody well. Make my love for my brothers and sisters sincere and observable. Teach me how to love deeply from my heart, just as you love us. I pray in your holy and loving name. Amen.

A Prayer about Jesus' Broad Shoulders

For to us a child is born,
to us a son is given,
and the government will be on his shoulders.
And he will be called
Wonderful Counselor, Mighty God,
Everlasting Father, Prince of Peace.
Of the greatness of his government and peace
there will be no end.
He will reign on David's throne
and over his kingdom,
establishing and upholding it
with justice and righteousness
from that time on and forever.
The zeal of the LORD Almighty
will accomplish this. (Isa. 9:6–7 NIV)

King Jesus, knowing the government of the whole world already rests on your shoulders profoundly humbles and gladdens us. It fills us with a joy second only to knowing your shoulders fully bore our sin.

Jesus, in you are hidden all the treasures of wisdom and knowledge. You are Wonderful Counselor. We look to you for knowledge of great mysteries and insight into things eternal, but you're also the one to whom we look for counsel on loving well—handling fresh disappointments, old hurts, and unfulfilled longings. You care about everything.

Jesus, you uphold all things by the power of your Word. You are Mighty God, the one who created and sustains the entire universe. You also give us power to boast in our weaknesses when we'd rather be self-sufficient.

Jesus, to see you is to see the Father, and by your work we know God as Father. You care so tenderly for the needs of the world—even the flowers of every field and the birds in every sky. But you also care about us. We are no longer orphans.

Jesus, no one else can pretend to be the Prince of Peace, for you alone paid the price of peace on the cross. Even as you are bringing the increase of your government and peace to all things, so you are advancing the reign of your grace in our lives. Forgive us when we look for wholeness, contentment, and healing somewhere else, for it cannot be found except in you.

For your broad shoulders, big heart, and coming kingdom, be glorified, O blessed Messiah and Redeemer. We pray in your matchless and merciful name. Amen.

A Prayer about Not Being Afraid

And there were shepherds living out in the fields nearby, keeping watch over their flocks at night. An angel of the Lord appeared to them, and the glory of the Lord shone around them, and they were terrified. But the angel said to them, "Do not be afraid. I bring you good news that will cause great joy for all the people. Today in the town of David a Savior has been born to you; he is the Messiah, the Lord. This will be a sign to you: You will find a baby wrapped in cloths and lying in a manger." (Luke 2:8–12 NIV)

Gracious Jesus, I'm confronted with the command "Do not be afraid" at both your birth and your resurrection (Luke 2:10; Matt. 28:5), like bookends of glory. Ever since our first parents sinned, feared, and hid, I've helped to keep the family tradition alive. At times fear has more power over my life than your love, and though I already know myself to be clothed in your righteousness, I still reach into my closet for fig leaves.

I join shepherds in hurrying off to come to you, Jesus, for you alone bring the good news of great joy for which my heart longs every day. You alone can charm my fears and set this prisoner more fully free.

Because the gospel is true, I can tell you what you already know to be true, Jesus. My fears aren't all that noble. I'm not really afraid of angelic hosts. I'm not really afraid to die. You've already set me free from that defining fear. I'm not even afraid of facing the final judgment, for I humbly cling to your cross as my judgment day. You've exhausted God's judgment against all my sins—past, present, and future. Hallelujah!

So what fears haunt me? For what fears do I need to obey the command "Do not be afraid"? I'll start with "the fear of man." Jesus, there are some people whose praise and disdain at times have more power over my heart than the gospel. It hurts to say it, but it's true.

Then there's the fear of redundancy—the fear of disappearing into a cloud of not mattering anymore. Jesus, even as I acknowledge this fear, I praise you for your noncondemning gaze. It's not easy to confess such weakness. May the joy of being used by you never supersede the much greater joy of simply being known and loved by you.

Jesus, I have other fears that need gospel charming. I bring these to you today with joy, for I've come to know you are not only a baby wrapped in cloths lying in a manger. I've also found you to be a Savior outside an empty tomb and now at the Father's right hand, ever living to advocate and pray for me. Thank you, thank you, thank you. I pray in your liberating name. Amen.

A Prayer about God's Favor
Resting on Us

Suddenly a great company of the heavenly host appeared with the angel, praising God and saying, "Glory to God in the highest heaven, and on earth peace to those on whom his favor rests." (Luke 2:13–14 NIV)

Heavenly Father, I've got to sit in these words for a bit: "peace to those on whom his favor rests." It's all right there in this doxological declaration, this angelic proclamation, this gospel-filled affirmation—everything my heart longs for, more than I could have ever hoped for or imagined. I know with certainty that you are at peace with me—that I'm someone upon whom your favor permanently rests—all because of what you've done for us in Jesus.

Father, if unredeemed angels were in awe of such good news, how much more should I be staggered and astonished, humbled and grateful, liberated and transformed?

We invest so much of our lives looking for favor—wanting to be wanted, longing to be celebrated, and seeking to be acceptable. Personally, I've looked to people and work, to education and exercise, to money and things, even to spiritual disciplines and ministry to give me what you alone give us so freely and fully in the gospel.

And what a freeing paradox, Father: the more we come alive to the riches of the gospel, the less we obsess about our own lives. We don't end up thinking more of ourselves or less of ourselves. We just think of ourselves less often. How liberating!

Jesus, may this old host of angels drive us into a new worship of you this Advent season. It's only because you submitted to the fullness of God's disfavor *for us* that we can boast of having the fullness of God's favor resting *on us*. We praise, honor, and adore you. We dare not look at your cradle without gazing at your cross. We pray in your holy and loving name. Amen.

A Prayer about No More Harm

The wolf will live with the lamb,
    the leopard will lie down with the goat,
and the calf and the lion and the yearling together;
    and a little child will lead them.
The cow will feed with the bear,
    their young will lie down together,
    and the lion will eat straw like the ox.
The infant will play near the cobra's den,
    the young child will put its hand into the viper's nest.
They will neither harm nor destroy
    on all my holy mountain;
for the earth will be filled with the knowledge of the LORD
    as the waters cover the sea. (Isa. 11:6–9 NIV)

Jesus, there are many things I love about the Advent season—the songs regaling your birth, the aroma of yuletide foods and spices, the dancing array of Christmas lights aglow in my neighborhood each evening. But I especially love fueling my faith and imagination with the promises God made surrounding your arrival. Every promise he has made finds its yes in you.

Today in particular, I'm stirred to think about the day of no more harm of any variety. "They will neither harm nor destroy on all my holy mountain" (Isa. 11:9 NIV).

Oh, for the day when all "tooth and claw" violence gives way to wolves frolicking with lambs; leopards and goats napping together; calves, lions, and young horses strolling through the new heaven and new earth as friends; cows and bears eating together rather than one another; snakes as pets rather than pests.

As much as I love the vision of shalom in the animal kingdom, ten thousand times over I long for the day when we, the two-legged image-bearers of the living God, no longer harm one another in any way. No more marginalizing or minimizing one another; no more demeaning or dismissing one another; no more vilifying or idolizing one another; no more hating or hurting one another; no more using or abusing one another in any way.

Hasten the day when we will finally and fully love one another as you love us, Jesus. Until that day, keep us groaning and growing in grace. Grant us quick repentances when we love poorly. May the world recognize us as your disciples by the way we love one another. We pray in your powerful and patient name. Amen.

A Prayer about God's Irrepressible Goodness

"Ask a sign of the LORD your God; let it be deep as Sheol or high as heaven."
But Ahaz said, "I will not ask, and I will not put the LORD to the test." And
[Isaiah] said, "Hear then, O house of David! Is it too little for you to weary
men, that you weary my God also? Therefore the Lord himself will give you
a sign. Behold, the virgin shall conceive and bear a son, and shall call his
name Immanuel." (Isa. 7:11–14)

Gracious Father, the more often and the more carefully I read your
Word the more I realize how little of your goodness I actually "get."
I love the name "Immanuel"—God with us—yet today I realize you
gave this hope in full view of unfaithfulness, unbelief, and unrighteousness.
What a God you are! What a story you're telling!

It was a time of local and international crisis, and King Ahaz had every
opportunity to repent and rely on you. You sent Isaiah with words of
wisdom and hope. But he refused. Feigning piety, King Ahaz remained
addicted to his illusion of control and self-sufficiency.

Father, as I read this story, I realize how much I'm like King Ahaz.
Often I go through the motions of acknowledging you, but on the inside
I'm far more resolved to trust in me than in you. I can't throw any stones
today at this wicked king. Rather, I grieve my own illusion of control and
self-sufficiency.

That's why the promise of Immanuel is so precious to me. Father, you've
proven yourself to be a God who is not only *with me* in Jesus, but a God
who is so very much *for me* in Jesus. Your love for us in the gospel is not
only unconditional, it's contraconditional. For you've met every condition
necessary to fulfill your commitment to redeem your pan-national people
and restore your broken creation. What a gospel you've given us in Jesus!

King Jesus, though I don't have the Assyrian army outside my door
threatening my existence, I do have no small number of challenges in front
of me this Advent season. By faith through grace, I purpose to rely on you
for gospel sanity and strength, just as I rely on you for my forgiveness and
my righteousness. You are with me and you are for me, and that is enough.
I pray in the glory of your name. Amen.

A Prayer about Seeming Impossibilities

"How will this be," Mary asked the angel, "since I am a virgin?" The angel answered, "The Holy Spirit will come on you, and the power of the Most High will overshadow you. So the holy one to be born will be called the Son of God. Even Elizabeth your relative is going to have a child in her old age, and she who was said to be unable to conceive is in her sixth month. For no word from God will ever fail." "I am the Lord's servant," Mary answered. "May your word to me be fulfilled." Then the angel left her. (Luke 1:34–38 NIV)

Heavenly Father, you gave Mary a calling no one else will ever share—to be the mother of God the Son. And yet I do have a lot in common with her. When I consider the enormity of the promises you've made accompanying the birth of Jesus, I too say and pray with incredulity, "How will this be?" And I hear you answer back in the gospel, "Nothing is impossible with God."

There's nothing you've promised, with respect to Jesus, that won't come to pass. This includes the transformation of this broken world into the new heaven and new earth. It includes the redeeming of a bride for Jesus from every single nation, tribe, people, and language. But it also includes your plans for my life. Just as surely as you placed the life of Jesus in Mary, you have done the same for me. Though in an entirely different way than Mary, I too am pregnant with glory (Rom. 8:18–27).

One day I will fully love with the kindness and compassion of Jesus. I will think and see only with the wisdom and eyes of heaven. I will completely embrace the will of God as my favorite bread and utter delight.

One day I will never be selfish, petty, or defensive again. I will never get my feelings hurt, insist on being right, or demand more. I will think of others more highly and more often than myself. I won't keep a record of anybody's wrongs, no longer remembering and rehearsing the ways others have failed me and the ways I've failed them. I will be free, so very free and whole.

To all of these promises I find myself saying, "How will this be, since I'm still so very much not like Jesus?" And you answer back so graciously, "Things impossible with man are possible with God." And I say and pray, "May it be as you have promised in the gospel, holy and faithful Father. I am yours and your servant." I pray in Jesus' name. Amen.

A Prayer about the Heart and Habits of the Gospel

And you, child, will be called the prophet of the Most High; for you will go before the Lord to prepare his ways, to give knowledge of salvation to his people in the forgiveness of their sins, because of the tender mercy of our God, whereby the sunrise shall visit us from on high to give light to those who sit in darkness and in the shadow of death, to guide our feet into the way of peace. (Luke 1:76–79)

Dear Father, I often forget about the other special baby promised and delivered in the Advent story: John the Baptist, the forerunner, the way-maker, the friend of the bridegroom. His birth and life are such a testimony to the way, the gospel.

Oh, to become a man like John, whose joy was to decrease as Jesus increased. Oh, to be a parent like Zechariah, wanting only what you want for our children and grandchildren.

What more could a father, like Zechariah, desire for his son than for him to be a powerful and passionate witness to Jesus, the Messiah—the one in whom we experience your tender mercy and full forgiveness? There needed to be only one John the Baptist, and yet there is an ongoing need for many others to live and love as John did.

What better story could we write or what other story would we choose than for our kids to be a means by which the rising sun of grace would bring the light of the gospel to the dark places and the broken people of the world?

Father, we lift our children and grandchildren to you. For those who don't know you, in light of your covenant promises, we ask you to bring them to a saving knowledge of Jesus. Rescue them from religion and non-religion. For those who do know you, we pray that the gospel would go deeper and deeper into their hearts, assuring them of your tender mercies and sufficient grace, transforming them into the likeness of Jesus, and freeing them for a life of living, loving, and serving in your church and kingdom.

Our prayer for our children and grandchildren is the same one we offer for ourselves: Lord Jesus, guide us into the heart and habits of the gospel; guide our feet more surely onto the path of peace; lead us deeper into the ways of shalom, into your commitment to redeem your people and make all things new. We pray in your name and for your glory. Amen.

A Prayer about Treasuring and Pondering

So they hurried off and found Mary and Joseph, and the baby, who was lying in the manger. When they had seen him, they spread the word concerning what had been told them about this child, and all who heard it were amazed at what the shepherds said to them. But Mary treasured up all these things and pondered them in her heart. (Luke 2:16–19 NIV)

Gracious Jesus, I'm very drawn to Mary's response early in her journey of nursing you and knowing you. Even as I write these words, I realize what a holy mystery the incarnation was. You, the very God who created all things, who sustains all things, and who is making all things new—you drew nourishment from a young maiden's breast.

And Mary "treasured up all these things and pondered them in her heart." "Hurrying off" like a shepherd to tell others about you has always been easier for me than sitting still and letting you tell me about yourself.

It's always been easier for me to talk than to listen, to stay busy than to relax, to be "productive" than to be meditative. I confess this as sin, Jesus. This isn't okay. It can be explained but not justified. For knowing about you is not the same thing as knowing you. An informed mind is not the same thing as an enflamed heart.

To know you is eternal life, and I do want to know you, Jesus, so much better than I already do. I want to treasure you in my heart and ponder who you are. I want to contemplate everything you've already accomplished through your life, death, and resurrection; everything you're presently doing as the King of Kings and Lord of Lords; and everything you will be in the new heaven and new earth as the bridegroom of your beloved bride. There's so much to treasure and so much to ponder.

It's not as though I'm a stranger to treasuring and pondering, for I treasure and ponder a lot of things, Jesus—things, however, that lead to a bankrupt spirit and an impoverished heart. May the gospel slow me, settle me, and center me, that I might say with the psalmist, "Whom have I in heaven but you? And there is nothing on earth that I desire besides you. My flesh and my heart may fail, but God is the strength of my heart and my portion forever" (Ps. 73:25–26). I pray in your peerless name. Amen.

A Prayer about a Standing Shepherd

"But you, Bethlehem Ephrathah,
  though you are small among the clans of Judah,
out of you will come for me
  one who will be ruler over Israel,
whose origins are from of old,
  from ancient times." . . .
He will stand and shepherd his flock
  in the strength of the LORD,
  in the majesty of the name of the LORD his God.
And they will live securely, for then his greatness
  will reach to the ends of the earth.
And he will be our peace. (Mic. 5:2, 4–5 NIV)

Most loving Jesus, there are so many reasons to love and worship you. First and foremost, you are God, who, along with the Father and the Holy Spirit, is singularly worthy to be worshiped with everything we have and are. The fact that I'm even tempted to worship other gods is irrefutable confirmation that I'm a broken, sinful man, desperate for the salvation that you alone can give.

Today I'm especially moved to worship you, Jesus, for being the Shepherd-Savior that you are. Having laid down your life as the Lamb of God, you've risen and are now *the standing shepherd*—relentlessly caring, vigilantly protecting, and faithfully providing for us. You never sleep or slumber. You are constantly caring for us. Be praised and worshiped, O good and engaged Shepherd.

Jesus, because of your great love for me in the gospel, I lack nothing that I need. I don't get all my wants, but I do have everything I need for life and godliness . . . and a whole lot more. I praise you that it's green pastures and quiet waters to which you lead me—all for the restoring of my tired, weary, broken, rebellious soul.

For your glory and my good, you guide me along paths of righteousness, goodness, truth, and grace. And even as that journey involves traversing places marked by decay and death, you are with me, and that's all I really need to know. I don't have to be afraid of anything or anyone, for you are with me.

You nourish me all the time, even when enemies are close by and threatening. Your generous anointing overflows for the blessing of others. To follow you is to be followed by the fragrance of your goodness and love. Even in the new heaven and new earth, you will be our shepherd, leading us to springs of living water (Rev. 7:17). Your greatness, Jesus, will reach to the ends of the earth, and we will always live securely, for you are our peace, now and forever.

In your great and gracious name we pray. Amen.

A Prayer about Immanuel's Presence and Presents

And we know that for those who love God all things work together for good, for those who are called according to his purpose. For those whom he foreknew he also predestined to be conformed to the image of his Son, in order that he might be the firstborn among many brothers. And those whom he predestined he also called, and those whom he called he also justified, and those whom he justified he also glorified. What then shall we say to these things? If God is for us, who can be against us? He who did not spare his own Son but gave him up for us all, how will he not also with him graciously give us all things? (Rom. 8:28–32)

Jesus, I'm thankful to know that every word of the Word, in one way or another, is ultimately about you. Every command drives me to you. Every promise is fulfilled in you. Every story whispers your name, points to your glory, and proffers your grace. This is why I love the Bible more than ever.

Yet there seem to be some Scriptures that are kind of like "homeroom" to me, like a favorite chair, jogging path, or scenic view. To go there puts everything into perspective. This portion of the Word is just such a place. All the Immanuel promises, all the carols and hymns of Advent converge right here. The hopes and fears of all my years are met right here.

Jesus, I praise you for being Immanuel—God with me and God for me. Your *presence* and your *presents* are all that I need, much more than I realize, and way beyond all I could have ever hoped for or imagined.

You're at work in all things for your glory and for my good—in the obvious and in the not-so-obvious, in my gains and in my pains, in what I "get" and in the things that seem to contradict what I know, when I'm "feeling the love" and when I'm feeling very lonely, when the gospel makes all the sense in the world to me and when I'm tempted to say with John the Baptist, "Are you the Messiah, or should we be looking for another?"

But there is no other Messiah, Savior, or Lord but you, Jesus. And absolutely nothing can separate me from your love, for I've been called according to the Father's purpose, which will never fail or falter. He "foreknew" me; he set his affection upon me before the world began, and he will continue to provide everything necessary to complete the work of the gospel in my life, in the whole family of God, and in the entire creation. "Thrice hallelujah!" I shout.

I pray by the light of this good news of great joy. Amen.

A Prayer about One Blessing
after Another

The Word became flesh and made his dwelling among us. We have seen his glory, the glory of the one and only Son, who came from the Father, full of grace and truth. (John testified concerning him. He cried out, saying, "This was the one I spoke about when I said, 'He who comes after me has surpassed me because he was before me.'") Out of his fullness we have all received grace in place of grace already given. (John 1:14–16 NIV)

Dear Jesus, I can understand why, of all the accounts of your birth, John's is least often chosen as the script for Sunday school Christmas pageants and programs. After all, what parts would the children play? What cute costumes could they wear? There's no manger, no Joseph and Mary, no shepherds and angels or wise men and lowing cattle. But there certainly is you. You're the only star on the horizon in this nativity scene, and how you shine.

I praise you, Lord Jesus, for becoming flesh and "tabernacling" among us for just the right amount of time. Though equal to yet distinct from the Father, you didn't consider your glory something to be tightly grasped or held on to selfishly. Rather, you emptied yourself by becoming a man—but not just any ordinary man but a servant-man, the servant of the Lord, the second Adam, our Savior . . . my Savior.

In your thirty-three years of incarnate life, you accomplished everything necessary for the redemption of the people for whom you lived and died but also for the restoration of the world you created and love. Be magnified, adored, regaled, worshiped, and loved, Lord Jesus. What a wonderful, merciful Savior you are! What a God who is so mighty to save!

I cannot sing Isaac Watts's great Advent hymn "Joy to the World" without thinking of John's Advent narrative. For you are presently ruling the world with your grace and truth—the grace and truth with which you are full. You're making the nations prove the wonders of your love as the gospel runs from heart to heart and nation to nation.

From the fullness of your grace I keep receiving one blessing after another and one blessing on top of another: the blessings of your imputed righteousness, the blessings of perpetual favor with God, the blessings of your intercession and advocacy, the blessings of your Spirit's work in my life, the blessings of citizenship in heaven, the blessing of knowing the good work you have begun in me, and in the cosmos, will be brought to completion! Hail the incarnate deity! Joy to the world, and to me, indeed! I pray in your most glorious name. Amen.

A Prayer about Singing Mary's Song

And Mary said, "My soul magnifies the Lord, and my spirit rejoices in God my Savior, for he has looked on the humble estate of his servant. For behold, from now on all generations will call me blessed; for he who is mighty has done great things for me, and holy is his name. And his mercy is for those who fear him from generation to generation." (Luke 1:46–50)

Jesus, I woke up today so thankful for the gift of music, especially the songs of Advent. I'm more likely to lose my inhibitions singing Christmas songs than any other genre. And it's not rocket science to figure out why this is so. Every Advent hymn, carol, and chorus I treasure—from your Word, in my hymnal, or on my iPod—propels me into hope and gratitude and more hope and more gratitude. And when my heart is fueled by these twin graces, I'm much freer and so much more full of faith.

I praise you for igniting my heart to sing your praise. I praise you for giving me a reason to sing, Lord Jesus. I praise you for songwriters who capture what I feel and give me the vehicle for expressing what I long to say to you.

Mary's story is different from mine, and yet I join her Advent refrain today. I can sing her song. I must sing her song, for you've been so mindful of my humble, broken, sinful state. I have nothing to boast in but you, Lord Jesus. You came to me when I wasn't seeking you. You are being formed in me as surely as you entered the world through Mary's womb.

I'm a blessed man because you've done great things for me, and you continue to do great things for me. Holy is your name, Lord Jesus! I have no concern for what any generation may say about me. It's enough to know what you say about me: that I'm yours, that I'm forgiven, that I'm righteous in you, and that nothing can separate me from your love.

Your mercy has been extended to my generation and to me personally. Therefore, my soul glorifies you, Jesus, and my spirit rejoices in you, my God and my Savior. As the gospel goes deeper into my heart, free me from all fears except the fear of the Lord. I want to be filled and freed with an affectionate reverence for you alone, Lord Jesus. I sing and pray, in your most glorious and gracious name. Amen.

A Prayer about a King, Not a Co-Pilot

Of the increase of his government and of peace
  there will be no end,
on the throne of David and over his kingdom,
  to establish and uphold it
with justice and righteousness
  from this time forth and forevermore.
The zeal of the LORD of hosts will do this. (Isa. 9:7)

Merciful Jesus, I thought I'd seen it all. I didn't really think there were many more surprises waiting for me . . . until yesterday. The SUV in front of me looked like a Christmas tree with blinking lights, ornaments, an angel on top and all. But right there on the bumper there it was—centered and unblemished, a 15-by-4-inch banner proclaiming, "Jesus Is My Co-Pilot."

After repenting of my cynicism, I was happy to affirm in busy traffic, as I do this early morning, that you're *not* a co-pilot. You're a king, the King of all kings, "the ruler of kings on earth" (Rev. 1:5) and everything else. The last thing I need in life, or in death, is a co-pilot. Co-crucifixion and co-resurrection with you, yes! Co-pilot, no.

Advent's the season in which we get to acknowledge there's only one government and one peace sufficient to meet the needs of our sinful hearts and this broken world. King David's throne has now become a throne of grace from which you rule the world, advancing your kingdom of peace, justice, and righteousness in the hearts of your people, among the nations of the world, and in every sphere of your creation.

Jesus, with zeal and grace you're working all things together after the counsel of your will. You—the Lamb of God, the Lord of Lords, and the Lamp of the New Jerusalem—are working in all things for your glory and for our good. No one and nothing can derail, deter, or distract you from bringing to completion your good work of redemption and restoration. Hallelujah! Hallelujah! Hallelujah!

As the gospel of your kingdom continues its transforming work in my life, Jesus, may it advance *through* my life. As you love me passionately, I would love you missionally, living in your redeeming story, to your matchless glory, with your unspeakable joy. I pray in your mighty and merciful name. Amen.

A Prayer about a Delightfully Huge Christmas

See, I will create
  new heavens and a new earth.
The former things will not be remembered,
  nor will they come to mind.
But be glad and rejoice forever
  in what I will create,
for I will create Jerusalem to be a delight
  and its people a joy.
I will rejoice over Jerusalem
  and take delight in my people;
the sound of weeping and of crying
  will be heard in it no more. (Isa. 65:17–19 NIV)

Heavenly Father, the long line at Costco gave me more than a chance to whine about the wait. Casual conversation with fellow shoppers once again highlighted the multiple ways the story of Christmas is told and experienced.

To start with, Bing Crosby was crooning, "Have yourself a merry little Christmas," but on top of that I kept hearing this shopping cart refrain: "We can't afford much Christmas this year" and "We're downsizing Christmas this year." I found myself grateful for the way you tell the story.

Father, we're not the ones who "do" Christmas; *you are*, and there's really nothing merely merry or little about the day. The size of our Christmas has absolutely nothing to do with how much discretionary money we have to spend on bigger and better gifts. How I praise you that *every* Christmas is *huge*, delightfully huge, irrespective of any economy or currency.

Through the gift of Jesus, you've promised to create a new heaven and new earth from the stuff of this very broken world—a new creation world in which you will find great delight. We praise you for your generosity and your joy, mighty Father.

You've promised to redeem a people from every race, tribe, tongue, and people group to live in that eternal world of peace and joy—a people in whom you find great delight and over whom you will rejoice forever. We praise you for your generosity and your joy, merciful Father.

Lord Jesus, I intend to fix my gaze on you today and not on my shopping cart. For you're the object, author, and perfecter of our faith. It's because you have come and are coming again that we live with the blessed assurance that all our sins have been wiped away and the glorious hope that all of our tears likewise will one day be wiped away. This is *huge*, delightfully huge! I pray in your holy and loving name. Amen.

A Prayer about the Most Holy Paradox

The Spirit of the Lord GOD is upon me,
  because the LORD has anointed me
to bring good news to the poor;
  he has sent me to bind up the brokenhearted,
to proclaim liberty to the captives,
  and the opening of the prison to those who are bound;
to proclaim the year of the LORD's favor,
  and the day of vengeance of our God;
  to comfort all who mourn;
to grant to those who mourn in Zion—
  to give them a beautiful headdress instead of ashes,
the oil of gladness instead of mourning,
  the garment of praise instead of a faint spirit;
that they may be called oaks of righteousness,
  the planting of the LORD, that he may be glorified. (Isa. 61:1–3)

Jesus, I'm marinating this morning in the holy paradox of the weakness of your birth and the magnitude of your calling. Who could've ever imagined that a baby whose birthing room was a stable would be the means by which God will ultimately stabilize and transform everything awry in the universe?

Who had any way of knowing that the child who nursed from a very young mother's breast was actually the Ancient of Days—the one who brings the nourishment of salvation, redemption, and restoration to God's pan-national people and much-beloved creation?

Who recognized that the cute, cuddly spirit of this infant was actually the Spirit of the Sovereign Lord by which one day all oppression will be stopped, all chains will be broken, all injustice will give way to justice, mourning will be replaced with gladness, broken hearts will become healed hearts, despairing hearts will become praising hearts, and the disfavored will become the favored of the Lord? Who possibly could've seen, known, and believed such a thing?

We praise you, Lord Jesus, for displaying your splendor most clearly in the gospel of your kingdom and of God's grace. May your splendor be more fully revealed in us and through us, until the day you return to finish making all things new. May we who have been declared righteous by faith in you live as a people who love your mercy, advocate for your justice, and walk humbly with you, our God. I pray in your most glorious name. Amen.

A Prayer about the Perfect Birthing Experience

But when the set time had fully come, God sent his Son, born of a woman, born under the law, to redeem those under the law, that we might receive adoption to sonship. Because you are his sons, God sent the Spirit of his Son into our hearts, the Spirit who calls out, "Abba, Father." So you are no longer a slave, but God's child; and since you are his child, God has made you also an heir. (Gal. 4:4–7 NIV)

Dear Jesus, like others, I often sentimentalize the circumstances of your birth, judging Jerusalem for missing the moment, criticizing innkeepers for gross inhospitality, and pitying Joseph and Mary for the birthing room they had to endure. Yet *everything happened* just as you, our Father, and the Holy Spirit planned. "Doing all things well" didn't just start happening after your resurrection.

"When the time had fully come" you came, not a day early and not a day late. As humbling as it was to be born under the ceiling of a stable, being born under the weight of the law was a far greater burden. Yet that's exactly why you came into the world—to be born under God's law to redeem us—to redeem me from my sin and my rebellion, to rescue me from my unwillingness and inability to love God as he deserves. There's no way in the world I could've ever fulfilled the demands of God's righteous, perfect, and holy law. Only you could and only you did. I worship, praise, and adore you, Lord Jesus.

Because you lived in my place and died in my place, I'm no longer a slave but a son of the living and loving God, with the full rights thereof. Abba, Father has robed this prodigal with your righteousness and has sent his Spirit to live in my heart. My future looks amazing, as I will co-inherit the new heaven and new earth with you! Oh my . . . what can I say but "Hallelujah, what a Savior! Hallelujah, what a salvation!"

I will not judge innkeepers, but I rejoice in the God of my salvation. I pray in your matchless name. Amen.

A Prayer about Christmas Memories

He [God] has performed mighty deeds with his arm; he has scattered those who are proud in their inmost thoughts. He has brought down rulers from their thrones but has lifted up the humble. He has filled the hungry with good things but has sent the rich away empty. He has helped his servant Israel, remembering to be merciful to Abraham and his descendants forever, just as he promised our ancestors. (Luke 1:51–55 NIV)

Heavenly Father, as the Holy Spirit prayed this magnificent prayer through a stunned Mary, little could she have imagined what was ahead. Her birth pains in nine months would be greatly surpassed by her heart pains thirty-three years later at the foot of her son's cross.

But there's one thing she did understand—at least one thing she took to heart from her years of growing up in a home of faith. She was taught that you are a God who remembers to be merciful. You have proved this beyond all doubt.

Father, I worship and adore you this morning for your memory and for your mercy. I've got a lot of great Christmas memories, but I am most thankful that Christmas is a celebration of what you did not forget and what you will never forget. With the gift of Jesus, you remembered all the promises you made to Abraham and to his descendants, which includes me. I'm humbled and overwhelmed.

You promised Abraham you would take him to a land of your choosing, make of him a great nation, and through that nation ultimately bless all the families on the face of the earth (Gen. 12–17). No one could fulfill these promises but you.

Like Mary, Abraham could not have begun to imagine how all of this would play out. But the promises you made to Abraham and the prayer prayed through Mary all find their fulfillment in your Son, Jesus. I praise you for your memory and your mercy, Father.

Indeed, Jesus, you are the fulfillment of all the covenant promises God has made. Because of your faithfulness, from the cradle to the cross, we live in the embrace of the Father of mercies, whose mercies are new every morning. Great is his faithfulness! Because of you, Jesus, the only sign of amnesia in our Father is his forgetting to remember our sins against us, forever! What peace, what joy, what hope this brings me today.

I pray with the faith of Abraham and the humility of Mary, in your gracious and loving name. Amen.

A Prayer about Jesus, Our Brother and Prophet

The LORD your God will raise up for you a prophet like me from among you, from your brothers—it is to him you shall listen—just as you desired of the LORD your God at Horeb on the day of the assembly, when you said, "Let us not hear the voice of the LORD my God or see this great fire any more, lest I die." And the LORD said to me, "They are right in what they have spoken. I will raise up for them a prophet like you from among their brothers. And I will put my words in his mouth, and he shall speak to them all that I command him." (Deut. 18:15–18)

Dear Jesus, of all the incredible promises made about your birth, I often overlook one of the first and most wonderful ones given. You are the greater Moses—our brother and prophet. What a joy it is to know that you rule the world with grace and truth, both of which you are full of (John 1:14).

Throughout the history of redemption, God spoke to our forefathers through the prophets, at many times and in various ways. But finally and fully, he spoke to us through you, his beloved Son—Creator and heir of all things (Heb. 1:1–3). You are the final Word, Jesus, the living Word, the loving Word, the incarnate Word! We worship and adore you.

Oh, the freedom and joy I have in knowing you've spoken and have not stuttered, Lord Jesus. Everything I need to know about God, about the world, about me, about the past, the present, and the future—about all things—I find in you. For all the treasures of wisdom and knowledge are hidden in you and revealed by you (Col. 1:3). You continually set me free from nonsense and no sense, from illusions and delusions, from all guessing and second-guessing.

Oh, the gladness of this Advent season that reminds me that I don't cower at the foot of Mount Sinai to hear you teach. No! I am a part of the joyful assembly that listens to you preach the gospel to my heart from Mount Zion (Heb. 12:18–25)! Therefore, I will listen. I will not refuse you, for you speak only words of grace and truth, words of comfort and joy, and words of peace and new creation. I pray in your glorious name. Amen.

A Prayer about Advent Tenderness

Who has believed our message
  and to whom has the arm of the LORD been revealed?
He grew up before him like a tender shoot,
  and like a root out of dry ground.
He had no beauty or majesty to attract us to him,
  nothing in his appearance that we should desire him.
He was despised and rejected by mankind,
  a man of suffering, and familiar with pain.
Like one from whom people hide their faces
  he was despised, and we held him in low esteem.
Surely he took up our pain
  and bore our suffering. (Isa. 53:1–4 NIV)

Gracious Jesus, before now I've never thought of the manger as the very place the Father "planted" you, the "tender shoot" of Isaiah's vision. But truly, you are the root that broke through the dry ground of a fallen universe. Who could have imagined that the humble estate of a stable would become such a garden of grace and glory? Who could have dreamed that the mighty arm of the Lord would be revealed most powerfully in the weakness of your birth?

Jesus, I praise you for the humility and tenderness of your incarnation. You who created the very category of beauty—you who are quintessential beauty—became the one with "no beauty," for us. Though I don't fully understand all that entailed, one glance beyond your cradle to your cross brings this hard prophecy to life.

You literally became everything ugly and vile about my sin. You became sin for me that in you I might be clothed and become the very righteousness of God. You who shared the eternal delight of the Godhead and the adoration and esteem of angels became the despised and rejected one for us—for me.

You who are the fountain of pleasures, whose laughter fills heaven, whose joy is our strength, became the man of sorrows for us—for me. And though you didn't remain a tender shoot, you have retained all tenderness. Lord Jesus, no one is familiar with suffering like you. In taking up your cross, you took up our infirmities and carried our sorrows. What a wonderful, merciful, tender Savior you are!

If I can make progress in only one thing this Advent season, Lord Jesus, may it be to have a much greater esteem for you. Intensify my love for you, deepen my awe of your manger and your cross, and make me much more the tender man that the gospel is calling me to become. I pray in your holy and gracious name. Amen.

371

A Prayer about Christmas Wisdom

When they [the Magi] saw the star, they rejoiced exceedingly with great joy. And going into the house they saw the child with Mary his mother, and they fell down and worshiped him. Then, opening their treasures, they presented him gifts, gold and frankincense and myrrh. (Matt. 2:10–11)

Dear Jesus, whether they were kings, magicians, or astrologers and whether there were two, three, or seventeen of them, it makes no difference. The Magi were wise men, and they show us the way of true wisdom because they lead us to the Person of true wisdom. Jesus, you have become wisdom from God for us—"our righteousness and sanctification and redemption" (1 Cor. 1:30). That's why we boast only in you and not in ourselves or our so-called wisdom.

In fact, you're the real seeker in the story of the Magi. Promises of your coming, an irrepressible calling, a providential star, a Spirit-generated joy—how we praise you for drawing men and women to yourself from every period of history, every family of humanity, and every segment of society. Come Herod or high water, those you've come to save will come to you, Jesus.

My prayer for this Advent season is quite simple: Jesus, please reveal more and more of your glory and grace to my heart. I want to bow quicker, lower, and with more joy than ever before you, my majestic and merciful King. Open the eyes of my heart a bit wider to behold the great hope to which you've called us in the gospel. Deepen my adoration of you, Jesus, and loosen my grip on my so-called treasures. What do I have that you have not given me? I pray in your most wise and worthy name. Amen.

A Prayer about the Quiet Certainty
of Jesus' Birth

In those days Caesar Augustus issued a decree that a census should be taken of the entire Roman world. (This was the first census that took place while Quirinius was governor of Syria.) And everyone went to their own town to register. So Joseph also went up from the town of Nazareth in Galilee to Judea, to Bethlehem the town of David, because he belonged to the house and line of David. He went there to register with Mary, who was pledged to be married to him and was expecting a child. While they were there, the time came for the baby to be born, and she gave birth to her firstborn, a son. She wrapped him in cloths and placed him in a manger, because there was no guest room available for them. (Luke 2:1–7 NIV)

Jesus, it's the beloved day we call Christmas Eve, the date we've set aside to remember and reflect upon your nativity. Luke took so much care to fix your birthday in the context of real history and a real world, but whether or not you were born anywhere close to December 25 is not important at all. That you were born—that you actually came from eternity into time and space—*that's* what's important, Jesus.

I sing to you today with all the passion and delight I can possibly muster, "Born that man (including me) no more may die, born to raise the sons of earth (including me), born to give them (including me) second birth." For the certainty of your birth, and therefore my rebirth, I give you great praise.

But for all the care Luke took to detail the *circumstances* of your birthday, it's the *quietness* of your birth that astounds me. Any other king would've come with great fanfare and a royal entourage. But you came into our world in utter stillness and profound humility. "No room in the inn" wasn't an insult to you. It was your choice, your plan, the way of the gospel.

We marvel, we wonder, we are in awe of you, Jesus. For you didn't consider your equality with God something to be selfishly hoarded and held on to. Rather, you made yourself "nothing," taking the very nature of a human servant—the "Servant of the Lord" of Isaiah's vision and songs— and in your humility, you died our death on the cross.

"Mild he lays his glory by . . . Veiled in flesh, the Godhead see . . . Hail, the incarnate Deity, pleased, as man, with men to dwell, Jesus, our Emmanuel! . . . Peace on earth and mercy mild, God and sinners reconciled!"

I so look forward to the day, Jesus, when every knee will bow and every tongue confess that you are Lord, to the glory of God the Father. It's going to be a loud and large day. But this Christmas Eve I say to myself, "Be still, my soul . . . behold calm glory, savor mild mercy, worship your newborn King with quiet certainty."

I pray in Jesus' great and gracious name. Amen.

A Prayer about Jesus

For unto you is born this day in the city of David a Savior, who is Christ the Lord. (Luke 2:11)

Dear Jesus, a most glorious and praise-filled "Happy birthday!" to you. Though you've existed forever in rich, joyful, pleasure-filled relationship with the Father and the Holy Spirit, today we celebrate your coming to us and for us.

I join brothers and sisters throughout the world and from all ages in celebrating that day on this day. Angels "harked," shepherds ran, and Mary pondered the very good news that fills my heart this early morning.

I praise you for being born in Bethlehem, the "house of bread." I was a famished man, binge eating at many empty buffets, spending my money "for that which is not bread" (Isa. 55:2). But you came as the Bread of Life, and you've brought the feast of the gospel to my soul. Now I'm a truly satisfied man.

Yes, I praise you for entering our world in the town of David, Israel's beloved shepherd-king. For what King David could never be, you've become for us—the Good Shepherd who laid down his life for his sheep and is now caring for us with relentless tenderness and persistent kindness.

You're the King of Kings, reigning over and working in all things, for your glory and our good. You're the ruler of all the kings of the earth, setting them up and sitting them down at your sovereign discretion. No other kingdom but yours is everlasting. Knowing these things to be true, I have a peace that passes all understanding.

I praise you, Jesus, that *you* are the long-time-promised and much-longed-for Christ—the Messiah. We're to look for no other, for in you every promise of God finds its fulfillment, its unequivocal "Yes!"

I praise you, Jesus, that you are the Lord—the Lord of all lords, very God of very God. Oh, for that magnificent day when every knee will bow and every tongue confess that you are indeed Lord, to the glory of God the Father! Happy birthday, indeed, Lord Jesus. You are so easy to love and so worthy to be adored. I pray in your matchless and merciful name. Amen.

A Prayer about the Day after Christmas

And the shepherds returned, glorifying and praising God for all they had heard and seen, as it had been told them. (Luke 2:20)

Heavenly Father, life just on the other side of Christmas day feels quite different to different people. For some of us, this was the "greatest" Christmas ever in terms of healthy, caring relationships; incredible "eats"; thoughtful gifts, both given and received; and above all, fresh gratitude for the indescribable gift of your Son, Jesus.

For others of us, it was a really difficult day of palpable tensions, dashed hopes, brokenness abounding. For still others, it was the first Christmas with an empty chair where a loved one used to sit, or a day spent all by ourselves in excruciating loneliness.

Father, my prayer today is for all of us, no matter what yesterday was like. For even our best days are in need of the gospel, and none of our worst days are beyond the reach of the gospel.

When the shepherds left Jesus' manger, they were still shepherds. They still couldn't worship at the temple; they still couldn't give testimony in a court of law; they still were stereotyped as thieves by many in their community. And we shouldn't romanticize what Joseph and Mary did the day after Jesus was born, as though all of a sudden a five-star inn in Bethlehem did open up, as though Mary's body would have been spared all the normal chaos and pain of birthing and afterbirth, and as though angels would've started showing up as round-the-clock nurses.

Father, thank you that we're Christians, not Gnostics. We don't have to pretend about anything. Christmas isn't a season in which we're supposed to be transported into a superspirituality, rising above reality. The gospel isn't about denial but is about learning to delight in you, no matter what is going on. We praise you that Jesus came into a real world where everything is broken, but he did come to make all things new, starting with us.

Please give each of us the special and the common grace you gave the shepherds. Let us hear and let us see more of Jesus, even if we remain "shepherds" the rest of our lives. Enable us to glorify and praise you, Father, for you are not a man, that you would lie about anything. Everything you have told us in your Word will come to pass. This is good news for shepherds and kings alike. I pray in Jesus' faithful name. Amen.

A Prayer about Jesus, the Preacher of Peace

And he [Jesus] came and preached peace to you who were far off and peace to those who were near. For through him we both have access in one Spirit to the Father. (Eph. 2:17–18)

Merciful Jesus, I don't usually think of you as a preacher. Yet this Scripture presents you as the preacher of peace. Having just celebrated Christmas, I have a brand-new appreciation for the wonder and the challenge of what this means.

What is Christmas? It's you, Jesus, coming as near as possible to us in your incarnation. You've come bringing the peace for which we are desperate—a peace that required your perfect obedience and your atoning death for us on the cross. Most definitely, Jesus, you are our peace. You destroyed the hostility between God and us. You are the peacemaker of all peacemakers.

Now, in your resurrection glory, you're the one who is constantly preaching the gospel of peace to us, through the widest array of preachers imaginable. Forgive us when we look to mere human preachers to do what you alone can do. For only you, Jesus, can apply the gospel to hearts dead in sin and trespasses (Eph. 2:1–7) and hearts, like mine, that are prone to wander away from the gospel.

Jesus, you preach the gospel to us not just as individuals but also as those who participate in a wide array of broken relationships. You came to reconcile us not just to God but also to one another. You're committed to destroying all kinds of hostilities and reconciling all kinds of people—in the body of Christ, in our families, in our communities, even with our enemies.

Glorious Prince of Peace, you who one day will reconcile wolves and lambs, leopards and goats, calves and lions—give me the desire, the humility, and the grace to be a man of peace. As far as it is in my own power (Rom. 12:18–21) and as far as the power of the gospel will take me, let me live as an agent of your reconciling love. I pray in your peerless and peace-full name. Amen.

A Prayer about the Pace of Peace

Simeon took him [Jesus] in his arms and praised God, saying: "Sovereign Lord, as you have promised, you may now dismiss your servant in peace. For my eyes have seen your salvation, which you have prepared in the sight of all nations: a light for revelation to the Gentiles, and the glory of your people Israel." (Luke 2:28–32 NIV)

Gracious Jesus, it's just a few days after Christmas and already many of my neighbors are taking down their lights and trees. It seems like we're always in a hurry for the next thing. Traffic never moves fast enough, waiters don't bring our food soon enough, and the mail isn't delivered quick enough. I'm no exception to this harried and hurried way of doing life.

I guess this is one of the reasons I'm drawn to Simeon, a man who seemed to live at a different pace than I do. We know so little about this "righteous and devout" man, but we do know he was "waiting for the consolation of Israel"—that is, longing for the arrival of the Messiah, anticipating the fulfillment of promises God alone can keep, hoping to see you, Jesus, though he didn't know your name.

Eight days after your birth, Jesus, Simeon took you into his arms—you, by whose arms all things have been made and are sustained. Whether or not he expected to die soon, the peace that resulted from that embrace changed everything.

Jesus, it's only because you have embraced me in the gospel that I have the same peace Simeon experienced. For you are God's promised salvation for Israel, for Gentiles, and for me. In you I have found the consolation that can be found nowhere else. You are my forgiveness, my righteousness, my sanity, my peace, and a whole lot more.

But as we're on the verge of beginning a new year, I want the peace of your grace to help me live by the pace of your peace in this next season. Slow me down, Jesus. Center me. Settle me. Focus me. If I'm going to be in a hurry about one thing this year, may it be to linger longer in your presence. Everything else will take care of itself. I pray in your glorious name. Amen.

A Prayer about Jesus
Transforming Worship

There was also a prophet, Anna, the daughter of Phanuel, of the tribe of Asher. She was very old; she had lived with her husband seven years after her marriage, and then was a widow until she was eighty-four. She never left the temple but worshiped night and day, fasting and praying. Coming up to them at that very moment, she gave thanks to God and spoke about the child [Jesus] to all who were looking forward to the redemption of Jerusalem. (Luke 2:36–38 NIV)

Jesus, there are so many reasons to love and praise you. Today I'm grateful for how you radically transformed the worship of God. The main reason we've been created is to glorify God and enjoy him forever, so nothing is more important than how we worship God.

Though I admire Anna for her life of devotion—worshiping God ceaselessly in the temple—I adore you for removing all the limitations temple worship imposed. You were just eight days old when Anna met you in the temple. There's no way she could have imagined you came into the world to fulfill and replace temple worship forever.

By giving yourself for us on the cross, you have once and for all atoned for our sins and exhausted God's righteous judgment against us. You fulfilled the entire sacrificial system. It will never resume. Hallelujah!

Not only is there now no condemnation, there is now full celebration, for we are fully and eternally acceptable to God in you. The sacrifice we make is one of praise, for you are the Lamb of God who has taken away our sin forever. The gospel put an end to all self-centered fears and concerns in worship.

I also praise you, Jesus, for removing all spatial and calendar limitations on God's worship. Because of what you have done for us, "true worshipers" are those who worship God in spirit and in truth (John 4:21–26), not just in one place but in every place. Though we are still to gather with our brothers and sisters for services of worship, you have transformed the entire Christian life into worship service.

Because of you, Jesus, one day the entire earth will be covered with the knowledge of the glory of God. The final sanctuary will be the new heaven and new earth. Every creature and all creation will be liberated for the praise of your glory and grace. Oh, hasten that glad and glorious day!

Until that day, Jesus, may the gospel free us to worship God more passionately and faithfully through prayer and fasting, like Anna, but also by everything else we do in life—with our thoughts, by our words, and through many gospel deeds. We pray in your holy and loving name. Amen.

A Prayer about a Most Beautiful Irony

When Joseph and Mary had done everything required by the Law of the Lord, they returned to Galilee to their own town of Nazareth. And the child grew and became strong; he was filled with wisdom and the grace of God was on him. (Luke 2:39–40 NIV)

*D*ear Jesus, I don't know if I've ever thought about irony being beautiful until today. But it seems that everything connected to you reveals beauty in one way or another. Joseph and Mary were such faithful and loving parents from your conception on, helping you grow and become strong. After you were born, they did "everything required by the Law of the Lord" on your behalf. But little did they realize it was you who was born to fulfill everything required by the law of the Lord for them . . . and for us!

Oh, wonder of wonders! My heart sings and soars as I reflect upon your humility, your kindness, and your servant love for us, Jesus. You came not to destroy the law but to fulfill it on our behalf. What I could never do, you've done for me. What I could never be, you became for me. The law demands a righteousness and a beauty that come to us freely and fully in you, Jesus.

Your last words from the cross, "It is finished," have become my first words of freedom. It's not my obedience but yours in which I trust. It's not my righteousness but yours in which I boast and rest. By the same grace you saved me and you are now changing me.

As this gospel continues to make me sane, I'm trusting it will make me more and more whole, more and more like you, Jesus. Fulfill in me everything you desire for me as a spouse, a parent, a grandparent, a child, a friend, a neighbor. Show me clearly and specifically what this will look like. There's nothing more I could possibly want from the rest of my days in this world. I pray in your most glorious and gracious name. Amen.

A Prayer about New Year's Eve

Not to us, O LORD, not to us, but to your name give glory,
  for the sake of your steadfast love and your faithfulness!
Why should the nations say,
  "Where is their God?"
Our God is in the heavens;
  he does all that he pleases.
Their idols are silver and gold,
  the work of human hands. (Ps. 115:1–4)

Heavenly Father, as I sit quietly before you on the eve of a new year, I've got a good case of sad and glad going on inside of me. Both of these themes are at work in my heart as I reflect on the past year. It's a good tension, one for which the gospel is more than sufficient.

Looking back over the past twelve months, I can easily say with the psalmist, "Be praised, adored and worshiped, O God, for your love and your faithfulness!" Abba, Father, you loved me all year long with an everlasting, engaged, unwavering love, irrespective of anything I did or didn't do.

You loved me as much as you love your Son, Jesus, for you've hidden my life in his. Thank you for your steadfast love and fresh mercies that came every single day this past year, when I was aware of them and when I wasn't. You remained faithful to everything you've promised in Jesus. Great is your faithfulness. You do everything that pleases you. This makes me very glad.

But Father, it's because of your love for me in Jesus that I can also own my sadness. This past year I also joined the nations in saying, "So where is your God?" You usually heard this complaint from me when you were busy doing what pleases *you*, and not what pleases *me*. Many times I trusted my voiceless, sightless, senseless, powerless idols more than I trusted you. I grieve my foolishness.

Here's where the gladness trumps the sadness: I will not always be a man of two minds and a divided heart. Father, you will bring to completion the good gospel work you have begun in me. One day I will no longer even be tempted to worship anything or anyone but you. Hasten that glad and glorious day.

But until that day, even on the eve of a new year, prepare me for twelve new months of groaning and growing in grace. Bring much glory to yourself as the gospel does its work in my life and through my life. I pray in Jesus' faithful name. Amen.

Scotty Smith is founding pastor of Christ Community Church (PCA) in Franklin, Tennessee, and has seen its membership grow to over three thousand. He has also planted five daughter churches in the Nashville area. Scotty is also an adjunct professor at Covenant Theological Seminary and regularly teaches at Reformed Theological Seminary in Orlando. He is the author of five books, including *Speechless* and *Restoring Broken Things* with Steven Curtis Chapman.